Ancient Gods and Heroes of East and West

Ancient Gods and Heroes of East and West

Marta Vannucci

D.K. Printworld (P) Ltd.
New Delhi

Cataloging in Publication Data — DK
[Courtesy: D.K. Agencies (P) Ltd. <docinfo@dkagencies.com>]

Vannucci, M. (Marta), 1921-
Ancient gods and heroes of East and West / by Marta Vannucci.
xxi, 468 p. 23 cm.
Includes bibliographical references (p.)
Includes index.
ISBN 8124604134

1. Gods, Hindu. 2. Gods, Greek. 3. Mythology, Hindu. 4. Mythology, Greeks. 5. Civilization, Hindu. 6. Civilization, Greco-Roman. 7. Indo-Europeans. I. Title.

DDC 202.11 22

ISBN 81-246-0413-4
First published in India in 2007

Published and printed by:
D.K. Printworld (P) Ltd.
Regd. Office: 'Sri Kunj', F-52, Bali Nagar
New Delhi-110 015
Phones: (011) 2545-3975; 2546-6019; *Fax*: (011) 2546-5926
E-mail: dkprintworld@vsnl.net
Website: www.dkprintworld.com

To the Memory of a
Great Soul and Great Master,
R.N. Dandekar

Preface

THE serendipitous discovery of familiar Indian traits and names on ancient Greek vases from Attika, was the starting point of a research delving into the question of the transfer of cultures between geographically distant civilizations. The first results of the studies were published (Vannucci, 1999b) in the annals of the Bhandarkar Oriental Research Institute. The study focused on the geographic spread of cultivated hexaploid wheat, or bread wheat, the commonest species of which is *Triticum aestivum*, over a vast area extending from Greece to India. From the "Fertile Crescent" where it originated as a natural hybrid not later than 6000 BC, it reached Greece towards the middle of the second millennium BC and perhaps earlier.

The overall conclusion of the first study was that "it should have taken a very long time for hexaploid wheat, a natural hybrid, to spread spontaneously to far away geographic places: hence the important role of cultural exchanges."

The present study is a continuation of the search for common cultural traits, material or behavioural, between people with a common Indo-European ancestry but widely separated geographically — India in the east and Greece and the Hellenic world in the west. The study has been a fascinating journey into the past and the finding of survival of ancestral characteristics and habits into the present. I will try to relate my findings into as succinct a form as possible though the abundance of material could be the matter of several volumes.

This book started as a short note to be published as a paper. It is not meant to establish a link or correspondence between Vedic and Hellenic gods and heroes. It is essentially meant to show substantive similarities between ideas, concepts, rituals and celebrations of different people, inherited from early prehistoric times. The study also intends to analyse how different environments and contacts with people from different stocks caused divergence of the philosophies of east and west. Perhaps the reader will find some bias in the approach followed, inevitable as it comes from a professional researcher in scientific ecology.

No clear-cut limits can be drawn between basic attitudes and thoughts of east and west Indo-Europeans. The cultural traits of each group were modified to a certain extent by mixing and exchanges with people of different extraction who were the earlier inhabitants of the lands into which they migrated. However I believe that the study provides sufficient elements to identify ancestral ideas and customs that engendered the gods and myths of east and west. Inputs by pre-existing cultures into the newly arrived immigrants can be identified since they are present in one group and not in the other. The mixing of people of various origins produced a cultural synchretism at variance between east and west though many of the differences can also be traced back to environmental and historic factors.

An attempt is also made to identify the causes of the divergent evolutions in east and west. Since evolution also means diversification and differential development, no attempt is made here to "recognize" the counterparts of gods and heroes of east and west. Indeed it is not possible to establish pairs of gods, one Indian or eastern, and one Greek or Western. There never is an exact correspondence, though Western authors have attempted, always unsuccessfully, to match pairs of gods and goddesses between east and west. What I do find is a meaningful parallelism of habits, gestures and techniques, as well as concepts and ideal representations of gods, though not their behaviour. The urge to participate in the cosmic drama when philosophy becomes religion, what Dandekar so aptly called "participatory magic," can be clearly perceived in cultic practices, ceremonies and rituals in east and west. Participatory magic is that which takes man from a being subservient to his god to a being who participates in the life and dynamics of the cosmos, as in the Vedic sacrifices, in the celebration of the Greek Mysteries or in the Eucharistic Communion in the "sacrifice" of the Christian Mass.

The passage from philosophy to religion was discussed in the west by the principal schools of philosophy of ancient Greece, the Stoics, the Epicureans, the Academicians, the Cynics and others, as summarized by Cicero in several studies, the most important being the "*De Natura deorum*" (= On the nature of the gods). At this time I will not enter into the discussion of other faiths and works, as for instance the imprint of ancient Semitic cultures on Christianity and tendencies of Catholicism. Christianity is not of Indo-European (IE) extraction or nature and it inherited fatalism from Judaism which became even stronger under Islam, where the word itself means "total submission to God." It took a long time for the West to accept partially and reluctantly the concept of the *Liber arbitrium* of the individual person. On the other hand, this was a subject rarely discussed in the east since it is an intrinsic idea of the concepts of *dharma* and *karma*.

This book refers exclusively to Indo-Europeans of east and west. Parallelism of myths and legends, specially of the early stages called the "*heroic age*" are obvious, but no identity or superposition of divinities or heroes is total and complete. The only general similarity refers to major nature gods, Dionysos and Demeter in the west and the abstract concepts of the Hindu Trinity in the east: Brahmā and Sarasvatī as Life and Knowledge, Viṣṇu and Lakṣmī as Beauty and Wealth and Śiva and Pārvatī as Action and Grace. As Dionysos and Demeter cover the entire existence of material life-sustaining reality, so does the Hindu Trinity cover the understanding of the material and immaterial reality of all aspects of the life of men, women and children, in their intrinsic quality of creation, maintenance of nature's cycles and recycling of matter and energy. All of these are life-dependent virtual realities linked to the essence of Life without which nothing could exist (Vannucci 1999 c).

On the other hand, the eternal human quest for immortality has no parallel between east and west. In the east, immortality is achieved through great deeds of knowledge and wisdom, the ancient seven sages are deified and in the Indian tradition they live forever in the mind of man as the stars of the constellation of the *Ursa Major*. In the west man was influenced by Egyptian and Semitic beliefs, immortality of the body was sought but could not be achieved, and man felt frustrated ever since.

More space is allotted to the discussion of Western Indo-European gods and heroes for the simple reason that the myths and legends related to Vedic gods and heroes are well known in India. To understand the full meaning of legends and myths it is essential to trace back their origin to find out how and why they were first created, what the background and environment that generated them was, what the symbolism and meaning under the beliefs and habits were of that time. It is for instance meaningful that archaic Rudra is "howling" and that primordial Dionysos is "noisy." Both were originally identified with the strong destructive winds of the steppes and of the mountains. Winds are overpowering forces to be respected, especially when nomadism was the rule and early settlements were precarious shelters. Also the primordial God of Mesopotamia was the God of Tempests. The Sun is everywhere recognised as the Life-giver and is described as "beautiful, generous and joyous" (St. Francis of Assisi) while Fire, lord Agni, gives light, warmth, and cooks food for better nutrition and is everywhere revered as the "most ancient."

As planned at first the book would include studies about Dionysos, Demeter, Viṣṇu, Varuṇa and the common man and woman. The book should also include studies of the traditional heroes: Perseus, Herakles, the Pāṇḍavas and perhaps Hanumān, but it soon became evident that such an extensive enterprise should best be broken up into parts. We will deal here only with the Greek nature gods and some of the heroes of the Greek epics. Briefly we shall also deal with some of the Vedic gods and heroes for the sake of comparison.

I offer apologies for what could appear to be un-necessary repetitions, but such a complex subject as dealt with here needs to be considered from as many viewpoints as possible, hence the repetitions of acts and facts as seen from different angles.

I am deeply grateful to my many Indian friends of different sorts who helped me understand the meaning and thinking of the Indian way of life, its tolerance and faith, first among them the late Dr.

Meenakshi Iyer. I am grateful to Dr Rajesh Kochhar for the time he spent in fruitful conversations and for his constructive criticism. To Dr H.K. Kaul, Director of the Library of the India International Centre in Delhi, I am indebted for the constant and free use of the library and its facilities and for the personal assistance given by Smt Sushma Zutshi in particular and all the staff. I am grateful to Dr M. Cristina Guidotti, Director of the Egyptian Museum at Florence, Italy; to Dr Marco Piccardi, Curator and Dr Monica Zavattaro, Deputy Curator of the Anthropological Sector of the Natural History Museum of the University of Florence, Italy; and to Prof. F. Pecchioli Daddi, Professor of Egyptology at the University of Florence, for their generous and learned interaction. I am grateful to the National Library at Florence and to the Biblioteca Marucelliana, Florence, for their always prompt assistance and collaboration. To Mr Ali Hooshmand, many thanks are due for the use of his personal library as also to my friend Jennifer Haslett for her patience and always interesting remarks. Last but not least I am extremely grateful to Prof. V. Giannellini of the University of Florence, for his unfailing help, constructive criticism and expert technical support.

Last and most important I wish to aknowledge the unfailing help and support received from Mr. Susheel Mittal on which I could always rely to report on the results of the studies of many years in different Universities and Museums in India and abroad.

Contents

Part II - Gods

Part III - Heroes

Part IV - Summary and Conclusions

List of Figures

Key to Transliteration

VOWELS

अ *a*	आ *ā*	इ *i*	ई *ī*	उ *u*	ऊ *ū*
(but)	(palm)	(it)	(beet)	(put)	(pool)
ऋ *ṛ*	ए *e*	ऐ *ai*	ओ *o*	औ *au*	
(rhythm)	(play)	(air)	(toe)	(loud)	

CONSONANTS

Guttural	क *ka*	ख* *kha*	ग *ga*	घ *gha*	ङ *ṅa*
	(skate)	(blockhead)	(gate)	(ghost)	(sing)
Palatal	च *ca*	छ* *cha*	ज *ja*	झ *jha*	ञ *ña*
	(chunk)	(catch him)	(john)	(hedgehog)	(bunch)
Cerebral	ट *ṭa*	ठ* *ṭha*	ड *ḍa*	ढ* *ḍha*	ण* *ṇa*
	(start)	(anthill)	(dart)	(godhead)	(under)
Dental	त *ta*	थ *tha*	द *da*	ध* *dha*	न *na*
	(path)	(thunder)	(that)	(breathe)	(numb)
Labial	प *pa*	फ* *pha*	ब *ba*	भ *bha*	म *ma*
	(spin)	(philosophy)	(bin)	(abhor)	(much)
Semi-	य *ya*	र *ra*	ल *la*	व *va*	
vowels	(young)	(drama)	(luck)	(vile)	
Sibilants	श *śa*	ष *ṣa*	स *sa*	ह *ha*	
	(shove)	(bushel)	(so)	(hum)	
Others	क्ष *kṣa*	त्र *tra*	ज्ञ *jña*	ळ* ḷ	ॠ* *ṝ*
	(*kṣatriya*)	(*triśūla*)	(*jñānī*)	(*play*)	

अं (-)*ṁ anusvāra* (nasalisation of preceding vowel) like *saṁskṛti*

अः *visarga* = *ḥ* (aspiration of preceding vowel) like (*prātaḥ*)

ऽ *Avagraha* consonant #'consonant (like:- *ime 'vasthitā*)

Anusvāra at the end of a line is presented by m (म्) and not ṁ

* No exact English equivalents for these letters.

Introduction

AFTER many years of studying, visiting museums and libraries and reading over again the Latin and Greek authors who wrote about the pre-historic and ancient historical periods of the west, and comparing cultural traits of east and west, I was greatly impressed by the astonishingly great similarities between the meanings and intentions underlining the rites, rituals, habits and even gestures of populations widely separated geographically, the Indian subcontinent, India for brevity, on one side and the Graeco-Roman Mediterranean on the other. I even wrote on this subject a paper read at a Seminar of the Indira Gandhi National Centre for the Arts (IGNCA) at Delhi, which I entitled "Common roots and transfer of culture?" (Vannucci 1988), the conclusion of which was that over centuries and under different circumstances, both processes had their saying. Later, in a paper published in the Annals of the Bhandarkar Oriental Research Institute (ABORI, Vannucci, 1999b), I drew arguments to show that goddess Demeter, who is known to have come to Greece from the east, introduced new varieties of wheat, namely hexaploid wheat in the Rharian plains in Attika near Athens, towards the middle of the second millennium BC. Tetraploid or *Triticum durum* wheat was cultivated in Greece since or earlier than *c.* 6000 BC by autochthonous pre-Hellenic non Indo-European people. On the other hand, hexaploid wheat, or bread wheat is a natural hybrid domesticated and first cultivated in the Fertile Crescent, most probably in Iran as suggested by archaeological research. There is evidence of the cultivation of hexaploid or bread wheat, *Triticum aestivum,* already in Mehrgarh Period I which ended about 6000 BC. Cultivation of hexaploid wheat became more and more popular in the following periods (Chakrabarti, D.K., 2001). Bread wheat remains, dated from *c.* 3000 BC were found in the Hafit horizon in the Omani peninsula.

The present book is the result of years of research that followed the conclusions drawn earlier from diffuse but significant evidence. It extends the research on Demeter to other ancient Greek gods and heroes, mainly Dionysos and Herakles and includes conclusions drawn from texts and detailed readings of common cultural trends between people of Indo-European extraction in east and west. In both east and west the fusion of Indo-European, Aryans and others, with local pre-existing cultures contributed to produce new cultures, the Vedic-brahminic-Hindu civilization in India and the Graeco-Roman in the west. In spite of different time lapses, different geographic and ecologic features, the Indian sub-continent and the western Mediterranean civilizations retained remarkable similarities derived from common roots. The continued presence from ancient times to the present of the personification of nature gods in the west, has been widely overlooked by western scholars who, from the nineteenth century onwards, were more concerned with the majestic Olympian gods, such as Zeus (or Jupiter) and Poseidon (or Neptune), than with the survival of nature gods and goddesses present in the folklore and traditional wisdom of the people, such as Dionysos (or Iacchos/Bacchus) and Demeter (or Cerere/Cybele). At present, early twenty-first century, there are signs of revival of ancient wisdom that had never been totally forgotten.

New studies confirmed the views expressed in the paper mentioned above (Vannucci, 1999b). Archaeology and related sciences were pursued scientifically especially since the nineteenth century. Much is known of the Mediterranean and European ancient cultures, with results published in a vast array of books and specialised periodicals. Recent comprehensive and scholarly overviews and reviews of the ancient past of India may be found in D.K. Chakrabarti, (2001) and R. Kochhar (2000). Studies of the Avesta, of the Vedas and of the oral tradition of the Indian civilization are indispensable to understand the past (Vannucci, 1999b) and to draw comparisons with the ancient Greek myths and the oral tradition of the west. The present book is an attempt to underline, as far as we can go, the similarities and dissimilarities between east and west as revealed by the personalities of gods and heroes.[1]

Finally a brief definition of words used here. The word "culture" is used in the sense given in Webster's Dictionary, the "totality of socially transmitted behaviour, patterns, arts, beliefs, institutions and all other produce of human thought typical of a population or community at a given time," to this definition we must add the words: "techniques and sciences." The word civilization is defined as: "an advanced stage of development in the arts and sciences accompanied by corresponding political, social and cultural complexity." The two terms, culture and civilization are occasionally, and under certain circumstances, interchangeable. The name "India" is used here to mean "Indian sub-continent," or South Asia and not just the area of present day India as a State. The "Indo-European East" includes areas where Indo-Aryan, Indo-Iranian and also other Indo-European clans migrated and at times lived in the ancient past. Some of them can still be identified and recognized from their language, habits, customs and dress, as for instance the Dards in Himalayan regions. Some Indo-European groups migrated as far as Vietnam where they founded the kingdom of Kampa that ruled over a vast area during a few centuries AD.[2] Standing Hindu temples with inscriptions in *nagarī* script are well preserved and attest to the presence of Indo-European settlements. At present their descendants live nomadic lives with no land of their own. The term "Indo-European West" is used here mainly to designate the area where ancient Indo-European clans, mainly Mycenean, Doric and Thracians established kingdoms or came under the influence of the Greek civilization. The term Indo-European of west includes both Indo-Aryans and Indo-Iranians as well as other Indo-Europeans. Migrations can be of many types. They may recur at seasonal intervals to escape from areas subject to seasonal droughts or floods, or the people may undertake regular transhumance, such as when shepherds take their herds to high-mountain pastures and spend months in simple semi-permanent huts in summer and return to the plains or valleys in winter. Transhumance may be annual or bi-annual, for instance going over high passes in the favourable season of one year and return to their permanent dwellings at low altitude valleys in the next season favourable for the return journey.[3] Migrations can also be permanent, when entire families, groups of families or clans go elsewhere, usually following the guidance of scouts who had searched for suitable lands for the group to move in. The latter people displacements are usually slow, with several or many generations between movements. Nomadism is the centuries or millennia old habit of people who never settle permanently, they do not own land and are always on the move as a way of life. The *Pax romana* refers to that long period of the first few centuries AD when imperial Rome ruled with an iron fist over a war-free western world.[4]

Part I

Indo-Europeans of the Euro-Asian Steppes

(A) The Scenario

THE environmental characteristics of the Indo-European original homeland, the steppes, distant horizons, cold winters, perennial winds and the presence of herds of wild horses contributed to the development of a nomadic culture. The people were not rooted to the land. Over centuries, many generations and long-term changes in climate would have triggered their search for greener pastures, for forests and their produce and for new places where they could develop semi-permanent, then permanent habitation. The urge to move and expand their oecumene is a trait typical of the Indo-European people, it has remained with them ever since. The Indo-Europeans over the centuries have become adapted to all varieties of climate and geographic features.

THE PLACE

We are not concerned here with the place of origin of the Indo-European people, or with the age when the great migrations took place, or where the Vedas were first formulated and the hymns composed. Certainly the Vedas were not born and grown in a single place or all at the same time. Focus is here on Central Asia, the Indian sub-continent at large, here called India or Major India in the east, Anatolia and Asia Minor, Greece and the Hellenic world in the west. This is where the acts and facts of the pre-historic, heroic and BC historic ages that are the subject of this book took place, at the cultural stage in the Central Asian scene where some of the Indic speaking people lived at some stage, from the fourth millennium BC onwards. From that time the characteristics of the populations started to turn towards different directions. The people were what they were, but their becoming would be moulded by new environments, by the places they migrated through and by those where they eventually settled, in east and west. The word environment is used here in its ecological sense which includes non-living geographic, geologic and climatic factors as well as living beings, from microbes through all species of plants and animals and the men, women and children of the same and other tribes, Indo-European or not, present in the domain where the migrating Indo-European tribes settled and where offsprings were conceived, born, lived and died.[1]

Recent methodic archaeological research started earlier in the west than in the east and the findings of those studies have relevance in the present context. Among them, scientific research based on analyses of DNA of various people of the world by Cavalli-Sforza (Cavalli-Sforza & Feldman, 1981) and the use of new techniques of chemical archaeological research (McGovern, 2003) amongst other methods, are important for the present study. Bhargava (2001) reviewed the information available about the people who went to India and called themselves Arya, Chakrabarti, D.K. (2001) published an update and discussed the present archaeological knowledge of the ancient past of India. Kochhar (2000) in addition to archaeological findings discussed also matters related to astronomy, history of technology, geomorphology, natural history, the Avesta and linguistics in his book on "The Vedic People — Their history and geography." Lahiri (1992) mapped the ancient trade routes of South and Central Asia. Dani & Masson (1992) report on the "Dawn of civilization in Central Asia." A look at the geography and climates of the places where the Asian people about whom we are concerned here lived, is the first step to try to understand how cultures evolved. The reader is referred to these publications for details and critical analysis of the findings of research todate.

I intend focusing only on the widely different scenarios from Greater Greece to the Indian sub-continent where people of Indo-European stock settled out of choice or necessity. Originally these ancient groups, tribes or clans were settled shepherds given to pastoralism always in search of greener pastures and favourable climates. Transhumance could have developed later, after agriculture was invented. Transhumance presupposes the existence of permanent settlements at lower altitude where shepherds and herds find shelter during winter months and where the fruits of tilled land provide food for a full year cycle. Agriculture presupposes fertile soils and abundant water supply as found in the plains, on alluvial deposits and river margins, preferably near mountains, because transhumance is often based on the existence of high mountain and good summer pastures for the herdsmen to take their cattle, sheep and goats for wool, hides, tendons, horns and hoofs, milk and its derivatives. Bread and cheese were the basic foods in Greece, and bread, curds and ghee in India, besides wheat, meat and vegetables. An important difference in food availability is the reduced variety in Greece, where olives and olive oil, figs, milk and derivatives, bread made of hard (tetraploid) wheat flour and some meat were about all there was as food.

The distribution of the Harappan civilization sites is typically regulated by hydrography. The Harappan or R. Indus Valley civilization is so far an undeciphered mystery, perhaps it pre-dates the arrival of the people known to be Indic speaking people. The Harappans and their script and even what their language was or where they came from or what caused the decline of their civilization, are still a heated subject of discussions among scholars. We are not concerned with them here. We are here concerned with the Indo-European who migrated to the "land of the seven rivers," the upper hydrographic basin of the Indus River where they found extensive lands and all requirements for pastoralism, animal husbandry and agriculture. They gradually expanded to all of north and peninsular India where they settled and eventually mixed with the pre-existing people, perhaps Dravidians in some areas, whose origin is also uncertain.

THE PEOPLE

Long before the advent of Indo-European people in the Mediterranean, the Egyptians had established contact and trading relations with the Semitic populations of West Asia, specially the Phoenicians who founded colonies throughout the Mediterranean region and ventured beyond the Columns of Hercules into the Atlantic Ocean. Tradition reports that "since ever" the Pelasgoi, sea people of the islands of the eastern Mediterranean and Crete in particular, were expert mariners who roamed the seas as pirates. Tradition, already recorded in the Iliad (II, 840; X, 429, seventh or eighth century

BC) also says that the Danai, Pelasgians from Crete, sided with the Troyans during the war that the Greeks waged against the city of Troy for supremacy in the Aegean Sea and the eastern Mediterranean and for access to the Sea of Marmara and the *Pontus Euxinus* (= Black Sea). Troy had been founded by ancestor *Dardanus* at the entrance of the Straits of the Dardanelles at a strategic place to supervise and control the traffic between the Aegean and the Black Sea. The other narrow strait between Asia Minor and Europe is at the Bosphorus that joins the Sea of Marmara and the Black Sea. Many centuries later, Xerxes, Achaemenid king of Persia, made a bridge built on floats and boats, crossed over the Bosphorus and led his army into Europe in the year 480 BC. The Indo-Europeans who migrated into Greece coming overland and over the Aegan Sea, did not find ample space there, though other advantages lured them into settling in the narrow valleys, small peninsulas and islands of Greece. The deciding attraction of that region was the sea.

The maritime routes have been at all times in the history of humankind, the means for widening horizons, for trade, for material and cultural enrichment. In the Indian Ocean the earliest maritime routes were established by the Harappans, though they were essentially land people. Kochhar (2000) mentions that "a marine trading post [of the Harappan civilization] has been identified at Ra'-s al-Junayz in Oman." I have myself seen remains of Harappan structures made of bricks in a mangrove island in the Indus River delta, besides those at Balakot near Somniani Hor (= Somniani lagoon) on the Makran coast. These sites bear testimony of the geographic expanse of the Harappans. According to Kramer (1959 1st ed., latest ed. 1994) and Bottero (1998), ancient Mesopotamian tradition says that the Sumerians "came from the sea," which can only be the Persian Gulf. Archaeologic evidence shows that they entered Mesopotamia in the fourth millennium BC. It is further known that their language was not a Semitic language. There are good reasons to believe that the maritime route between the Arabian Gulf and the Indus River system was a trade route of the ancient past, but it is not known when trade started, certainly not later than the fourth millennium BC. Navigation and trading must have been from east to west and vice versa and initially it must have been "hugging the coast" until when the mythical Greek mariner called Hippalos showed how to ride the south-west monsoon winds to sail a straight course across the Arabian Sea from west to east. The south-west monsoon winds were called "Hippalos" by ancient Greeks and into the Middle Ages of Europe. Open sea navigation implies the architectural ability to build sea-worthy ships. The earliest such ships were probably those built in Oman, where the city of Salala is still well-known for the high quality of the ships built there. During the times of Imperial Rome and the so-called *Pax romana,* maritime trade routes were well-known and used in the Arabian Sea and east coast of Africa, as far as India. Hence the importance of the good harbours of the Malabar coast where transhipment of goods to ships travelling as far as the Molucca islands and further was regular seasonal routine already in the first centuries of the Christian Era. The history of the Malabar coast and its princely states is recorded and well-known since BC times.[2]

The Macedonian and the Mycenean civilizations were the older Indo-European civilizations developed to high standards in that part of southern Europe. The people who became known as Greeks had migrated into the Greek peninsula coming from the plains of R. Danube and moving southwards along the western border of the Black Sea. The Indo-Europeans of the east, including the invading Persians (= Iranians) and Mitanni who eventually reached the islands and mainland Greece, arrived there via Asia Minor. Soon after settling in Greece the people (= *demos*) had to expand to new areas with enough arable land for agriculture. With the founding of Syracuse (734 BC), of *Massilia* (or *Massalia,* now Marseille) and others about 600 BC, *Magna Graecia* (= Great Greece) was born. *Magna Graecia* is a term that designates a loose league of numerous semi-independent "colonies" linked with each other and to mainland Greece by strong cultural affinities, trade and political bonds. The cities of *Magna Graecia,* including those of the islands of the Aegean Sea and of the western coast of Asia Minor had a profound influence on the development of the western world. Greek cities and colonies were also founded over the northern coasts of the Mediterranean Sea, especially in the Italian peninsula, Sicily and the western shores. One Pytheas from Massilia sailed clockwise along western Europe as far as the extreme north called "Ultimate Thule."[3] The Greeks followed closely the example given by the Phoenicians, a Semitic race of seamen who had founded Carthage, *Alalia* in Corsica and other colonies and may have sailed earlier than the Greek, into the Atlantic Ocean well beyond the pillars of Hercules (= Straits of Gibraltar) and perhaps as far as Cornwall in search of tin ores, cassiterite and others. Cassiterite often comes in large beautiful lead-coloured often geminate, shining, opaque and hard crystals that may have originally been used as ornaments.[4]

All over the world as known then, before alloys were made of copper and tin (Cu and Sn) which is bronze, most people were confronted with using copper implements not hard or strong enough for heavy work or weapons. The heroic ages of east and west coincide with the development of the metallurgy of bronze, the metal for weapons, shields, helmets, pegs and other parts of the wheels of chariots and heavy duty carts, nails of ships and wagons and other heavy duty machines. In the east copper was also smelted from chalcopyrite and other ores and fused with zinc to make brass, an alloy which together with bronze, retained its prestige and acquired an almost sacred character. Copper ore was one of the first metals to be mined and later fused into alloys in both east and west and to this day copper and brass, also bronze implements are traditionally used in India as temple-ware, though iron and steel had been produced in India since the second millennium BC. Archaeological studies have found copper implements at Mehrgarh sites dated from the fifth or early fourth millennium BC, when copper became widespread (Chakrabarti, D.K. 1999). There was already in early days an extensive network of trade in Europe as well as in major India, with very long inter-connecting overland routes and maritime traffic in the Mediterranean and in the Arabian Sea, then called *Red Sea.* Nodal and terminal points in the web are now becoming known to archaeologists, maritime routes were more frequently used in the ancient past than is usually supposed. Planks of seagoing, fishing and village craft in the Indian Ocean were until very recently and even now made with planks sewed up with coconut fibre ropes imbibed with tar and other resins. Coconut fibres do not become rusted, tar makes them water tight and avoids fouling by marine organisms.

EXPANSION OF THE INHABITED WORLD

The expansion of the Indo-European civilizations of the west took place mostly by sea. From 2000 BC onwards, the Greek civilization learned in the island of Crete, earlier inhabited by people who had come from Asia, features of continental west Asian cultures (Pope 1969), such as the building of large palaces and other impressive structures. The maximum splendour of Knossos was reached about 1700 BC. This tendency was followed by the Minoan civilization but was not influenced by the architectural design and structure of the Egyptian colossal buildings. The Indo-Europeans who colonized mainland Greece, were not the first to arrive there. Phoenicians and other Semitic people from Asia Minor, Pelasgoi of uncertain origin in the eastern Mediterranean Sea, Italics of various denominations in Italy and Sicily, Indo-European tribes and other people roamed the Mediterranean Sea and were already settled at places around it since olden times. Some of the Indo-European clans who entered into Greece, mainly Thracians, were not sea people, they had migrated overland from the plains of River Danube and quick adaptation to the new environment was necessary, hence culture evolved rapidly.

The same happened also in the east, in the areas where local people lived before the arrival and settlement of the Indo-Europeans of east. The clans and tribes that migrated towards Kashmir and Punjab in India settled into environments not too different from what they already knew. There was no urgent need to change habits and customs. They were confronted with high mountains on the horizon, fertile valleys, lush plains, high forests and abundant water.[5] What was new to them was a monsoonal climate, with an alternation of very dry and very wet seasons. The arts of storing water and irrigation are very ancient, the most ancient works, many of them still in use, are to be found in Mesopotamia, Iran and India. Practical implications of a monsoonal climate are described in detail in hymn *Ṛ̥V* VII.103, the "Maṇḍūka," by *ṛṣi* Vaśiṣṭha (Vannucci 1999) and is ritualistically recalled as part of one of the most important Śrauta rites, the Soma sacrifice. The "Maṇḍūka" is a good example of the learning that the sages obtained from observing nature, how they bowed to it and how they transformed the knowledge acquired into a religious rite for the consecration of knowledge, for thanksgiving to the gods, Viṣṇu in this case, for peace of mind and to impose on themselves and others lifestyles attuned to the environment through the sacralisation of life. In both east and west the newcomers adapted as quickly as necessary to the new environment, however the process took several or many generations to mature and was slower in the east where the environment was not too different from where they had come from. Caste systems more or less rigid developed in east and west, they brought unending strifes, but persisted everywhere because in a developing society artisans and manual workers had to become specialized and be proficient in different jobs and duties. In addition to developing expertise in arts and crafts, in both east and west the invention of agriculture created two distinct classes of people: the rural and the urban. With the development of agriculture, population density increased as well as class antagonism and differences in the ethical and social approach to life. The urban elite had more time available for wars of conquest or defence and for the development of martial and other arts, philosophy and religion. The rural people lived in villages, usually small and scattered over extensive areas, they had to follow the biological dictates of nature. Rural life requires collective action of the community for pastoralism and transhumance, for defence against wild animals, intruders, invaders and the urban overlords. Rural communities are conservative, based on traditional experience of ancestors.

Many villages or clusters of villages in India had a peculiarity of their own which ensured to a point their long-term survival. Villages in India often include, or included members of different castes, arts and crafts. In a sense this was a significant achievement for self-sufficiency and for protection agains possible abuse of authority by any urban, domestic or foreign dominant group. However the oral tradition and law could not be the same in the urban or in the rural environment, customs and ethics became more and more divergent, increasing the variance among castes. In the west the *ilota*s of Sparta as a State, or the rural population of India seen as a large sub-continent, would have to be ruled and judged by canons different from those of the noble, warrior upper caste, such as that of Sparta or the warriors and the learned brāhmaṇas of India. As cities grew, problems also became more complex and they were never permanently solved. There is, however, one class of people that has always been similar all over the world due to the need of common understanding. These are traders and merchants who are an important link between different cultures and an efficient vehicle for the transfer of knowledge as well as technical and professional development, especially in the natural sciences and medicine.[6]

URBAN DEVELOPMENT

Mainly due to space limitations, competition and warfare between clans, the number and size of cities grew fast in the west, city people were concentrated inside walled cities ready for defence, while the rural people lived in open spaces, in villages protected by hedges of prickly plants, some of them poisonous. Cities had permanent structures built with fired bricks or stone, more easily protected by huge walls, the prototypes of which, in the Hellenic world, were the urban centres of the Cretan and the Mycenean civilizations. The latter flourished between 1400 and 1150 BC and had a definite influence on the Greek epics that sing about acts and facts that happened at that time. Archaeologists find a rich amount of remains and artefacts that enable them to reconstruct down to details the culture of the Indo-Europeans of Europe and of the Hellenic world in particular. In the east there were vast territories, scarcity of easily accessible quarries to obtain stones for building permanent structures and large forests that provided abundant timber for building palisades and wooden structures, including temples. Wooden temples open to the sky, in use and sanctified as sacred enclosures, still existed some years ago and were taken care of by the Kalash people of Gilgit and Hunza. They were described by Loude (1987; Loude & Lièvre 1980, 1984; Lièvre & Loude 1990) but have been destroyed or used otherwise, following the Islamisation of the area. Archaeological remains are relatively scarce in the Indian territory, wood does not keep well over centuries, it decays leaving no remains to tell the story, but baked pottery and other clay and metal artefacts are abundant and well-studied by ethnologists, anthropologists and archaeologists. New archaeological techniques, especially in the fields of nano-chemistry, are promising of new discoveries and chronological studies (McGovern 2003).

CITIES AND LANGUAGE

In this context I would recall that Kochhar (2000) mentions that studies by Rau (1976) indicate that "the word *pur* in Sanskrit is etymologically related to the Greek word *polis*, fortified city." This is not correct. The two words *"pur"* and *"polis"* do not come from the same root and their meaning is different. *Pur* is a city fortified for strategic protection against enemies, it has defensive structures, such as palisades, walls or bastions made of stone or wood logs usually standing side by side, with upper tops trimmed down to points hardened by fire. *Purah* or *pur* is a structurally fortified city, a city protected to stay materially intact. The word *polis* is the concept of a city fortified by wisdom and knowledge, it is a word having a philosophical, religious, political meaning, whether the city itself has defensive boundary walls or not. It is the *nābhi*, the navel, if I may say so, of the Athenian and the Hellenistic civilizations. The epitome of the *polis* is the Acropolis of Athens, built around 570 BC. Acropolis is a word where the root *akros* means the summit, the uppermost, the maximum and *polis* means city. The Indo-European root *pu-r* (long *u*) and the alternative *pewe* means "to purify." In Greek, Hittite and Germanic languages the theme *pu-r* suggests purification, hence fire (gr = *pyr* = became *Feuer* in German). Fire is the excellent purifier. The word *polis* in Greek refers to the political structure characterised by the participation of all citizens in the government of the city. The word *polites* means "citizen" and the latin word *politica* refers to the science and art of government of the State.

Herodotus (VII, 101-105, 135) recognizes the courage and qualities of the Persian soldiers under the invading King Xerxes, but concludes that the Greeks are superior to the Persians in one single essential point: "the Greek people live in the *polis* which is a community of free men exclusively ruled by The Law and they are not under the sceptre of a despot." The acropolis of Athens was the religious and political centre of the *polis,* the city-state and the two, religion and politics during those days could not and should not be dissociated. Since Athens was the paradigm of the Greek civilization, the *acropolis* of Athens became the emblem and symbol of the city-state, fortified by wisdom, knowledge, philosophy as natural and political science, hence the universally used words "politics" and "political." With time, other cities had their citadel with this or other name, for instance the fortified Capitol Hill of Rome. The original meaning of "*Pur*" or "*purah*"in Sanskrit as a city fortified structurally, survived as such in the ample lands of the east, but the word *polis* was "philosophied," if I may say so, into the restricted area of Athens, the ideal city-state in Greece. We may remember that the Capitol Hill of Rome during the early times of the Republic, had only temples and geese for its protection. Once, during the Republic, when barbarian hordes attempted to escalade the hill by night, the startled geese sacred to Juno made such an uproar that the entire city was awakened and ran outdoors to expel the intruders. The sacred anonymous geese played successfully their protective role, as the saying goes.

Often the divergence of philosophies of east and west stems from the different concept or meaning of words which may have the same origin but have changed differently in the course of time. Philosophy in the east was born as a natural or ecological science, it has basically remained as such, unpolluted. In the west, out of population and environmental pressures, philosophy became speculative and bound to undiscussed and unrestricted respect of the *polis*, or whatever other authority, as the word political and policy imply. In India the word *pur* was extensively used in the heroic age sung in the *Mahābhārata*. *Pur* has maintained its down-to-earth meaning of a fort, a fortified city or village materially reinforced, even if at present the fortification may be just a spiny hedge and the root *pur* is not more than a suffix added to the name of the place which may or may not have been an important city in the past. In the west no fort or walled city was ever called a *pur.*

NOMADISM AND SETTLEMENTS

Coming back to the scattered distribution of rural populations, the routes of communication had to be very long in India because of the size of the country. The establishment of routes which could be used the year round developed very early, as mentioned by Chakrabarti, D.K. (1999). The network of permanent routes favoured trade and the development of a special class of people, the artisans, as well as good means of conveyance, such as carts and wagons for horse or bullock traction and later, the very Indian travel device, the *palky* of which there were many varieties. India developed a special breed of "trotting bullocks," specially reared for travel by palanquins. It must be noted that very few roads could be year round, all weather routes, because of the inconvenience of travelling under monsoon rains which flooded the plains and swelled the high reaches of rivers to dangerous proportions.

To this day in India *loharis* are wandering iron-smiths who move from village to village and spend weeks or months at crossroads, villages or private estates to make and repair the metal implements of the people, of the landlords and in the past, the armament of local princes. The *Roman* or gypsies still lived in wagons and called from the gates of the farm when I was a child in Italy, and elsewhere in Europe. The men were known to be skilled ironsmiths and the women were fortune tellers, somewhat feared like revived Cassandras for their accurate even if often unfortunate predictions. The gypsies are known to be far-wandering artisans — descendants of people from the Indian subcontinent who are unwilling to forgo their traditional habits.

The horse used by the *kurgan* culture was already full grown to its present stature and fully domesticated, while the horses of the early Indo-Europeans were of small size and were reared essentially for meat. Specially prepared and preserved horse meat was still eaten in France and Italy well into the twentieth century. The wandering horse of the honoured great sacrifice called *aśvameda* and some habits of the Kurgan culture reflect attitudes much older than the *Manu-Smṛti*, and many indicate aspects of very ancient accepted ways of defining boundaries between fields and ancestral properties.[7] Much later in Rome *Janus bifrons*, the two-faced head of a deity called *Janus*, marked the boundary between fields under different ownership. The underlying original principle is that boundaries defined by the wandering horse, or by man in his fields, should be accepted since they reflect natural limits as much as human dominance and limitations. In rural areas of India and Italy where land over the centuries was divided and subdivided, single trees or rows of trees were lawful demarcation of individual properties. The practical meaning and usefulness may have changed, rows of trees nowadays are planted as wind breakers, bunds and dykes to control run-off waters, most naturally they often coincide with the wisdom of traditional topographic or geographic boundaries. In both rural India and all of southern Europe, rows of prickly bushes, often blackberry in France and Italy, are still planted as source of abundant edible fruits and obstacle to human or cattle trespassers or marauding carnivores. Unlike the ramparts of the *pur* or the *polis,* field boundaries are made of living vegetation. Soon after her advent in Greece and the spreading of her teachings, goddess Demeter was responsible also for surveying the distribution and demarcation of arable lands in a fair and honest manner.

In the east, the nomadic Aryan tribes eventually settled in the Punjab and gradually expanded throughout the entire Gangetic plains, however this could not be accomplished without the usual violent expression of human frailties: jealousy, envy, greed and competition, the main outburst of which was the great Bhārata War. Kochhar (*l.c.*) knowingly concludes that: "the bloodshed seems to have been a part of the transition that the Indo-Aryans had to make from the autonomous Ṛgvedic nomadism to settled life which entailed assimilation of native cultural and ethnic elements."

Evidently technicalities and laws must be appropriate to the setting and the times. The development of agriculture required the development of appropriate technologies for tilling, ploughing, sowing, reaping, threshing and for storing the harvest. New and more plants were introduced in the west where the last glaciation had destroyed a major part of plant species for food, construction, textiles and dyes. In the east the use of minerals, plants, animals and all natural products in general for food, medicine, textiles, utensils and weapons could be invented and improved upon earlier than in Europe. The arriving Indo-Aryans learned the arts from local people and had ample space, time, variety of materials and opportunities with which to work. The Indo-Iranians of Persia were more advanced in arts and crafts than contemporary western Indo-Europeans of Greece. Later, though he defeated the Achaemenid rulers of the Great Persian Empire, Alexander the Great of Macedonia in the fourth century BC was duly impressed by those he conquered on the battlefield and by those he could not conquer in wisdom, the brāhmaṇas (or Jains?) whom he called "naked sophists," where sophists means learned men. With time specialisation was necessary, to this day artisans of east and west have their special trademarks. In India, for instance, cloth made in Kerala has a woven-in trademark, different from textiles of Gujarat and other places.

The sea routes in the Indian Ocean were used since very ancient times with such frequency that the "Red Sea," as the Arabian Sea was known at that time, appeared to be as familiar as a large pool of water. Recently Cavalli-Sforza (1996) drew conclusions from DNA studies that suggest that groups of people from various populations may have gradually spread from coastal east Africa, moved around the Indian Ocean and perhaps reached as far as the western Pacific Ocean, following the coastline. Friends in Fiji told this author that they could trace ancestors many generations back as having come perhaps from the area of modern time northern Tanzania which they left after a devastating pestilence. They stopped for an unspecified length of time or generations perhaps in Sri Lanka and other places before reaching their present land, the islands of Fiji in the Pacific Ocean. The finding of remains of ancient civilizations such as the Harappan, in coastal areas far from their normal region of settled residence, confirm the view that ancient people travelled more often and wider than usually presumed, overland and over the oceans to distant places for trade or to establish new settlements. The time tables are in general agreement with the dates given here.

In ancient times, specially in the rural area east and west, horizons were far and wide, planets and stars could be observed easily and their motion studied the year round through an atmosphere unpolluted by the glare of modern lighting of roads and cities, by smog and other benefits and malefits of present day civilizations. It was better and easier to attune the life of the individual, of the family, of the clan, of the entire village to nature's ways and wander far and wide without getting lost.

INDO-EUROPEAN SETTLEMENTS IN EAST AND WEST

Groups of men belonging to the subspecies *Homo sapiens sapiens* are found in Europe since 6000 or perhaps 9700 BC, agriculture was introduced in Greece and Crete, about 6000 BC. Grey pottery, different from the later grey pottery of India, was found in Crete dated from the Minoan period while, according to Georgiew (in Chakrabarti, check also Renfrew, 1988) there was at least another language spoken in Greece before the advent of the Indo-Europeans. Chadwick, based on linguistic evidence, times the advent of the Indo-Europeans in Greece about the first half of the second millennium BC. There are reasons to believe that Demeter arrived at Athens from the east towards the middle of the second millennium BC (Vannucci 1999b) and brought with her the knowledge of improved agriculture.

The Indo-Europeans arrived in Hellas over two routes. One was from the plains of the Danube and the other from Asia Minor, coming from the east over Anatolia and Asia Minor, then proceeding to the island-dotted Aegean Sea and mainland Greece. In either case when they settled in Greece they were confronted with topography and natural resources different from what they knew. There were mountains from which building materials could be quarried, narrow valleys with good water, but small open fields for extensive agriculture, few species of trees, shrubs, plants and animals in general, but a very extensive coastline. The Indo-Europeans had to learn everything about the sea, from resources it offered, to the art of navigation. The Cretan and Mycenean civilizations developed massive buildings in which were preserved large amounts of artefacts and libraries (Casson 2001) a boon for present day archaeologists and scientists. Nowhere similar palaces, walled cities or burial places were left by man from the same age in India. Maybe they have not yet been found or perhaps they were destroyed by wars and intensive agriculture and extensive irrigation works. A sad example of recent destruction of important archaeological remains, is the destruction of much of the ancient city of Moenjo-Daro by Cunningham who used the bricks of the ancient Harappan city to pave roads and railways of the lower delta of R. Indus.[6]

There has been more archaeological digging in the west where ancient urban population density and urban cultures yield more and more significant information for less digging time, than in the east where the scattered nature of rural cultures multiplies efforts for lesser results. The Greek civilization was developed in islands or inside walled cities surrounded by villages, a situation that favoured the formation of a privileged urban class at odds with the rural population often, if not always, kept in bondage to ensure the provision of food and other raw materials for the ruling or dominant city. Graeco-Roman culture admitted slavery of men, women and children as normal while Arrian in his *Indika* (Arrian was born between 85 and 90 AD) on the strength of Greek historians and Megasthenes in particular, says that there were no slaves in India. Social life in ancient Greece developed different values than in the east. Ethics, philosophy and religion became centered on the relations between man and the *polis* or city-state, rather than on the relations between man and nature, nature gods and the personified forces of nature, as in India.

In the east man could not but observe and analyse the cause-effect relationships of all natural phenomena. People had faith because they were taught to rationalise the observed natural phenomena which are what they are, cannot be changed by man and are inescapable. The concept of *Ṛta,* the Law of the Cosmos, that "**Is what Is**" fixed and eternal, as for instance the movements of the planets, was firmly established in the mind of Man. Man acquired understanding of how the world system works and out of observation, logical deduction and experience he believed in the repetitive cycles of natural phenomena. Because he believed in what experience and reason had shown to be correct and true, man had Faith and Fear of the Forces and Powers of Nature, which he called gods. In the west, under the influence of ancient Egyptian and Semitic religions, man was told to have faith and to believe, *before* he understood or tried to understand the nature of things. Man was told that it is meritorious to have blind faith, this he did whether he had or not the knowledge of ancestral wisdom. The Greek schools of philosophy started experimental science only in the second half of the first millennium BC and early AD centuries. Theoretical debates took place among philosophers, notable among those that have come down to us the *De natura deorum* of Cicero (106-43 BC) and the *De rerum natura* of Lucretius (100?-57? BC). It took centuries before the Graeco-Roman world understood that one can have *conscious* faith only *after,* and not *before* having convincing knowledge of beliefs. In the east the ancient sages acquired knowledge with the purpose of becoming wise. They repeatedly remembered with reverence the "ancients" or "elders" also called the "fathers" who lived before them. In the west acquisition of knowledge was and has increasingly become the stated means for acquiring more and more power and material wealth. After centuries the process of divergence and diversification between east and west is still going on. The changes are fast and the east experiences difficulties in both being and becoming, while the west does not know how to handle what it has become.

CONCLUSION

Ghirshman (1977), based on the evidence from ethnological and archaeological findings and linguistic affinities, including his own research, summarizes what is known of the origin and migrations of the Indo-European people. New evidence acquired after the publication of his book tends to support and confirm his conclusions (see: Kochhar, R. 2000; Lahiri, N. 1992; Parpola, A. 1999; Renfrew, C. 1988, others) *fig.* 1 is reproduced from Ghirshman (1977) and summarizes graphically the routes taken by the Indo-European migrations. The author concludes convincingly that an early wave of migrations began in the fourth millennium BC. These people he calls the Indo-Aryans who moved over many centuries away from the Indo-European homeland in the Euro-Asian steppes north of the Black and Caspian Seas and around the latter's eastern shores. Many centuries later, they split in two groups. One moved in an eastern direction and eventually entered India, the other group moved westwards along the borders of the southern Caspian Sea and eventually entered Asia Minor via Anatolia and occupied most of Asia Minor.

About two millennia later, other Indo-European people, the Indo-Iranians, migrated away from the original Indo-European homeland. They soon split in two groups, one circled the eastern margins of the Caspian Sea and at the southern margin of the Caspian they again split in two branches. One branch of these Indo-Iranians moved towards the plains south of the Aral Sea, and went as far as the *doab* between the rivers Amu Darya and Syr Darya, later called Oxus and Jaxartes by Alexander. The other branch of these Indo-Iranians moved south-eastwards towards India and Baluchistan. Another group of Indo-Iranians migrated in the second millennium BC away from the original homeland and circled the western margins of the Caspian Sea. They eventually entered South Iran and reached the land called Phars and the Zagros mountains. The picture proposed by Ghirshman is based on archaeological and ethnological studies. We may conclude that it is now established that Indo-Aryans and Indo-Iranians belong to the same stock of Indo-Europeans who called themselves Aryans — they are an eastern branch of Indo-Europeans (Ghirshman, 1977). This author's conclusions are at present widely accepted and explain also the cultural evolution along these routes. They clarify the results of the hybridisation with other Indo-European and non-Indo-European cultures that took place in the course of centuries, both east and west. Ghirshman's interpretation of the data relating to Indo-Aryans stop at the approach to the River Indus hydrological system.

The studies referred to in this book go only as far as the beginning of the Christian Era. The scenario described here refers to the people as seen in their geographical perspective of space and time.

(B) The Problem and the Very Ancient Past

A few millennia ago the proto-Indo-Europeans inhabited the Eurasian steppes, north of the Caucasus mountains and the lands and steppes north of the Black and Caspian Seas from where they eventually migrated. After different groups were separated by migrations and other causes, each evolved separately. The problem therefore is to find how much of the original traits, if any, can be recognised in each group at present.

MYTHOLOGY

The search here refers to different times, all of them ancient or very ancient. Migrations and displacements in general did not take place suddenly as single episodic events, more often they dragged over many generations and were triggered by climatic changes or cataclysms, famines, feuds among tribes, the capacity to domesticate new plants and animals, devastating epidemic diseases of humans or their animals, invading hordes of enemies and so on. As far as geologic time is concerned, we will not deal here with the Palaeolithic, when *Homo sapiens* emerged as a separate species or as an invader into areas new to the species. Proto-history and pre-history are concerned with culture before the invention of writing. However, the terms "writing" and "script" are themselves difficult to define. At what stage do symbols, paintings, knots made on strings, the way they are represented and spatially arranged, acquire the designation and value of proper writing or script? Was there a single time or place when and where writing was invented? For instance, there are 419 distinct signs in the Harappan script and the longest inscription has 26 signs, but more often there are only a few on single artefacts of the Harappan civilization (Kochhar *p.c.*). The Harappan is so far an undeciphered script, but are these signs arranged in sequence, do they form a sentence, or are they just symbols, as is suggested from the fact that there are only very few of them, not more than 17 at any single place? We will forego the important question of script and writing and at this stage we will concentrate on the oral tradition. Testimonials of ancient cultures exist independently and beyond of what is conventionally defined *script.*

Cave paintings of early man are a case in point. An old question was alive among zoologists who were puzzled about the presence and disappearance of lions or tigers in Europe. The skeleton of lions and tigers are identical and cannot be told apart except for a single minor point. The tip of the tail of the male lion has a small claw-like horn in the middle of the hairy terminal tuft. The two species may interbreed but their territories do not normally overlap. The lion is much more specific than the tiger in its environmental requirements, and its presence in southern Europe was a hint on the climate prevailing at the time of the paintings. Finally the question was solved by a young zoologist who noticed that the cubs painted on the walls of the Altamira caves by pre-historic man, showed the cubs with a spotted fur. Tiger cubs are not spotted, and the spots on the fur of the young lions disappear not long after birth. The faithful rendering of details of the fur of lion cubs is in some sort an eloquent form of script. History does *not* begin with the invention of a script, in my opinion it begins much earlier under a variety of forms. I feel confident that archaeologists would agree.

Myths and legends refer essentially to facts, acts and beings that may have lived or taken place in early periods and survived as tradition in the collective memory of the people. Distance from past times adds mystery and glory to the story, but truth and reality become blurred by enthusiasm. Enthusiasm, we must remember, literally means "having God inside the self" which is the same as "to be possessed by a god." Enthusiasm is not faithlessness, on the contrary, enthusiasm with the passage of time, enriches traditional myths at every re-telling. The older the deities and heroes, the more numerous and phantastic are the myths telling about their feats and glory. It could be difficult to winnow the chaff from the grain, but patient search may help to visualise what ideas, understanding or concept the god or hero stood for **in the beginning**. The pair Dionysos/Demeter offers a clue to the question of the passage from the free use of wild nature to the methodical care and use of forests or pastureland, such as agriculture, animal husbandry and forestry. It is this big step forward from proto-history to pre-history that induces the emergence of traditional wisdom, socio-economic patterns, diversification of cultures and writing. This is the central theme of this book.

The symbolisms of the proto-history of *Homo sapiens* refer mainly to the fertility of his own species: from the virility of man and feminine reproduction, to the fertility of Mother Earth, the universal nourisher, and Sun and Water without which there is no life. The Indo-European root for water is *Akwa*, from which Aqua derives in Latin and all neo-latin languages. Virility is evident in the widespread occurrence of menhirs, lingams and other monoliths usually represented as rough or carefully carved standing stones or as rocks and cave paintings and later by paintings on pottery, carvings and sculptures in the round, often ithyphallic. Standing rocks, carved or not may also have been used as territorial markings. Fertility of women and of Mother Earth is usually symbolised as the feminine isosceles triangle, the *yoni*, or as feminine figurines, often with exaggerated secondary sexual characters. Some of these characters have survived into modern times, as for instance the praised steatopygia of women among some African and other people. Water is represented by undulating lines or ditches, as later became common in the chordate pottery. Most of these symbols have remained unchanged and are still used or have reached a secondary degree of symbolism wherever man has gone. Many of the ideograms of various cultures, like some of the hieroglyphs of Egypt or the *kanji* of China have the same origin, a stereotyped representation of an idea or thing.

One of the many important teachings of R.N. Dandekar (1997, 1981, 1979 a, b, c) is that everything evolves, therefore changes with time: "even the gods evolved" during the long history of the cultural evolution of the people of the world. The subject-matter of this book is the evolution of the most ancient gods of the Indo-Aryans and Indo-Iranians and of the Graeco-Roman pantheon. The Indo-Europeans were people of different lineages related by languages having common verbal roots, similar grammar and syntaxis. After many generations and extensive migrations from their place of origin, different clans settled in lands for which they fought and eventually called their own. Those who called themselves Arya settled and gave their name to the Indian sub-continent including India and Iran. Their influence and culture reached Hellas or Greater Greece in the west, passing through Asia Minor. We postulate here that divergence in philosophical attitudes, religion and social habits were much greater and quicker among the Indo-Europeans of the Graeco-Roman urban civilization than among the Indo-Europeans of the Indo-Iranian long period of pastoral/agrarian civilization. No chronological study in absolute time is attempted here, emphasis is on the processes and trends of development and changes in the cultures and philosophies in east and west, rather than on the description of historical facts. Of special interest are the changes in the philosophical and religious attitudes of the two groups, the Indo-Europeans of the east, mainly Indo-Iranian, and the Indo-Europeans of the west, both derived most probably from the same ancestral heritage with inputs from cultures of people with whom they had extensive contact and with whom they intermingled or ruled over. We may anticipate here that some of the basic characteristics have remained unchanged, such as some gestures[8] or the great, fundamental importance given to Truth and speaking only the truth, to the horse, and the patriarchal social pattern with the key role of the mother as the binding element of the family circle. To this day among many Indo-European people, the "womb (or uterine) cousin-brother or cousin-sister" is considered to be closer by blood than the paternal cousin-brother or cousin-sister. Much, however, changed or acquired new values in the course of centuries because of different environmental conditions, including other people with whom the Indo-Europeans mixed, as well as different foods and materials available. The myths of different people reflect the story of changes of customs and habits.

INDO-EUROPEAN CULTURES

Filippo Sassetti (born 1540 in Florence, Italy) arrived at Cochin (now Kochi) in 1583, died at Goa in 1588. Sassetti was a writer and traveller and, as far as I know, one of the first Europeans who mentions in letters to his friends Bernardo Davanzati and Pier Vettori of Florence, that the languages spoken in India are derived from Sanskrit (written by Sassetti: *sanscruta*) and are closely related to Italian and other Latin languages. Volumes of "Collected Letters" and other writings of Sassetti, a learned and perspicacious observer, are kept in the "Biblioteca Marucelliana" (Marucelliana Library), in the National Library and Archives of Florence. Indo-European is a term invented in 1813 by Thomas Young and generally accepted since, though not without some reservations. The term refers to people speaking languages with a common origin, as redefined by Renfrew (1988). It is generally accepted that the land of origin of the Indo-European were the Eurasian steppes, from where they expanded west and east, Europe and Central Asia, as far as the Altai mountains region. After the groups were separated by centrifugal migrations, each evolved in a different direction. The problem therefore is: how much of the original characters and traits can be recognised in each group at present? Are the parallelisms recorded in historical times generally valid? What factors induced specific differentiations? What weight did inputs from other cultures have? What were the influences from different environments? We will try to throw some light on these and other questions, many of which unresolved so far.

Ghirshman (1977) described and discussed the role played by the Indo-Aryan branches of the Indo-Europeans in the great development of martial arts achieved in the second millennium BC in the kingdoms of Mitanni and Hatti, capital city of the Hittites. When they were living in the Gorgan (= Gurgan) plains, east of the southern Caspian Sea, the Indo-Europeans had already bred a race of horses which is still nowadays very appreciated and is called the "turkoman" horse.[7] These horses are taller, stronger and faster than those originally bred in Central Asia which were not much bigger than a pony. The Indo-Aryans had also improved the early solid wheel into the spoked type, initially with four, then six and finally with eight spokes, best suited for the war chariot. The "turkoman" horse was so famous that the Egyptians waged several military campaigns into Syria for the procurement of horses, after the turkoman race had been introduced there by the Hittites. The Egyptians frequently requested chariots and horses from the Mitanni king and when Pharaoh Amenophis III wooed the hand of the daughter of the Indo-European Hittite king Tushratta (a name of Sanskrit extraction), the king agreed to the marriage by sending horses and chariots as a gift and pledge. Earlier, after the battle of Megiddo (1480 BC in N. Palestine), the Egyptians had captured 924 chariots as booty. It is interesting to point out that the Greeks met camels used in battle and for riding only much later, since they were used by Medes and Persians only as late as the Great Graeco-Persian Wars moved by the Achaemenid kings of Persia, as mentioned in "The Birds," one of the "comedies" by Aristophanes.

Kikkuli was a Mitanni horse trainer who served under the Hittites. He wrote a treatise on the breeding and training of horses. The language used includes typical Indo-Aryan words, such as orders given for the performance of the horses in parades and in battle. It also includes the notion of circle, distances are measured in *āryan* (sic) numerals, and the word *stadia*, race course and other specialised words are common. *Aspa* (= horse) is used for *ashwa,* and *ratha* (= war chariot) occurs frequently in the text of the treatises as well as in the compound names of members of the ruling Indo-Aryan class. The bulk of the population was autochthonous, had a different ethnicity and spoke a different language. They had come from the mountains in the third millennium BC before the advent of the Indo-Aryan Hittites and Mitanni.

Another item important for the development of the martial arts was invented by the Indo-Aryans. This was the trumpet. It was used to transmit commands to the various units during parades and deployment in battle. Among the many prized gifts given by king Tushratta to Pharaoh Amenophis III were also 40 trumpets. Some of these were made with or ornamented with gold or silver and precious stones, and were obviously intended to be used during ceremonial occasions. Others were simple, made of brass and must have been used to train horses for battle and parades, as well as on the battle field to direct troops and chariots (Ghirshman, *l.c.*).

EVOLUTION FROM THE HEROIC TIMES

The age that antedates the art of writing is the "heroic" age of all people, when myths and legends are born, nurtured and embellished according to the whims and inventiveness of the story tellers and of the mental, psychological and political needs of the audience and of the rulers. The proto-history of the Indo-Europeans begins in the Eurasian steppes according to present day knowledge. Incidentally, the word *samudra* which means Sea in Sanskrit as used in the older Vedic hymns, surely refers to the Black, the Caspian and the Aral Sea which are all centered about lat. 35°N-45°N, which means that seasons and calendar fixes, such as solstices and equinoxes define the same pattern of daylight duration and night/darkness in all the latitudinal belt. Daylight duration is of fundamental importance for agriculture, pastoralism and climate forecast and seasonal rhythms. It also leads to easy geographical orientation during displacements and migrations. These three Seas had salty waters and are ocean relicts, a fact which early man could not know, but is significant for his perception of the environment in which he moved. Marine mammals such as seals and other species of marine origin are survivals of the fauna of the archaic ocean in these "seas" where they are relicts of the species present in the ancient Thetis Sea. In all the ancient and very ancient Asian legends of the great deluge, the Caucasus is recalled as the only or the principal part of the surface of the Earth that was not flooded over. These three large inland seas where the distant margin is hidden below the horizon, were designated with the same word: *samudra*, which may have been later used also to designate the Arabian Sea and Indian Ocean, though the word *sāgara* was a more common name later used for the open ocean. It is not likely that the noun *samudra* in the *ṚV* refers to the Indian Ocean, though marine shells, including the conch, are found at Mehrgarh Level One, hundreds of miles away from the sea. Remains of marine animals and other materials of marine origin inland are rightly considered to be indicative of trade, rather than direct personal contact and knowledge of inland people with the ocean.

The great achievements of the Indo-European cultures at the very beginning were, first: domestication of farm animals, which meant independence from obligatory hunting for food, second: domestication of the horse, which initially was reared for its meat, and was then trained for traction and later, for riding and war, and third: the most probably independent invention of the wheel. Of these they had two types, the old, heavy, solid type wheel for ox-drawn carts and wagons, and the light spoked wheel for horse driven hunting and war chariots that carried one, two, or exceptionally three men. From hunting wild horses for meat to using them for traction and riding, the proto-Indo-Europeans became great travellers and had then the capacity to expand their frontiers east, west and south. For ever after the Indo-Europeans and their descendants had the horse as the "noble animal" par excellence, as praised by Swift in "Gulliver's Travels." They had the oxen as a draft animal for heavy duties and the cow, giver of plenty. One of the main centres of domestication of the horse had been the Gorgan plain, at the feet of the Elburz Mountains, on the south-east corner of the Caspian Sea. The horse was thoroughlly bred between 3000 and 2250 BC (Hancar,F. 1934; 1956, *apud* Ghirshman, also Cambridge Natural History of Iran, 1968, v.1, p. 301). Careful breeding produced the *turkoman race*, famous to this day for its endurance, strength and swiftness and capable of going into a jouste or battle himself covered by a heavy armour and at the same time carrying a cavalier inside his own armour inflicting heavy blows to a similar heavily armed opponent. Man and horse armours could weigh as much as 30-40 kg.[7]

Among all Aryan clans and their descendants the cow became the "second mother" of the people, producer of milk and milk products, butter, curds, ghee, also manure, bullocks for traction (trotting bullocks are praised even at present in India), for ploughing, for horns, tendons and hides. Sheep and goats provide hides, wool, milk and cheese. Domesticated animals made it possible to colonise different environments, sheep and goats took herdsmen to the high pastures and paved the way to nomadism and seasonal transhumance. The production of varieties of cereals adapted to different climates ensured livelihood during displacements and after reaching new settlements.

SOURCES

People would have lived the nomadic existence of shepherds and herdsmen who had domesticated the horse, cattle, sheep, goats, wild pigs and dogs when the families settled in temporary or permanent villages. The horse became the cultural fingerprint of the Indo-Europeans. The camel and its variety, the one hump dromedary, and donkeys were domesticated by Semitic people in desert areas. The wagons for transport of people and goods were also used as granaries, traction of wagons was a heavy duty exclusively given to the bullocks. Well bred and nurtured, the horse grew in stature, agility and speed and was trained for parades, war and riding. The stirrup was introduced much later by the Mongolian invaders. Before them, even the Roman Emperors rode bare back or with simple leather or felt covers over the horse and no stirrups. The experience with diversified foods and means of transport enabled the Indo-Europeans to expand over more fertile lands, eastwards, westwards and southwards. Migrations brought the Indo-Aryans into the very large area conventionally called Major India and the Indian sub-continent. Artefacts obtained from searches in the Swat valleys in present-day Pakistan, give a date of *c.* 1744 BC for the earliest Indo-European settlements in the Indian subcontinent, however more ancient remains could be found in Afghanistan, where little archaeological research has been carried out. On these matters more information is available in Ghirshman (1977), Lahiri (1992), Chakrabarti, D.K. (1999), Kochhar (2000), Bhargava (2001), Guidotti and Daddi (2002 eds. of a multi-author book and multimedia reconstruction of the battle of Kadesh and of the plain and times when it took place), and others. The reconstruction of the Vedic culture in the east, where major archaeological remains are few, is mainly represented by beads, mud-brick structures, pottery, metal artifacts, granaries and kitchen left-overs. Vedic and Avestic cultures are still centered on the study of the Vedas and Vedānta, the Avesta, the Indian epics and Purāṇas, the Itihāsa and the very rich ancient Indian literature, ethnology and linguistics, the oral tradition and myths. In the west, reconstruction of the Greek culture is, exhaustive though of course, not complete. Archaeology, the critical reading of the classics, of the epics beyond Homer and Virgil and of the philosophical literature of Greece and Rome are very well known and of common domain.

Summarizing the present knowledge, Kochhar (*l.c.*) concludes correctly that "The proto-Indo-Europeans are allotted the continuous territory to the south of the Finno-Ugric lands, that is the resource-poor steppes bordering the Caspian and Black Seas. It is noteworthy that this territory has not been associated with any other language group." He adds (p.147): "Significantly, the evidence for the domestication of the horse comes from the steppe zone already suggested as the proto-Indo-European homeland on linguistic grounds."

CONCLUSION

Summing up, it is generally accepted that the Indo-Europeans were a group of people not necessarily all of the same ethnicity who originally lived in the same region, had a common language, similar customs, habits and beliefs. They were pastoralists and also agriculturists. From their homeland in the Euro-Asian steppes, they migrated to Europe and Central Asia following the eastern and western margins of the Caspian Sea, and over the Caucasus mountains into eastern Turkey. The people who called themselves Arya, here called Indo-Europeans of the east, migrated southwards into the Iranian plateau, eastwards into Major India, and westward towards Anatolia and Asia Minor, the Aegean Sea islands and mainland Greece. Different groups of the proto Indo-Aryans who migrated eastwards moved towards the Altaï mountains (we are not concerned with them here) while others moved towards Sapta-Sindhava, the Punjab and India. Other groups of Indo-European people also arrived in Greece and Macedonia coming from the plains of the western littoral zone of the Black Sea and the plains of R. Danube. The most numerous of these were Thracians. Wherever the Indo-Europeans migrated, they met autochthonous people with whom they fought, submitted peacefully or absorbed, or all of these at the same or successive times. In the east they met people probably of Dravidian origin and the Harappans about whose origin little is known for sure. In Central Asia the Indo-Europeans had ample interaction with people of Semitic origin, in West Asia they came in contact with Phoenicians (Semitic), Egyptians, Pelasgoi and other autochthonous people of Greece and Italy.

As mentioned above, there are no sure data about the arrival of the Indo-Europeans in India. There was surely more than one wave of arrivals spaced over undeterminable lapses of time and there were not only Aryans but other Indo-European clans as well, such as the Saka (a branch of the Scyths?). In Central and West Asia there were several different groups of Indo-European people beyond the Indo-Aryans and the Indo-Iranians. They were Medes, Mitanni and others. Though the Indo-Europeans maintained most of their habits, they also acquired some of those of the people with whom they came in contact or subjugated. Some of the cultural exchanges are well known and the most important acquisition was the use of the cuneiform script because the Indo-Europeans did not have a script of their own. The syllabic phonetic cuneiform script had been developed in Sumer, centuries earlier and could be used to write different languages, including Semitic languages of Babylon, Akkad, and that of the Hurrites(?) among others.

Details are well-known of what today would be called the balance of powers between West Asia and the Pharaohs of Egypt, because of the war for the supremacy over Amurru, roughly present-day Syria. The army of young Pharaoh Ramses II (ruled 1292-1225 BC) clashed with the Hittite army of king Muwatalli II whose capital was the city of Hattusha in the kingdom of Hatti created in the sixteenth century BC by the Indo-Aryan king Hattusilli I. King Hattusilli III signed the Final Peace Treaty between Hatti and Egypt in 1259. The site where Hattusha flourished has been the object of extensive archaeological diggings in the twentieth century (Gimbutas 1970, 1974), specially in the area that is now Boghazkoy. In the plains of present-day Syria at Kadesh, in about 1270 BC (?1275) a famous battle was fought between the Egyptian army of Ramses II and the Hittite army of Muwatalli II. About this battle there is abundant information in cuneiform, hieroglyphic and Egyptian ancient cursive script, as well as inscriptions on monuments in Egypt and elsewhere. The battle of Kadesh marked the northern-most extent on the Mediterranean coast of West Asia of the dominion of the Pharaohs. North of Kadesh lands were traditionally occupied by Semitic people and in later times were ruled and partially occupied by Indo-Europeans of the east. The battle of Kadesh facilitated the access of the Indo-Aryans to the eastern Mediterranean, while the northern approaches to the Aegean Sea and parts of the Peloponnesus were already dominated by them. The Indic speaking Indo-Aryans who had already conquered an opening on the Mediterranean Sea needed to strengthen their position on the access to the sea, hence their eagerness to conquer the area of present-day Syria. Cultural exchanges between Hittites, Egyptian and Semitic people were greatly intensified after the recognized uselessness of the battle for the hegemony over Amurru undertaken at Kadesh by the two kings, the young Egyptian pharaoh Ramses II and the Hittite Muwatalli II. As a matter of fact, after the third day of battle, the kings came to an agreement as they recognized that neither could establish an absolute victory on the battlefield, a rare and notable example of royal wisdom. The battle of Kadesh *c.* 1275 BC marks the northernmost limit of Egyptian expansion into West Asia as well as the southern extent of the Indo-Aryan dominance. The international boundary was respected during two centuries but further historical developments eventually rearranged the political map of the region.

In conclusion, both Egyptians and Indo-Aryans, retained their front on the Mediterranean shores, shared with Phoenicians, Canaanites, Amurrans and other people, where the famous cities of Ugarit, Biblos, Sidon, Tyre and others were located. Only the battles of Marathon (490 BC) and Salamina (480 BC) more than seven hundred years later, were comparably decisive in setting the course of the history of the western World. At Salamina and Marathon the advance of the navy and army of the Indo-Iranian Achaemenid Persian Empire was blocked by the Indo-Europeans of Greece, many of which were of Indo-Aryan origin while others were of Thracian descent.

About eight centuries after Kadesh, the defeat of the great Persian Kings by the Greeks re-oriented and determined the course of European history and civilization and blocked the access of the Indo-Iranians into South Europe.

The battle of Kadesh is more important for its ideologic and cultural implications than for the military "success" or "failure" of the sides. It was the first time that the "Great King," the Pharaoh could not subjugate "barbarious people" such as the "treacherous Hittites" and had to admit that he was not the exclusive, single, "legitimate Power on Earth." Ramses II returned home without having achieved his goal, and the kingdom of Amurru, remained a Semitic enclave between the kingdom of Egypt, under the rule of the pharaohs in the South and the kingdom of Hatti in the North, under the rule of the Indo-Aryan Hittites. In spite of the language, ethnic and ideological barriers, the Egyptian and the Hittite leaders had reached the agreement to respect the *status quo.* Such was the subject and decision documented in the first *interim* treaties and in the final "Peace Treaty" sealed in 1259 BC that followed the battle of Kadesh. The clashes happened approximately at the time usually considered to be that of the Great Bhārata War in India. The important point in the context of this book is that the final treaty drawn between Ramses II of Egypt and Hatusilli III, the new king of Hatti and brother of Muwatalli II who had died in the meantime, was written and sealed according to the form used by the Hittite Chancellery which was well versed in such matters because of the experience gained during the long expansion of the Indo-Aryans westwards, after leaving the plains of R. Gurgaun. On the Egyptian side, never before the Great King, the Pharaoh of Egypt had lowered himself to the same level of a king of another "Great Country." He had to rely and bow to a double text written in cuneiform script and Indo-Aryan language and the corresponding text written in cursive Egyptian script and language. The Indo-Aryans did not have their own script at that time. The strategy and the technicalities of the Hittites are very similar to those described in the *Mahābhārata,* also the war tactics shown in sculpture on the Hoysala temples of Central India, and described in the Iliad and in the many accounts of the Persian wars are practically the same. The young pharaoh Ramses II was taken aback by the war strategy of the Hittites. The wars of the Egyptian pharaohs had been until then typically not much more than ceremonial performances of the Great King who showed off his Great Army and his World Power and over-ruling intent. The Great King had seldom, if ever, been confronted by fighting troops and the planned war tactics of the "barbarian Hittites" intent on winning the war.

Another significant detail of the text of the final Treaty drawn after the battle of Kadesh and of the ensuing correspondence between the two great kings that followed the Battle, was the preparation of elaborate arrangements for the weddings that took place between the parties, the gifts exchanged and the rich dowry given to the young Hittite princesses. About one century prior to the battle of Kadesh, the great Hittite king Suppiliulima I had signed a treaty with the Indo-European Mitanni king Matiuwaza, son of Tushratta after invocations and calling to witness R̥gvedic gods. Significantly all the gods called to witness are the ancient-most gods of the Indo-Aryans. This indicates that the groups of Indo-Aryans **coming** from the east, were separated at a very early stage from the bulk of the Indo-Aryans who **migrated eastwards** into India. There is no mention of Vedic or Avestic gods further west than Asia Minor, with the only exception of the very important god Mithra, supervisor of obedience to Law and Justice, the Indo-Aryan Mitra, or Mithra for the Indo-Iranian. After the battle of Kadesh, the protection of the Egyptian god Seth is now repeatedly requested by the Egyptians.

The kingdom of Hatti was created and became established in the seventeenth-sixteenth centuries by the Indo-Aryan king Hattusili I, with its capital Hattusha, modern Boghazkoy. Very soon the Hittites were engaged in wars with the Mitanni kingdom and in about 1350 BC a peace treaty was sealed between king Matiwaza of the Mitanni and King Suppiliulima of Hatti (Kochhar, 2000), during the reign of the eighteenth dynasty of Egypt, mentioned here only for chronological reference. Vedic gods called to witness as guarantors of the treaty were the Vedic Mitra, Varuṇa, Indra and the Aśvinis (= Nasatyas). After the reign of the Hittite Suppiliulima I and the reign of Muwatalli II, the Hittite kings were Arnuwanda II and Mursili II, a period that coincides with the time of the sixteenth-seventeeth Egyptian dynasties (1640-1540 BC) which includes the short lived Hyksos rule. The name Hyksos is an Egyptian abbreviation of "*hekau-khasut*" meaning "princes of foreign countries." The Hyksos brought with them to Egypt the horse, the two-horse war charriot and the spoked wheel that replaced the solid wheel. The earliest spoked wheels had four spokes, they were replaced by the six-spoked wheel, later by the eight spoked wheel. The older model of the war chariot was a Sumerian invention, it had solid wheels, was drawn by two donkeys or mules, not horses and carried two men, occasionally could carry a third one. The driver was usually the warrior who carried bow and arrows and lances.

In contemporary publications there is some chronological confusion arising from the fact that there were two Hatti kings with the name Suppiliulima. Suppiliulima I lived during the reign of the thirteenth-fourteenth (1750-1640 BC) Egyptian dynasties and Suppiluliuma II during the twenty-third Egyptian dynasty (818-715 BC). Also there were two Muwatalli kings of Hatti. Muwatalli I lived at the time of the seventh-tenth Egyptian dynasties (2150-2100 BC) while Muwatalli II is the Hatti king of the battle of Kadesh (1275 BC). There were at least three kings named Hattusili of the Hittites. The acceptance of a common god identified with the sun, called Seth or Mithra also indicates the respect and perhaps partial acceptance by both sides, Hittites and Egyptians, of each other's ideology and religion as well as the growing influence of other cultures on the Indo-Europeans following their displacements westwards. Mithra has the double personality of law maker and obedience to the law, he was identified with the sun and acquired some importance also in Rome, specially during the Empire, his cult flourished even in the early centuries AD. Well preserved temples dedicated to Mithra have been found under the city of Rome, where the bull is usually associated to the god Mitra. It is interesting to note that the seal of the dynasty of Suppiliulima has in the centre top, a winged solar disc which suggests that the ruling dynasty of Hatti claimed Solar descent, a suggestive Indo-Aryan trait.

(C) Proto-history and Pre-history

Some scholars define pre-history as the times prior to the invention of writing. Gimbutas (in Renfrew 1994) defines writing a "characteristic of urban civilizations that have reached the level of States." It is however not true that geographic names have come down to us "only through the neighbours who had a script." Experience shows that the transfer of knowledge by the oral tradition can be more pointed, correct and more deeply rooted than the transfer from the written word; illiterate masses have a very good individual and collective memory. The oral tradition, often in metric form such as songs and poetry, is more easily and correctly memorised and undergoes only minor changes as the language itself evolves. The written texts are usually in prose and suffer from translations, changes, "improvements" and errors entered willingly or not by scribes, translators and reviewers. To this day foreigners coming to countries with ancient civilizations, as for instance India, Italy or Greece, are amazed at the wealth of knowledge of the common people specially in the rural area, in terms of practicalities, myths, legends, value and use of plants and animals, medicinal plants and minerals, agricultural practices, health and nutrition, culture in general and above all, popular wisdom. In fact we would not be here if our ancestors had not been knowledgeable and wise. Apart from the sacerdotal classes, womenfolk were and still are, the main preservers of the traditional lore on which they feed children and grandchildren. Recently, Capila (2002) produced a collection and explanation of the songs usually improvised by the women of Garhwal, their relationship with the forest and their daily life of toil. Sax (1991) recorded songs recited during the pilgrimage to Nandadevī, the contents of which are reminders of the ancient-most traditions from the most remote past.

Proto-history can be seen as the stage when people or groups of people lived in isolation during long periods of time, during winters, monsoons or natural catastrophes, without any or only very little interaction with other people or groups. Isolation requires self-sufficiency for survival. Pre-history begins when different people or groups of people interact and mutually enrich their factual knowledge and genetic potential. Trade is one of the most efficient means of transfer of knowledge and expertise, of material and mythological culture.

ORAL AND WRITTEN TRADITION

Darius the Great, king of ancient Persia who ruled 521-486 BC left in 520 BC the following message for posterity: "I invented a writing of a different type for the Aryan language, which did not exist earlier." The script of the Greeks in Bactria was *kharoṣṭī*. The coins of king Menander I Soter (155-130 BC) and of other Greek kings of Bactriana were engraved in a Sanskrit-derived Indic language and *kharoshthi* script, as was also the famous *Milindapanha*. The "Tokarian" language of Tarin, also an Indo-European language, was written in *brahmi* script since the eighth and seventh centuries BC, the manuscripts were written on palm leaf or wooden tablets. It should be noted that the language of the Indo-Aryan Hittites was earlier written in cuneiform, the script of their neighbours. At another time and other lands, the language spoken by the Medes (Young 1967), a people of Indo-European origin, has partially survived as Kurdish under the form of four closely related dialects, the Northern, Central and Southern Kermanji and the Gurani. Kurdish is an Aryan language closely related to ancient Persian (Soane E.B. 1918).

Proto-historic times were characterised by diffuse knowledge and transmission of culture mainly by example rather than teaching. In pre-historic times, language was gradually enriched with new words. Expanding grammar allowed for better and more precise explanations and teaching while knowledge contributed to create the roots of experience and wisdom. The mythical deeds of gods and heroes were told and retold and enriched by community story-tellers and elders, for better education of the new generations and when required, also for self-praise and glorification of the family, clan or tribe. Mime, and figurative representations, besides songs would have started very early and contributed to brain development and facial expression.[8] Stories can be told just with mime and gestures. During pre-historic times myths were canonised and gradually enriched by new and more significant details. Anecdotic enrichments are a feed-back mechanism that creates the culture and sense of belonging and integration of each individual and of the families into the community. Enrichment of culture gives a purpose to create lifestyles greater and nobler than just eating, sleeping and reproducing.

SOURCES

Philosophic ideas, including material and structural techniques, methods and science are born in pre-historic times, which could also be called the "heroic times" when being and becoming create customs and habits that evolve into a more complex culture and may become great civilizations.[8] Recorded in the oral tradition, pre-historic knowledge refers to personalities, facts and places which may have existed really and evolve into legendary history. The epics are based on the oral tradition. Kochhar, based on anthropological, archaeological and linguistic studies has convincingly confirmed what others before him, had said, namely that some of the Indo-European people migrated into the Indian sub-continent towards the second millennium BC. Pre-Vedic and Vedic lore are valid and essentially the only reliable sources to give some insight into the beliefs of the "ancients." Similarly the Homeric epics, the Iliad and the Odyssey, whether or not produced by a single poet called Homer (eighth century BC), as well as the so-called "Homeric hymns," probably produced by more than one anonymous ancient poet, the *aedes*, the *rhapsodists*, the *citharists* and story tellers of ancient Greece, refer to proto-historic and pre-historic times when man was at the doorstep of the developing European, usually called western, civilizations, their religion and literature. The great leap forward took place when agricultural activities were added to the until-then only hunting and pastoral way of life. Methodical agriculture, including irrigation, brought an immense improvement of lifestyles, life expectancy and health as well as decrease of infantile mortality through better nutrition. When Indic speaking people arrived in Greece, they already had an array of domestic animals, including the horse for traction, riding and warfare, they had the wheel and bronze. They met people who spoke archaic greek and cultivated *Triticum durum* and other species of tetraploid wheat which were already acclimatised locally since about 6000 BC. What probably was not yet practised at any critical level was irrigation, though the art was already well-developed and common in Asia.

FOSSIL, ARCHAEOLOGICAL AND CULTURAL REMAINS

Abundant fossil remains in south Europe also indicate the presence of settlements of Neanderthal-type people and the arrival of *Homo sapiens sapiens*, or modern man, the so-called Cro-Magnon Man. For a period Neanderthal and Cro-Magnon may have coexisted and perhaps interbred at places in southern Europe. Modern man arrived in Europe probably from West Asia about 40,000 to 45,000 yrs BC (Cavalli-Sforza, 1996) but nothing can be said about their perception of the world they lived in.[9] There is only conjectural and scattered evidence of the very ancient past, it is in itself subject to a variety of interpretations and is a frequent object of debate among anthropologists, archaeologists and ethnologists. What matters here is to point out that the Indo-Europeans of the west did not arrive into a cultural vacuum when they settled in the areas of southern Europe new to them. Some knowledge about daily habits, weapons and customs of the earlier people can be inferred from archaeologicaly datable remains or cave paintings, which may have been known to the new immigrants. Though the gap is large and ancient, I will enter directly into that part of pre-history that is referred to as the "knowledge of the ancients," the Indian sages, the *ṛṣis*, and referred to as "legends" and "wisdom of the elders" and mythology in the western Helladic tradition called Hellenism. The Vedas were written very late, not without opposition by the priestly class, and used a script adapted from Mediterranean phonetic alphabets, especially Phoenician and Greek.

What should be pointed out is that expansion did not happen as mass migrations of entire populations or a major part of it. There are many examples that show that expansion into new territories was often realised by small wandering groups even in proto- and pre-historic ages. Two historically recorded examples in Asia may be mentioned. The first refers to the people that became known as Sumerians. It is known from cuneiform texts that they "arrived from the sea in small numbers." They were gradually absorbed into the local population which was at that time already present in the lower reaches of the Tigris and Euphrates rivers that had separate outlets into the Persian Gulf. The lower reaches of the two great rivers merged into a single channel, the Shatt-al-Arab in historical times. The Sumerians gradually organized the highly structured civilization that bears their name and invented what is considered to be the earliest non-pictographic, syllabic form of script, the cuneiform script. The second example is that of the Hittites who established a powerful nation, well organized militarily, though the bulk of the people were ethnically different from them and spoke a different language.

The "God of Tempests" of the ancient Mesopotamians, under this or other names is the early god of most primitive cultures. The proto-historic figure of Dionysos in the west is very ancient and much older than the Indo-European expansion into Europe, it is originally the personified aspect of wild nature, violent and gentle, generous only if respected and followed obediently. In the proto-history of Greece, there are different names for basically the same God, the counterpart of the proto-Dionysos. His personality was the catalyser for the domestication of plants and animals, for taming rivers and conquering the fear of navigation in the "boundless seas." Dionysos, the personification of wild nature and its bounties, closes the great cycle of nature by teaching mankind how to use nature itself and how to participate in its rites. This was achieved first by instituting the Dionysiac Mysteries, then by bringing Demeter to Greece. By being her *"paredros"* Dionysos agrees to teach healthy nature's ways to mankind.[10] Demeter (= Cerere for the Romans) is an imported personality, brought to Greece from the east by Dionysos himself. She is the one who showed to the Greek people how to produce better and more nourishing food with better varieties of cereals, methodical agriculture and perhaps also irrigation, hence the propitiatory rites to River Ilyssos (Vannucci 1999b) that waters the Rharyan plains in Attika. Irrigation gives freedom from dependence on rains that only too often fail. Extensive irrigation probably started as far back as the third millennium BC in Iran.[11] Legends also tell us that it was a woman who acquired the habit of planting rice and showed man how to cultivate it in what is now north-east India. In the *R̥V* wild nature and its bounties are beautifully represented by the elusive personality of Araṇyāni (Vannucci 1999), the Lady of the Forest, "who tills not, yet has stores of food" for those who respect her.

An updated synthesis of the present knowledge of archaeological findings in India may be found in D.K. Chakrabarti, (2001) and will not be repeated here. A critical summary and updated bibliography of ancient archaeological remains in the lands where the Indo-Iranians settled, which is mainly present-day Iran and parts of Iraq, can be found in Girshman (1977).[12]

The third and second millennia BC witnessed a great advance in cultural development in east and west, which took place before writing was invented or used. We do not discuss here Mesopotamian and Semitic civilizations. The great changes of the cultures in and around the Aegean Sea came as late as the early second millennium

BC in the island of Crete, the Mynoan civilization and about four centuries later in Mycenae, the Mycenean civilization in the Argolid area of the Peloponnesus, in peninsular Greece. Expansion of the Greek culture started with the founding of Syracusa (734 BC) outside Greece, on the Ionian Sea coast of south-east Sicily. The making of other colonies followed, such as Massilia (present day Marseille), around 600 BC. Records of the pre-historic culture and religion of the Indo-Europeans of the west who migrated into Europe are mainly to be found in the songs of the *aedes*, the ancient poets and singers who, similarly to the bards and singing poets many centuries later, related the heroic acts of the rulers and forefathers at the courts of princes and in the cities of Europe. The Iliad and the Odyssey were put in written form not earlier than the eighth century BC, though they refer to happenings that took place in the Mycenean age (fifteenth to twelfth centuries BC). In a way the Greek epics correspond to the *Rāmāyaṇa* and the *Mahābhārata*, which refer to history that took place in the Indian sub-continent at about the same time, eleventh to ninth centuries BC or earlier and also to happenings of the distant past.[13]

THE QUEST FOR KNOWLEDGE

Contrary to several contemporary authors (Càssola 2000, notes to Homeric Hymn XXIII to Zeus) who "hypothesize" that "personification [of Greek divinities] precedes the abstract concept" or idea, I have argued earlier (Vannucci 1994) that most ancient Vedic gods are first of all concepts, ideas, convictions derived from observation of natural phenomena and experimentation with man-made artefacts. The conclusions derived therefrom are later personified as a short-cut for the mental representation of the "Truth" or "Vision" (To see = *vedere* as in Lt., same word-root as *Veda*) arrived at by reason. In the Italian language, inflections of the word: *vedere* (= to see), are often used as a short-cut meaning "I understand or do you undersand?" Such a short-cut is convenient, perhaps necessary, to facilitate conscientious worship and for developing intimacy, care and love for the deity. Intimacy is necessary for the process of "unveiling Truth," which in contemporary parlance we would call "scientific research." The Vedas are not only the narration of Truth revealed to the mind by Reason, but they are also the expressions of knowledge acquired by man through observation and experimentation in his quest to figure out the structure and function of material reality, to search for causes and effects of natural phenomena and to understand their meaning, their being and becoming. It is the close relationship and understanding between man and gods that is the basic philosophy of the Vedas which has in turn generated the vitality of Advaita Vedānta and the concept of Sanathana Dharma. A similar expression: "I have found beauty, I am happy," was the secret formula of the *mystai,* the initiated to the mysteries of Dionysos where *Beauty* is taken as a paragon of *Truth.*

Philosophy as the "love of knowledge" and of knowledge applied to wisdom for better everyday living, is a scientific attitude which sets the foundation of the Vedic religion. The Vedic philosophy and religion has survived to the present days, albeit with the changes and developments which are inevitable and necessary over time. Already Plutarch (46?-120?BC) realised this truth when in his studies of the Delphic Oracle he wrote: "Theologians state and sing, in poetry or prose, that God is incorruptible but that on account of Fate it undergoes transformations. It [God] sometimes burns in the fire of its own nature, merging all substances in a single *magma,* and at other times it multiplies itself in all sorts of forms . . . and . . . is called world" (Plutarch, E.-F 388). Aristotle emphasized the simple truth that "thirst for knowledge is inherent in human nature."

FROM PHILOSOPHY TO RELIGION

In ancient Vedic times, from what we can perceive throughout the *R̥gveda,* man had a strong will to participate in the working of the cosmos and to live in harmony with the environment in which we, as a species, have evolved (Vannucci 1999).

Recent authors are correct (see Càssola, above) only when they see personification of gods *"preceding"* the abstract concept, but the words "Greek Olympian gods" must be introduced in the sentence because otherwise this is not true. Greek gods were created by man as individuals, same as the *personae* of the Greek theatre. It is evident from Hesiod's Theogony, from Homer and from the writings of Cicero (*De natura deorum; De Fato*) and in the discussions of the Greek schools of philosophy on this subject, stoics, academicians, epicureans, cynics and others, that the classic Greek gods were first of all personifications of human concepts, emotions, virtues and vices, as clearly expressed in the *Theogonia*. The personification and existence of the Olympian gods made at the image of man, was not doubted. What *was* discussed was what they did and did not do, and their relation with mankind. This is obviously a late stage in the evolution of the religion of the Indo-Europeans of Greece. It happened in relatively recent times and under the influence of Egyptian and ancient Semitic religions.

Among the ancient Indo-Europeans of the east, gods are worshipped for what they are and they do not bodily mix with man, except some of them who are clearly deified humans, personified and endowed with human characteristics and frailties, as for instance Indra. I will not enter here in the discussion of ancient Semitic and Mesopotamian religions and cultures, so profoundly studied and summarised by Kramer, Bottero, and others. Nor will I enter into a comparative study of religions. However it should be noted that Judaism, Christianity and Islam are essentially directed towards the adult, while nature religions are strongly oriented towards the next generation and children. In the philosophies based on the reality of nature, the "Great Passage" from Life to Death is not a final step or the end of something, a once-for-all life-time. It is the natural evolution and development of the cycle of birth, death of the body and rebirth, the inevitable recycling of matter and energy that keeps the universe alive and moving. Hinduism incorporated the ancient concept of natural cycles with the care of children who are minds purified by the Great Passage entering into new bodies. Christianity accepted the important role of children in the community, but vigorously rejected the idea of cycles of birth, death and rebirth, an idea or conviction perhaps first born in the west in ancient Egypt and endorsed in Greece by Orphism and by Plato. The important role of children for the cultural improvement and ethical evolution of the community is stressed already in the Vedic lore with the stories of Nachiketās, Dhruv, Prahlāda and others which illustrate the respect for the purity and innate logic and wisdom of the yet unspoiled young. The sacredeness and continuity of life are repeatedly stressed, for instance in *R̥V* X,85 with the celebration of the wedding of the daughter of the Sun, the giver of all life on Earth (Vannucci 1999).

EXPANSION OF THE INDO-EUROPEANS

In the late third and early second millennium BC different clans migrated in various directions from the original Indo-European homeland. We are concerned here with those who called themselves Arya. They spread and settled in the vast region that extends from Asia Minor to India. Other Indo-Europeans followed the route overland, probably moving counter clockwise around the northern coast of the Black Sea, to the plains of the Danube and then descended into Greece, and the whole of Hellas and its colonies. Other clans came around the southern coast of the Black Sea. Some Indo-European tribes or clans reached the Mediterranean Sea by way of Asia Minor. The remnants of the city of Ilio (= Troy) on the north-west Asia Minor coast at the western entrance to the Straits of the Dardanelles, then called Hellespont, bears testimony of the presence of those Indo-Europeans who followed the Asia Minor route before reaching the Peloponnesus. Archaeological findings confirm Homer's Iliad in establishing the date of the arson of Ilio (= Troy) in the second half of the thirteenth century BC, which is very close to the date assigned by tradition to the arson of Troy.

During pre-historic times wars and battles among the different clans of Indo-European people in both east and west continued over centuries before they could definitely call certain areas as their own. The memory of some of these wars is still now live embers under cinders. During their wanderings and expansion, the Indo-Europeans learned many arts and crafts from local people, including the cultivation of rice and perhaps also the domestication of the grape vine and later metallurgy, especially important the metallurgy of iron. They brought with them domestic animals, the wheel, carts, wagons and, most important, the horse for riding, for parades and for war. Battles were mainly waged from war chariots drawn by two horses or on foot after the contenders dismounted from their chariot, driven by an *auriga*. In the east the collective term *anarya* refers to the local people, the designation could mean both "non Aryan" or "no nose = chubby nose" as compared to the Indo-European's long noses. They were physically different and discriminated against; they formed the lower level of society without being actually reduced into slavery as were the ilotas of Sparta in the west. Slavery was unknown in India, *apud* Arrian (born between 85 and 92 AD, died prob. 145/146 AD, who quotes from Megasthenes and Eratosthenes): says the "Indian people who live east of the Indus river are of darker skin, the tallest and most brave in Asia, they do not keep slaves."[14]

There are many references to local people in the Vedas and in the Indian epics, as there are also in the Greek epics about the people who were there before them. Like the Vedas, the Purāṇas and the Epics, also the Greek texts describe the genealogies of heroes and kings and the mixture of gods with local people. Western epics and legends, the epics and historical accounts refer also to the ancient Italics, to Etruscans, Egyptians, Phoenicians, other Semitic people and specially to the Pelasgoi (= people of the seas) repeatedly mentioned as autochthonous, who sided with Troy against the mainstream Greeks (Iliad and Odyssey). Most of these myths and legends of both east and west have come down to us from the oral tradition, Indian and Graeco-Roman respectively. In both east and west the Indo-Europeans were stronger in battle and much of the bloody wars described in the epics were fought between different lineages of the Indo-Europeans themselves.

Little is known about the Pelasgoi, except that they lived in the islands and lands bordering the southern Aegean Sea before the advent of the Greeks. They are mentioned in the Odyssey (XIX, 179) where they can be read as people from the island of Crete. In the Iliad they are mentioned twice (II, 840; X, 429) where they are said to have spears and to be one of the people who moved in support of the city of Troy against the Achaeans. They were worthy sailors, well versed in boat building, seamanship and the art of navigation. They also had knowledge of the routes to and from the many islands and the mainland. It is not known for sure who they were or where they came from, most probably they were not Indo-European. They were absorbed into the Hellenic culture for the benefit of both people because Danaus, a Pelasgian, founded the acropolis of Argo in the north-east Peloponnesus (Strabo VI, 9).

The Indo-Aryans who settled in the east, continued to be land people, hunters, shepherds, agriculturists spread in many villages, small and large. The reference to *samudra* as sea in the Vedas most probably refers to the large land locked bodies of water of Central

Asia, the Caspian and Aral seas, to which the Black Sea earlier called Pontus Euxinus, was added later. The word *samudra* has generally been translated as "Ocean" or Sea, with reference to the Indian Ocean or more properly, to the Arabian Sea. From internal evidence in the Vedas however, it seems likely that the word refers to these large Central Asian bodies of saline water, rather than to the Indian Ocean, normally called *sāgara*. The latter became known as the Red Sea only late and was taken by the ancient Greeks to be the mythical ocean which girdles the entire Earth.[15]

It was to describe the Earth's coastline along the "Red Sea" (= Indian Ocean) that Alexander the Great, in the fourth century BC built a fleet of about 2000 ships, including cargo boats and ships for the transport of horses, under the overall command of his nominated admiral Nearchus. Alexander's orders were to navigate down R. Hydaspes (= Jhelum) and then R. Indus down to the sea, then follow the coastline westwards and northwards along the Persian Gulf. Nearchus and his colleagues were to describe the people and the resources available from the hinterland and coasts, from the Indus River delta to an assigned meeting point at the mouth of the Euphrates, a city called Diridotis, the remains of which have never been found. It is probably buried under several metres of alluvium brought by Rs. Tigris and Euphrates. At that time (fourth century BC) the Shatt-al-Arab, which is formed by the confluence of the two rivers, was not yet formed and each river had its separate mouth into the Persian Gulf. The Indo-Europeans of the east had probably heard about or perhaps even come in contact with the Arabian Sea earlier. There are archaeological remains of ocean materials, including the Conch (*Xanchus*), at Mehrgarh Level I, (earlier than 4700 BC). These findings are now correctly interpreted as evidence of trade between inland people, with the original people of the coastal area. We should recall here that there was trade also between Harappa and Sumer that is recorded on tablets from Sumer in cuneiform script and that the people who came to be called Sumerians had arrived in Mesopotamia from the sea **in small numbers**. They had colonized the land around and between the lower Euphrates and Tigris River, they were experts in irrigation works and did not speak a Semitic language (Kramer 1994, Bottero 1994, 1998; Kramer & Bottero 1989).

CONCLUSION

Symbols and symbolic gestures and sounds are typical and were most important before actual writing was invented. Unfortunately they do not keep well and when they are sculpted, carved, painted or designed, they are often difficult or impossible to decipher. Stereotyped gestures and sounds would evidently have had more relevance before the development of grammar, in the ancient past than at present, when writing usually precedes the symbol and explains it. Verbal and written signs and symbols function as reminders and quick reference. This is actually the idea behind shorthand script and codes that in one way or other are still in use.

Though it is true that cuneiform is the most ancient form of writing so far known, it is wrong to consider that "history begins at Sumer. . ." (Bottero) because the first alphabetic script we know of was invented there. The written tradition is only one of the many methods available to educate offsprings and future generations and thus put history on record in the collective memory of the people. There are many ways to put history on record and to transfer knowledge, experience and wisdom other than writing. The most important is by example and second by the participation of the younger generation in the doings of the elders. Drafting, singing, dancing, games (= sports), sacrifices, rituals and ceremonies are some of the many ways useful to educate and memorize history and myths. But there were elaborate cultures and high levels of civilization in many places of the world that were illiterate. In my opinion however, numbers and arithmetics were the first great basic step forward, though there is no doubt that writing was an important bench mark in the history of the intellectual evolution of Man, one that had become an inescapable necessity in view of travels, trade and exchange of experience, expertise, knowledge, wisdom, "folly of man" and wars. Reports and accounts of "other" places and people, political treaties, marriages and other contracts, land tenure, ancient myths and personalities had to be written down; they become history.

The most abundant material in Mesopotamia was clay. It is malleable and once sun-dried or baked can preserve forever the engraved signs of the cuneiform script that correspond to sounds and syllables. The cuneiform script was the first alphabetic and phonetic script, a major innovation after older records made of pictographs and ideograms. The oldest so far known cuneiform inscribed tablets are about 5000 years old. The only trouble is that clay tablets are fragile, bulky and heavy. The need therefore arose for building libraries for the storage of accounts, knowledge and history. This has been the good fortune of modern scholars, the beginning of written texts and the need to organize libraries for storage and retrieval of knowledge (Casson 2001).

In fact history was born with the development of the standing posture, beginning probably with that species of our ancestral line called *Homo habilis* (2,500,000 years ago), the stone tool-maker who walked erect like his successor: *Homo erectus* 1,000,000 to 2,000,000 years ago. About 43,000 *Homo sapiens sapiens* enters Europe probably from west Asia, relatively a short time before the disappearance of the Neanderthal man (Cavalli-Sforza 1996).[9] Finally our own species: *Homo sapiens sapiens* emerged only about one hundred thousand years ago. The standing posture gave man freedom of gestures of arms and hands and increased the variety of facial expressions. Above all history was born with the development of speech, which is recorded mentally. Memory and the knowledge of his own past and conjectural perspective of the future, are the most human of all human attributes. This type of knowledge made history and was recorded in many ways, including in writing.

Very ancient history is known best from the oral tradition, from the knowledge and experience of traders and merchants who walked the lands and sailed the seas, and from the wisdom of those who stayed home to listen, observe, study and codify knowledge, even if initially this was not done in writing. It was done, for instance by tying knots or beads on strings, counting boards, the *abacus* or the "maps" of the Polynesians where reeds represent the propagation of ocean waves and winds and cowry shells mark the position of the islands. Memory was served better and developed faster by repetition of metrical poems which told about gods and heroes, their acts and facts, at home and elsewhere. Ancient history can best be known from the ancient oral tradition, from the knowledge and wisdom of the "ancients," the sages, those "who were before us," the "wizards," *aedes* and *kitharistes* (= players on the *kithara*), poets, from the figurative and performing arts. This last category includes sages, story tellers, shamans and priests, but *not* warriors.

Written history began late among Indo-Europeans of east and west. As late as the first century AD there still was in India a strong opposition by the learned classes, mainly the priesthood, to put in writing the sacred texts, the *Śruti* and the *Smṛti*. The opposition was worldwide, but lasted longer in the east. Though Alexander had been a disciple of Aristotle, he probably was not an expert in writing. He might have been barely capable of writing his name, but he was wise enough to sponsor science and culture. He took with him several learned men who wrote books on the observations made during his campaigns. Apparently he forgot very soon the teachings of his master, and in one of his well known fits of anger and show-off, Alexander gave the order to burn the sacred hide (= leather) on which parts of the Avesta were engraved in golden letters. On the other hand, one of the few constructive virtues of Napoleon Bonaparte (1769-1821 AD) was to emulate Alexander, he took scientists with him on some of his campaigns. One notable result was the decoding of the hieroglyph script of ancient Egypt by Champollion (1790-1832).[16]

History does not comprise only the written word. It includes also results of research in archaeology, ethnology, astronomy and all the sciences, and the inputs of the oral tradition. The experience of millions of story-tellers and common people, like the *kaṭha-putlī* (= puppet shows) operators of India who are as much part of history as the artists engaged in figurative and performing arts, or those engaged in the art of healing body and mind, or the architects who built the great ziggurats, monumental palaces and temples or extensive irrigation works are all builders of history.

Though the oral tradition is often blown up and fantastic, the written history is often just as false. I have lived long enough to see history books of my childhood, college, mature and old age change over and over again and in particular instances, more than once and I have seen the same "historic" facts told in different, often contrasting ways according to political dictates. In fact, the pharaonic accounts of the battle of Kadesh are different from the

Hittite accounts of the same battle, its causes and consequences, and also vary somewhat from what we learn from the text of the treaties drawn between the parties.

There are many points of convergence among the great riverine civilizations which differ widely from basic viewpoints of maritime or landlocked civilizations. Affinities and transfer of knowledge and ideas are numerous among the pharaonic R.Nile civilization, the ancient Mesopotamian civilizations and the civilizations that developed in the geographic region of the *Saptasindhava,* the often quoted "land of the seven rivers," which is north-west and part of the hydrographical system of the Upper R.Indus. It is mentioned in Aeneis IX,30 (. . . *Seu septem surgens sedatis amnibus altus per tacitum Ganges* . . . = like Turnus, [a great Italic warrior] who inflates [his chest] like the deep Gaṅgā that is inflated in its quiet bed by the seven full rivers . . .), here Virgil confuses the Indus with the Gaṅgā. This is one of the many places where Virgil is carried away by lyricism rather than accuracy, though the "seven rivers" is a correct statement.

(D) Evolution of Cultures and Ancient Historical Times

At the time when centrifugal migrations started from their original homeland, the Indo-Europeans had already achieved a remarkable level of culture. They had domesticated cattle, including as draft animals, had bred and trained horses, had perfected different types of carts, chariots and wheels and their social organization was such that enabled them not only to undertake extensive migrations, but also to adapt to different environments, climates, food and most important, to overcome by arms, dialogue or political ability the people who came in their way. By a combination of all these factors and above all by an unshakable faith in their gods, the Indo-Aryans coming from the east gradually reached the shores of the Aegean Sea and eastern Mediterranean, after having crossed Anatolia and the length of Asia Minor. Another branch of the Indo-Aryans had earlier moved eastward and settled in India. The Indo-Iranians settled in what is now Iran and parts of Iraq, as far south as the land of Phars, the Zagros Mountains, the Arabian Sea and the eastern coast of the Persian Gulf. The ancestors of the Indo-Europeans of Asia

Minor and Central Asia and of those of Greece, Rome and the Aegean islands include other Indo-European branches besides the Indo-Iranians and Indo-Aryans; also other clans of Indo-Europeans arrived at different times from beyond the Caucasus and settled in parts of Central Asia, among them the Medes were probably the more important numerically.

The world of the Indo-Europeans of the west includes a variety of Indo-European clans and is geographically, climatically, ethnologically, linguistically and anhropologically complex. The evolution of the western Indo-European cultures is correspondingly at variance with the evolution of the Indo-Aryan and Indo-Iranian cultures and civilizations of the east.

The world of the Indo-Europeans of the east has, amongst others, two distinctive features: first, in the east the Indo-Europeans lived in climates mostly of the continental type, seasons are well defined and the orography includes the largest and highest mountain ranges on earth. Second, the open sea is not a determinant geographical feature in the east, rivers are dominant and they directed the course of the evolution of inland cultures. The wide Indian Ocean comes into the picture only at a late stage of advanced development of the cultures of the Indo-Europeans of the east. The "oceans" (= *samudra*) mentioned in the ancient texts are not extensive, they are the Caspian and the Aral Seas, both below mean sea level and centered around 35°-45° lat.N. Later the Black Sea may have also been characterized with the word *samudra*, all three seas have waters saline to different levels of salinity and are relicts of the *Tethys Sea* that linked the Indian to the Atlantic Ocean before the Mediterranean was closed off from the Indian Ocean. Calendar fixes (equinoxes and solstices) are easily marked, seasons are well defined, agriculture and other aspects of culture follow an established pattern and festivals are suitable markers of a well studied calendar.

As mentioned above (see *fig.* 1) the Indo-Europeans who had settled in the plains of R. Gurgan (or Gorgan) east of the south Caspian Sea, split in two groups, one moved westwards and eventually, after many generations reached the Aegean islands and mainland Greece, while the other moved eastwards. The Greek peninsula and the Aegean Sea islands are placed around 40°lat. which is roughly the same approximate general latitude of the route followed by the eastward moving Indo-Aryan clans. These Indo-Aryans entered north Pakistan after moving in the plains and plateau of southern Turkmenistan. Numerous archaeological sites, more than 30 have been excavated and studied, provided abundant archaeological material that are witness to these movements, they range in the large area from Tepe Hissar in the Elburz mountains area and Tureng Tepe in R. Gorgan basin in the west, to Zaraf Chan beyond the Amu Darya in the east. The Indo-European crossed the Hindukush and settled in the fertile lands and valleys at altitudes ranging from 1000 to 4000 metres that are well irrigated by pure waters from melting snow and glaciers. Life was based on pastoralism, subsistence agriculture and hunting. The earliest archaeological sites of the Swat culture, in the open and wide Swat valley, are dated 3000 BC, a date that agrees with the presumed date of the separation between eastward and westward-moving clans of the Indo-Aryans, south-east of the Caspian Sea. The area where the Indo-Aryans of the east moved into, is one of the most beautiful and fertile parts of the world, it justifies the legend of the fabulous "land of the Seven Rivers." After an undetermined period, when the urge to move on arose, nothing would be more natural than to follow the course of the rivers, which includes the "land of the Five Rivers," or Punjab, R.Indus and its affluents. From the region at the foothills of the Hindukush, all doors were open for further migrations and permanent settlements.

It is not clear whether the earliest remains of the "Swat culture" are those of Indo-European people or not. What is known is that the oldest "neolithic" remains are clearly those of a pastoral society, becoming gradually more refined. Kochhar, following earlier authors, considers the "Ghaligai" neolithic culture to be different from the more evolved "Swat" culture that later developed on the same sites. However a break in an archaeological sequence does not necessarily mean that the earlier culture was eliminated or displaced by later arrivals. In my opinion therefore, it cannot be excluded that the early Ghaligai culture was also an Indo-European or Indo-Aryan primitive culture — dates point in this direction and would further confirm that migrations were not massive displacements of all the people of a clan. The archaeological remains of the "Ghaligai neolithic" culture could be the remains left by forerunners, the scouts who were later followed by the migration and settlement of the bulk of the clan, including women and men of reproductive age. The earlier explorers would not have been burdened with agricultural implements and bullocks trained for ploughing. Before undertaking the displacement of all the group, there would have been time enough for the development of an improved material culture, as that found in the typical "Swat culture" that settled in selected areas of the valley. More searches will answer the question whether the Ghaligai culture people were ancestors of the Swat culture people or had altogether different roots.

It must have taken many generations for the people who had arrived and settled in the hydrographic system fed by the Hindukush mountain ranges, before they evolved into a mature culture. Arrival and mixing with people of a more evolved culture would facilitate the technical development of the earlier occupants. Pastoralism and subsistence agriculture remained until recently the usual way of life for people living in the "hills" (= lower mountain ranges and high valleys), it is associated with seasonal transhumance. Dardic and Kafiri are Indo-European languages still spoken in the areas of the high ranges of the rivers. When again the urge to move and colonize new areas arose, there were two routes to be followed, they were the hydrological systems of rivers Indus and Gaṅgā, born on two opposite watersheds of the Himalayas.

Geographic expansion continued eastwards and southwards to Sri Lanka, variously called *Suvarnabhumi* and *Suvarnadwipa*. Among the Jataka stories, the *Kathasaritsāgara* tells that the kingdom of Champa (= Kampa) in present day Vietnam that was founded by Chams who were Hindu people coming from the island of Java (Skt. *Yava*) and *Yavadwipa* is already mentioned in the *Rāmāyaṇa*. There were early Indian colonies also in *Kamboj* (= Kampuchea). The story of the Champa dynasty goes back to about 150-200 AD. A well settled Indian colony in Java is known from the fifth century AD and the Bali Indian kingdom is known from earlier than the eighth century AD. In Java there are Gupta, Pallava and Chola style sculptures, then Buddha images in the Amarāvatī style and great monuments in all of south-east Asia, including Angkor-Wat. The reason underlying the expansionism of the Indo-Aryans had, the main purpose of trade. However as everywhere else, mixing with local people was inevitable and higly productive, it brought with it enrichment of all the people and cultures involved in the process. The great development of Buddhism followed the conversion of King Ashoka and his famous edict dated 256 BC. However, remains of the earlier Hindu culture are still alive, from Sri Lanka to the Ryukyu Islands of south Japan.

Expansionism trends continued also among the Indo-Aryans who entered into present-day north Pakistan. Unfortunately archaeological remains may suggest that people who became known as the "Harappan culture" occupied some parts of the upper reaches of the rivers and followed their course towards R. Indus and the Arabian Sea. Other clans followed the R. Gaṅgā hydrological basin eastward and onwards to the Sundarbans of Bengal and beyond. Gradually Indian people visited places favourable for local agriculture and established colonies all around the Bay of Bengal and always further with greater or lesser success.

The islanders of Yae-Yama group of islands of the Ryukyu archipelago of Japan "remember" a powerful god from the west called "*Mayur Ganasu*" (= Ganesh?). He is represented in sculptures in the round to be very tall, powerful and fat, with a very very long nose, very very large ears and brings with him all sorts of blessings, he is represented in the likeness of Ganesh. The powerful Mayur Ganasu is joyous, happy and very good.

The spread and knowledge of the *Rāmāyaṇa* eastwards is earlier than the arrival of Buddhism, but there are no clear traces of the *Mahābhārata*. From the eastern coastline of the Bay of Bengal, from Burma proceeding to Thailand and South-east Asia, including Cambodia and Laos as far as Vietnam and Indonesia and in the distant Ryukyu islands, there are echoes of the *Rāmāyaṇa* among all the people. The Indo-Aryans' expansion eastwards, outside the Indian sub-continent was not of the colonial type; other people and other kingdoms were influenced but not colonized by India. Unlike what happened in the Mediterranean region, there were no political ties between the culturally "Indianized" states outside of India and the Indian sub-continent, though the religious ties were firmly established and continue to be so in the island of Bali. Within India itself there was much open-mindedness and great autonomy of the various political states, the binding elements were lifestyles and philosophical aspects of behaviour, habits and religious beliefs. Each place or State kept its tradition and independence intact. Similar to the Greek expansionism, the Indian expansionism was mainly ocean or sea-borne.

Trade and the items traded between India, the Arabian peninsula, the island of Madagascar and mainland west and south-west Africa and between India, Sri Lanka and eastwards as far as the Ryukyu islands continued well into modern times (Keswani, 1980). Apart from trade, Major India remained isolated from the rest of the world. Megasthenes says (*in* Strabo; 15, 1, 5) that the Indians had never organized any expedition against other people nor had any foreign army invaded their lands earlier than Alexander the Macedonian, though Dionysos and Heracles were known to have gone to India.

The consequences of these and other geographic and ecological factors are such as favoured relatively peaceful rural, pastoral and agricultural cultures among the ancient Indo-Europeans of the east, while the Indo-Europeans of the west found themselves living in restricted lands and small islands. There were initially fierce battles on ancient Indian soil, especially among different clans of the Indo-Aryans themselves, but there was no need to wage wars of conquest or expansion beyond the Indian sub-continent. Overseas travels of the Indo-Aryans of the east are a story of trading reltionships. The Indo-Aryan culture of india developed essentially from self-generated energy and knowledge. The Indo-Aryans of Central Asia were warriors and conquerors as attested by the historical Persian wars against the Pan-Hellenic League formed by different tribes of western Indo-Europeans and the wars waged by Alexander the Great who extended his dominions from Egypt to the Indus. Circumstantial evidence suggests that the migrating groups of Indo-Aryans and Indo-Iranians were not very large. They are often present in not more than the relatively small numbers of the ruling class, the noblemen and warriors, such was the Hittite society.[17]

SOURCES AND THE PASSAGE FROM PROTO-HISTORY AND PRE-HISTORY TO HISTORY

There is only indirect evidence from palaeontology of very early man's cultures, or lack of culture. More evidence is to be found in archaeology, cultural anthropology and, most important, in the oral tradition, myths, legends, habits and, much later, the written texts. To these we should add the powerful tools of present day "molecular biology" and "chemical archaeology," as recently shown by Cavalli-Sforza (1996), McGovern (2003) and others. At some stage of the evolution of cultures, religions were born, created, organized by specially gifted persons, prophets or others. The transition from proto-history to pre-history and history, can never be understood clearly, first of all because proto-history is by definition, strictly indefinable in space, time or detail and second because most studies are usually relative to one another and mutually dependent; therefore conclusions tend to run in circles. Knowledge of the ancient past relies to a great extent on the analysis of beliefs and myths, studies of artefacts and technical development, studies of the lists of items offered for trade, of observational and experimental ancient knowledge and traditional wisdom. Religious and literary texts are indicators of the origin and evolution of gods and heroes of different or related cultures. Except for artefacts and implements, real dates can seldom be precisely defined. Recorded exceptional astronomic phenomena can be helpful to date particular events.[18]

The oral tradition is never fixed in time, it is self-generated, like *swayambhu liṅgams* it is represented and evolves from its own creative power, it is unlimitedly enriched by phantasy and increasing environmental and practical know-how. It is not easy to unravel the truth underlying myths and "superstitions" from the superstructure made of stories that camouflage the jewel hidden under the corner stone of the historical building. The oral tradition survives for very long times when it is in metric form, but the structure of myths usually breaks up when the oral tradition is not in poetical or musical form. Development of all cultures at all times tends to grow by leaps and bounds and is usually a product of interchanges with different cultures.[19]

The ancient past of the Indo-Europeans of the east is relatively easy to understand because their languages are the root of well known classical languages such as Sanskrit, Avestan, Greek, Latin, Neo-Latin, Russian and Germanic languages, Kurdish and others, many of them still alive in one form or other. Languages also evolve, changes may be indicative of migrations, trade and mixing with other people and cultures, birth of new religions, technical and scientific development and political interests. Archaeological findings in the nineteenth and twentieth centuries and decipherment of the phonetic cuneiform script brought to light texts written in different Semitic and Indo-European languages and improved our knowledge of the past history of mankind.

Within the scope of this book the early sources can be divided in two phases. The first refers to the passage from proto-history to the pre-history of the Indo-Europeans with whom we are concerned here. The second refers to the Indo-Aryans and Indo-Iranians in particular. There is at present enough material available to draw reliable working hypotheses. Follows a condensed version of recent views based on known facts of the evolution of the cultures of the Indo-Europeans. There are many and often contrasting views in modern publications concerned with the Graeco-Roman and Indo-European mythology and literature; they will not be repeated here. Classic and modern studies and literature have their merits but can be used as reliable information to trace the evolution of cultures only, and *only if* myths and legends are taken in the correct chronological order and place when and where they were born. The best example is the well known encyclopaedic book by Graves, *The Greek Myths* first published in 1955, where everything that was ever said on the 171 topics discussed by the author is lumped together with impressive wealth of information. However the value of the information provided is meaningful *only* when origin and authorship are given. Roughly 80% or more of all stories given in the book are derived from authors who lived in AD times when the original myths and legends had undergone changes, additions and deletions caused by two major religious innovations, the Homer/Hesiod new Olympian religion and later, the new Christian religion. These two revolutions masked or disguised in different ways the meaning, sense and logics of the very ancient myths and legends of the Graeco-

Roman tradition, even before St. Augustine (354-430 AD) produced his *Civitas dei* (= The City of God). We are here concerned essentially with the archaic and ancient tradition, with pre-history and ancient history up to the beginning of the Christian era.

The transition of the religious thought and behaviour of the Myceanean and earlier Indo-European cultures and civilizations to the Graeco-Roman culture coincides with the Doric invasion of Greece (about twelfth century BC) celebrated by Homer's epics and Hesiod's *Theogonia* produced in the eighth-seventh centuries BC. The ancient-most nature gods and the Earth-Mother, or Great Mother, and other archaic gods were never abandoned though the focus of cultic practices became centered on the formidable new Olympic pantheon. Old gods may survive under new names and new cultic practices, human customs and habits rarely change completely. Conversely gods may keep their names but their character may change gradually or they can be entirely altered, like Dionysos, a pure nature god who became an orgiastic deity under the late orgiastic culture of Rome. Other gods may change names but retain their intrinsic characteristics. The history of each one must be worked out specifically and the best tool is to consider details of the original myths in relation to the cultic world in which they were born spontaneously or were created by man.

The ancient Indo-Iranians did not abandon entirely the gods of the ancient Indo-European cultural period, as far as can be understood from the Avesta. Under the new Zoroastrian religion most gods became secondary figures though they were still alive in the folklore, myths and legends. The cult of Fire, the Great God, giver of all life became the exclusive all encompassing God worthy of worship. Knowledge of the religions and history of the ancient Indo-Iranians survived until modern times partly thanks to the Shah-Namah of Firdusi (940?-1020? AD); much ancient tradition would be unknown to us if there had not been a Firdusi. After the first great damage caused by the destruction of the sacred texts by Alexander the Great, the Zend-Avesta suffered again nearly total destruction under Islam. Our present knowledge of the ancient history of the Indo-Iranians is to a great extent not more than the tid-bits that survived by chance.

There is no marker for the entry into pre-history and history of the Indo-Aryan culture and civilization. Even the Great Bhārata War, greatly destructive and described down to the most crude details in many passages of the *Mahābhārata*, did not cause drastic or sudden changes in the culture and civilization of the kingdoms, republics and other nations or people that emerged intact to various degrees, from the great war. The destruction and high price paid by all sides was material and human but not ethical or religious, of course culture and religion evolved and mythology continued to be enriched. No culture in the world other than the Indian, has been able to evolve more or less peacefully since archaic times to present.

Some of the common cultural roots of the Indo-Europeans were recorded in cuneiform script by the Indo-Aryan Hittite rulers in their own language. They show that there are essential points in common between western and eastern Indo-European cultures as considered for the purpose of this book. The Indo-European *original* religion must have been like elsewhere throughout the world, a nature religion for the simple reason that man would not be able to see himself dissociated from the rest of nature. Initial instinctive thinking devoid of mental representation would gradually evolve into figurative myths and stories created to "explain" natural facts. Cultic practices would then develop as participatory rites and prayers begging for help and protection. The attempt to understand and perhaps predict the most frightful forces of nature, created demons and monsters in the mind of early man.

In the older nature religions, Typhaeus (from which= *Typhoon*) and the Titans are monsters of the Greek mythology. Ullikummi and Illuyanka are monsters of the Hittite ancient tradition. Daeva Apaosha of the Avesta (*Yasht* VIII, 20-22) and Vṛtra and the Asuras of the Indian mythology are comparable monsters that represent the difficulties that mankind had to overcome and protect itself to survive in a frequently hostile environment, prior to the development of agriculture. In the evolution of nature religions, monsters gradually become milder, less frightening and shed much of their super-human power as much as men gradually become stronger, more *virile heroes,* and more powerful. It is the humanistic phase in which warriors are not superhuman beings and saintly men and women continue to be men and women without becoming gods even if capable of performing miracles.

The most ancient religions are centered on the figure of the Mother, variously called Great Mother, Earth Mother, Aditi, **the** Infinitely Great Mother which held united groups of men, women and children. She was Gaya the Earth in the west, the śakti and consort of Uranus (= Ouranos, sky, tempest), the original man/ woman couple. Uranus had a violent temper, he was castrated by their son Chronos (= Time) with the help of mother Gaya who provided the sickle to cut off the genitals of Uranus. His semen flowed into the sea and was collected by Gaya who generated more offsprings from Uranus even after his castration (*Theogonia, 155 seq*). Matriarchy has survived in open or disguised forms, or is forcibly repressed in most present day civilizations. The new religion organised by Hesiod then created Zeus, son of Chronos (= Time, son of Uranus) who will himself defeat (castrate) Chronos after which, armed with lightning, thunder and flaming arrows made for him by the Cyclops (with steel?) he fights the monsters of Nature, first the Titans, then Typhaeus and then many others whom he sent to Tartarus (= Hades, the nether world, hell). Typhaeus subjugated by Zeus, later became the Master and personification of fearful, destructive winds. Prometheus, another rebellious Titan, stole fire from the gods and gifted it to man.

The Hittite texts describe how the God of Tempests Kumarpi (= Kumarbi, time, corresponds to Chronos) "hits and wrenches to pieces like a mortal man, like an ant he crushes under his feet the demon Ullikummi and Kumarpi, the Great king [here god= powerful entity], will scatter away all gods and will break them to pieces as empty boats." The second monster defeated in battle by the God of Tempests is Illuyanka. In Ṛgvedic mythology it is Indra, born from Puruṣa's mouth who, aided by the powerful Māruts, destroys the Asuras with his thunderbolt, he then destroys amongst other demons his great enemy Vṛtra whose brother Vala had stolen and hidden in a cave the cows of the gods. In the evolution of knowledge into recorded history, man gradually accepts the bad forces that he cannot defeat and begins to understand how to obey and tame the helpful forces of Nature through hard work, cultic practices and propitiatory rites. The latter are often the description of practical methods and techniques, codified from experience. Indra, initially a strong nature god, becomes humanised with the passage of time only to become again deified in the *Ṛgveda*. It takes a human-god or a godly-human to unravel the long way from pre-history to history.

There are no episodes in the ancient texts as violent as the castration of Uranus at the hands of Zeus, and of Alalu (= the highest) by Kumarpi who swallows his father's genitals. The transition from proto-history to history via pre-history of the Indo-Aryans is a long way, not regularly smooth, not deprived of violence, horrors and fantasy, but never forgetful of the fact that man is part of the nature in which he lives and out of which it would be unthinkable to try to survive.[20]

Indra was gradually "humanized" as Kumarpi and Zeus were also humanized, but gradual cultural evolution never stopped in India and there were no drastic, massive religious changes in the many centuries of its existence. Even the birth and evolution of Jainism, Buddhism and many other sects born from brahmanism and Hinduism were, and still are peaceful. All forms survived because there are merits and demerits in all aspects of human endeavours and no human being or creed is omniscient, perfect or totally impartial. Humility and tolerance are a product of intelligent and rational thinking. This is why Indra survives as a great human king of gods and humans, but Zeus, the conqueror who defeats Typhaeus, father of gods and humans and the great Kumarpi gradually disappeared in the nebulous religious past of the cultures where they were first created. The isolationism of India and Indians has been over the centuries the guardian of traditional values and the custodian of smooth evolution in tune with growing factual knowledge.

ANCIENT HISTORICAL CULTURES

Over centuries and millennia and under the influence of the new environments into which they had migrated the Indo-European cultures of east and west evolved into different civilizations, the Indian and Iranian civilizations in the east and the Graeco-Roman in the west. In the pre-historic period, late third and early second millennium BC, the divergent trends of the evolution of cultures was already clear. A culture centered on nature and nature forces in the east and one centered on man and his achievements in the west. Man lived as a function of the environment in the east, while man spared no efforts to shape the environment to his will in the west. We must not forget however, that no such generalisations can be entirely true, but they do reflect the attitudes which still linger unspoken among the people of both east and west. We will not enter here in the discussion of ancient Iranian cultures, and reference to their ancient gods and heroes will be made below.

Though the civilizations of east and west acquired characteristics of their own, they carried with them many of the same fundamental Indo-European traits. If a personal diversion may be permitted here, I would say that as an Italian brought up traditionally in the first quarter of the twentieth century, I did not feel uprooted when I first went to India and finally lived there for much over 30 years, in spite of the many differences in lifestyles that may intrigue other foreigners. Family life, personal care of body and health, family and social habits, customs and beliefs correspond closely in the two worlds only apparently at odds. I could learn quickly to be an Indian in India and a Florentine in Florence, my home town. I concluded that the superficially different attitudes in India and Italy stem from different ecological environments and from recent historical developments. Earlier Jawahar Lal Nehru (1889-1964) had arrived at similar conclusions in his comparative study of the two countries and cultures.

EAST AND WEST

Two factors dominated the divergence between east and west. First were the inputs from the cultures of the people new to them with whom the Indo-Europeans came in contact. Second was the different physical and biological environment in which they now lived. The eastern Indo-Europeans migrated into vast fertile lands which proved to be suitable for agriculture or pastoralism. The plains of Asia were dominated by extensive ranges of the highest mountains on earth and watered by the mightiest rivers. Some of the clans moved to the mountains, and there is a passage in the *R̥V* which says that the "tribe of Kanva went its own way and was lost forever," they could well be the people of Swat and other parts of the Hindukush,

Himachal Pradesh, Kashmir and the Himalayan high ranges where different but closely related people live in Gilgit, Hunza, Swat, Garhwal, Kumaon, high ranges of R. Beās and others. Many of these people were semi-isolated from those of the plains until relatively recent times.

Other groups or clans settled in river valleys while still others gradually moved southwards to the very tip of peninsular India and beyond into the land masses and large islands of South-east Asia. The western Indo-European found themselves confined into relatively small mountainous regions of Macedonia and Greece, with narrow valleys, several peninsulas and many small islands surrounded by the sea and broken up by channels, gulfs and bays. In the east the Indo-Aryan civilization first remained by and large pastoral. Even after agriculture was developed, nomadism and transhumance remained the regular life pattern of many people and families. Lifestyle and economics was vastly the same all over India since a distant past and at present in the rural regions and mountains. Over the centuries, people of other origins who settled in India acquired traits which mark them as Indian in spite of the initial differences. Many of the earliest forms of developed agriculture and domestication of wild varieties of cereals and other edible plants were developed in "Major India."

Among the Indo-Europeans of the east, many aspects of the ancient Iranian culture are well known. Also much is known of the ancient kingdom of Mitanni, where the bulk of the population was formed by Hurrite people who migrated from the mountains into the area of northern Syria and Mesopotamia towards the third millennium BC. During its greatest expansion in the fifteenth and fourteenth centuries BC the kingdom occupied all the area between the mouth of R. Euphrates to Palestine and from the Mediterranean to the Zagros Mountains. The Mitanni lost its power with the arrival of the Indo-European Hittites. The local people spoke, a language that was neither Semitic nor Indo-European, some authors believe that they were Indo-Aryans who had arrived in Mesopotamia from the east, probably around the eighteenth or seventeenth centuries BC. The Indic language spoken by the dominant Hittites was more archaic than the Sanskrit spoken in India and their gods were the ancient-most Vedic gods. There are clear indications that the Hittites were a group of the Indo-Aryans who had become cut off from the main branch at an early stage of the migrations and clan displacements. The first Indo-Aryan Hittite kings are achaeologically dated from the seventeenth or sixteenth centuries BC. The twelve Hittite kings who ruled the kingdom from the end of the sixteenth to thirteenth century BC were worshippers of Varuṇa, Mitra (= Mithra), Indra and the Nasatyas or Aśvini, the ancient-most Indo-Aryan gods. The nobility of the kingdom included the *mariyanni* (= warriors on chariots, warriors who fight from chariots).

According to Ghirshman (1977) and others, the Indo-Iranian language is closely related but different from the language of the Indo-Aryans. Archaeological findings indicate that the Indo-Iranians entered Iran by two separate waves of migration (*fig*. 1, from Ghirshman) towards the end of the second millennium BC, which corresponds to the early Iron Age in Iran. One of the Indo-European migrating waves was that of the western Iranians, who became known as Persians and the Indo-European Medes who arrived from over the Caucasus Mountains and from the plains western of the Caspian Sea. The other migration wave was that of the eastern Indo-Iranians who arrived later, during the last millennium BC when the use of iron was already well developed. The eastern Iranians were those called, according to Ghirshman, Hyrcanians, Parthas, Bactrians, Arya, Chorasmians, Sogdians on which there is abundant historical information from classic Greek and Roman authors. Eastern and western Indo-Iranians were always at odds, as referred in the Shah-Namah of Firdusi, where the easterners are lumped together under the general name of Turanians.[20]

The evolution of the Indo-Iranian culture was different from that of the Indo-Aryan. Under environmental constraints of climate and availability of building materials, the Indo-Iranians developed to a high degree all aspects of water resources engineering and management as well as architecture. Similarities and differences between Indo-Aryans on one side and Indo-Iranians (western Indo-Iranians) and Turanians (eastern Indo-Iranians) can best be studied in the Avesta and in the Shah-Namah of Firdusi. The religion of the Indo-Iranians diverged early from that of the Vedic people, it clearly can be seen from studying the birth and development of Zoroastrianism. One important feature remained common to all Indo-Europeans throughout their history, especially among Indo-Iranian and Indo-Aryans. This is the sacredeness, respect and worship of mountains, hence the construction of ziggurats, the colossal gopurams of south Indian temple architecture, *śikhara*s of north India, the stepped temple of Myanmar such as the Dhamma Yan Gyi Bagan built by Buddhist non-ethnic Indo-European people (= Tibeto-Burmese) and others of south-east Asia. To this day, mountan climbers have respectfully agreed to the request made by the King of Bhutan not to step on the very top of Annapūrṇā to avoid defiling its purity and sacredeness. Flags, markers and other records of mountaineering achievements are considered to be valid testimony of reaching the top even if planted at a slightly lower altitude.

The contribution of the wise men and priests of the Medes, the *magi*, influenced Europe since the beginning of Christianity, the birth of Jesus Christ was glorified by the arrival of the three wise men (= *magi*) from the east. Later, oriental wise men were specially invited to the Concilium of Florence (begun in 1439, lasted over ten years) to participate in the debates for the unification of eastern and western religions, though what was then meant by Oriental religion, was mainly the Christian Syrian and the Greek Orthodox doctrines as different from the Catholic doctrine of the Church of Rome.

CITY STATES AND VILLAGES

In the west civilizations broke up into townships that relied on the surrounding fields to produce their food. The development of city-states capable of self-defence was inevitable in the west, as was equally inevitable the rise of a multitude of villages in the east, like the "*gaon*" of all sorts and sizes scattered all over the Indian sub-continent and the Iranian plateau. There are relatively few remains of structural or architectural importance in India later than the Harappan civilization and prior to AD times, except for *all* types of engineering structures small and large for the management of water resources. Villages do not leave behind them much in terms of archaeologically meaningful artefacts or other archaeological fossils, such as signs of ploughing, ditches, wells, tools. The already ancient custom of cremation of dead bodies also deprives the archaeologist of many clues about customs of the ancient societies. More reliable information is available from palynology and from the remains of the practices of metallurgy, from the smelting of ores to the final production of artefacts. Studies and diggings carried out in ancient village sites in many parts of India and Iran produced information about agriculture, domestication of plants and animals, agricultural techniques, nutrition, health and funerary rites. However the bulk of reliable information comes from the oral tradition and from epic poems. Village life implies growing of food for family and clan and for export to the nearest city if any, but above all it implies the development of harvest and water storage techniques, hence the ancient art of hand or wheel-made, sun-dried or kiln-burned bricks and pottery, ancient arts common to all Indo-Europeans.

In the east as well as in the west there were well-known communication or trade routes since pre-historic times. They were further developed into a considerable network with the growth of human population density and increase of trade in the Iron Age. Since proto-historic times there was communication overland and by river and coastal navigation, that led to the transfer of cultures, from the western parts of the Indian sub-continent to far east Bay of Bengal. Communication routes by sea extended west up to the Arabian Gulf and overland from the Gangetic plain and the Indus River System Harappan civilization, to Southern Europe and western Asia respectively. A seldom-mentioned example of the intensive trade in BC times, is given by Arrian who says, on the strength of Megasthenes, Greek ambassador at the court of Chandragupta Maurya, that the Indians east of the Indus River have no gold, they have to import it from Bactriana. The vastness of the geographic area available to the Indo-European in the east is in contrast with the small area under Indo-European influence in Greece where cultural expanse had to extend overseas into the island — dotted Aegean Sea and other distant shores. Rather than dividers, the seas, the Mediterranean in particular, performed well as links between people and civilizations. States were confined to small areas hence the decisive role of the city-state, the *polis* of the Hellenic civilization, a concept developed since early historical times that survived up to present as "political science."

INCREASE OF CULTURAL DIVERSIFICATION

In both east and west the need and greed for land and its returns in terms of ores and other minerals, building materials, clay, water, agricultural produce, pasture land or forest, were the causes of migrations, exploratory travels by land or sea and fierce battles and wars to establish ownership and rule over disputed territories and mines. Land available for each clan was relatively scarce in Greece and Italy. Because there was no need of defence, large cities developed late in the east and were until relatively late, represented mainly or only by temple cities, universities and monasteries or royal estates. Wars in the east were mainly open field battles. The sacredeness of the temples was a better and more reliable defence for the safekeeping of the harvest and other riches than the walls of the Greek or Roman cities that were never spared pillage, arson or treason. The *"purah"* or fortified city and urban establishments in general mentioned throughout the Vedas and the epics must have initially been built mostly in wood and burnt brick small forts for the protection of the kings, their household, their armed men and stores. Large fortress towns of Rajasthan came up very late and are indicative of preparedness against enemy invasions. Fortified royal palaces of the princes of the small kingdoms on the Malabar coast, like the Padmanabha Swami temple and residence of the local royal family still exist in Kerala, where the nearby ocean required defence preparedness against pirates and intruders. The builders, warriors and artists of south India reached remarkable levels of engineering ability, bodily strength, agility and artistic performance. The martial arts of Kerala and the physical strength and agility of the Kerala youth and mature men, are amongst the most remarkable. Physical fitness was not only used for bodily combat but also for the performing arts that reached highest levels of artistic and intellectual development, witness kathakalī, bhāratanātyam and other related perfomances that are among the most highly refined arts that involve music, song, dance, philosophy and religion. Knowledge and devotion are never separated from all and any form of perfomance in India.

The forests that covered the plains of the east offered abundant first quality timber. In the Indian sub-continent large stone structures were developed late, mainly with the advent of the Buddhist universities and monasteries and the development of the large Hindu temple cities, while impressive architecture was developed in all ancient Greece, such as the Minoan and Mycenean civilizations of the second millennium BC, and later in Magna Graecia already in the last millennium BC. Arrian (born at Nicomedia about 85 or 92 AD) in his "*Indika*" writes that though Greece and Rome produced great cities and buildings, the culture and philosophy of India east of the Indus River, is greater in the sense that "India has not waged wars of conquest like the Persian emperors, and the learned men are great philosophers." Quoting from earlier authors, Eratosthenes and Megasthenes, he also mentions the general use of wood, including for fortifications.[21]

Wood is more easily transported and worked, but is perishable, hence the relative scarcity of archaeological remains in present day India except for later days cave and rock hewn temples, chaithyas, shalas and stupas. Though hard woods are still used to make the plough-share in India, wood is not entirely satisfactory as a material for agricultural tools. Copper is also relatively soft. These may have been incentives for the development of harder and stronger metals like bronze and then iron. Steel was produced very early in India, it was called *ferrum candidum* (= white iron) and highly praised by Greeks and Romans. Even very large fortifications and palaces were made of wood and not of long-lasting archaeological materials; sooner or later fire destroyed most wooden historical structures everywhere in the world. The church of "Santa Croce" in Venice was built with wood and straw as late as 967 AD and had to be rebuilt in stone, after a devastating fire in 1149 AD.

In Greece and later in Italy there were many quarries from where stone material of good quality could be had for the construction of permanent cities with massive ramparts, walls, towers, palaces, castles, temples and forts. There is a rich amount of archaeological remains of the Mediterranean civilizations. Restricted habitable space and availability of marble and other stones instead of wood and other biological materials, is one factor that caused the divergent evolution of arts and crafts in east and west. From roofs to manuscripts palm leaves provided excellent but perishable material for a variety of uses. Wooden tables for writing are typical of the east and the most ancient Indian cultures, as in Orissa. Individual small slates are still vastly used in the elementary schools of India. Semitic Mesopotamian civilizations had clay for making tablets on which to write, later the western Indo-Europeans learned how to make paper from the Egyptians and Phoenicians, or otherwise used parchment and leather made from hides. Different climates and availability of raw materials defined divergence of physical aspects of culture, of political life and of the institution of the city-state. In the east even at the time of the large empires, such as the Maurya or the Gupta, and even into the present, the village *pañcāyat* continued to be the traditional type of the basic administrative and political organisation of India and Nepal.

In the west weapons such as swords, daggers, axes and double axes, called *labrys* in Latin, by the Indo-European of the west, arrow and spear tips and protective devices such as helmets and shields made of bronze, were still the common attire of the Mycenean warrior (1500-1150 BC). Copper and iron were used to make utensils and tools. Iron and steel were initially rare and more costly than gold. Baked terracotta and wooden utensils are common even at present in east and west; they remained largely in use among the Indo-Europeans of west even at a time when metals, bronze, brass and steel were already commonly used in the east. For what concerns material aspects of culture, remains of pre-historic metallurgy of copper, tin and iron (Cu, Sn and Fe) and their alloys are well known (Chakrabarti, Kochhar) and are a rich source of information on arts, crafts, trading routes, mining and smelting sites. Workshop left-overs indicate the direction and magnitude of the web of exchanges of artefacts, though there are at present only few and scattered remains of archaic and ancient permanent or temporary settlements in India. High population density in India must have disturbed many archaeological sites. The *lohari* ironsmiths are mostly wandering artisans to this day. In the east copper and iron were well worked and used for utensils, tools and weapons since the third millennium BC (Chakrabarti) but archaeological remains are widely scattered geographically. Kiln-baked terracotta utensils and pots of all sizes are common to east and west and remained largely in use for the storage of grain. Indian iron ore has an exceptionally high percentage of iron and is among the best in the world hence the value given since ancient times to Indian steel: *"ferrum candidum."*

GEOGRAPHY AND CULTURAL SYNCRETISM

The geographic constraints imposed on man in the west in terms of space, orography and hydrography in contrast with the ecological opportunities available in the east in terms of flora and fauna diversity and natural products including availability of minerals in general and ores in particular were, it is postulated here, the decisive factors which caused divergence of the evolution of cultures and civilizations, including philosophical and religious traits in the eastern and western Indo-European worlds.

Modern authors interpret differently the affinities between Uranus/Chronos/Zeus/Titans/Typhaeus/Prometheus myths and the Hittite cuneiform recorded Kumarbi/Illuyanka/Ullikummi myths. Some interpret the affinity as a transfer between cultures, others interpret them as evidence of common origin. Still others believe in similarities and parallelisms in the evolution of basic themes of the myths of *all* cultures. Aristotle defined *mythos* (= myth) a "combination of actions that follow each other in a typical, almost stereotyped sequence from the beginning." This series of actions Aristotle listed as: *arché* (= beginning, hence the word archaic), *peripeteia* (= peripety, running around or course of events), *lysis* or *katastrophé* (= the end, dissolution or catastrophe). In fact the two points of view, on one side the borrowing and on the other the common origin of myths, are not mutually contradictory. Two or more myths may coalesce to produce single larger myths rich in episodes that could even contradict each other in time, place or sequence because they were produced by different cultures at different times, or by the same culture at different times, though the human and psychologic value of the myth continues to be the same. In other words, there can be transfer and syncretism of cultures whether the two have a common origin or not. The older version of the myth of the Indo-Aryan Hittites has much in common with the older version of the Greek myth of the castration of father Uranos by son Chronos and of the latter by Zeus before he became the great god, and the swallowing of the genitalia of the original great king by Kumarbi. However, there is no parallelism and no castration of the

Father Progenitor in the Vedic lore. This is consistent with the fact that Vedic gods are neither generated nor begotten by gods, men or other superior beings. Vedic gods just *exist, they are, they are Reality, Truth.* Apart from this fundamental point, the battles between Indra and Vṛtra or Vala have close affinity with the battles between Zeus, the Titans and Typhaeus (= typhoon), later made the god of destructive winds, and the battles between Kumarpi and Illuyanka and the demons. These and other myths are the imaginary representation of the eternal battle between Good and Evil that pre-historic man witnessed in the material reality of everyday struggle for survival. These myths are deeply rooted in the original Indo-European culture as they are rooted also in the mythology of other people. They are specially remembered by those cultures that have cultivated the memory of the past, such as the Indo-Iranians and Indo-Aryans who never abandoned many of the ancient traditions of the Indo-Europeans. Later versions of the myth of Typhaeus (Apollodorus, fifth century BC) and late cuneiform texts indicate transfer of culture between different lineages of various people including between Indo-European and non-Indo-European cultures. The eagerness for strict "scientific" definitions and classifications of twentieth century authors caused many misunderstandings because they did not realise how intense was and has been in the past, the transfer of knowledge and expertise in all fields of culture between different "races" of human beings.

The evolution of the Olympian gods and the entire Greek civilization are the result of the interaction of very ancient traditions of the incoming Indo-European migrants with the new environment, the sea and the pre-existing Mediterranean and west-Asia people. The arts of navigation and ship-building, as well as the art of writing, the manufacture of dyes, glass and paper were also imported from Semitic Phoenicians and Egyptians. From Egypt several religious and philosophical doctrines were incorporated in the Graeco-Roman culture. Greek science was developed more *extra muram* (= outside the walls, outside the city) than in peninsular Greece, it grew in the colonies scattered over the Aegean Sea, the lands bordering the eastern Mediterranean and further west, specially in Sicily, more than in the mainland cities, including Athens. With the fusion of east and west the Peloponnesus and Magna Graecia became the fertile soil for the growth of Hellenism. Myths of Olympian and non-Olympian gods and heroes flourished over the centuries well into the Christian Era. Many have remained alive under different attire in the official and popular practices of Christianity, as for instance the Saturnalia of Rome, in honour of god Saturn, that survive in present day carnival. In trying to find out how the very ancient Greeks reasoned and what their beliefs were, it is necessary to go back to Homer and pre-Homeric times. The descriptions of later authors and philosophers added many myths and legends to the original culture and religion. Personified deities may become unrecognisable by assuming new personalities with the passage of time. From the very beginning most Greek gods received new names in Rome, a typical example are the changes in the personality of Dionysos, who became an almost unrecognisable figure with the name of Bacchus in Rome and colonies. Another example is the changes imposed on the pre-historic figure of Demeter, also called Cybele or Cerere in Rome. The goddess as she became at the time of imperial Rome and of the writers of the early Christian centuries exhibits a shocking difference from the shining goddess who tried to give immortality to a human child. Also her young innocent and sweet maiden daughter Kore became the powerful matron Persephone of the Romans!

IN THE EAST

There were no ecological constraints of space, no scarcity of land, no urgent need of distant voyages by sea fcr the ancient Indo-Europeans of the east. There had not been a glaciation that wiped out 70% or more of plants and animal species of Europe, there were instead fertile valleys and plains, richness of plants, animals and water. Rains, however, came in abundance only during a short period of a few months yearly. In ancient Iran and India ways and means for storing and distributing the precious liquid in small family quantity or large amounts for entire villages and cities and for agriculture had to be developed. Machines to elevate water, construction of irrigation systems were invented to use water wisely and to subdivide it in sufficient quantity to the largest area possible for the sake of agriculture, of man and of his animals. The autochthonous populations which the Indo-Europeans encountered in the east were mild and were subjugated or ruled with no great pain. The newcomers had a lot to learn from the local people, specially in the arts of metallurgy, domestication of plants and animals, health care and medicinal plants, nutrition and, as mentioned, water resources management. Both newcomers and locals were trained observers of nature and in the process of acculturation the gods were spontaneously born from the ideas and concepts arrived at by observation and logical deduction, not perhaps so much as an act of will or reason, but rather as a corollary of the conscious effort made by the sages to try to understand the working of the world that all had to live in. Once the gods became real in the minds of man, myths and legends took shape to glorify the divinity they saw in everything.

It is necessary to return to the origins to understand what was the primordial idea or concept, or thought that created gods and deities. In doing this we find that in the first place, since early times, the ways of east and west bifurcated. In the west, in Homer and in Hesiod, the philosophy was aggressively man-centered, which is very clear from the meaning of the names given to the gods, goddesses, demons, deities, muses and even the men or women with whom the gods and goddesses had relations. In the east, Indo-Europeans always considered man as a part of the world he lives in: *Homo sapiens,* as a Mammal is physically and biologically similar to other creatures. Mentally, however, Man is endowed with the power of Reason and Discrimination, and at the same time he is seen as a partner rather than the master of other living beings. From Reason, Man developed his Spirituality.

In the west, under the influence of the older Semitic cultures, where the belief was that the world was made by God for the pleasure and use of mankind, the Olympian gods were created by the Greek and made as man's image, with the same attributes and needs, same virtues and vices, weaknesses and valour and were then endowed with the great powers that man would like to have.The *Theogonia* was a political necessity and it served its purpose, it created the great binding culture called Hellenism. Indirectly it promoted rationalism and the revolt and liberation of men from the man-made gods.The world of the philosophers and of speculative sciences was born almost as soon as Hesiod produced the *Theogonia* in the eighth century BC. Thales (seventh-sixth century BC) was one of the first and upmost "naturalistic iconic philosophers."

Among the Indo-Aryans and the Indo-Iranians, the firm belief was that the gods **exist;** they are not generated spontaneously nor created by man. What learned men and sages do is just to "uncover Truth," expose the naked reality of the being and becoming.

GODS AND BELIEFS

Having created or identified gods, the Graeco-Roman culture tried to imagine what their acts were or would be. Because gods would be gods, there is no limit to their power. Myths are a test and proof of the power and capability of the gods made at the image of man, as in Mesopotamia and among other ancient Semitic people. Differently, in the east only **few** gods are the materialised sublimation of personalities that really existed. Out of respect and admiration for great souls and leaders, man arbitrarily deified them, apparently a normal psychological trait of human minds. Myths and legends are created to justify the divine nature of a newly discovered particular "god." In the east man did not seek immortality of the body, differently from ancient Mesopotamians where the defeat of Gilgamesh in his quest for immortality of the body, defines the limiting difference between man and gods. In the east immortality is reached through knowledge and wisdom, as happened to the seven ancient sages who became the seven stars of the constellation of the Ursa Major, or Dhruv who is immortalized as the Pole Star, because of the very Indo-European persistent quest for Truth.

At the early stages, beliefs were expressed as myths respectively by the *ṛṣis* in India and the *aedes* in pre-Homeric and pre-Vedic times. Among the Greek, mythology existed before Homer, but the great Olympian gods took shape only with the Homeric epics and the so-called Homeric Hymns and were finally codified in Hesiod's Theogony. Deities and divinities had been preceded by well-established facts and partially-understood principles concerning the physical world and general human behaviour of a not-yet formalized society. This is what Greek gods stood for. In the east the reasoning was different. In the history of the Vedic intellectual evolution, first came the observation of natural phenomena, then the observations were codified as stereotypes that became the virtual personification of gods. Something like mathematical formulas, which are powerful virtual entities linked to rules and subject to a unique type of Truth, eastern myths are truths embellished by imagination and built on ancient tradition, wisdom and knowledge. Archaeology has shown that there often is a kernel of truth in ancient legends about people, heroes and facts that happened in the past. However, since nothing is ever static, once created or recognised by man, even the gods evolve.

The Iliad and the Odyssey refer to facts and people who lived long before Homer's time. The facts are from the Indo-European Thracian and Mycenean cultures, but it is known that thinkers and heroes existed even earlier than Mycaene and earlier than Homer well into the ancient, nebulous though real heroic age, and it was the wandering poets and singers, the *aedi,* who kept the tradition alive. The *aedi,* improvised the songs according to the request and questions of the audience, but in the west the *aedi* sang for men, while in the east the *ṛṣi* sang to the gods which were **the Truth** which the singer "saw" with the "eyes of the mind." It is said of the sages that "even with their eyes closed, they see," which is very much like the concept of "*Idea*" in the "Discourse of the Pure Reason" by Kant. **Veda** comes from the same root as the Latin *vedere*, which means "to see," even if just with the mind, a form of virtual vision of virtual **forms**. Accordingly, having perceived the Truth, though not the **Absolute Truth**, the Vedas were memorised; only much later they were written and codified. The Vedas entered in the collective memory of the people and were not forgotten even if only ideally and subconsciously. In a comparable manner the *Rāmāyaṇa* and the *Mahābhārata* mark the crystallisation of the legends of the ancient oral tradition.

Myths continued to be enriched in both east and west. By being told and re-told new details and new stories were added to the amazing stories of the lives of heroes and deities. With the passage of time, myths became more and more phantastic.

ORAL TRADITION AND FACTUAL FINDINGS

In the east the vigour of the oral tradition was preserved thanks to the memorization of the Vedas by the brāhmaṇas in India and the *magi*, the priesthood of the Indo-European Medes, who were the sages who knew the Avesta by heart, in Iran. The word *magus, magi* in the plural form means, in Latin, a man with a very powerful mind, very learned and capable of extraordinary feats, hence the words magic and magician. In the Hellenic world the ancient oral tradition of the *aedi* was never written down because the songs were largely improvised on well-known basic theoretical and worldly themes and were opportunistic to suit any situation and audience, rather than philosophical for the sake of knowledge (Vannucci 1999). In India, story tellers, using shadow puppets or real puppets and theatre shows by living men in costume draw massive audiences even in the capital cities and are a powerful tool for nurturing the collective memory of the people, but the texts are never written.

The written tradition took over from the oral tradition, but in the west it is only partially known from scattered references mainly in Hesiod, Plutarch, Eratosthenes, Anassimander, Anassagoras, Pausanias and above all from the texts of the Mysteries that have come down to us. We know from the Epics, from Hesiod and the metamorphoses of Ovid (48 BC-18 AD) among others, that much more was known and told, but not written down in olden times, during the heroic or pre-historic period, in the last millennium BC and earlier. Even Homer and Hesiod must have known much more than what they left in writing. It is also known that the Vedas as they have come down to us, are only a fraction of the entire Vedic lore.

Most Greek "Mysteries" and philosophers have left written texts and have been studied and commented upon by scores of scholars. Unlike other Mysteries, such as the Orphic Mysteries, not even a single text was ever written down of the "Mysteries" of Goddess Demeter of Eleusis. These Mysteries were celebrated since the second half of the second millennium BC, during almost 2000 years, well into the Christian Era, but all the teachings and rites were oral and the initiates were bound by an oath of secrecy not to divulge the doctrine. Differently the Orphic Mysteries left a body of teachings in the written form.

In India, though much of the pre-Vedic tradition was lost, there is enough in what we now have of the Vedas to tell us how man thought and what his beliefs were prior to the written record. The oral tradition was still well alive in the nineteenth and twentieth centuries AD. Most unfortunately most of the Avestic texts were destroyed, first by Alexander the Great Conqueror, and later by the Islamisation of Greater Iran including Kurdistan, the ancient land of the Medes. What has come down to us from the knowledge and wisdom of the *magi*, the learned men of the Avestan tradition, is indeed only a very small fraction of what the entire tradition would have been. The people of Europe and Asia, throughout Christianity and Islam, have retained the word *magic*, meaning the representation, understanding, familiarity and practice of the uncommon and supernatural. The ancient *magi*, masters of wonderful arts, were chosen as the symbol of mysterious and divine knowledge in the tradition of the Christian lore: the three wise men were "kings," they were the ***Magi*** coming from the east and they are represented as visiting and paying homage to the newly born Jesus of Nazareth. Hence the saying: *ex oriente lux* (= light comes from the east).

Most of the details of the religion of the Indo-Iranians is lost. What we know are the parts that have come down to us of the Avesta, perhaps first codified in the fourteenth-twelve centuries BC, and from the Shah-Namah of Firdusi (940?-1020? AD) which was written many centuries after the acts and facts that he describes and that took place in the distant past of pre-Islamic history.

Archaeological findings show that early agriculture goes as far back as 6000 BC or earlier. The migration of the Indo-Iranians from the original Indo-European homeland took place in the second millennium BC. Around the fourteenth century BC a new type of pottery similar to the pottery of north-east Iran and India appears suddenly in western Iran. This pottery is known as gray or black pottery and coincides with the Iron (= Fe) horizon. The black pottery of the Indo-Iranians is similar to the black pottery unearthed at Shah Tepe, in the plains of R. Gurgan whose mouth opens in the south-eastern corner of the Caspian Sea, the plains where the Indo-Aryans split into two groups, one going towards India and the other towards Asia Minor.

CONCLUSION

All the Indo-Europeans absorbed during their migrations cultural traits of the people and of the lands which they occupied for longer or shorter periods. An example is the use of cuneiform script by the Hittite chancellery which drafted the Peace Treaty between the Hittites and Egypt after the battle of Kadesh that had ended in a draw. On the other hand much was also contributed by the Indo-European to other people, important among others are the cultivation of bread wheat (= *Triticum aestivum*), the domestication of the horse and the invention of the spoked wheel. The arts of ship building and navigation the Indo-Europeans learned from the Pelasgoi and Semitic Phoenicians. The value of medicinal plants and the usefulness of timber the Indo-Europeans learned from local people everywhere they went, as well as the adaptations needed to live under different climates, different physical and biological environments. What the Indo-European culture cultivated and maintained since the earliest beginnings was the respect and the observance of Truth, knowledge and science, law making, different types of carts, the chariot and above all, the care of the horse and the trumpet to guide the horses and chariots in parades and in battle.

The institution of the *polis*, the city as the political corner-stone of civilized nations as opposed to cities which are only an assemblage of houses and huts around the king's mansion, is typical of the Greek civilization and has its counterpart in the great ancient Buddhist university cities and the temple cities of medieval India. Roman legislature remained the basic Code of Conduct in the western world since it was first formulated, but the Graeco-Roman religion was lost as a religion and evolved into lay philosophies and arts. In India philosophy remained basically unchanged since Vedic times, though cultic practices, ceremonies and religious beliefs evolved into Brahmanism and Hinduism and different philosophical schools. Jainism and Buddhism were born as shoots from common beliefs and the respect of nature of the earlier philosophy and religion.

Part II

Gods

(A) The Indelible Link Between Man and God

ALL the definitions of the word "god" in Webster's Dictionary refer to a "being." The "definition" given by "Christian Science" in Webster's for the noun god, is more of an explanation and is more acceptable because of its neutrality. It reads: Infinite mind; Spirit; Soul; Principle; Life; Truth; Love.

From the "definition" itself, the word god is indefinable, it is an unlimited, unbound concept or idea. Perhaps the concept among the early Indo-Europeans was that Truth is omnipotent and omnipresent and therefore **is** god. Truth is taken to be what man can touch, see, smell, hear, taste or **just think about**. It is what exists above and independently of anything else. Truth is self-governing and permeates the entire Cosmos. The respect and adherence to Truth is a common characteristic of all Indo-Europeans. Truth is sacrosanct. Falsehood and lies are seldom if ever forgiven, in one way or other the culprit is punished. Truth is reality. To tell a lie is a sin greater even than stealing or robbing, because a lie is an attempt to deceive or fool God, the indefinable **Absolute.**

Manifestations of the Universal godhead were seen by early thinking man in all nature and natural phenomena good and bad. The manifestations had characteristics of their own and were personified when relationships between cause and effect became better-known following the observation of nature. Nature gods exist to this day and are obeyed — or should be obeyed — though their names may have changed.

Mythologies are stories and statements related to facts of nature or wishful thinking, or both. They often express the wish of predicting the future on the basis of "understanding" or "discovering" the will of the gods. Since early science was often inaccurate or wrong, myths were added upon myths to justify the "conclusions" obtained and perpetuated by the oral tradition. Phantasy (= fantasy, from the Gk *phainein*= to make visible, to show) is like magics, misunderstood and misused science. *Phanes* (= visible, from Gk *phaneros*) is one who has become visible, a manifestation, and it is one of the earliest names of Dionysos, the nature god who is what man can see and perceive with the senses and rationalize with the mind. It is the nature-man interaction.

Among the Indo-Europeans of the west, at some stage the philosophy of nature was codified by Homer and by Hesiod into a humanistic philosophy. The genealogy and character of the Great Olympian gods of the classical Greek religion was described, along-with that of minor deities. The characterization of the gods remained static as long as the gods themselves lived, and after they were forgotten the ideas/concepts/moods which they represented, persisted and inspired the arts of western civilizations, their names were used in science to characterize processes and phenomena. The early systematization of the Greek and Roman religion is found in the *Theogonia* by Hesiod, in the Epics, namely the Iliad and the Odyssey by Homer and in the Aeneis by Virgil. It is present in special treatises, such as the beautiful *De Rerum Natura* of Lucretius, the *De natura deorum* and the *De Fato* of Cicero, the *Metamorphoses* and *The Fasts* of Ovid, the texts of the Orphic and other Mysteries and in the writings of the philosophers (= scientists) beginning with Thales and including Euclidean geometry.

Among the Indo-Europeans of the east knowledge, mythologies and teachings constitute the *Saṁhitās* which include texts in poetry and prose, they are *Śruti* (= truth revealed by Reason), the Vedas and Vedānta to which we must conceptually add also the Avesta. The *Smṛti*, differently from the *Śruti*, rather than a fruit of revelation, are a fruit of man's studies, offered to mankind for his benefit and well-being. Though the Vedas and the Avesta are religious texts, they are compositions that go beyond religion. The hymns and prose texts may even contradict each other on details, as contemporary scientists and doctors also do, they are not dogmatic utterances. Dogmas are man-made, the reality or Absolute Truth exists independently of man who is not perfect or omniscient and cannot go beyond knowing that everything is always relative to something else.

Everything and anything evolves in nature as much as the perception that man has of nature which varies at different places and times. Consistent with this way of thinking, in both archaic and ancient east and west the "voice within," the "self within" is as real as the godhead of which it is a part. Not so long ago scientists discussed about the nature of the "instinct" of animals and people, without ever reaching a conclusion of what the word really means or is. In one or other way, seen from different angles, the nature of these debates is at the root of all religions. Hence, as I see it, philosophy comes before religion.

GODS AND TRUTH

The old-English word god, other words like Īśwaran, Bhagavān, Deva, Deus, Dio, Theo, Allah or others, have different meanings and belong to different cultures, though they may all be approximately translated with the word god. The only common denominator of the many definitions of the word god is that whatever its nature, God is an entity with infinite power and capability. Agnostics do not believe in the existence of God or gods and are convinced that science will be able to explain and perhaps predict everything. Others believe that it will never be possible for science to explain and understand everything down to its minutest details, causative forces and consequences. These are subjective questions, debatable as beliefs are; they cannot be proved right or wrong. Faith like belief, are words that neither carry nor admit explanations. The understanding of the meaning of the word god varies even among people of the same religion, in the same person they may change with age, at subsequent times and under different conditions and situations. Blind belief and blind faith engender lack of tolerance and fanaticism, they are a source of discussions, arguments, disputes, wars. In the end everybody is wrong.

The ancient Indian sages pointed out that logical thinking implies that man will be unable to fully understand or explain the "Ultimate Reality," or "Ultimate Truth" or "The Absolute" because of man's mental limitations which exist in spite of his power of reason and discrimination. Follows from this the intrinsic difference between the gods of east and west. Gods for the Vedic man were the essence, the **forma** of some basic truth or reality whose function he had understood up to the threshold of his intellectual capacity. In the west the gods of the ancient Greeks were said to be the creators and actors of the phenomenal world, physical, mental and personal. As argued earlier (Vannucci 1999) most gods worshipped by Vedic man were the result of an analysis of the cause-and-effect of natural phenomena of the world around him, each represented a step forward towards understanding the world of which we are a part. What man could not explain entered into the realm of myths. As knowledge progresses, the gods also evolved. With time leaders and specially honoured and competent men and women were also deified. Newly acquired knowledge, as for instance the nature of infectious diseases, such as smallpox, acquired the rank of smaller divinities, even if evil, such as the *sapta mātṛkā* (= seven mothers) who had to be propitiated to avoid wrong-doing, specially as cause of children's diseases. Divinities are the powers and forces that may bring about particular results, or are just the power or force itself. When a concept, or idea, or mental representation took shape in man's mind it was personified and represented as a separate entity: a *quantum* of understanding, a god, or a mathematical formula, or the Greek letters **Pi** and **Phi** as later used in mathematics. The "unveiling" of Truth, or acquisition of knowledge was the aim of the ancient sages.[1]

In ancient Mesopotamia, when facts and processes were witnessed but not yet explained, the gods were made as the image of man because man was the highest and best that man himself could imagine: gods were powerful creatures to be served by man and who would in turn extend to man all that was needed. It was an innate, probably sub-conscious astute process to explain, excuse and pardon man's own ignorance and weakness, to highlight man's positive qualities and pardon the negative traits. In the evolution of civilizations most probably the made-to-man's image of gods came later than the nature gods who are essentially the manifestation and personification of observed causes and effects of nature's forces. The great gods made as the image of man pass away as the civilizations for which they were tailor-made decline, while nature and nature gods or rather gods true to nature, hindered or not by man, follow their course. Unfortunately the gods themselves are not listened to when tempers flare up.

About the word God or gods, the only conclusion possible is that expressed by the Latin aphorism: "*De gustibus non est disputandum*" (do not argue about tastes or preferences; tastes or colours cannot be described and therefore are not arguable, or disputable. "Do not argue about preferences"). In contemporary terms I would say: "*De deibus non est disputandum*" or: "There should be no arguments about gods." The corollary is also true: "There are no indisputable proofs of God or gods." Whatever is said or has been said about the noun God may be believed or not, therefore here we will take the word God at the conventional face value of this indefinable word. The Italian author Pirandello, in his play "*Così è se vi pare*" (= This is so, if you please), arrives at the lapidary sentence:, *io sono colei che mi si crede*" (= I am the one who each one of you believes I am). This was the simple truth under a family situation where the only way to maintain family unity and mental sanity was to confirm with unflinching courage what had to be said, this is that each one of us sees others from a different angle, whether the image is true or not, but each and everyone has to be accepted. Personal images and human "truths" are inevitably biased, they are always relative, but there is only one Absolute Truth which is beyond human grasp. Nowhere Pirandello considers Mrs Ponza anything more than just a wise woman who has to extricate herself from the difficult position of a mature woman accused of perjury. Mrs Ponza achieves the miracle of a new lease of normal life for the family, though the culprit was never found. In fact, did it exist at all? What is truth and how far does truth go? Pirandello closes the drama with the Inspector's words: "*Ed ecco, o signori, come parla la verità* (= And this is, gentlemen, how Truth speaks). Comparably in Rajasthan, Bengal and elsewhere in India, the wife and other respected ladies are usually addressed as *Devī*, whether we admit it or not, the mother is always as right as a goddess. *Devī* is mother and mother is *Devī*.

GODS

In the context of the theme of this book, I dare say that the best course is always to try to understand the structure and function of natural systems, accept the existence of unsolved mysteries and live in accordance with material and immaterial reality, even if not fully understood. After all, trying to explain everything is a form of pride, conceit and narcissism. Radhakṛṣṇan (1953) in the Introduction to the Isa Upanishad writes: "its main purpose is to teach the essential unity of God and the world, being and becoming," then he further points out that "It is interested [the Isa Upanishad] not so much in the Absolute itself, Parabrahman, as in the Absolute in relation to the world, Parameśwaran. It teaches that life in the world and life in the Divine Spirit are not incompatible." Is there a difference between a single Absolute Truth with an infinite variety of facets or many facets compounded in The Absolute? We should say: above all we should remember that sacred texts, the *Theogonia* or the *Smṛti* are written by man for men, women and children, for the younger generation which will be adult tomorrow. The question is whether *to believe only in revelations expressed in words or to admit that there can be wordless revelations.*

NATURE GODS

Naturally archaic man would have been afraid of powerful visible forces of nature such as lightnings, winds, floods, landslides or ferocious animals. He would have been afraid also of invisible forces such as the effect of poisons, diseases, birth, old age and death. Dangers were ever present in the world he lived in and he would imagine the good and favourable forces as his own image, while dangers would be represented by demons and monsters. Gods made as man's image are authoritative and command respect while the similarity creates self-respect and understanding. Gods should be propitiated to ensure natural fulfilment of the unending requests of man. Prayers would come naturally and they would become stereotypes only after generations of supplicants had addressed God or gods. Mental representation is a form of understanding that precedes characterization and identification.

There is probably no exception to the rule that all primitive cultures have eulogised, invoked or worshipped nature's forces. Dionysos is a late name given to a pre-historic Mediterranean god who is at present known only indirectly and from tradition. Rudra is an ancient Vedic god named about 60 times in the *ṚV* alone. Four hymns are especially meaningful in the present context. In *ṚV* II, 33 Rudra, father of the Maruts is eulogised as the "strong bull," "sovereign of the world, dreaded beast of the forest." He is armed with bow, arrows and thunder; he is described as the mightiest of the mighty, giver of most saving medicines and the best of all physicians. He is fair-faced, giver of food and protects the worshipper from injury. In *ṚV* II, 34; *ṚV* VI, 48, 12-13 and *ṚV* VI 50, the Maruts are said to be sons of Rudra and of his consort Rodasi, who may be identified with the Earth and could be an old name of Pṛśni. Undoubtedly Rudra, the Maruts and Rodasi represent the wild destructive forces of nature, who could occasionally be benign, while the Aśvins in *ṚV* VIII, 22, 6-7 who come at dawn are credited with teaching how to plough, and are therefore teachers of methodical agriculture; accordingly they appear relatively late in Vedism. Work in the fields begins at dawn and agriculture was recognised to be the first important step for the acculturation of man.

In the east, nature gods evolved with the evolution of culture, but they were not *substituted* by other gods. They continued to be worshipped and are alive as members of the Hindu pantheon. In Greece an entirely new pantheon was created under the influence of the cultures of West Asia. Ancient nature gods of Greece were by-passed by the development of the new religion of Olympian gods because historic imperatives had to be methodically codified. Nature gods became the substratum needed to define the evolution of the principles and characteristics of Greek lifestyles and to justify the cultural and geographic expansion of the Greek civilization. Hellenism was thus conceived, born, nurtured and expanded.

HOMER AND HESIOD

It is not known if pre-Hellenic Pelasgians had specific names for their gods. According to Herodotus (II, 51) they were the first who made ithyphallic statues of their gods, but names are not given and the time when they did so is not specified.

Greek religion was first put in written form by Homer (ninth century BC) based on the foundation created during the "heroic" or archaic pre-Homeric period which includes, as defined here, the myths and legends of the proto-historic and pre-historic periods of the Greek culture and civilization, the duration of which is not much more than guesswork. Homer himself is a semi-legendary figure who most probably existed in human form in the ninth century BC.

Homer is credited with having composed the two great epics of the Greek civilization, the Iliad and the Odyssey. The epics refer to the long-drawn war and siege that the confederate city-states of peninsular Greece waged against the city of Ilyo (= Troy), four to five centuries before Homer. The remains of a walled city identified as ancient Ilyo are still visible near the shores of Asia Minor, not far from the western entrance to the Strait of the Dardanelles, connecting the Aegean Sea with the Sea of Marmara that separates Europe from Asia Minor, an obviously important strategic point. The poetic cause of the war was the abduction of a Greek princess of Sparta, Helen by the Trojan prince Paris. The Iliad sings about the heroes and the battles that preceded the fall and arson of Troy by the Achaeans (= Greek) in the second half of thirteenth century BC, as approximately confirmed by archaeological findings. The Odyssey refers to the fall, the sack and arson of Ilyo and the return of the Greek hero-king Odysseus (= Ulysses) to his home-state, the island of Ithaca, in the Ionian Sea, traditionally but only tentatively identified with the island of Thiaki. The epics gave the opportunity, or were perhaps written mainly for the purpose of accounting for past history and for recording the ancient beliefs regarding cosmogony, theogony and theology and for defining and eulogizing the rules of the new Greek culture created by Homer and Hesiod.

Traditionally the Greek *aedi,* the *rhapsodysts* and the *cytharists* respected scrupulously their anonymity and this may be the main reason why we have almost no knowledge about Homer the blind poet as a person, though there are sculptures believed to be his portraits. Homer recorded much of the knowledge and myths which existed before him, but it was Hesiod who organised the Greek pantheon into a complete whole, which he expressed in the 1020 verses of the "*Theogonia.*" Homer presumably came from Smirne or perhaps from the island of Kios. Hesiod came from Central Greece but more than Homer he had direct contacts with Asia Minor where his father spent most of his life. Hesiod arranged the Great Olympian gods and minor deities and divinities into a system where the names reflect the world we live in as well as mental, psychological and emotional characteristics of man. Arrighetti (1984, Introduction to the Theogonia of Hesiod, *transl. mine*) writes: ". . . reality is multiform and [Greek] gods represent both the personification and hypostasis of the various aspects of reality which is their own jurisdiction, their *timai.*"

The *Theogonia* (= The Origin of gods) is a methodical presentation of theogony and cosmogony of the material world in which each deity and god has its function and attributes. Both Homer and Hesiod, respectively in the epics and in the *Theogonia,* express their understanding and reliance on a rich *corpus* of knowledge contained in the earlier songs of the *aedi,* the myths and legends they sang and whose ancient roots are lost in time. Homer and Hesiod set the clock for the recording and evolution of the Greek civilization. Herodotus (fifth century BC) in II, 53 says about Homer and Hesiod: "they are those who created for the Greek the history of the birth of their gods, gave them names, described their figure, their competence and activities." This sentence sounds almost as if man had defined the *dharma* or *timai* of each one of his gods. Evidently Hesiod's century was ready for the assimilation of cultural and religious traits of the civilizations of West Asia and Egypt, the most relevant being the making of gods as man's image. This is a far cry from taking the lofty gods to witness for the preservation, respect and obedience to **human** treatises as the one that was drawn in the first quarter of the second millennium BC, between the victorious Indo-Aryan Hittite King Suppiluliuma I and the defeated king of Mitanni, contemporary with the thirteenth-fourteenth Egyptian dynasties (1750-1640 BC).

HESIOD

Hesiod's family was from Baeotia, where the Mycenean culture had flourished. His father had lived for many years in the coastal city of Cuma in Asia Minor from where he would have brought home first-hand knowledge of the religion and wisdom of the Anatolian and other cultures of Asia. The task given to Hesiod by the Muses, was to sing "Truth and Justice" as the poet himself states in the Invocation. By saying this he means that tradition is to be weeded of the phantasy and imaginary and should be reduced to the truthful representation of the reality of the world of the gods and their interaction and relations with man. Children are only mentioned in the context of their birth, especially those sired by the Great Zeus by as many different mortal and divine women. The *Theogonia* is a book of the acts of the adult generations, godly and human, past and present. The authority of Hesiod's teachings remained alive and respected well into the Era of Imperial Rome. From the point of view of the present study, the remarkable aspect of Hesiod's philosophical religion is his study of "eastern" ideas, concerns and motivations. I shall follow the advice given by Herodotus and take Homer and Hesiod as the bench-mark to distinguish "classic" Greek culture and religion from the earlier "archaic, mythological tradition." Hesiod also started a new style, as the *Theogonia* begins with an unusually long invocation that is a panegyric of the Muses who *"ordered"* him to write and gave him the gift of truthfulness (vv. 22/23). Hesiod here breaks away from tradition which was to invoke the Muses to *inspire* the poet, rather than *ordering* the poet to sing the Truth. The order given by the Muses establishes a gap between Homer and Hesiod, between the old and the new tradition, namely the will to define and interpret, rather than accept blindly the myths and legends of the earlier Archaic, or Heroic Age. Hesiod accepts the self-imposed challenge to spread the truth about the myths, a responsibility new to a Greek poet; it was a new approach to religion since it is man and not Zeus or Fate, who now defines the *timai* of each god or deity. It is tempting to interpret the *timai* of each god, now defined by man, as the individual *dharma* attributed by Hesiod to every god and goddess. This duty Hesiod, himself a man, takes up to fulfil the order received from the nine muses. He creates a highly structured pantheon and by putting himself in an entirely new position he creates a new philosophy, the humanism of ancient Greece nowhere expressed better than in the classic tragedies of Aeschylus (525-455 BC), Sophocles (496-406 BC) and Euripides (485-406 BC).

TRADITIONAL GODS

Neither Homer nor Hesiod care much about nature gods, they are reticent in mentioning them, almost as if they were embarrassed by the acts of the rustic divinities in the presence of the great civilized Olympian gods, lords of the world and of mankind. In the east ancient sages had already understood that man is far from being the Lord of Creation, they looked for Truth or Reality beyond man and these they recognised as their gods and goddesses. When men had to create divinities out of historical necessity or some other compulsion, they did not hesitate to give them human titles, such as King or Lord and to invest these gods and other divinities with frailties similar to those of man. This is how Indra and Zeus are Kings of gods and man. The mystery of life is central in the Vedic religion, but the very ancient original Greek Mysteries of Eleusis, or the Orphic Mysteries of the Greek tradition initially had no place in the official religion of the rulers of the Graeco-Roman world — they attained their position only very late. They had initially been overshadowed and hidden under the majesty of the great gods. The celebration of the Mysteries of Eleusis was held annually for over 400 to 500 years or more before Homer's and Hesiod's time, yet they are not mentioned, or only very briefly, in the latter's writings. Demeter appears in the epics, mainly because of her daughter Kore, sired by Zeus, rather than as the creator of the Eleusinian mysteries and teacher of the agriculture of hexaploid (= bread) wheat and other cereals, an art which she had brought with her from the East (Vannucci 1999b).

Homer's epics are the last recorded documents of the ancient pre-historic period, at the same time they are the ground knowledge and set the scene for the evolution of the Hellenic philosophic civilization, with prominence on political science, the administration of the "*polis*," natural sciences, religion and arts. Pausanias (2nd century AD) takes Homer as the correct recorder of the traditional religion and culture of the ancient Greeks. Trails of Greek influence were still alive when St. Agustin (354-430 AD) father of the Christian church, entitled his master work *Civitas Dei* (The city of God).

FROM PRE-HISTORY TO HISTORY

Homer's epics and Hesiod's Theogony mark the passage from pre-history to history in Greece. The collected myths and legends are taken from a rich *corpus* of traditional lore that preceded them. The two epics and the Theogony show the influence that the civilizations of Asia Minor had on the development of the Greek culture and of the great cultural movement called Hellenism. The *Theogonia* of Hesiod describes the succession of kings and gods beginning with Ouranos (= Uranus), king of the sky. Gea or Gaya (= Earth) was his consort. Because of his tyrannical nature, Uranos was dethroned by his son Chronos (= Time) who castrated him. Chronos then swallowed all his children as they were born, until when Rhea, his wife, gave him a brick to swallow instead of the baby and thus saved Zeus (= Jupiter), the last born. Gaya then advises Rhea, her daughter-in-law, to resuscitate all the offsprings previously swallowed by Chronos, Zeus becomes the next king of gods and shares the world with his siblings.[2]

A Hittite text of the thirteenth century BC puts on record an originally Hurrite myth much older than Homer and Hesiod. The Hittite text written in cuneiform script refers to the Hurrite non-Indo-European language text which gives the following hierarchy of the heavenly kings (Arrighetti 2000).[3] First Alalu was king in the sky. He was served by Anu (= sky) who became the next king of the sky, then Kumarpi (= Kumarbi) who descends from the lineage of Alalu, defeats Anu and castrates him. His victory is short-lived because Anu introduces in Kumarpi the god of Storms (= God of Tempests) which corresponds to the powerful River Tigris prone to sudden flooding, and other deities. Zeus therefore corresponds to the god of Storms. In conclusion, the two genealogies, the Greek and the Hurrite are almost identical. Thus the corner stone of Hesiod's Theogony is taken from the Semitic (?) or otherwise local tradition transferred to Greece via Asia Minor and West Asia most probably through trade and other cultural exchanges. The language as well as the details of the myth may have been Semitic, however they also reflect the original thought of the proto-Indo-Europeans since they are nature-based, which is an archaic attempt to "explain" cosmogony and theogony, besides representing it. Such attempts are common among all emerging cultures.[3]

A well known text of the probably Indo-Aryan Kassite dynasty of Babylon (c. 1750-1170 BC), written in a non-Indo-European language contains Arya names, such as a sun-god named *Suriyas*, the war-god *Marutas,* which corresponds to the Sanskrit *Marutta* and of a king *Abirattas,* which can be interpreted as *abhi-ratha* (= facing [war] chariots). The warriors on horse-back were called *mariyanna,* while the Maruts are called *maryah* (*ṚV* I 64,2; VII 56.1); acc. Chakravarty, U. (1997), the Maruts are described as *maryah* (from Skt. *marya*), "a band of young men moving in groups." Many more important details are given by Harmatta (1996). Chakravarty also points out correctly that the "Maruts, storm gods, are only apparently anthropomorphic. . .they are nature anthropomorphised" . . . "after an initiation which resembles death (cf. Skt. *dvija*) they were considered as reborn." The rites of initiation bound the young men to the observance of special rites and duties as warriors. Also the names of princess of Akkad (c. 1500-1300 BC) are Aryan names written in cuneiform script and in Akkadian, a Semitic language. Documents in Assyrian contain the Aryan names of nobles. Rulers of surrounding territories have Aryan names. From Harmatta (*l.c. p.372*): "It seems . . . that simultaneously with the movements of the Kassites — and before 1700 BC at the latest, or perhaps even earlier, at the end of the third millennium BC, immigration of proto-Indian groups into Hurrian territory began, led by the class of war-charioteers (*maryanna*)."[4, 5]

Another important document that illustrates the religious thought of the Indo-Aryans of the second half of the second millennium BC, is a well known Peace Treaty drawn in 1350 BC after the Mitanni king was defeated by the Hittite king of Hatti (Kochhar 2000). The treaty was written in cuneiform script, in an Indo-European language. In the treaty sealed beween the king of Mitanni and the king of the Hittites, Vedic gods are mentioned in the same sequence as in *ṚV* X; 125,1, where Vāk, the Word or Speech personified, upholds the dignity and importance of the dual divinities Mitra-Varuṇa — Indra-Agni — the Nasatyas or Aśvini as well as Ādityā and Viśvedevā. Kochhar points out the occurrence and significance of the invocation to these Vedic deities which are called to witness: "May the gods of the secret and may the gods whom we call lords of the oath, whom we are herewith calling, stand by, may they hear and may they be witness . . . of the Treaty [sealed hereby]." The language used to draft the treaty reflects the original religious thoughts of the Indo-Aryans, it confirms the view that the Indo-Aryans who migrated westwards towards Asia Minor, were a shoot that separated early from the bulk of the Indo-Aryan population that was settled in the plains of R. Gurgan, off the south-eastern shores of the Caspian Sea. A major and different group of the eastern branch of Indo-Aryans migrated eastwards and eventually settled in the hydrographic basin of R. Indus and beyond. Another group of the eastern branch of Indo-Aryans migrated eastwards and settled at higher latitudes, around 45-50° N. lat, in the Altaï Mountains region.[5] Kochhar points out the occurrence and significance of the invocation to the Vedic deities which are called to witness, however the document cannot be taken as a proof of the local origin of the proto-Indo-Aryans. The Indo-Aryans at that stage already had a long history behind them. The chronological sequence of events (Tabs, A, B) is known, dates are confirmed by comparison with Egyptian records besides being calculated from archaeological data. As quoted above from Harmatta, the kingdom of Hatti was well established already in the early sixteenth century BC and Babylon was conquered by the Hittites in 1531. The Hittites had a developed civilization and were experienced in warfare.

The Peace Treaty sealed by the Mitanni and Hittite kings was drawn in the city called Hatti or Hattusha, seat of the Hittites, one of the farthest and westernmost areas of the Indo-Aryan habitat, in the second millennium BC and the gods quoted are familiar and well-known. Kochhar (*l.c.*) mentions that the wording of the Treaty shows that "R̥gvedic concepts were already *fully developed in about 1400* BC" (italics mine). Here I strongly differ from Kochhar because dates indicate that concepts were **still alive** and not, as mentioned by Kochhar, that they ***"were already fully developed"*** at least by 1400 BC. The wording of the treaty shows that the basic concepts were alive, but the Vedic culture was **not yet** fully developed. The Indo-Aryans had come from the east and at that time Asia Minor was their farthest expansion before crossing the Aegean Sea and before being assimilated and mixed with locally more ancient civilizations. The Indo-Aryans **were not** moving from west to east, as argued by Kochhar; in fact Harmatta (*l.c.*) confirms that they had arrived in Anatolia coming from the east.[5]

R̥gvedic concepts had by 1400 BC **survived** intact or almost so over a long history of geographic expansion and cultural development. R̥gvedic ideology however gradually became diluted in the west. The wording of the Treaty also indicates the rule and practice of the Vedic religion among the ruling class of Hitta. Vannucci (1999) pointed out the important meaning of hymn *R̥V* X, 125, in another context, Mitra (= Mithra in the Avesta) is a close associate of Varuṇa and supervises the faithful observance of accords, laws, treaties and the like, under the overseeing personality of the great Asura Varuṇa, the ideal and personification of Truthfulness. Significantly Mitra-Varuṇa and the other Vedic gods mentioned are among the ancient-most gods of the Vedic Indo-Aryan people and they are the gods who herald and certify the advance westwards of the Vedic rulers who had been separated early from the eastern branch of the Indo-Aryans who eventually settled in the lands irrigated by R. Indus and tributaries, and beyond. Indra with his *vajra* is the great overlord and conqueror associated to Lord Agni. The *vajra* is the most powerful of weapons. The *Aświni* or "Nāsātyas'" role is to promote and preserve the sanity of body, mind and spirit of the individual and of the relations among humans. The mention of these gods in this treaty drawn at the then western far-end of the great Indo-Aryan habitat and the historically recorded date of the treaty, are highly significant to show the extent and time of the spread westwards of the eastern Indo-Europeans, the Indo-Aryans, in Asia Minor and as far as the eastern Mediterranean (*fig.* 1).

Later, after the wars with the Mitanni, the Hittites were engaged in another war, this time with the Egyptians. The battle of Kadesh was waged between the young pharaoh Ramses II and the Hittite king Muwatalli II in *c.* 1275 BC. The Peace Treaty between Egypt and Hatti was sealed only as late as 1259 BC by Ramses II and Hattusili III for Hatti, since king Muwatalli II of Hatti had died in the interval. The war that resulted in the Battle of Kadesh had been carefully planned and Mursili II, the then King of Hatti, had duly consulted and sacrificed to the gods, the Indo-Aryan gods, prior to the declaration of hostilities.

There is a long gap of about, or almost, one thousand years between the date of the conquest of Babylon by the Hittite king Mursili I in 1531 and the lives of Homer and Hesiod and there had been much mixing of people and cultures in the interval. This may be part of the reason why the very ancient Ṛgvedic or Indo-European tradition had become blurred and discoloured in Greece in Homer's time. The names of Arya gods and Kings were forgotten in Greece, leaving behind them a vacuum which was occupied by recent influences on Greek philosophy and religion that had come mainly from Crete, Egypt, Phoenicians and ancient Semitic people from Mesopotamia.[6]

The dates and texts also show the split between the Vedic and the Avestan cultures on one side, and on the other side the people who migrated over different routes from their original Indo-European homeland. The names and dates also indicate clearly that the ruling class of the Hittites was Indo-Aryan and not Indo-Iranian because, as well known, the "*devas*" of the Indo-Aryan had become the demons of the Indo-Iranians. The people who eventually built the Graeco-Roman civilization included also Indo-European coming from continental Europe, Macedonia and Thracia who were at an earlier and less developed cultural level than the I.E. of the east and of the other people, Asian and Egyptian who influenced the development of the Graeco-Roman civilization. Considering etymological and other cultural affinities, the most significant cultural input came to Greece from the Indo-Europeans of the east, both Indo Aryans and Indo-Iranians who had arrived culturally from Asia Minor.

The door must be left open for refinements or corrections to be added when further archaeological evidence will be found. We are mainly interested here in the ideological and intellectual processes that culminated with the large corpus of knowledge included in the Indian oral and written traditions. Tradition and internal evidence show beyond doubt that the foundations of the immense cultural edifice are the Vedas. All the Vedas, and the *Ṛgveda* in particular, are an assemblage of the oral tradition of the Indo-Arya lineages or *gotra,* the families and the descendants or lineages from ancient patriarchs (among others, Bhargava, ed. 2001), though various lineages have variants of beliefs and ritual practices. The Vedas are not a mosaic of heterogenous beliefs, they are rather their record and synthesis, encompassing all, or as much as possible of the archaic tradition, even if various lineages are followers of different branches of tradition, ritual practices, habits and customs. With time differences arose due to geographic and environmental isolation, differential acquisition of knowledge, development of various lifestyles, habits and customs, but the fundamental ideology remained the same and unchanged during the long life of the culture and religion inherited from the Indo-Aryan ancestors. Other texts, particularly the Brāhmaṇas, clearly show the intention to incorporate and consider all views into a general doctrine which would not erase the "information" or viewpoints of different lineages even if followers of other branches of tradition. This intellectual tolerance has enabled contrasting remarks and details to survive intact in contemporary daily habits and in the performance of rites and rituals. The essential tolerance of Brāhmanism is one of the driving forces of its vitality and historical survival. Beliefs and religious practices are man-made; they are wise or faulty depending on the individual point of view and may vary with caste or lineage. Dogmas are man-made, only the Absolute is Perfect, the individual actions are the personal responsibility of each one of us.

Summing up, we find Indo-Aryan Sanskrit names in texts of the Kassite dynasty of Babylon, 1750-1170 BC (Kochhar 2000; Guidotti & Pecchioli-Daddi 2002), then again in 1500-1300 BC texts from the Mitanni and Hatti kingdoms. Finally we have the rich source of information from the Hittite sources discovered by the searches made at the Hittite capital Hattusha (now Boghazkoy) in Anatolia and in the Final Treaty that followed the battle of Kadesh and was sealed in 1259 BC by Ramses II of Egypt and Hattusili III, the then Hittite king who suceeded Muwatalli II, the Hittite king of the battle of Kadesh (1275 BC). The cycle is thus closed with the "legal" acceptance in the Hittite Treaty of the Egyptian god Seth, counterpart of the Semitic nature god, the god of Tempests who could also be admitted into the personality of Rudra.[7]

THE INDIAN AND GREEK SOURCES

Unlike what happened in Greece, in the vast Indian territory there was not just one single singer called Homer, followed by a major poet-singer/philosopher called Hesiod who collected, selected and joined into an almost logical perfunctory whole the oral tradition of the people who preceded them. The sheer amount of knowledge and wisdom, the myths and legends themselves with the inherent variants of the centuries-old oral tradition alive in widely dispersed clans and families, made it impossible for Vedic man to establish for Vedism a basic formal, rigidly structured book comparable to the *Theogonia* of Hesiod, or the Old Testament of the Hebrews. Ancient and evolving tradition was instead incorporated in the Indian epics. Finally, from the epistemological (ethical and critical) Indian point of view, there cannot be a *man-made Absolute Truth*, hence even contradictory statements could be correct or not, who knows? which man can decide? It is therefore worth mentioning all points of view and let each one live his religious beliefs the way he considers most adequate. Vedic man did not formulate religious dogmas. Though over the centuries fanaticism has occasionally flared up in Greater India, it has been short-lived and only a consequence of external or political compulsion.

There is no single author of the Vedas, of the Brāhmaṇa, Saṁhitā, Purāṇa or any other religious text. The earliest and condensed result of the immense learning and phantasy of the "forefathers," is the *Ṛgveda* of which we have what is believed to be the major part. It was put in written form after centuries, probably after over twenty centuries of oral tradition. Since the general practice was and still is never to discard whatever knowledge has been acquired, variants of form and details were compounded in a manner comparable but not similar to what happened later to Greek mythology.

Greek mythology was inflated not as a result of the search for truth, but as the opportunistic or nationalistic embellishment and upgrading of places and people, as evident from the works of late authors, such as Pausanias, to mention only one of the best known. As an example we may quote Virgilius himself, author of the *Aeneis,* who gives details of the divine origin of the mythical ancestor of the Roman people: *Aenaeas,* son of goddess Aphrodite (= Venus). It is an attitude not exclusive of Rome and Romans. Recently, it is said that Napoleon grabbed the crown that was about to be placed on his head during the coronation ceremony, saying: "God gave it to me, and I will put it on." Among the Greek, new temples and isles were given historical status with exclusive mythological details and legendary acts of gods and heroes, not only in the Aegean Sea, but throughout the Mediterranean Sea, Asia Minor, West Asia and as far as India, west of R. Indus. Modern and contemporary western scholars and writers also inflated and confused Greek mythology by lumping all the myths related to single gods or happenings into long texts where place and time of origin of the myths were not taken into account. Myths and legends can be deciphered, if ever, only when seen under a geographic, historic and chronological perspective. For this reason Homer and Hesiod on one side and the

Ṛgveda on the other have to be taken as the bench-mark on which a superstructure, partly phantastic and partly truthful was repeatedly built and rebuilt. Both the Greek and the Vedic texts are fundamental, themselves the epilogue of a very rich earlier tradition which is mostly lost to us, except for the contents of the sacred texts or the proverbs, songs and stories of the popular lore.

The Avesta and the Shah-Namah of Firdusi are the principal sources available for studying and trying to understand the Indo-Iranian mythology and the pre-Zoroastrian and Zoroastrian religions.

MYTHOLOGY IN THE EAST

I wish to recall here only a few basic myths which are particularly relevant towards trying to understand the development of the human intellect, the building of the personal and collective conscience and the sense and feeling of belonging. The first refers to the myths of the origin and personalities of Indra and Zeus, both of them kings of the gods. They both ascended to this position in the same manner, by slaying a superhuman being, demon, dragon, *rākṣas*, Titan or whatever powerful being. The great feat of Indra was the slaying of Vṛtra for which gods and men were forever thankful. The same is true for Zeus and the slaying of Typhaeus. Both Vṛtra and Typhaeus are superhuman beings, very strong and choleric, apt to cause much damage to Great Mother Earth. In either case without this act of valour Indra or Zeus would not have ascended to the throne or received the undisputed support and praise from other gods and all men. A trustworthy leader is essential for technical (material), mental (unwavering belief in the success of the king) and spiritual (acceptance of the new king as a god by other gods) development of the people, especially if the group has a heterogeneous ancestry. Indra is a very ancient figure, probably one of the original gods of the Indo-Europeans. The name itself is akin to the Greek word for man: *andros,* where the Indo-European prefix *aner, andr* indicates either the male sex in Greek, or the word man. *Mann* is the root-word for man as a thinking being, or a mortal man among the Indo-European of northern Europe from Armenians to Celts and Germanic people. The Latin word *humus* refers to earth as soil, it gave the word *homo* (= man) and is one of the most ancient roots for *man* and similar in earliest Indo-European languages such as Tocarian, Indic languages, Hittite, Slavic and Baltic. The Gk. *khthron* refers to earth, underground, underworld and its gods such as Ades or Aidoneus and gave the English word chthonic or the rarely used Italian *ctonio* (= underground).

Indra is the Great Man, similarly to Zeus who was earlier a man, or Uranus and Gaya, the original couple. Both Indra and Zeus were so great that they became gods because of their heroic feats. This position they conquered through acts that endeared them to men and gods who believed in the success of their leadership and enabled them to achieve the goals of a superman. The origin of the personality of Indra emerges from the distant past. According to the older myths (*R̥V* IV;18,1) after a gestation of thousands (meaning an extremely long time) of months, Indra insisted to be born in an unusual manner, not from the usual channel, to accomplish much which was yet to be done (Chakravarty 1997). Indra's mother may have been Aditi, Mother of Infinity and of the concept of *infinite*, itself Nature, who endowed him with infinite valour that filled the Earth and Sky as soon as he was born, according to sage Vāmadeva (*R̥V* IV 4; 12). According to the Taittirīya tradition of the *Yajurveda*, as soon as born Indra killed his father Vyamsa, a demon. The greatest feat of Indra, for which he is repeatedly remembered, is the slaying of Vr̥tra and other demons like Ahi, Namuci, Vala. Indra emerges from the distant past as the conqueror of the destructive forces of wild nature, epitomized with the killing of Vr̥tra — Indra Vr̥trahan is the most common designation for the frequently eulogised Indra. The killing of Vr̥tra and his nature have been unendingly discussed. By all accounts Vr̥tra is the symbol of all violent forces of material nature, winds, landslides, earthquakes, burst of bunds and floods as well as droughts, against which puny man alone is helpless. Hence the creation of the myth of the Great Superman, conquerer of human or superhuman foes, unopposed by man or demon. He is to be eulogised and encouraged with a fortified drink (*soma*) and to him praises are offered mixed with the request for rewards such as the booty to be had at the end of the battle. Indra never sheds his human characteristics, as when he is afraid of darkness, ignorance and night (Vannucci 1999) or when he would gladly run away and has to be heartened by his admirers, the common men. Indra remains the natural leader, for many centuries. Hence the suggestion that the name Indra became with time, a title for honoured leaders, like "Caesar" an honourific for kings, used since the age of Imperial Rome down to the present. Evidently, Indra is the personality who could lead the very early Ṛgvedic people during their migrations towards and to the east, beyond the Indus River. Indra, the Great King, would conquer for his people ample land in which they would settle permanently. From the viewpoint of this book, the notable points are: Indra's ancient origin and very long gestation period (the pre-historic era), the slaying of his tyrannical father symbolizing man's freedom from fear, his courage and superhuman nature (idealized by man), the slaying of demons, the most troublesome being Vṛtra and Ahi (*ṚV* IV;19 *et al.*). Vṛtra in the course of time, finally agrees to serve god Indra by becoming his food. We are tempted to see in this epilogue of the rebellious character of Vṛtra a suggestion of the surge of the art of agriculture. Agriculture is wild nature conquered by man's patient work and perseverance under correct guidance over many generations and finally producing man's basic food.

In this context, we should note that the Nasatyas, or Aśvini, are not only knowledgeable of medicinal plants, but also have something to do with agriculture since they are mentioned as teachers of agriculture in *ṚV* VIII; 22,6, where they are said to have ploughed the fields for the first harvest "in the sky." The proto-historic heroic Rudra, the "howling," a nature god, gradually gives way to the majestic power of Indra who then becomes less godly and more human in the course of centuries, probably because fights among clans decreased as they settled each in their own area. Indra however remained for ever the warrior king, patron and guardian of the Indo-Aryans who, by eulogising Indra also praised themselves and other leaders. Indra is an archaic personality and is classified a demon in the Avesta.

MYTHOLOGY IN THE WEST

In the west the proto-historic gestation period of the traditional Greek culture built the foundation on which Homer and Hesiod produced the scaffolding for the evolution of the Greek civilization, rich in philosophy, arts and science. The wild nature personified by

Dionysos was the driving force of the archaic period. The Muses "ordered" Hesiod to winnow off the chaff from the grain of the lengthy repertoire of the acts of gods and heroes of the past. As briefly mentioned above, in terms of cosmogony Hesiod's condensation led to the establishment of an original pair: Uranos (= Ouranus) and Gaya or Gaea, respectively Sky or Heaven, and Earth. One of their sons, Chronos (= Time) liberates mother and brothers from the tyranny of father Uranos by castrating him. Chronos had three sons from Rhea. The eldest, Zeus (= Jupiter for the Romans), overpowered Chronos and made the division of the Cosmos in Sky (= heaven), Hell and Ocean. He kept the brilliant day/sky under his rule, put the Ocean under the lordship of Poseidon (= Neptune) and the Nether world or Hell, under Ades. Chronos, unable to generate new progeny, had from then on to live in the underworld with Titans, demons and other malevolent deities. The Greek symbolic hierarchy of the first three brothers and rulers of the world: Uranos, Chronos and Zeus has no parallel in Vedism, but corresponds closely to the Hurrite cosmogony described in the Hittite text of the thirteenth century BC, mentioned above, where the succession of the gods is Alalu, dethroned by Anu, who corresponds to Uranos, who was dethroned and mutilated by Kumarpi (= Kumarbi) who corresponds to Chronos (= Time) and the last one, who corresponds to Zeus, is the Lord of Tempests and Storms who reigns supreme in this world and on all living beings.

The Hurrite theogony is described in detail in a Hittite text in Hurrite language and cuneiform script of the thirteenth century BC, at least six or seven centuries before Hesiod. There are differences in details between the Hittite text and Hesiod's succession of heavenly kings, but the vision of the divine superhuman world is basically the same in both traditions. Both culminate with the victory of a powerful man-made god, respectively Zeus armed with terrible thunderbolts and the god of Tempests. Both these myths are important in that they demonstrate the holistic view of the physical and divine worlds that local Greek and Hurrite people had in first and second millennia BC. This view in effect derives from a correct ecological perspective as would be expected from people living under natural conditions with a materially simple lifestyle. They were people who knew well the power of the violent aspects of nature.

These myths actually set the basis for a realistic approach to the understanding and use of nature, for this reason they matched easily and naturally the Hittite world-view. They evolved into the ideals of the Greek civilization that was born with Homer. The biological aspects of wild nature are present in the oral tradition and folklore of a very large part of the eastern Mediterranean and West Asia, they are represented by Dionysos who eventually tames wild nature with the aid of Demeter whom he "brought from the East" and of his expert pastoral ancestors. We have good descriptions of the early developments of Graeco-Roman culture in the Georgicae of Virgilius. We can still sense the presence of Dionysos when talking, eating and drinking with peasants in the Mediterranean regions of Europe.

The god-kings described by Hesiod became the Olympian gods of Greece, but Dionysos and Demeter were only much later, almost reluctantly, admitted to Olympus. To achieve the elevation to the god's abode, Dionysos was made to be born from the thigh of Zeus himself and Demeter gave birth to Kore, daughter of Zeus, even though chronologically both Dionysos and Demeter are older than the certified Olympian gods who are the latest generation of the official pantheon. Homer is believed to have lived in the ninth century BC, Hesiod lived in the eighth century BC. These dates coincide with the institution of the Olympic games first celebrated in honour of the Greek gods at Olympia in 776 BC, first quarter of the eighth century BC. The gods were man-made, but the nature of the celebrations was the same as in the most ancient Indo-European oral tradition and folklore: games, songs, dances, banquets and libations.

Essentially both the Greek and the Hittite tradition reflect the presence of a decided leader, respectively Zeus and the Lord of Tempests (= Rudra) who establish a logical, though artificial theology to explain how the world is governed as it is. From this point on, the poet/philosopher Hesiod proceeds to "explain" the being and becoming of the world. The mutilation of Chronos and the slaying of Kumarpi mark the beginning of a new era, when the gods and other divinities are given a meaning by Hesiod, **a man**, following the order given to him by the Muses, daughters of Zeus. The Muses had in turn been generated by Mnemosine, goddess of memory, herself, as far as we can tell, created by Hesiod in the *Theogonia*. The decisive proof of valour given by Zeus was his victory over the giant Typhaeus, last son of Gaia (= Gaea, Earth, consort of Uranos), sired by Tartarus after the castration of Uranos and after Zeus had expelled the Titans from heaven (*Tartarus* = Erebus, the dark, frightening underground reign of the dead). The Titans were monstruous giants sons of Uranos and Gaia, who wanted to be the rulers of heaven, hence the importance of having to kill Typhaeus, the vicious monster endowed with many voices and the power of ferocious animals, a Titan who aimed at ruling man and gods, "mortals and immortals." The victory of Zeus over Typhaeus signifies freedom from fear for mankind to pursue and develop its own culture. It is the liberation of man, who could now obtain rewards or punishments according to his merits or demerits and sins. The victory over Typhaeus represents the conquest of the *Liber arbitrium,* the free will of man. Free will is such a great responsibility that later philosophers trimmed it down by creating *Fatum,* Fate in Latin. About Fate we will talk later. What matters here is that by the last single act of valour, which was throwing Typhaeus into the Tartarus, Zeus was finally entitled to be consecrated king of gods and men (Theogonia, vv. 820-868). With his victory over Typhaeus, Zeus ascertains his right to the highest seat in Olympus, declares the beginning of new times, the victory of the new gods, not only over the Titans, but also over the "ancient" gods and the victory of light over darkness, which had already been achieved earlier in the Vedas with the victory of light over darkness and in the Avesta with the victory of Ahura Mazda.

Indra, on the other hand, is already created so great that he does not need to start a new era; he incorporates the old tradition into the new. By reaffirming his sacred power over destructive nature he enables man to develop the means to adjust to the forces that cannot be conquered or defeated. Human enemies, unlike unleashed violent natural forces, can be vanquished in battle. Indra, as an autochthonous very ancient human god still "reigns supreme" *because* he has become also the leader of men. The Olympian gods were made by man and this is how mortal kings, righteously or not were forever afterwards given divine titles and status.

It should be noted that the late Hurrite/Hittite myths of the thirteenth century BC, recorded in cuneiform script refer to the battle delivered by the chronologically last of the four gods of the Hurrite/

Hittite theogony, the god of Tempests. In this "Ullikummi" (= the stationary), blind and deaf giant who reaches distant lands by expanding his size without moving from his stance, is vanquished by cutting the land or soil under him. Typhaeus from the Greek mythology of approximately the same period, also had the ability to grow in size at will. These myths evidently refer to the expansion of the initial settlements when mankind was not numerous but had an unlimited eagerness for geographic expansion into the unknown, the new or different. Both the Hittite and the Greek myths reflect respectively the expansion of the areas under Hittite kings and the geographic expansion of the Greek concept of a civilized world represented by the *poleis* that were the nuclei of the urban civilization of the Hellenic world in and beyond peninsular Greece; they were the knots in the web called "Hellenism." Ullikummi had to be destroyed by "cutting the earth under his feet," which evidently was the only trick that could render him vulnerable, the connection with earth had to be severed and this is what the god of Tempests did. Typhaeus had no connections with earth, he remains active as the storms, typhoons, tempests, destructive winds, particularly dangerous at sea, the normal means of communication between the *poleis* and the rest of the world, symbolically Zeus maintains his control over Typhaeus, the world. The Hittite Ullikummi myth is linked to an older Hittite myth of about the sixteenth century BC, which is the battle between the god of Tempests and a dragon called Illuyankas. The twin battles against the two monsters were delivered at a wide interval of time, the second was a reminder of ancient glory in battle and of the power marked by successive stages in the expansion and conquests of Asia Minor by the Hittites and other Indo-European people. Similarly Zeus had to regain his position of absolute power with two major battles and victories, first over the Titans and later over Typhaeus. What is not clear is whether the myths were created by the Hittites themselves or whether they were taken and incorporated in their own traditional Indo-Aryan mythology from older Hurrite legends; probably both versions have some truth. The Hurrite were non Indo-European people governed by Indo-European (Indo-Aryan) Hittites. There is only one geographic place named after Typhaeus, it is in Baeotia in peninsular Greece, place and time of the origin of the monster or the myths that refer to him suggest the great antiquity and origin of the giant's name.[7]

We should note here the Greek word *timé* (= *timai*) the meaning of which is the exclusive personal attribute of the Greek gods. In the Theogonia, the word *timai* is first to be found in v. 81. The meaning of the word is occasionally explained, as for instance under v. 347 *et seq*. where it is said that spring waters have the *timai*, or *duty*, to protect youth, or at v. 34 *et seq*. and v. 50 where Zeus promises to all gods that each would receive his or her due share of honours, his or her *timai*, if they sided with the Olympians. The word *timai*, as noted above, is further explained in *Theogonia* vv. 411-452, the so-called hymn to Hekates, the only goddess apart from Zeus, whose *timai* or jurisdiction extends over land, sea and sky. In fact Zeus conferred upon Hekates **all** the privileges of the earlier ancient gods and therefore she has the duty to bless or condemn **all** activities of mankind. The *timai* of the gods can be approximately rendered as their "jurisdiction," with duties and rewards. To a certain extent the concept of "*timai*" of Hesiod corresponds to the concept of *dharma;* however, contrary to the intrinsic value and meaning of the word *dharma,* the *timai* was attributed by Hesiod **a man, to the gods**.

Man-made gods were repeatedly a historical necessity, at all levels and times of the history of mankind. The *Theogonia* served well and in good time the historical necessity for which it was planned.

Other myths worth mentioning in this context are aspects of theriomorphy. Theriomorphic deities are common in most cultures, specially in their early stages. Theriomorphism derives from the recognition that many animals are physically better endowed than puny man. They can fly and run faster and longer, they have more strength and agility and their sense organs are usually more sensitive and accurate, giving them a better perception of the environment. From the adoration of animals, they became the god's associates and carriers in the east, their faithful *vahanas*. In Greece they became the object of opportunistic metamorphoses, in the east Ganesha is endowed with human attributes, including very human weaknesses and thereby becomes the **ego and conscience** of each one of us.

CONCLUSION

It would indeed be an exercise in futility to try to establish parallels between Graeco-Roman and Indo-Aryan or Indo-Iranian gods. The "Greek gods" were made by man as man's own image and were listed in the carefully, planned *Theogonia.* Apart from nature gods the "official" Greek gods have only rare similarities with Vedic gods. Further, these similarities occur only among the gods who are divinised humans, like the late form of the Great Leader Indra and Zeus (= Jupiter) wielder of the thunderbolt as Indra is wielder of the *vajra.* The Indo-Aryan gods have maintained over the centuries the basic traits of the Indo-European nature gods, conceptual divinities and sacred natural principles expressed by *ṛta,* which **Is what IS,** as is made clear in the Vedas. Divinised human sages and kings were occasionally elevated to the rank of gods, they occur in both east and west. Similarities and "parallels" between east and west have been frequently discussed by modern authors who never reached any convincing conclusion. At most they describe superficial and fortuitous coincidences. The reason for this state of affairs is that in the east, gods imposed themselves on man's mind and spirit because of their intrinsic existence, concrete or virtual. In the Graeco-Roman west most gods were a product of man's reason and were deeply rooted in the incipient Greek humanism, they were the object of philosophical discussions rather than conclusions drawn from the observation of nature and of man's biology, behaviour and place in the world of Great Mother Earth. The fundamental but hidden and still surviving aspects of the Greek pantheon were not that of the Olympian gods, but that of the mysteries and nature gods. The Olympian gods survive as philosophical creations and subjects of different art forms.

The humanism of the Greek culture had no place prior to the Olympic religion; it expressed itself only *after* the gods were created by man. Greek humanism appears as man's revolt against the man-made gods who were not better than himself. Greek man sides with the revolting Titans, like Atlas or Prometheus or the rebellious characters of the tragedies, like the passionate Medea or the criminal Phaedra. The humanism of the ancient Indo-European of east expressed itself through the praise of "simple lifestyles" in tune with the environment. Man accepted his role of being just one element of nature, *though a significantly special pawn, thanks to his power of reason and discrimination.* It has remained so for many centuries among the Indo-Aryans. The Indo-Iranians, however, soon became lovers of luxury, impressive architecture and very "refined" lifestyles. Oriental lifestyles adopted by the great Conqueror Alexander under Persian influence were highly criticized by his friends and followers.

(B) Dionysos - The Forces and Vitality of all Nature

The archaic god Dionysos[7] with whom we are concerned here, is probably the ancient-most god of the Indo-European of the west. He has survived to this day in remote regions and rural places. The evolution of the personality of Dionysos since the most remote past to the present, reflects the evolution of man's understanding of the phenomena of Nature. Phenomenon (= singular form of phenomena) is what is directly perceived by man mentally and through the sense organs. The evolution of the personality of the god known to the greeks as Dionysos (= Bacchus, Iacchos) indicates man's understanding of himself and of his place in nature and of how this evolution may have taken place. From this point of view there is a distant similarity between Ganesha, the personification of the human Ego and Dionysos.

NATURE GODS

Herodotus considers the Pelasgians to be the autochthonous people of Greece. We do not know who their gods were, perhaps the Sea and the god of Tempests and Storms were the highest authorities of their religious beliefs, we shall do no further guesswork about them here.

Neither Homer nor Hesiod says much about Dionysos. The name occurs in the epics and in the Theogony, but both authors are equally reticent about the personality of the god, though the Mysteries of Dionysos were being celebrated already many centuries before Homer's time. For this reason, neither Homer nor Hesiod can be taken as benchmarks of the origin of this god. We must rely on Herodotus (born between 490 and 480 BC) to give us reliable information on the ancient myths related to the birth, character and *timai* of Dionysos. Since the ancient-most past Dionysos, the god of living nature was given its rightful place and importance among the common people. His name is variously spelt in Greek, in Attik and Aeolic dialects and becomes Bacchus in Latin. Bakkos or Iacchos are the esoteric names of Dionysos, as he is called in "The Frogs" by Aristophanes (448?-380?BC) and various ancient texts. There is no doubt that Dionysos is an archaic pre-Hellenic god as suggested also by the many widespread places called *Nisa* which claim to be his birthplace. Many of them were well-known and much older than the fourth century BC when Alexander conquered or visited them. The antiquity of Dionysos is probably greater than the second millennium BC and may be older than the third millennium.

There are different views on the origin of the name. It is sometimes explained as "god of Nysa," because the several places so called are said to have been called Nysa in honour of the god. Cities called Nysa or Nisa occur in the ancient Mediterranean, in West Asia and one also in Upper Egypt or Ethiopia, though with different spellings. In Iliad II, 508, a place in Baeotia is named "divine Nisa" and Dionysos' name occurs twice in the Iliad VI, 132, 135 and XIV, 325 where he is called the "joy of mankind." In the Odyssey Dionysos is mentioned in XI, 325 and XXIV, 74 in relation to myths of the ancient heroic age, one in connection with Ariadne (the name is spelt *Ariadene,* akin to *Āranyani*), and the other as giving a golden amphora to Achilles' mother Thetis to preserve the bones of her son and of his friend Patroklos, key Achaean heroes killed in the Trojan war, after they were cremated. The various spellings of the name of both Dionysos and Nysa, the obscure origin of the ancient deity and the many claims for Dionysos' birthplace indicate that the presence of the god is "ubiquitous" and lost in very ancient times. He had no origin but existed since ever and was seen as existing forever in the future. The original Olympian founding dynasty: Uranos, Chronos, Zeus, as characterised in Homer and Hesiod, is undoubtedly younger than Dionysos and symbolizes the forces of material nature as opposed to the forces and energy of the Life Principle Dionysos. The intrinsic nature of the three Great Brothers and gods, sons of Chronos: Zeus (= Jupiter), Poseidon (= Neptune) and Aidoneus (= Hades) was established by Homer and Hesiod **after** the nature of Dionysos as the Life Principle of Nature had been firmly established by ancient tradition. Homer and Hesiod circumscribed the powers of material nature by dividing the cosmos among these three divine brothers. The Great Olympian gods, having been made by man as man's image, were of course also living entities, they would not be able to function if they were not alive as man also is.[8]

The Olympians being by definition super-humans, interacted with man as creatures imbued with great normal **and** magical power. It thus became necessary to officialise also the divine nature of Dionysos by giving him an unusual birth. Therefore, after his mother Semele died at the sixth month of pregnancy, foetus Dionysos was incubated in the thigh of Zeus and then released at maturity to attest for his divine origin. Thus Dionysos has two births, one human and one divine. Dionysos, who in the distant past **was** Living Nature, **becomes and is,** in the official Homeric/Hesiodan religion, its symbol, while the thunderbolt-waving Zeus is made the undisputed King and Father of gods and men and controller of material nature. Rituals and ceremonies related to a double birth, one human and one divine, are common among Indo-European people ancient and modern, such as the *Upanayana* ceremony among Hindus and the Confirmation (= Lat. *chrisma*, from Gk. *khrisma* = anointed) and First Communion ceremonies among Christians. From the texts of the Orphic Mysteries that have come down to us it is possible to understand that the core of the Dionysian and later of the Orphic Mysteries, and of the initiation rites was to confirm the double births and to insufflate the divine spirit in the reborn believer, a *dwija*.

The "twice born" are those who, after a first birth into worldly life, are secretely "reborn" (= introduced, admitted, initiated or anointed) into the spiritual community. They become "cenobites," "mystai," "initiated," *dwija*, or whatever word was used by different people. Among most people of the world, ceremonies and rites of initiation at puberty of boys and girls have basically the same meaning; adulthood lifts the adolescent to a higher level of knowledge, maturity and responsibility.

Dionysos became and **IS,** rather than symbolizes Living Nature. The passage of Dionysos from "representing" to "becoming" Nature itself, symbolically takes place only after and not before the thunderbolt-waving Father Zeus becomes the undisputed King and

Father of gods and men and controller of the wild forces of material Nature, *physis* in Greek. Dionysos more than other gods is subordinate to Zeus because he is said to have been actually born from the body of the Father, as he was earlier born of the body of the Mother. There is always a male and a female principle in nature and being Nature itself, Dionysos incorporates both principles, without being hermaphroditic.

DIONYSOS, UNTAMED NATURE

The personality of Dionysos is the result of the syncretism of at least three mythical divinities. The usual present day image of Dionysos is that of a divinity in whose honour the Athenians created the most powerful dramas of the western (European) classic theatrical culture. They are stories that after three millennia continue to impress western civilizations, as Freud showed by giving the names of Greek theatrical characters to the moves and moods of the personalities of the psychoanalysis theory he created.

Directly or indirectly, Dionysos is one of the most popular personalities of the literature and mind of the people of the west. Already towards the end of the third millennium BC, Dionysos was known as the god of grapes and wine. Even before he acquired the grandiose image he obtained in Athens, he was the ubiquitous god of all vegetation and of fertile nature. He later became a powerful urban figure for political reasons at the time of Pisistratus (sixth century BC), the tyrant of Athens who needed the support of the rural masses to strengthen his position. The greatness of the god expanded from Athens and Rome throughout the Roman Empire during the centuries of the *Pax Romana*. The name of the "pagan" god Dionysos became very common in the Christian Era and the name was later given to mortal men in its vulgate forms: Dennis (English), Denis (French), Dionigi and Luigi (Italian), Dioniso (Sardinia), Dionisio (Portuguese) and other names that recall the god, such as Silvio, Silvano, Silvana, Silvia in Italian, Portuguese and other Latin languages. Some of the many men named after the god were sanctified by the Church of Rome and one of them, Saint Denis, is the patron saint of France. The popularity of this pagan god in whose honour festivals of beauty and of the joy of living were celebrated for centuries, is attested by the writings of the Christian authors of the first half of the first millennium AD who could not grasp the hidden meaning of the rites and spared no efforts to ridicule and denounce them as "infamous." The *mysti,* the devotees, the men and women who celebrated festivals in honour of Dionysos were ridiculed and eventually branded as vicious heretics. The ceremonial harvesting, pressing and control of the initial phase of fermentation of grapes' juice are closely observed and carried out by European people and peasants to this day. The rituals of wine making during the celebrations of the winter solstice by the Kalash people of the Hindukush are described in detail by Loude and Lièvre (1980).

Much of what is known of the traditional Dionysan rites as practised during the first centuries AD is due to two authors, Longo (author of a poem written in the second century AD) and Nonnos of Nicomedia (middle fifth century AD). Very litlle is known about the "Bucolic Novel" in 48 books (*boukolos* = shepherd in Greek) by Longo, except that it was written in the second century AD and that the action takes place in an idealised island called Lesbos (not the same as the island of Lesbos, now called Metelinos, home of seventh century BC poetess Sappho). Merkelbach (1988) considers that the text allegorically describes in detail the rites performed during the Dionysan mysteries and believes that the poem must be read at two levels: one as the story itself and the other as the interpretation of the religious meaning of the rites. The poem, is to be understood as written for the education and performance of the initiation rites of the *mysti,* the postulants and of the *epoptai,* the already initiated to the mysteries. All the details of the poem have a double meaning, one evident and the other symbolic, often difficult to detect. Essentially the *mysti* spent much time celebrating and serving Beauty in tune with Nature and the *Horae* (= Seasons).

About Nonnos we know very little, he is known as coming from Panopolis in Egypt, and to have lived in the fifth century AD. The *Dionysiacs* (written in 440 AD) of Nonnos are an epic poem in 39 books in which the life and acts of the god are described in the style of the classic Homeric epics. A large part of the poem refers to the "conquest" of "India" by Dionysos. It is interesting to point out that the author was evidently familiar with the new Christian religion and may have been a Christian himself. There is much phantasy in the epic poem of Nonnos, but also much admiration and sincere praise for the personality of the god of Nature, Beauty, Joy and Happiness. Nonnos misses no opportunity to underline the points of similarity between the "pagan" and the Christian faiths. Like most authors from the first centuries AD onwards, Nonnos includes in his story as many myths, legends and details as he has ever heard of, whether authentic or not and often invented by himself. He also does not hesitate to create new details and entirely new stories; it is therefore difficult to extricate the grain from the chaff. Nonnos' poem is not a reliable source of information, though modern authors often relied on his never-verifiable testimony.

Contemporary authors very often lump in a single description all the information on ancient gods that they could glean out from earlier works. The results are composite figures of difficult interpretation. This procedure of course blurs our understanding of the original personality of the gods or goddesses, Dionysos in the present study. Care must be taken to select the traits of the pre-historic god, hidden under many layers of later additions. New characteristics, new myths and legends are superimposed on old ones that are not discarded, and the final description and reading of the personality of the gods and heroes, produce the current image which is often very different from the original one. This is particularly true of nature gods, such as Dionysos and Demeter. Nonnos' poem however, shows beyond doubt that the personality of the god and the rites of the Dionysian Faith were still current among the people of his time, though often under disguise. Contemporary studies by Vian (1976, 1990, 1995), Chuvin (1992), specially Merkelbach (1988) and others have put in the correct perspective the personality of the god, of his mysteries and of the word "orgy" (= *orgia*), the original meaning of which had been vitiated by the extremes of the rich patricians of Imperial Rome and the zeal of the converts to Christianity in the first half of the first millennium AD. The Lat. and Gk. word *orgia,* comes from *ergon*= work, that could mean ceremony or rite.

THE YOUNG GOD DIONYSOS

Three ancient divinities of Greece under the same name are well-known. The most ancient Dionysos,[9] is a pre-Hellenic character, perhaps known also elsewhere and under other names. He was probably the embodiment of the spirit of wild nature which later merged with the personification of Dionysos who was to become a god. One of the major tasks of this very ancient young god was that of taming the oceans by teaching to the Greeks, and perhaps much of mankind, the art of navigation and the use of the wealth of the sea, as evidenced by the myth of the young Dionysos captured by the pirates and saved by dolphins, of course with the "acquiescence and protection of the Great Olympians." The myth is a syncretism of ancient and new, it defines the identity of the *young* god who has to prove his divinity by performing miracles, punishing the pirates and creating out of nothing fruiting grapevine that climb over the mast of the ship. The faithful helmsman is duly rewarded and the pirates providentially changed into dolphins, become friends of mankind ever since. The fact that grapevines grew on the mast and sails of the ship of the pirates, mentioned by some as Tyrrhenian (= Etruscan) and by others as Phokaies (= Phoceians, inhabitants of the island of Skeria, different from Phoenicians) suggests that the young god had to be confirmed as a persisting god from ancient times, in new attire and new capacity. The Phoenicians were the great navigators and traders of the eastern Mediterranean. They had established a colony at Alalia in Corsica, as early as 564 BC.

This archaic myth evidently grew in details and meaning with the passing of centuries. It proves first of all the mastering of physical entities: sea, winds, waves, storms, caves and the mastering of the art of navigation. A secondary meaning of the myth is the expansion of the Greek culture in the Mediterranean Sea which was probably the last major and violent encounter of Dionysos with natural physical forces. Finally, the myth also illustrates the technical enrichment of the Greek culture with the cultivation of grapes and the production of wine. After the episode of the capture of the very young god by the pirates, Dionysos recognizes with gratitude special divinities in charge of taking care and enlivening entities such as seas, lakes, caves, rocks, springs of fresh waters that thereby acquire a life and personality of their own. Youngsters are to be instructed about the new living places, their role in the great symphony of nature and their very special type of life. It is a reminder of the care that nymphs, fauns, satyrs, maenads and all the good spirits of nature had of the infant Dionysos hidden in a cave to escape the wrath of jealous Hera (= Juno). Grapes are known to have been cultivated in Egypt already by 2500 BC, but it is not known for sure how the grapevine arrived in Egypt.[15]

The Greek, as far as we know, acquired the art of navigation and the use of the sea for transport, of its shores as a living place and of the waters as a source of food, from the Pelasgoi (= people of the sea). The Pelasgoi inhabited the island of Crete, some of them having come from West Asia, while the origin of most of them is not known. Also the Phoenicians, Semitic pirates from the eastern coasts of West Asia were expert navigators. Pelasgians, Feacians and Phoenicians are historically known to have been able sailors "since ever," probably many centuries before the epics were composed. Though Dionysos is not credited with having "conquered" the Sea he can confidently be credited with having *hellenised* most of the Mediterranean Sea, and the western lands beyond the Aegean. The dolphins are said to be descendents of the repentful "Thyrrenian" (= Etruscan, this ethnicity of the pirates is clearly a late addition though it is true that the Etruscans also practised piracy) pirates who had captured the young Dionysos and had been thrown overboard and then pardoned by the god after they had tried in vain to bind and enslave him. Bad pirates are transformed into friendly animals. The abduction of the young god by the pirates and the metamorphosis of the wicked humans into good friendly animals signifies that Dionysos learned and taught how to control the sea for the "benefit of mankind," or rather, for the benefit of his *demos*.

Centuries later Hesiod took away from Dionysos the lordship of the seas and handed it over to Poseidon without even mentioning Dionysos. Hesiod explains that the Ocean is one component of the tripartite division of the cosmos following the castration of Chronos. Herodotus (fifth century BC) tendentiously states that Dionysos and Demeter are gods younger than the Olympians, though we know from the writings of Homer that the Olympian gods were created chronologically later than the original nature gods of the archaic or heroic period of Greece, they had already lived for centuries before the Olympians took over. Many of the myths related to Dionysos are late myths, as for instance the legend of the abduction by pirates which seems to be superimposed on probable pre-historic facts.

However, to understand the "young god Dionysos," we must look back at his predecessors.

THE ARCHAIC GOD

The very ancient Dionysos, or proto-Dionysos, is found all over the ancient Graeco-Roman world, his fame and acts were sung by the ancient *aedes* and *cytharists,* he was respected as Nature's Life Principle, his presence was implicit in the life cycle of plants and animals. Dionysos and his retinue cover all aspects of living nature on earth. His symbol was most probably the *phallus* which survived in cultic practices well into the Christian Era, as the *lingam* is alive, respected and worshipped in India. The covered phallus was placed on the winnowing basket (= Gk. *khistaphora,* L. *cysta mystica, vannus* shaped like the present day winnowing basket still in use in Italy and India) on ceremonial occasions and during the Lower Mysteries' annual procession from Eleusis to Athens. The original Mediterranean god of nature had many names; four of them have come down to us. *Phanes* (= the Manifest, the First Visible); *Eros primigenius* (= the first engendered, the power of generation, regeneration and reproduction), *Protogonos* (= the originally created), *Proteurhythmos* (= the first true, real rhythmic and recurrent principle, or god). Most often he is invoked as Dionysos Protogonos or *Eros cosmogonicus* which represents the human urge to unite or relate opposite entities. The intimacy of Man with Nature produced in the east the many nature gods of the Indian pantheon. Among them, one of the most important in this context, is the reserved and mysterious *Āranyani,* the Lady of the Forest (*R̥V* X; 146) who is celebrated with a short hymn of only six stanzas, but is one of fundamental meaning and importance. In the east there never was the need to visualise a Dionysos because everything is sacred as part of the whole nature and Dionysos exists in all the parts of the whole, as long as they are alive. The inevitable intimacy of man with the nature of which man was conceived to be a part, produced cultures based on man's power of observation and logical thinking, the Mysteries in Greece and the Vedas and Vedānta in India. Science as the **will to understand** was still in its initial empirical stage (Vannucci 1999) when nature gods entered into the realm of the Indian culture.[9]

The entity, later called Dionysos, was the ubiquitous spirit of untamed living nature, biologically incorruptible and exclusively deterministic. This original deity still lives in the Mediterranean world in the collective sub-conscious memory of rural, as opposed to urban people and populations, especially in secluded places and mountainous regions. He is both the vigour of nature and the beginning of domestication, as attested by the fact that Dionysos is known since the early stages as the god of grapes and wine and is crowned with ivy, a species of creeper that strangles to death the tree on which it grows, if left untrained. He is also crowned with laurel, a strong scented shrub, producer of a praised aromatic substance. This implies that the god had learned how to use plants that play a significant role for human welfare. We cannot say where and how he learned the art, probably everywhere and at all times, together with the multitude of minor deities of nature, scattered over all the specifically sacred places of Sacred Nature.

During the early stages Dionysos under other names, was the ubiquitous and immaterial spirit and power of life in nature not yet domesticated by man, gradually he became involved in the evolving human culture, in all types of bucolic and silvan activities and in the cultivation of grapes and wine making. The urbanization of Dionysos at the time of Pisistratus was boisterous and energetic enough to put in motion and sustain over centuries a culture based on reason and constructive criticism. A less sudden and boisterous, but more profound cultural development came in India with the growth and development of the Vedas and Vedānta and other Indian philosophical systems. The initial assignment of Dionysos was to define the duties and powers of various natural elements good or not so good, such as nymphs, maenads, satyrs and theriomorphic creatures, like Pan or the Centaurs, as well as plants and animals. The initial personality gradually evolved into the second Dionysos who leaves to other deities the violent aspects of nature, such as Pan, the satyr with goat legs who occasionally falls victim to bursts of violence, known as *"furor Panicus"* (= the fury of Pan), an expression still used in modern Latin languages. Dionysos is the one who puts in order the forces of nature and has them under his control, but only up to a point. At this second stage he recognizes natural cycles, like the seasons called *Horae* (= hours), of which there are only three at the beginning, like the main seasons in ancient Egypt and India. They later became four, like the Mediterranean seasons, or six as they are in India, by splitting each of the original three in two halves. The seasons are not the only cycles recognized and monitored by Dionysos, many other natural cycles are also idealised and worshipped in the Dionysian mysteries, such as flowering and fruiting and all life-cycles of plants and animals such as seasonal metamorphosis of frogs remembered also in Aristophanes' "comedy" Frogs where Dionysos descends to Hades in search of a wise philosopher who can bring Athens back to earlier standards of rectitude and wisdom. There are some parallels here between Lord Viṣṇu and Dionysos who is often represented with the *Horae* (= seasons) going "round in circles" (Orphic hymn 53,7), while Viṣṇu (*R̥V* VII, 103) duly controls the *mantras* as they go "round and round," during the Atiratra and the Visvajit rituals of the Soma sacrifice (Vannucci 1999).

URBANIZATION OF DIONYSOS

The ancient nature god was "urbanized" when Athens' tyrant Pisistratus (died 527 BC) needed the support of the masses who were "living in front of the city," meaning that they were living in rural lands outside the urban walls and fortifications. Before this happened at Athens in Attika, the festivals of Dionysos were celebrated in the fields, in tune with the seasons, mainly involving shepherds and peasants, the *bukoloi.* The most important rites, methodically organised, were related to the culture and cycle of the grape-vine, the collection and pressing of grapes and the making of wine in late autumn, probably to coincide with the winter solstice. A detailed description of the festival of the winter solstice among the Indo-European Kalash people of Gilgit-Hunza given by Loude and Lièvre (second half of twentieth century) are astonishingly similar to the descriptions of the ritual festivals of ancient Greece, though the natural setting is different. The rigours of winter in the Hindukush are in contrast with the mild winter in Greece, where even snow is a rare event, nevertheless the habits of the people are remarkably similar. Among the Kalash the main god, Imra (= Indra) arrives on horseback and is present in the merry making, singing, dancing and pressing of grapes and making of wine during the festival of the winter solstice, though nobody can see either him or his horse, except the "oracle," who also interprets Imra's predictions and sayings. After a few days of his and his horse's invisible presence, when the sun is still in its northern abode, after staying in his traditionally roofless and open-to-the-sky temple, Imra departs. The head and neck of two horses, cut in wood, were placed at horse height on both sides of the temple's closed entrance. The most interesting detail is that in the late nineteenth century there were no more horses in those mountains when Robertson visited those areas for long periods of time, yet Imra was still remembered as a god on horseback. The Kalash lived in isolation, by the late nineteenth century they were still practically "cut-off" from other populations. One of the horses, with the god or a respected ancestor (?) on its back, is now guarded in the Anthropology and Ethnography Museum of Florence, together with other horse heads, including those that were at the sides of goddess Jestak sanctuary, carvings of ancestors and a rich collection representative of the Kalash culture. The life-size wooden house and the wooden "ancestor" it carries was specially made locally and purchased by the "Spedizione Italiana al Karakorum K_2–1955-1960" (= Italian Expedition to the Karakorum K_2–1955-1960). It was made according to traditional rules and had to be sawed into three pieces for the transfer to Florence. Also the Musée Guimé of Paris shows in its exhibits, tools even now used by the Kalash people that are characteristically similar to other ancient tools and utensils of early Indo-European elsewhere. The Kalash were called "Kafirs" by outsiders and they speak "Kafiri" a dialect belonging to the Indo-European family of languages (Harmatta, 1996).

When Dionysos was brought to Athens, festivities were organised in the city on the same principles as the village festivals but with different performances. All the Dionysian rites celebrated the joy of living and the cult of beauty and goodness as the wholesome procedure for a peaceful and tranquil passage from this life to another, after bodily death. The presiding god of these rites was the Dionysos we are at present not familiar with, but who was still present in the recitations, music, dance and mimes of the early "Dionysian" festivals of Athens, during which the urban and rural people mixed and revelled together at the sound of Pan's flute. The official entrance of Dionysos in Athens was the beginning of the involvement of the god with urban civilizations, the god in whose honour the dramas of the classical Greek theatre were oganized. Later, in the first millennium BC, other cities organized similar festivals. At the religious and philosophical levels the Mysteries of Dionysos had many points in common with the Orphic Mysteries which will not be discussed here.

According to some later versions there was another Dionysos, sometimes called the "second Dionysos" who was the bucolic god of the fields and newly domesticated nature. Dionysos is the third and the one usually known at present, he was called Bacchus in Rome and his esoteric name was Iacchos. There are many more patronymics given to Dionysos over the god's very large mythical and geographic domain.

MYTHS

There are several different versions of the myths relating to god Dionysos, this indicates a protracted period of oral tradition with the implicit recording of various variants. The third Dionysos, is Dionysos Zagreus (= from the name *Zagros*), a Thracian god. The third Dionysos is not an exclusive Hellenic god and is not in chronological succession of the earlier two, he is an element interpolated and grafted into the building of the "official" Greek mythology. This third Dionysos was brought back to light by Herodotus late in the mythological corpus of the Greek tradition and legends, when the concept of Dionysos grew in complexity. The myths tell us that Zagreus (=? the twice born, reborn, the restored to life) perhaps son of Zeus himself and of Persephone, daughter of Demeter, was slain and torn to pieces by the Titans during or after the episode of their revolt against Zeus. Zagreus was later reborn as Dionysos *"in very ancient times."* Therefore, according to this late myth, Dionysos is not only the first man who was competing for kingship, rather he represents the evolution of the relations of man with nature, at the same time he also represents the original excellent Man. This Dionysos was torn to pieces by the Titans because of their revolt, jealousy and desire of vengeance against Zeus. Dionysos Zagreus was an important god brought to the Greek world by the

Thracians, Indo-European people who reached Macedonia and peninsular Greece coming from the north, the plains of R. Danube and the western margins of the Black Sea.[10]

The myth of Dionysos Zagreus brings to memory the dismemberment of Puruṣa (*R̥V* X, 90), described in the so-called *Puruṣasukta*, admittedly a late introduction in the *R̥V*. Also Puruṣa is, according to some myths, the first man and he was torn to pieces as Dionysos was torn by the Titans. In the west, the myth also tells us that goddess Aphrodite (= Venus) collected the scattered pieces of the very young Dionysos after his dismemberment by the Titans. She brought them to Zeus who managed to have them put together and thus salvaged the new creature. We are not told and it would be idle to speculate about what happened to the pieces of the torn body of Puruṣa. Puruṣa was a spirit, he had a virtual existence and "he is *one* with all created life." In this sense he is Lord of Immortality (*R̥V* X; 90) being both the father and the son of Viraj, he immortalizes the cycle of Life, Death and Rebirth. Every point in a circle is both beginning and end, or there is neither beginning nor end in a circle. Every truth is relative, it depends on its point in the circle and on other truths, and there is only one Absolute Truth, **THE** Absolute. This is how Adi-Puruṣa became the eternal spirit, or essence of all living beings, but he himself is not re-constituted as Dionysos was. The original embodied spirit permeates all sentient living beings as the Life Principle itself. Perhaps this is why Puruṣa had to be fragmented into "*thousand*" parts so that he could continue to exist as the ubiquitous spirit of all living beings. This Life-Principle is what discriminates living from non-living. The pieces of Puruṣa are immortal and life-giving. In contrast Dionysos was made to pieces because of the treacherous jealousy of the Titans who selfishly sought power for themselves and therefore unsuccessfully tried to destroy him. It would be ugly if Dionysos did not exist; this is why Aphrodite, Goddess of Love and Beauty, pieced the torn parts together. The pieces of slain Dionysos are put together to reconstruct Dionysos himself, and no more.

Puruṣa, or Adi-Puruṣa is different from Prajāpati, who is not a virtual being, but the actual Lord of all creatures, under this guise, Prajāpati reminds Dionysos.

THE MYTHICAL PERSONALITIES OF DIONYSOS

As a nature god, as Dionysos *agroteros* (= hunter, lord of the land) he has in his entourage deities of all bounties, trees, springs, lakes, nymphs, also satyrs, maenads, fauns and Silenes are parts of his world, because they are all different aspects of wild nature, good and bad. These imaginary beings with time conquered more and more presence and space in the festivals, called in Greek and in Latin *"orgia."* The word "orgy" became under imperial Rome a synonym of unrestrained indulgence, including sexual activities, while originally in ancient Greece it meant to "exhibit the sacred objects." The present meaning of "orgy" is different from the original Greek/Latin *orgia*, which signified only "secret rites," it is understood at present as an aspect of the cult of Dionysos or Bacchus during Roman times. As Merkelbach (1988) reports, during the time of Imperial Rome, the mysteries of Bacchus included a number of games, with prominence of music, mime and dance, re-enacting the episodes of the garland of myths about Dionysos' life and acts that grew around the central figure, the god himself. In this sense they recall the *"Kṛṣṇa Līlā"* of India. The cult of Dionysos remained, as long as it was openly celebrated, a religion of nature, notwithstanding the distortions and excesses due to the changes imposed by urban life in Imperial Rome and in the entire western world at the time of the *Pax romana*. The three or four or more divine personalities that go under the name of Dionysos are differently represented by various ancient authors. The above is a synthesis that makes sense. The licentiousness of the Dionysian orgies of later times brings to mind the institution of the *devadāsī* in the temple cities of south India, though here again, there is no parallelism between the two phenomena because the underlying realities, meaning, circumstances and purpose of the two are entirely different.

Summing up, there are at least three major mythical personalities listed as forming the complex figure of Dionysos. As mentioned, he was originally a god of the entire wild nature, living and non-living. His jurisdiction or *timai* was very large and had to be trimmed down to the role of a god of living nature, of plants and animals. This was done with the agreement of Zeus, king of gods and master of the thunderbolt. To avoid restraining the authority of the Great Zeus,

Homer and Hesiod barely acknowledge the existence of Dionysos, but they cannot ignore him entirely. Dionysos therefore was given a spectacular origin and is made to be "younger" than the Olympian gods, which in fact means that he was elevated to the company of the Olympians only very late, after a very long existence as an ancient deity, a wildling. It is well established that the Olympians are the last generation of Greek gods (in *Theogonia;* also Arrighetti, 1984, X ed. 2000).

Dionysos is mentioned in the Iliad (XIV, 325) as *"joy, happiness of mankind,"* son of Semele, daughter of Kadmos, a man. Kadmos is a very ancient legendary figure who had come during the heroic era from Thebes in Egypt to Greece and founded the citadel of the city of Thebes in Baeotia (*apud* Herodotus) in the Peloponnesus, peninsular Greece. Child Dionysos was hiddenly conceived by Semele, sired by Zeus in the palace of Kadmos. Jealous Hera found out the proofs of one more infidelity of her brother and spouse Zeus and vowed to destroy the fruits of it. Hera caused the death of Semele, the prematurely delivered baby was salvaged by Hermes who brought it to father Zeus who sealed it in his thigh and gave it birth when the time of incubation, rather than gestation, was completed. Over and beyond the evolution of the legends about Dionysos this myth gives evidence of the transfer of culture in general and of particular techniques among the people of three different origins. Kadmos was father of Semele. He was from Tyre in Phoenicia from where he had gone to Thebes in Egypt and then migrated to Greece and founded the citadel of the Greek city of Thebes. Kadmos represents the fusion of Semitic, Egyptian and Indo-European knowledge that began earlier than the middle of the second millennium BC in the eastern Mediterranen. Dionysos, Kadmos' grandson by Semele is no longer only the representative of man, at this stage and time Dionysos becomes an important representative of the entire eastern Mediterranean civilizations.

The legend of the displacements of Kadmos illustrates the expansion of knowledge from the coasts of western Asia and North Africa (= here Egypt) through the eastern Mediterranean and Greece to the entire Hellenic world. One of the oldest Greek colonies was that of the Focei (not to be confused with the Semitic Phoenicians) and the pirates who kidnapped young Dionysos, described as Thyrrenian (= Etruscan or Phokaies), who lived in an island of the Ionian Sea. According to Herodotus (I, 165) one of the first Phoenician colonies was Alalia in the island of Corsica (founded 564 BC). Earlier Syracusa, had become one of the leading colonies of Magna Graecia, founded 734 BC by Corynthian Greeks on the south-east coast of Sicily on the Ionian Sea. It was only natural that the son of Semele, grandson of Kadmos, namely Dionysos who incorporates ancient indigenous nature gods, would become the great god of living nature of **all** the people of the Hellenic world, and later the god of nature cults of the west.

After the birth from the thigh of Zeus, Hermes handed the infant to old Silenus, the patriarch of the satyrs, who in turn entrusted him to the nymphs to raise him. He was nursed by a she-goat. He grew wildly in the natural world to which he belonged. Symbolically, one of his first feats was the mastering of the Sea, in fact all the people of the then-known western world are united by the Mediterranean Sea. Dionysos is more often represented under his human form as Lover of Beauty, of Joy and Happiness and to this day he is indirectly remembered, especially with joyful singing, dancing and drinking at the time of pressing grapes and fermentation of the juice to produce wine. Though at present he is not remembered nominally, the spirit of Dionysos at the time of vintage, harvesting and pressing grapes lingers in the songs, dances, merry-making and drinking of the newly fermented grapes' juice and the new wine, like the Kalash people of Gilgit and Hunza of the Hindukush area of Pakistan, did at the festivals of the winter solstice and in all the places in Europe where grapes are grown and wine is made. The winter solstice traditionally marked the beginning of the New Year. Only later the New Year was transferred, in some cultures to the spring equinox, a more easily observed and measured astronomical marker of the renewal of nature after the winter stasis.

The unbridled licentiousness that grew at the time of Imperial Rome spread also to the Dionysian rites. The licentiousness that dominated Rome was purposefully highlighted during later centuries with the aim of pointing an accusing finger at Dionysos and his rites and to defame "pagan" customs as most evil.

Dionysos is above all the god of the beauty and purity of uncontaminated lands. The first cry of the *mysti* after the initiation ceremony was: "I am happy, I have seen Beauty" and "I have escaped from evil, I have found Goodness."

ANCIENT POEMS ABOUT DIONYSOS AND DIONYSAN RITES

We have no texts describing or explaining the mysteries of Dionysos. It is doubtful that any was ever written, and if any was written, it would have been so secretly guarded that none survived the changed political supremacies and new religious beliefs and attitudes. Much however was written about the god, his acts and those of his associates during the past two millennia. Nietzsche (1844-1900), for instance considers Dionysos to be the god of violent uncontrolled passions. His views were sustained by most scholars and people in general and are still the most common. However, much of what was written is conjectural, legendary and mostly produced by the common fascination with the spectacular and the forbidden, rather than by the detailed study of the old texts and of the oral tradition.

The love story of Daphnis and Chloe was sung by poets, especially during the Renaissance and in the Italian Humanistic period. The story of Daphnis and Chloe is the subject of the open poem by Longo. It is thanks to H.H.O. Chalk, A. Geyer, R. Tureau, *apud* Merkelbach, and the latter author himself that the bucolic poem of Longo was interpreted as representing the Dionysan religion. Merkelbach (*l.c.*) reads the novel/poem by Longo as a direct reference, almost a transcription of the mysteries of Dionysos, as he clearly demonstrates by clarifying the parallels of what we know of the traditional religion of Dionysos, which is the religion of nature, at the time of Imperial Rome with what we know at present of the Dionysan religion. Throughout the story there are symbols, places, names, habits and customs related to Dionysos, who is usually not mentioned by name but whose presence is, or would be felt throughout the poem. At many places there are paraphrases of what is now known of cultic practices of the Mysteries and of the education and initiation of children and youth. For instance the lustral bath at birth was considered to be the first step to initiation and it has remained a sacrament in many religions, including Christianity. Even though not everybody was fully initiated to the mysteries, members of the religion of Dionysos formed a closely knit elite that lived in joy and happiness through proper ethical behaviour, as dictated by the principles of nature and Dionysism.

The story covers a period of less than 20 years and is located in a bucolic (= pastoral) environment of fairy tale beauty. The hero, Daphnis (from Daphne = laurel, the name of a nymph) is the baby boy of a well-being family devoted to Dionysos, who is abandoned in a *paradeisos* (= paradise or garden) with an altar and a shrine to Dionysos. The heroine is baby Chloe (= green) who is abandoned by her wealthy parents two years later in the cave of the Nymphs, in a site also sacred to Dionysos and next to the pasture where Daphnis tends the cattle and goats. The two children are brought up by two couples of foster parents who carefully keep in hiding the identification objects that were found lying together with the abandoned babies. The children grow ignorant of their real parents, they are taken care of by the *boukolos* (= shepherds) and educated by the nymphs. They pay homage to Pan, their protective deity, half human with hind quarters, ears and horns of a goat, symbolising the wholeness of man and his domestic animals. The components of the environment are reminders of plants, animals, companions and acts of Dionysos. The education of the two children runs parallel and every detail and episode marks stages of their upbringing into the mysteries of life and nature. How much of this actually represents the steps of the initiation of the adult to the mysteries is not known. What is evident is that it is the preparation for a healthy future life in tune with the natural environment on which finally we all depend, including the wealthy urban parents of the children. The poem is dedicated to Eros, the nymphs and Pan (= everything in Nature). It declares that the poem was written for all men, "it will appease from love sickness, will comfort the discouraged, will recall Eros (as Love) to those who have already loved and will prepare for Love those who have not yet loved" . . . "because nobody will ever be able to escape love so long as there will be beauty for the eyes to see" . . . finally it supplicates . . . "may Eros allow us to write about other's love and to have the virtues of moderation and chastity."

It is not possible to summarise here this gentle and marvellous poem that describes the education and development of an ideal couple since the first lustral bath to the final recognition of Daphnis and Chloe by their parents, which marks the fulfilment of the initiation of the *mysti* and the entrance into adulthood and married life. The Mysteries take the *mysti* back to the Golden Age of Happiness, Rhythm, Love and Moderation, the Golden Age of Mankind. In this context it is interesting to recall the long Vedic hymn about the wedding of Sūryā, daughter of the Sun God Sūryā that illustrates the many steps of the initiation of the boy and the girl to wedded life (Vannucci 1999, *R̥V* X, 85).

DIONYSISM, ORPHISM AND VEDISM

Orphism (sixth century BC) may be seen as a synthesis of pre-Hellenic archaic beliefs of the Thracian cult of Zagreus, later called Dionysos Zagreus. Thrace is, or was called the region that extends from River Danube southwards to the north of the Aegean Sea. Thracians spoke an Indo-European language and later became an important component of the Hellenic world.[11]

The Orphic doctrine says that the original Golden Egg was broken in half, thus Earth and Sky came into being. Orphic hymns number VI and VII, describe Dionysos as "he who wanders in the Ether, who moves impulsively and noisily and who can traverse the Cosmos in just one stroke of his golden wings." Dionysos therefore brings to memory both Rudra and Viṣṇu, but he is neither and more. Dionysos is also *Phanes* (= manifest, visible, the one who *becomes* visible). He is also *Eros Primigenius* or *Proterogonos* (= the first born, first generated), not to be confused with later Eros, son of Aphrodite (= Vẹnus) and Ares (= Mars). *Eros Proterogonos* is he who illumines the world, the Earth and the stars and brings together the pair of opposites, as it did by bringing together Sky and Earth. Dionysos is further known as *Proteurhythmos* (= Original rhythm, from Latin Rhythmus and Greek Rhythmos), Dionysos himself is the *Executor* of natural cycles, therefore the original god of all nature, later restricted to God of *living* Nature. This original, extremely ancient Dionysos had jurisdiction over Sky, Earth and Sea and administered Justice among the gods. Jane Harrison (*apud* Merkelbach, §144) identifies *Protogonos-Phanes-Eros Proteurhythmos*, with still one more primary divinity: *Erikepaios* (doubtful etymology), since this was done at the initiation ceremony of the Iobacchi (= the good or correct followers of Bacchus) of Smirne, in Asia Minor, on the Mediterranean sea-front. Aristotle and Plato agree with Hesiod that *Eros [Primigenius]* was one of the "first principles." The myth of the archaic progenitors of the lineage that culminates with Dionysos summarise the pre-Homeric Greek views about cosmogony and evolution of the natural world.

Dionysos Proteurhythmos is not the *Preserver,* but the *Executor* and as such is not comparable to Lord Viṣṇu who is essentially the *Preserver* of natural cycles or even natural cycles themselves, in tune with *ṛta.* Dionysos Proteurhythmos as the Executor, is the one who implements the seasonal cycles, personified by the *Horae* (= hours, seasons). These are the closest companions of Dionysos who, under the guidance of the god, perform some duties comparable to the *mantras* (= metres, measures) which helped Indra conquers the fear of cold, darkness and death (Vannucci 1999). As a living person, or a god, a symbol or a persuasion, Dionysos travelled extensively and was present everywhere in one form or other, in the myths, folklore and mind of many people in Europe and Asia Minor. In the Orphic hymn 53, 7 seasons are described, or better defined as those "who run around in circles," as we read also about the *mantras* (*ṚV* VII, 103). Another close similarity with the older Vedas is Ariadne, the spirit of trees, specially the oak the most majestic of them. Ariadne is for a period consort of Dionysos and brings to memory Āraṇyāni (*ṚV* X; 1, 46), the Lady of the Forest. We must always bear in mind that Homer and Hesiod structured the classical Greek religion as we know it, on the basis of the Uranos-Cronos-Zeus dynasty and on the strength of the Olympian pantheon, while some of the nature gods belong to the Heroic or pre-historic period or earlier and were only very late, not earlier than the middle or last quarter of the last millennium BC, admitted into the Olympian pantheon.

It is not astonishing that neither the Orphic nor the Eleusinian Mysteries are mentioned in the Iliad, the Odyssey or the Homeric hymns. The reason is that they were kept secret and they refer, probably unchanged, to archaic times which were restructured and stylised by Homer and Hesiod. Herodotus (fifth century BC) mistakingly believed that both the Orphic and Bacchic ancient mysteries had an Egyptian and Pithagoric origin. His opinion was influenced by the fact that both Orphic and Bacchic mysteries believed in metempsychosis, whose origin was in the west, in ancient Egypt. The belief in reincarntion entered late and under different forms in the Mysteries of the west.

EVOLUTION WITH TIME

In the course of centuries, several ideas, principles and duties were lumped together in the classic Greek Olympian religion; many original myths and beliefs were not discarded but were preserved with honour, though most of them are confused by contrasting details. Many of the myths have some points of similarity and contact with the original myths of the Indo-European people and with the Indo-European of the east in particular, as for instance the myth of the original golden egg and the separation of the original Cosmos into Heaven and Earth. There are several points of similarity with *ṚV* X, 85, the "Wedding of Sūryā," daughter of Sūrya the sun, one of the longest hymns of the entire *ṚV* giving details of the preparation, ceremony and consummation of one of the most sacred rites: marriage. There is also some affinity with the so-called Creation Hymn of the *ṚV* as well as the myths on the origin of earth. Affinities and similarities recall the ancient-most myths and beliefs rather than the "official" new religion of Homer and Hesiod. Vannucci (1988) concluded the paper entitled "Common Roots and Transfer of Culture?" saying that in the history of the evolution of cultures there are many examples of both modalities. The story of the development of the figure of Dionysos shows very clearly that both common roots and transfer from other cultures are active in the evolution of the personality of god Dionysos.

The Indo-Europeans of east and west were obsessed with Truth, or the force of Truth, an abstract concept not personalised. In the west, the Indo-Europeans were fascinated by Beauty and War, an ideal symbolized by the marriage of Ares (= Mars) with Aphrodite (= Venus) a fundamental concept of the humanistic Greek culture materialised through architecture, sculpture, paintings, tragedies and comedies, songs and dances. In the east the Indo-Europeans were fascinated by Truth expressed as material and immaterial reality, because there is nothing more sublime or sacred than Truth under whatever form it appears. In either case, in east and west, all Indo-

Europeans found harmony in Love and Wisdom. In the Middle Ages, Dante Alighieri defines the ascent of man to Paradise as made possible by "LOVE that moves the Sun and other Stars" and the Greek represent love by the wedding of Kadmos (father of Semele, mother of Dionysos) with Harmos (= Harmony, daughter of Aphrodite, goddess of Beauty and Love). At the wedding, the Muses sang: "we like what is beautiful." The powers of Truth, of Love and of Beauty are the recurring themes of Humanistic Greece and of the Renaissance of Italy, which is the art of living well, according to the saying "may we agree, if it is honest and beautiful." For the Greek, wedding was always an initiation rite, a sacrament to be performed meticulously, as also in the *R̥V*, the wedding of Sūryā. According to Pausanias, during his time (second century AD) weddings in Attika were often celebrated according to the Dionysan ritual, with music, songs, dances and dramatic performances.

Dionysan beliefs and the prescribed way of life bring to memory another great lover of Love and Nature, the Great Persian mathematician/astronomer/philosopher Omar Khayyam (1050-1123 AD), popularly well known as the author of the Rubayyat, a poem devoted to the glory and joy of living, with happiness, love, wine, beautiful women, but with measure and self-control.

NONNOS AND THE DIONYSIACS

As mentioned above, the aristocratic urban society of ancient Greece was not interested in this wild, pre-Hellenic nature god without whom, however, it would not be able to survive. Gradually the Greeks changed the nature of the god of the Hellenic world and made him Dionysos *agroteros* (= hunter, disciplined lord of the lands) and paladin of the nine Muses, daughters of Mnemosine (= Memory) and sponsors of all arts and sciences. About one thousand years later, as some thinkers were reconsidering the traditional values of the society of Imperial Rome and its social and economic problems, Nonnos wrote the epic poem *Dionysiacs* in 48 books, as many as those of the Iliad and Odyssey taken together. The core subject and aim of the book is to enhance the personality of god Dionysos as the *civilizer* (word derived from *civilis* = civil and from *civitas* = city) of the people of the world. According to Nonnos' phantasy, this Dionysos and his court achieve victory through wars of conquest which begin with singing, dancing, copious libations of wine probably mixed with water, honey and other substances, and much music, mime and pantomime. As and when the cultural war fails, Dionysos engages his retinue in bloody battles, described by Nonnos down to awful details. Similar descriptions occur also in Homer, a model closely followed by Nonnos, though in the older epics they were not under the protection and inspiration of Dionysus but under the frequent participation of the Olympian gods.[12,13]

Much of the image of intellectually refined though ambivalent Greek culture that has come down to us over the centuries, such as the orgiastic activities of the Dionysan Mysteries, is due to the complex personality of Dionysos as his character was changed with the passage of time and under the influence of centuries of political, economic and social upheavals in Imperial Rome. The result in the west was a culture where pairs of opposites: Good and Evil; Beauty and Ugliness; Ignorance and Wisdom; Peace and War; Knowledge and Phantasy; Religion and Superstition; Devotion and Bigotry; Purity and Vice; Science and Deceit; Normality and Abnormality; Real and Unreal, Restraint and Orgy, and others, could meet and coexist without loss of balance. Nonnos' poem must be read under this perspective. The same happened in the east, not under the influence of a single God, but from an experienced intimacy with nature where the pairs of opposite, the Good and the Bad, the Mild and the Violent, the Material and the Immaterial, the Normal and Monstruous, the Friendly and Terrifying coexist inevitably and forever, because such is the balance in Nature; Truth governed by *ṛta* which is the Natural Order that IS what IS.

The bucolic poem of Longo (II century AD?) shows that the original faith in the Mysteries had remained alive and was still cultivated, partly in secrecy and probably in a highly stylized manner. It survived until when in the fourth century AD, an Imperial Edict condemned all "pagan" cults and religions.

The Dionysiacs of Nonnos on the other hand, are an attempt to show the greatness of Dionysos in all domains, during peace and war. Nonnos' Dionysos is still *Dionysos agroteros* during peace, but in wartime he is not much more than a poor copy of the Homeric heroes, influenced by the historical period in which Nonnos lived, when the greatness of Imperial Rome was beginning to be eroded at the frontiers which could no longer be efficiently guarded, and eroded at home by revolts and economic impoverishment caused by the extravagant lifestyle of the Roman patricians. In the Poem the decaying economic situation of Rome is evident in many ways, including in the accounts of the trade with India, where the value in weight of the metal became greater than the face value of the Roman coins.

The attraction of the Dionysiacs of Nonnos lies in the far flung imagination of the poet and baroque poetical style. What the masses inherited in Europe was mainly the Dionysos of Nonnos, who wrote in Latin, a language that became much better known than the older classic Greek. What has to be clarified at this stage is that "India" for Nonnos and his contemporaries, begins in West Asia and the Arabian peninsula and does not extend eastwards beyond River Indus, if it goes at all that far. India is still for Nonnos the vast area where the Indo-Aryans and the Indo-Iranians lived and ruled over many centuries. Nonnos also includes Ethiopians, Erythreans, Arabs, Kabiri and other people in a complex story in which myths and history are irretrievably mixed and geography is by-passed. Though one of the main sources are the reports of the campaigns of Alexander the Great, which had taken place about one thousand years earlier, the value of the text lies not with its historical reliability, but with the descripion of genealogies, the retelling and embellishment of ancient myths and legends and above all, the poetic aspects of the description of habits and customs of various people. The Dionysiacs of Nonnos makes interesting reading, but for the purpose of this book, they have no historical, factual, correct, geographic or philosophic interest or meaning. It is, on the other hand, a good example of the fruits of the fertile imagination which is shared equally by Indo-Europeans of east and west. As such the poem was well read and commented upon down to present days, though it cannot be taken as a correct representation of the personality of Dionysos or his times.

The Dionysiacs are meant to be the apotheosis of an archaic nature god who had to do something spectacular to attain his place in the lofty heights of Olympus. Nonnos recalls the myths of the god's divine paternity and unusual birth, but he places major emphasis on the "war against the Indians" and the "conquest of India" as the great feat that would have entitled Dionysos to ascend to the stature of an Olympian god, as opposed to the majority of the numerous offsprings of Zeus who had less glamorous careers. In fact, in ascending to Olympian heights Dionysos drops many of his characteristics of an all-encompassing nature god. He becomes one of the smaller Olympians, though he continues to reign supreme among the people. To these days a non-elegant but not rude and very popular swear in Italy is "per Bacco barile!" (= by the wine barrels of Bacchus = Roman Dionysos), or just "per Bacco!," the latter expression being assertive of something absolutely certain and good.

Dionysos is mentioned very briefly — only twice in the Odyssey, thrice in the Iliad and there are only three Homeric hymns dedicated to Dionysos, one of them refers mainly to Pan. The esoteric meaning of Dionysos must be sought in the Mysteries of his cult, of which nothing has come down to us in writing. What we know can be gleaned from the texts of the Orphic Mysteries and through classic Greek and Roman authors; also from Longo (see Merkelbach) which is one of the latest but most reliable.

HOMERIC HYMNS TO DIONYSOS AND NONNOS' OTHER WRITINGS

The three Homeric hymns (about seventh and sixth centuries BC) dedicated to Dionysos, probably reflect archaic beliefs. Hymn I mentions the three births of the god: first the premature birth from mother Semele, daughter of Kadmos; second from the thigh of father Zeus where he had been sewed in to allow for the full development of the foetus, forcibly aborted by mother Semele due to the jealousy of Hera (= Juno). The third birth was when the body of the infant was put together after being broken up into pieces by the defeated Titans. The first two births could symbolize the seasonal cycles and the vitality of nature and the third refers to the initiation of the god to the cult born with him and also to the metamorphoses of nature.

Dionysos often makes his appearance as a bull, or, at other times, as a lion or other animals. Homeric hymn XIII describes the handsome dark-eyed and dark-haired adolescent clad in regal purple and abducted by Thyrrhenian pirates. It describes the miracles, or "magics" created by the youngster as he resists capture, the punishment inflicted on the captain and crew who are thrown overboard and changed into dolphins and the reward given to the faithful helmsman who recognizes him as a god when grapevines grow spontaneously and fructify on the mast and sails. The symbolism is clear, emphasis on the "dark" youngster indicates ethnic mixture and the ubiquitous presence in Hellas, North Africa and West Asia of a God of Nature; it also suggests that grapevine was introduced in Greece from the lands of the eastern or southern Mediterranean.[14] McGovern (2003) found traces of a "royal winemaking industry . . . thriving in the wide alluvial plains of Nile River Delta by at least Dynasty III (*c.* 2700 BC)." Grapes cultivation, wine-making and libations of wine are shown in detail in many Egyptian tombs, as for instance the very well preserved tomb of the architect named Kha and his consort Mirit of the XVIII dynasty in the valley of Deir-el-Medinet, studied by Schiapparelli (1856-1928). The hymn, besides giving a good description of the boat and of the rudimentary art of navigation of those very ancient times, also indicates clearly that god Dionysos not only existed long before the advent of the fair Indo-Europeans in Greece but also tamed wild animals at sea as on land for the benefit of the newcomers that would be called Greeks or Hellenes. He instructed the late comers not only on the science of viticulture and on the art of making grapes' wine or viniculture, but also on sailing over the sea, following the invocation made by the faithful helmsman: "Hail, o son of lovely Semele, if you will be forgotten, it will not be possible to compose sweet songs." Hymn XXVI sings about the god crowned with ivy and laurel, of his infancy and childhood, his education by the nymphs and by the spirits of nature and the outcry during his wanderings in the wild forest. His taming of nature is recognized and acknowledged as he is thanked for annual abundant grapes.[15]

Nonnos of Panopolis, a city about 200km downstream of the ancient city of Thebes in Egypt, wrote the "Dionysiacs," in the fifth century AD. The poem is interesting to assess how the image of the god, the interpretation of the myths and legends and the personality of Dionysos evolved in the first centuries AD at a time when the Christian theology had not yet been finally structured. St. Agustine, the Father of the Christian Churches (354-430 AD) lived at about the same time. The poem has been widely used by modern authors, including Merkelbach who pointedly remarks that his own analysis of Dionysos and of the Dionysan Mysteries refers to the time of Imperial Rome. The Dionysiacs of Nonnos carried no weight on subsequent literature in Latin and they remained vastly ignored until the twentieth century when they were retrieved from obscurity in the European drive to retell and re-analyse past history. Nonnos also produced a "Paraphrasis of the Gospel of St. John" in 3650 hexameters in which he repeatedly draws parallelisms between pagan stories and rites and those of the New Testament of the Bible.

Before Nonnos, Plutarch (46?-120 AD) who lived shortly after the reign of Emperor Tiberius, composed a dialogue which he entitled "The sunset of the oracles" in which he mentions a "voice" announcing that the Great God Pan was dead. According to some, Pan (= everything), who was the semi-human and semi-goat incarnation who plays on his flute chanting and eulogizing the unity and harmony of all nature, had been one of the "First Principles" of creation. The "Eternal Pan" was since those early times the constant and most faithful companion (= *com+panis*, from *com*, together+*panis*, bread; companion = the one with whom we eat bread, the basic nourishment of man) and follower of Dionysos. Most authors of the first centuries AD are usually violently critical of faiths other than Christianity, but at the same time attempts were made to harmonize old habits with new beliefs and customs. Nature, which was earlier seen as the source of life and all goods, to be feared and obeyed, gradually became the handmaid, then the slave and a tool at the service of man, only exceptionally respected and most often outraged. We bear at present the drastic consequences of this attitude.

Almost every author, ancient or modern who has written about Dionysos, mentions the "successful war" against the Indians, without clarifying that all the people of various descent from Asia Minor and West Asia to the Indus River, were indiscriminately called Indians. The "successful war" probably means that much was gained during centuries of exchange and transfer of culture, knowledge, goods, plants and animals and above all trade with different people. There is no single myth about the "expedition to India" that could be considered true and original. After Nonnos, every poet added episodes and interpretations born out of his own imagination or understanding of tradition. The correct view is that there was much interaction and movement among the different people and different clans of the Indo-European of east, Indo-Aryans and Indo-Iranians and those of the west, as well as interaction between Indo-Europeans and other people, even before 1275 BC when the battle of Kadesh took place in what is now Palestine and stopped the advance of the Hittites into Egyptian territory, and the advance of the Egyptians into West Asia.[14]

LEGENDS ABOUT DIONYSOS

Most of what is known of the god and his entourage, of the rites and rituals, comes from sculpted sarcophagi, painted Greek pottery, Roman frescoes and mosaics of the luxury villas of Herculaneum and Pompei, cities buried under the ashes of the eruption of the volcano Vesuvius near Naples (79 AD) that also killed the curious naturalist Plinius the Elder who ventured too near to nature's fury to watch the volcanic eruption. It is from such sources that musical instruments are well known and many resemble closely musical instruments of the early Indo-Europeans of the east, such as cymbals, cythars and the lyre. The frequency of Dionysian scenes and symbols on Etruscan sarcophagi testifies to the general belief in the philosophy of Dionysos and in the Orphic mysteries concerning the cycle of life and death of the body, the cycle of the seasons and of the moon, the cycle of day and night and all nature's cycles, each with its works and rewards.

The original "noisy Dionysos," *Phanes* (= the manifest) brings to memory the "howling" Rudra.[15] Dionysos suffered as many rebirths in his vast domain from the Mediterranean Sea in the west to River Indus in the east, as Rudra suffered in the vast domain of the Indo-Arya. There is no doubt that there is some overlap of the beliefs and cult of the two gods, in time and space. However Rudra and Dionysos on the whole run on divergent and independent paths and have a different evolution, except for a significant detail: Dionysos is the god of wine, the inebriating powerful drink and will keep this attribute for ever after, up to present. Rudra after the fusion with

Indra, becomes the *soma* drinker, though on most attributes he merges with Śiva. *Soma* continues to be the very special preparation made in restricted quantities for very special rites and special occasions. About the evolution of Rudra, we will talk later. I believe that what was and still is described in Nonnos' *Conquest of India*, the major feat of god Dionysos, the ubiquitous god, represents the late advance of the Indo-Europeans of the west into territories occupied by the Indo-Europeans of the east. I refer here to the campaigns of Alexander, the satrapies he conquered and the new ones he founded. The Persian Empire created by Xerxes (519-465 BC) was very well organised politically and administratively when Alexander defeated the last Achaemenid king. The satrapies instituted by Alexander followed the system that already existed and had functioned successfully for a long time. The "great conquest" must be read in reverse, it really means that Dionysos brought to the Hellenic world much knowledge, technical and otherwise from the various Indo-European and other people and older cultures with which the Greeks came in contact in Asia. One such example is that Dionysos is credited with having brought Demeter to Attika, probably from Indo-Iranian settlements, where she instituted agricultural rites and rituals, many of them long since practised in the east (Vannucci, 1999b).

In other words, the original Dionysos is not only the god of untamed nature, he is also one of the most important instruments for the transfer of knowledge and experience between east and west, not limited to Indo-European people in general.

After Homer and Hesiod systematized the Olympian religion and when Dionysos was finally admitted among the Olympians, his *timé* (= jurisdiction) was restricted to a smaller sphere of action. On the religious/philosophical side, he was involved with Orphism; on the naturalistic side he was mainly involved with seasonal cycles, specially the cycle of the grapes-vine and the making of wine. From a violent beginning his character, comparable to that of the God of Tempests, again became more and more gentle and centered on love and the cult of beauty. His latest personality occasionally reappears in the Dionysiacs of Nonnos, it is credited with condemning bloody sacrifices, he recommends to be satisfied with the offer of cheese and olives instead of meat. These simple habits, conveyed to us by

Nonnos are those of a convinced and convincing philosopher who may have acquired them during his wanderings in Central Asia and India in particular, under the influence of Buddhism and Brāhmaṇism.

DIONYSOS, SUMMARY AND CONCLUSIONS

Dionysos is one of the ancient Greek gods more often discussed in prose and poetry in the ancient and modern worlds, in the oral and in the written tradition. Dionysos is a measure of the human personality that may faintly remind the personality of the *laddoo-eating* Gaṇeśa.

Dionysos is the name arbitrarily given to an archaic, proto-historic divinity of the pre-Hellenic people living in the part of the world that later came to be called Greece or Hellas. The primordial divinity is better designated as *Phanes* (= The Manifest, what can be seen). He is frightful and violent, he has all the powers of nature that keep man subjugated and terrified by the unknown and unexplained. He is awe inspiring and boisterous as the very ancient howling Vedic Rudra also is. Besides *Phanes,* Dionysos incorporates other "original principles" (Aristotle, 384-322 BC), designated as *Eros primigenius* and *Eros proteurhythmos.* As such Dionysos is both gentle and violent in all his aspects, including the biological aspects. In pre-historic times, violent natural phenomena would be considered inevitable manifestations of divinities or gods who personified the power of winds, earthquakes, floods, storms and other manifestations of nature, identified with the loud-voiced roaming divinity called *Phanes,* the archaic proto-Dionysos. To this day, thunders are jokingly said in Italy to be "Jupiter (= Zeus) moving around his wine barrels." As the early imaginary personification of *Phanes,* god Dionysos, not always named as such, is known to the pre-Hellenic people of the eastern Mediterranean, probably arrived from Crete, and present on land and sea. The people of Crete are well known as a *demos* (= people, population) perhaps even a nation and they were called Pelasgian (= *Pelasgoi*), they travelled all over the Aegean and the eastern Mediterranean. Other pre-Hellenic people are mentioned, as the Thyrrenians, reputed to be pirates like the Ionians and the Pelasgians. At present some authors identify the

Thyrrhenians with Etruscans. Gradually new and greater achievements were attributed to the infant and the young Dionysos, legends were added to myths and many of these reflect growing knowledge of geography and natural sciences.

The Greek and Roman myths refer to at least three successive wild nature gods. One of the adjectives given to the name Dionysos, was *Dionysos agroteros*, it first appears late in the literature but refers to the god said to have existed since very ancient times, presumably earlier or sometime during the third millennium BC, when not yet culturally developed Indo-Europeans came to the Greek peninsula from the north, overland and bordering the shores of the Black Sea. Other Indo-European people came by sea from the western shores of Asia Minor or over the Dardanelle Straits and were already familiar with an evolved Dionysos. The third or fourth Dionysos was called Bacchus in Latin or Iacchos in Greek, which may be the esoteric name of the god, acquired in the second half of the last millennium BC. Bacchus is the name currently given to the god presiding over the Roman orgies of the decadence period which were celebrated with licentious festivals called *Bacchanalia* (= bacchanals).

Dionysos, follower of nature's cycles and "creator of grapes vine and wine the divine drink," at some stage started the inevitable domestication of nature, a knowledge secretely guarded by the Mysteries. This knowledge is revealed symbolically in the poem by Longo (second century AD) which stresses the need and the advantages of living a healthy life in tune with nature's rules and reality. It is evident from the growing number of myths and legends, that most aspects of biological nature were gradually incorporated in the personality of Dionysos and in those of his entourage, such as the appearance on the scene of his faithful spouse Ariadne, the goddess of trees and forests. Over the centuries Dionysos became the personification of the compound knowledge and understanding of nature under the process of domestication, underlined by his association with "Chloe, the Green" which is Demeter in her relations with Dionysos. The Olympian gods had to be told that they and man would not exist in isolation and outside the world of the forces and energy of nature. This understanding however, was new to the humanistic Hellenic society eternally centered on man and it took very long to be recognised and admitted. During the second half of the last millennium BC and the first AD centuries, Greek science and Roman praxis grew on firm bases, new and realistic attributes were given to Dionysos or Bacchus as the protector, called *paredros* (= accompanying figure as of a husband or son) of Demeter and agriculture. Later the Phrygian cult of goddess Cybele (= cereal) was identified with Demeter and was also introduced in Rome from West Asia for political and practical purposes.

Myths and legends refer to pre-historic or early historic times. The evolving characteristics and increasing complexity of the archaic personification of wild nature reflect the ever-growing factual knowledge of nature in Greece, which had its origin towards the early second millennium BC and was well established in the last BC centuries, when Graeco-Roman science and technology began to fructify. The powerful sometimes violent archaic, proto- and pre-historic nature god, eventually called Dionysos, survived until recently in remote and mountainous places under the influence of Indo-European traditions, as for instance in remote mountains of the island of Sardinia, called Barbagia (= barbarous land), where some of the characteristics of the original noisy proto-Dionysos or *Phanes* and the habit of consuming raw meat and other primitive habits forgotten elsewhere, such as human flagellation and perhaps also human sacrifices had to be abolished by law in the first quarter of the twentieth century (Sanna & Lorettu, 2000).

As primitive culture developed into an organised complex civilization, the rustic proto-Dionysos had to conquer a place among the "higher" gods of the institutionalised religion of Greece, thus myths were multiplied by spontaneous generation among the people of the Hellenic world. New myths relating to his unorthodox birth, his nursing by a nanny, hidden upbringing by nymphs in caves, tutoring by the obese *Silenus* head of the satyrs and by the rustic ubiquitous *Pan* were multiplied. Dionysos gradually became more and more familiar with imaginary but symbolic theriomorphic figures like the centaurs, and with the metamorphoses of nature and its creatures, including the gods. The understanding of nature enabled Dionysos to become the interpreter who could teach and "explain" the unexplainable through the Mysteries, to appease the curiosity of man. Great and unheard-of unparalleled actions had to be performed, even if only in the mind of men for the rustic "*Dionysos agroteros*" to be identified with the formidable Zagreus, specially venerated in Thrace. The god's several personifications, not necessarily arranged in chronologic or geographic order, were vastly distributed, from the Greek world and all the way through Central Asia as far as Greater India. Temples and oracles, shrines, sacred caves, sacred groves and springs dedicated to Dionysos and his many personifications occur from southern Europe to Africa, Asia Minor and as far of what is now northern Iran.

The passage from the wild to the divine condition had to go through a process of humanisation to ensure the god's bilateral communion with gods and men. This process was long and troubled; it occupies most of the career of the god before he could finally ascend to Mount Olympus. Dionysos' exploits are many and wonderful, from archaic wild feasts and eating raw meat of newly sacrificed offerings together with the infuriated maenads, to finally condemning both bloody sacrifices and the eating of meat. Dionysos is the pagan god who survived longer among the Indo-European stocks of the west, even though he is at present alive mostly only in the collective subconsciousness of the masses as a frequent name given to newly born children. One of the first exploits of the boisterous god of winds and storms, which recalls the Sumerian god of tempests, was expressed with the creation of dolphins that were punished humans and the teachings of navigation at sea. The Indo-European culture was born on wind-swept open steppes, on fertile plains or mountains, the people had developed their culture on land, the sea was new to them so the myth of the abduction of young Dionysos by the Thyrrhenian pirates had to be created to indicate that those Indo-European now living around the Mediterranean Sea had mastered the art of navigation and had harnessed the wind, so that Greeks could face Pelasgians, Etruscans, Phoenicians, Feacians and traders or pirates on their own realm: the sea, with the blessings of the young ancient god, now introduced into Hellas. The Aegean Sea and most of the northern rim of the Mediterranean thus came under the influence of Hellenism. To a great extent Dionysos represents the evolution of the original Greek culture into a refined civilization. Rather than a man-made god, he is the whole, the entire Nature, a first and greater *Pan* playing on his magic flute to create harmony from disorder. Thanks to his achievements Dionysos obtained his position among the greatest gods by acclamation. Cheers to Dionysos still echo all over the world where at some stage there was Graeco-Roman influence. The career of Dionysos calls to mind the career of Lord Kṛṣṇa, born under unusual circumstances, somewhat uncouth, unconventional, truthful, free and happy, jovial and giver of joy, player on his magic flute who is nevertheless so wise as to become a god in spite of his human nature.

Finally Dionysos is represented on late (AD centuries) Etruscan and Roman sarcophagi as a bearded well clothed senior adult, leading the *Horae* (= seasons, hours) as he guides funeral processions, a reminder that death of the body is a promise of resurrection into a future life if, and only if, one has been initiated to the mysteries and has behaved accordingly. Of all the acts of Dionysos, bringing Demeter to Attika "from the "East" was his crowning glory, because through good nutrition due to methodical agriculture, man became strong in body and mind. Dionysos guarantees that the teachings which Demeter, whose symbol were ears of wheat, imparted to Triptolemus would not be lost.

There is no single deity among the Indo-Europeans of the east, comparable to the pre-Hellenic personality of Dionysos in the west. He is one who on his own and together with his companions and retinue male, female and theriomorphic, encompasses all the forces, powers and rhythms of natural elements, living or material. In the east, the Vedas themselves, as we have them, are not a complete record of the original beliefs of the Indo-Aryans who migrated as far as east of R. Indus coming from the plains around the Caspian Sea. Internal evidence shows that the Vedas are not exhaustive of the ancient tradition of the Aryans and other clans which lived or migrated into what is now known as Greater India. However we can confidently say that if there had been in ancient times a single God of all Nature, it would have been identified in the Vedas. What is described instead is that very early, after the world came into being, the forces of nature imbued with immense power and energy, divided the Cosmos into Sky and Earth, and then there were two groups who fought each other and will continue to fight each other to the bitter end of time. Both parties were imbued with many forces and much energy and it so happened that the elements of one party, the *Devas* (= Deus, Theo, God), were all Goodness and Righteousness, while the defeated party, the *Asuras* (= endowed with great magical power) were left with the not-so-good qualities, they could even use their power for evil doing. Every aspect of nature, of both Devas and Asuras was identified singly, each became a god or other deity and everything was recognised as sacred for the simple reason of its existence. As knowledge of nature increased, divinities were multiplied. There is no moral implication in "evil doing," the right or wrong resides in how, at what time and for what purpose the power is used and not in the doing itself. The concepts of "good" and "evil" vary under different circumstances and different habits. The *magi* of ancient Iran saw matters in the same manner, but inverted the roles of the *Deva* with those of *Ahura* (= *asura*). Ahura Mazda is imbued with all Good and Righteousness. The mythology of the Indo-Aryans and of the Indo-Iranians are very close, almost a specular image of each other.

Nature in the Vedas is not personalized, though it is acknowledged as an integrating whole known as Reality, material and immaterial (Vannucci 1999). The methodical objectivity and tendency to analyse everything led the ancient *r̥ṣis* to bow low to the reality of what they saw in nature and had to admit that there is a god or other divinity or nymph or fairy or demon or any other kind of *energy* in all the aspects of nature, constructive or destructive. Each and all are integrated in *r̥ta,* the supreme Rule and Order of the entire Cosmos. The stated goal of the Vedic seers was to obtain wisdom which should and would be applied to daily life. Wisdom would be obtained through knowledge. As Dionysos is the master of the seasons, Lord Viṣṇu is the energy, the One who preserves, but does not control seasons. Seasons are not personified or included in the world of Viṣṇu; they just exist as part of *r̥ta* and cannot be represented.

This is perhaps the first and most important observation that marks the difference between ancient religions of east and west. The contrast was already noticed by ancient Greek authors who textually say: "The Indians unlike the Greek do not make statues or otherwise represent their gods." In India representation of gods started very late, and only under the influence of western Indo-Europeans, it also did not take place in Avestic Iran. Vedic and Avestic gods are either mental representations of natural phenomena or intangible ideas or concepts. The first "visualisation" of a god was Fire, which exists as such and does not need to be represented. Fire is the manifestation of Lord Agni and at the same time Lord Agni himself (Vannucci 1999). Most Vedic gods are personifications of principles, concepts, ideas or they represent sages and elders imbued with knowledge and wisdom. A few others are divinized human beings, great kings or warriors. A large percentage of the hymns of the *Ṛgveda* that have come down to us and are alive in the collective memory of the people, are eulogies of the Great Conqueror Indra and are prayers for his victory in battle and for rich booty for his followers. Indra is frequently remembered, eulogized and prayed to, as the greatest god, but because he is in fact the most human of the gods, a warrior, leader and king, giver of material riches and other benefits and as such more readily and easily understood by man.

The migration and settlement of the Indo-European clans in India was not peaceful, nor did it happen all at once, following a single migratory wave. There were wars between the invaders and the local people and the most fierce battles took place among different clans of the Indo-Aryans themselves. Witness to this is the Great War described and discussed in all details in the *Mahābhārata*, the longest epic poem in history.

The legendary "conquest of India" could be a faint reminder of archaic exchanges between east and west added to more recent and better known travels and trade in both directions, between India and ancient Greece and much earlier at the time of the great migrations in the "Heroic" proto-historic period.

The Indo-European clans arrived in "Major India" at different times, probably by different routes and naturally the earlier settlers would be unhappy with the arrival of new people competing for land, even though closely related to them, having similar habits and customs and speaking similar languages. Aryans were not the only Indo-Europeans who came to India, but they are singled out already in Herodotus, who even defines the borders of the extensive territory that they occupied. Much later Strabo again describes the areas occupied by different Indo-European and other people. We find for instance the Arya and the Saka in eastern Central Asia and others which also inhabit lands east of River Indus. Some of them retain many of their original habits to this day: A curious detail is the way the Kalash women part their hair, it is similar to the way some women among the Indo-Europeans of the west parted theirs, as shown on Greek statuary, terracotta vases and Etruscan sarcophagi and to this day Indian women traditionally part their hair in the middle. The women of the Dard people, Indo-European nomads in the Himalayas, part their hair, make tresses and wear flowers in them, very much the way the Greek women did. The name Dard is the word-root of the name of the Strait of the Dardanelles that connects the Aegean Sea in the west to the Sea of Marmara in the east and near to the access of which was built the ancient city of Troy. In Strabo (XII, IV,6), Eneas, a Trojan hero of the War, was known as Chief of the Dardanians, Greek word-root of the name of the *Dard* people. The description of the war chariots of the heroes of the Indian epics is very close or almost identical to the paintings showing the war chariots of the Hittites. Also the role of the *auriga* (= chariot driver) is the same as that of the Vedic *sārathy*. The Saka were considered by Strabo (XI, VI, 2; VIII 2,4; VIII 4-5; VIII 8-9) to be "oriental Scyths" who occupied, before their final migration into " India," the vast territory south of the Aral Sea. The Saka clan eventually settled in the Gangetic plains and Siddharth, who eventually became the Buddha, belonged to the Saka lineage. The *Sindoi* (Sindhi) were people who lived north of the Caucasus and north of R. Hypanis, beween the Black and the Caspian Seas, another part of the territory occupied by the expanding populations of Indo-Europeans of Central Asia. They would have migrated in later times to the region now known as Sindh, in present day Pakistan. The word *samudra* in the Veda, usually translated as ocean, refers to the Black Sea, the Caspian Sea and Lake Aral and not to the Indian Ocean, as often suggested by modern commentators. Reference to the Indian Ocean as *samudra* comes late, usually as a synonym of the word *sāgara*, when the Indian Ocean became known directly, after having earlier been known only indirectly through traders as evidenced by the finding of the conch, and other rare objects of marine origin, already at Mehrgarh Level One. The first sure sign of direct contact with the ocean comes in the texts of the Indo-Europeans of the west, who were astonished at the high salinity of the waters and talk of the "infertile sea," such as those of the Aegean Sea and the Mediterranean in general. River Halys, in Asia Minor, flows near to the ancient city of *Gaṅgāra* and discharges its waters in the southern coast of the Pontus Euxinus (= Black Sea) where there are also salt water springs. It is singled out here because of the salt content of its waters as the name Halys indicates and because there is a village called Gangra in the high Kumaon, in the State of Uttaranchal in India. High salt content makes the waters unsuitable for agriculture as for instance those of R. Halys. High salt content occurs also in smaller land-locked bodies of water of Central Asia and were well known in ancient times.

Migrations of the original Indo-European people undoubtedly occurred from the centre of dispersion of the original Indo-European homeland north of the Caspian and Black Sea in all directions and maybe also in a return direction as the displacement of the name "Dard" indicates: first westwards, then eastwards or vice versa. God Dionysos travelled with the people and is remembered all over the ancient world.

Cities named Nysa or Nisa, people named after Dionysos, temples, sacred forests, sacred springs and meadows dedicated to him and above all the memory of the beloved god Dionysos may be found from the Mediterranean to all of Central Asia. At present they stop short in what are now Afghanistan and Iran.

Finally, translating from Prof. Menghi (2003, 162), "Greek tragedy [Aeschylus, Sophocles, Euripides, VI and V centuries BC] has deep roots in the rituals that were celebrated in honour of Dionysos, the god of liberation [= evasion, escape] from the [mental, psychological] contrast between the urge to act [= need of action] and predetermined destiny."

(C) Demeter — The Domestication of Nature

Domestication means: to make homely (*domus* = home). The merit of goddess Demeter is to have taught mankind how to transform agriculture (= cult of the field) into a routine, a frame of mind, a homely methodical activity. By introducing and teaching how to cultivate species of cereals in Attika and other lands of the Mediterranean, she made some of the most important food species *homely* rather than *exotic*. Archaeological research has shown that the science new to Greece which Demeter brought from the east, was known there since many centuries earlier.

MYTHOLOGY AND PRE-HISTORIC EVIDENCE

Vannucci (1999b) points out similarities between the Greek mythology of goddess Demeter and some traits of pre- and post-Vedic mythology and religion. Demeter is traditionally known to have come to Greece from the east. She is mentioned as having arrived in Attika, more precisely at Athens, during the reign of the eighth king of Athens, called Pandion, in the fifteenth century BC. According to tradition, she was brought to Greece by Dionysos himself. In late Greek mythology she is deemed to be the daughter of Mother Rhea, the earth, Good Mother Earth that sustains all living creatures, including mankind. Rhea was the consort of Chronos (= time) and mother of Zeus.[16]

In Homeric Hymn II to Demeter, she is represented as a mortal woman who had a daughter sired by Zeus, but her own parentage is not mentioned. Zeus, the god and king of gods had many sons and daughters by mortal women, but rarely and doubtfully from goddesses, a sign that Demeter was indeed a mortal woman to begin with and became a goddess only later thanks to her great service to mankind (Iliad IX, 457, 569). Her daughter was Kore (= young girl, maiden) who was abducted, then married by Zeus' brother Aidoneus (= Hades, Pluto, king of the Nether world or Hell). Demeter was outraged by this vicious behaviour and the neglect of father Zeus, so she caused a terrible drought to destroy everything on earth until when Zeus finally convinced Aidoneus to permit that Kore, now called Queen Persephone, should spend two thirds of the year on light-drenched earth, and one third, during the four winter months in the darkness of Hell with her spouse. On this condition, both Demeter and Persephone became goddesses in their own right. Following this agreement, Demeter instructed the Athenians on how to perform her rites, she created the Lower and the Great Mysteries and she taught Triptolemus (= sharp minded) how to cultivate, harvest and store cereals, especially bread wheat.

Some of the philosophic and esoteric meanings of Demeter's teachings are: *First* — Nature works in cycles which must be understood and obeyed. Thus the seed germinates, grows and reproduces on land at definite seasons, it then produces more seeds that will first rest (= hibernate) below ground, during winter. The cultivation of cereals and care of the field and its produce which is agriculture, must therefore follow defined methods and techniques. Seasonal or long-term annual or longer cycles, as for instance human birth, growth, reproduction, death of the body and again birth and death also run in cycles. Cycles are the normal rule and reality in nature. The purpose of the Mysteries of Demeter celebrated annually at Eleusis near Athens, was first: to "merit the privilege of death" (the term used is to **conquer the privilege**). Since birth, life and death are one and all, there is no birth without death and no death without birth. Death is a privilege because it opens the opportunity of a new and better incarnation; *Second* — practicalities about agriculture, including tools, ploughing, sowing, weeding, irrigation and storing of the grain were introduced and their use explained by Demeter; *Third* — finally another important teaching that has not, to my knowledge, been satisfactorily explained by commentators is that Demeter failed in her attempt to give immortality to the *body* of baby Demophont (= he who gives light to the people), son of noble Celeo (= Keleo) and his wife Metaneira, hosts of Demeter when she came to Athens. The episode stresses the fact that it is not possible for humans to achieve immortality of the body; hence it is better to acquire the privilege of death and rebirth. Celeids (= Keleids) and Eumolpids were traditionally the two families from which the *hyerophant* (= revealer or interpreter of secret knowledge) was alternately selected for the celebration of the Mysteries. It was the *hyerophant* who disclosed the Great Secret and gave the personal "secret formula" (= *mantra*) to the initiates during the rituals of the Great Mysteries. Initiation is indeed a second birth, the Dwija.

THE PERSONALITY OF DEMETER

To our knowledge, the first written source of knowledge about the personality of Demeter is the Homeric Hymn II, composed around the eighth century BC which coincides with the time when Hesiod lived and completed his *Theogonia* (= origin or genealogy of the gods).

According to Hesiod the hymn is the ancient-most source of the myth. Earlier notice of Demeter, of Kore later Persephone, and Ades would have been found in the oral tradition and the chants of the *aedes* (ancient poet/singers, comparable to medieval minstrels in Europe) and those of the rhapsodists (= epic singers) of pre-Homeric times. The Greek themselves interpret her name as derived from *D* or *Da* (= Earth) and *mater* (= mother). Aeschylus (525-456 BC) in his tragedy *Prometheus, v.*566-568 uses the syllable *Da* as a synonym of God as the Mother Goddess, he spells the name *Dametre* as written in Ionic language. *Da* is a very ancient syllable which the Greek considered to be derived from ancient Doric language, like *dada* and *dadi* in common parlance in India. Both Doric and Ionic are dialects of ancient Greek, therefore dialects of Indo-European Greek language. Demeter would be seen initially as the original Mother, as the soil which produces nourishment for all living beings, mankind included. She is the land that begs to be cultivated with care. The first task of agriculture is to work the soil, weeding, ploughing, irrigating with care. With time, the personality of the goddess as seen by human eyes evolved and she was identified with the Great Goddess worshipped at Eleusis in Attika, where the mysterious rituals which she created were performed during about two millennia, well into the Christian era. She taught how to cultivate hexaploid varieties of wheat and by extension she is credited with having imparted methodical agriculture. Nothing about the mysteries or her teachings was ever given in writing; secrecy was the first requirement to be imposed on the *mystai* at the initiation rites.

The names of Demeter or Kore/Persephone are not mentioned in the Cretan or Mycenean epochs. The original cult of Mother Earth, the good-earth that produces the basic food items as described in Hesiod's Theogony, may have its roots in the third millennium BC or, as ancient authors said: "since very ancient times." These dates coincide with the early presence of barley and tetraploid species of wheat of the *durum* varieties in Greece, which existed before the arrival of Indo-Europeans coming from Asia Minor or from those coming from the plains of R. Danube who first settled in Thessaly. The very ancient Earth Goddess (= Great Mother Goddess) of the Eteocretans, the "true Cretans" arrived in the eastern part of the island of Crete probably in the last quarter of the third millennium

BC and reached their maximum development around year 2000 BC, was the Great Mother Goddess. It is appropriate to use the capital letter *D* as the symbol of the Mother Goddess, as Aeschylus did, because capital letter *delta* up-side-down is in fact the symbol of the female gender. Finally, as a cultivator of cereals, Demeter would inevitably be involved in seasonal cycles, hence the myth of Persephone knitted into that of Demeter.

Over the centuries a large number of myths were associated to Demeter's name. Many, if not most of them were divulged during the time of Imperial Rome in the first three or four centuries AD by authors who had no access to the genuine ancient sources. Late myths usually enhanced or invented spectacular, improbable or obscene aspects of the rituals, e.g. Tertullian (160?-230? AD). Unfortunately many modern authors have relied heavily on late, often apocryphal sources of doubtful validity (Vannucci 1999b) and most popular books on Greek mythology repeat a hotchpotch of stories without any critical analysis of their origin or of the place, time, move and mood when they first appeared and were told and repeated.

KORE, DAUGHTER OF DEMETER

Kore is the virgin daughter of Demeter,[16] sired by Zeus and abducted by Hades. Zeus, the king of kings and gods, greatest of the Olympians had a large number of offsprings from mortal women; a few of them were later divinised. The maiden Kore, after abduction becomes the woman, Queen and Goddess of Hell named Persephone. Because she is allowed to spend yearly four months in Hell and eight months on Earth with her mother Demeter, she is the symbol of the alternation of generations (seed-plant-seed) and of the different agricultural stages at a time when cereals were, even more than now, the basic crop for the sustenance of the masses and of the armies. Wars, military campaigns and battles were timed "until after harvest time" to ensure that no damage would affect the crops and starve the soldiers. The worse offense of invading armies was to burn the crops before retreat.

Persephone, the maiden-Kore-made-woman became the mother of a son sired by Ades and conceived in the Nether world. She is a goddess because she is the consort of a god. She reigns on the rites of passage at puberty of virgin girls and on the passage from one stage of life on earth into another in the realm of the dead. The annual emergence into the lighted world symbolizes the germination of the next crop, while the seasonal descent to the underworld is the entombment of the seed into the dark, cold soil until when warmth and light will give it a new living body. Ades (= Aidoneus), the god and king of the deceased, good and bad, sinful and holy, is the treacherous god who tries unsuccessfully to keep Kore permanently in Hell. He is to some extent comparable to Rāvaṇa who had achieved much merit before he committed the fault of abducting Sītā. Also Rāvaṇa tries unsuccessfully to keep Sītā a captive, but he is overpowered by the spirit of justice and fairness embodied in prince Rāma. The determination and strong will of *mother* Demeter to obtain periodical relief from the horror of a life in darkness to which her daughter had been condemned, was stronger than the biased will of father Zeus himself. Ades proves to be equal to Zeus by reaching a compromise which is more like a defeat. He is forced to agree to keep Persephone for only four cold winter months yearly with him. Many species of plants and animals need regular periods of rest; this is one of the rare instances in Greek mythology when it is conceded that nature may have the last word when at variance with the arrogance of the Olympians and of man. Archaic matriarchal cults of the Earth Goddess/Mother Earth survived in the myths born with the arrival of Demeter in Greece in the middle of the second millennium BC. It is superfluous to discuss here the basic role of the figure of the Mother, disguised or not it survives in the habits and customs of all cultures.

The name of Persephone is written in various forms, depending on the place and dialect. According to experts, the name sounds pre-Hellenic, which is correct since the tetraploid species of wheat and barley were planted in Greece since about 6000 BC, before the advent of the Indo-European Doric tribes and the introduction of hexaploid varieties of wheat. This is one reason why I believe that the "wheat" that Demeter is said to have brought to Attika, is not the common "hard" wheat, the *durum* types which are tetraploid species, but something new to Greece, some other more valuable species of wheat, which are the "bread" varieties that are genetically hexaploid species.

DEMETER AND HER CULT[17]

According to tradition Demeter arrived in Attika probably during the reign of the eighth king of Athens, called Pandion (*circa* 1462-1423 BC). Herodotus (fifth century BC, I, 173) reports that Pandion was eventually exiled by his enemies. Later his four sons recaptured power over the city, but the youngest, Lycos (= wolf) was exiled to the country in western Asia Minor bordering the Aegean Sea that later took his name: Lycia. Herodotus remarks that the Lycians were the only people who observed matriarchy, a strange custom, he says, different from that of all other people who follow patriarchal systems of inheritance, for naming their children and recording their genealogy. It should be noted that this is the rule in much of south India to this day and most probably was so during the rule of the many-centuries-later Pandian dynasty in the area of Madurai (= *Mathurai,* old city = *Mathura* in North India) in Tamil Nadu.

When Demeter, disguised as an old woman was questioned by queen Metaneira in Athens, she lied bluntly to conceal her identity and origin saying that she was abducted by pirates from Crete. The mystery of Demeter's origin is a heated point of debate. To this day, several authors ancient and modern discussed many possible origins of goddess Demeter, including Crete, but archaeologists and linguists have found no sign of Demeter in Crete or in the texts retrieved from the Minoan libraries, nor anywhere else. Herodotus (II, 59) mistakenly identified Demeter with the Egyptian goddess Isis, wife of Osiris her brother, which somehow reminds Rhea, wife of her brother Chronos. Further Herodotus (II, 171) mentions that the *Thesmophoria,* a three-day annual festival in honour of Demeter which was celebrated on the occasion of sowing winter wheat (= *durum* variety, not bread wheat), were brought from Egypt to Greece by the daughters of Danaos who also taught the rites and ceremonies to the Pelasgian women in pre-Hellenic times. Later the rites were lost when the Doric people, Indo-Europeans coming from the plains of R. Danube, evicted the Pelasgians from the Peloponnesus. The *Thesmophoria* rites were celebrated only in Arcadia, a mountainous area of the Peloponnesus. These rites, in which only married women could take part, are obvious remains of the past archaic culture, most probably the culture of *durum* wheat, which is older than the arrival of the Indo-European people in the southern Peloponnesus. They are evidently also reminders of matriarchy.

The devotion to Demeter and her cult is attested also by the fact that very ancient temples and sanctuaries to the goddess are found over a wide geographical area, not only in the Peloponnesus, but also in Baeotia, Thessalia, Thracia, Rome, Phrygia and places in Asia Minor and are often quoted by ancient authors, such as Strabo (VIII). In the Iliad (II, 696; XV, 335) areas sacred to Demeter are mentioned from Pirasus and Filake, both places in Thessaly. Herodotus (IV, 53) mentions a sanctuary to Demeter in the land between the rivers Hypanis and Borysthenes (= R. Dnieper) in Scythia, probably not very far from the present-day city of Kiew. Some, if not all the Scyth tribes came from Asia to Europe by the western routes circling the *Pontus Euxinus* (= Black Sea), from the twentieth or nineteenth centuries BC onwards.

A temple in the city of Enna in Sicily was traditionally considered to be the place where Ades (= Pluto) abducted Kore, according to Cicero (in: *In Verre*) who describes it as surrounded by lakes, sacred groves and ever-flowering prairies. All these places are related to the culture of cereals, wheat, barley, more rarely also rye. Fertility of the land was gauged by the degree of production of grain. In the Iliad (XIII 322), it is said of Ajax Telamonius that "he would not be second to any man who eats Demeter's flour," meaning that great supernormal strength comes from consuming bread flour (hexaploid wheat). Again in Iliad (VI 5; X, 100) men are classed as those who "eat bread and salt" and those who do not. The daily routine of making bread is mentioned as a sure sign of civilized habits.

Partly because of the prayers of grateful men, Demeter accepted to ascend to Olympus where she became the "first of all the goddesses of fertility." Herodotus (IV,198) measures "Demeter's gift" or "Demeter's fruit" in terms of production of grain, he gives figures for places in Lybia as producing 100 to 1, or even 300 times to one sowed grain in terms of weight. These figures are probably inflated, but are compared by him to the figures for Babylon, where they are "highest than anywhere else."[16]

The importance of wheat, first the *durum* tetraploid species (genetically AABB) and later the bread type, hexaploid wheat *Triticum aestivum* (genetically AABBDD) cannot be overestimated. Herodotus (I, 193) attributes the wealth of Mesopotamia to Demeter's gift, the cereals, though other plants are important, such as fruit trees and vines, specially figs and grapes. Herodotus (III, 22) mentions a curious episode to illustrate the value of bread. He gives details of a dialogue that took place between the king of Ethiopia and the emissaries of king Cambyses of Persia (died 522 BC). Replying to a question by the king, the emissaries said to the astonished king that Cambyses ate bread and that the average life span of a Persian was 80 years because of the habit of eating bread as regular food. In the west as well as in the east barley, which is perhaps the first cereal domesticated by man, was and still is offered for salutations, worship and thanksgiving to the gods. Among contemporary authors, the geneticist Cavalli-Sforza (1996) and other modern and ancient authors, mention that agriculture of cereals and farming in general is what strengthened physically the human species and promoted demographic growth.

The "gift of Demeter" or development of methodical agriculture, was the acculturation necessary to promote the evolution of the Greek *culture* to what we now call the Greek *civilization* and Hellenism. The term "civilization" implies the existence of a structured society capable of living beyond just eating, sleeping and reproducing, with spare time for the pursuit of knowledge, philosophy, creative arts and unfortunately, also wars of conquest and migrations for land seizure and occupation. Demeter showed the merit of following with intelligence and method all nature's laws. This is the recognition of what the ancient *ṛṣis* called *ṛta,* the cosmic law from which no man or god can escape.[17]

DEMETER'S ACTS AND MISSION

All important gods and heroes are mentioned in the epics with a stereotyped qualification.[18] Demeter is known as the "fair haired" and "the one with beautiful fair curls" to emphasize physical characteristics which assign her to a particular stock, in this case the Hellenes or Greeks of Indo-European descent, different from pre-Hellenic people. One is tempted to see in the fair, blond and long hair of the goddess a generous field of ripe golden wheat waving in the breeze, ready to be harvested. Demeter is not only a beautiful woman, she is also persevering to the extreme since she knows how things should be done and she has the determination to carry her mission to the end because she has the certainty and assurance that her teachings are correct. It is the inflexibility of her convictions that succeeds in redressing the cycles of nature that had been upset by the forcible coercion of Persephone in hell. It is the same conviction that gives her the power of programming and organizing the Mysteries and it is her own fortitude which she imparts to all around her. Sub-consciously her presence in Christian Europe is alive down to present days, especially when the fields are blessed after ploughing and before sowing after the soil is thoroughly mixed and aerated to prepare it for receiving the seed. In a way, Demeter is what Pṛthvī is in the east: good original Mother Earth. She is the soil fertilized by rain, the semen of father Sky. She produces grains to nourish the body and she gives serenity to the soul of the "reborn" or, in the west as in the east, the "twice born" who duly fulfilled her rites. The performance of agricultural work, which are the "rites of goddess Demeter" cannot be but basically the same in east and west. Demeter is Pṛthvī, Bhūmi, Devī, Kālī, Mahādevī all in one, but the myths related to these simple basic natural truths and activities may be different, and so are also the explanations that are given according to local environmental realities.

The story of Demophont and the attempt to give immortality to man shows how much Demeter was devoted to her mission, the more so after her disappoinment with the Olympian gods during her strife to save Kore from spending all eternity in the nether world as consort of Aidoneus. Demeter gave to man food for the body with wheat, and food for the spirit with the Mysteries. But all her determination and the magic powers she had acquired were not sufficient to transgress the laws of Nature. By her failed attempt at imparting immortality to the human child Demophont, Demeter gave to man the fortitude to conquer the fear of death. She shows that bodily death is only the Great Passage to another life. In her own words, she gave man "the *privilege* of Death." Death of the body should be regarded as the happy ending of a life well spent and made possible by a full and conscientious initiation. Immortality can be achieved by man with the memories he leaves behind him, through his teachings, like the *ṛṣis* did, or by steadfastness, like the unwavering faith shown by child Dhruv later immortalised as the Pole Star, or by their teachings, like the saints and great masters of all faiths.

THE RITES, THE KYKEON

Vannucci (1999b) mentions the most striking parallelism between details of the Lesser Mysteries and the procession that took place annually on the 19th day of October from Eleusis to Athens and back to Eleusis, with habits and rituals in India and the importance given to singing and "*dancing on prescribed steps.*" The Lesser Mysteries were open to everybody who wished to participate, they are known in detail, but what we know with certainty about the Greater Mysteries is very little indeed. What is actually known is that on the last night of the initiation, after days of prayers, meditation, fast and silence, the great revelation took place. What happened was never revealed by either the *Mystai* (first initiates) or the *Epoptai* (veterans) and the most far-fetched conjectural guesses were made by authors ancient and modern. Wasson (*et al.* 1978) in an important book which, I did not know when I wrote the paper on Demeter and hexaploid wheat (1999b), puts emphasis on "what the "Great Mysteries" actually were. Wasson hypothesizes rather convincingly that the *kykeon*, the ritual beverage of the ritualistic libation of the last night, could have been naturally laced with a microscopic fungus named *Claviceps purpureus* (= mace-shaped, purple coloured), commonly called *ergot* and related species which grow on the ears of cultivated and wild cereals and produce bioactive alkaloids. Ergotamine, produced by *ergot*, is used in small quantities in obstetrics to induce and intensify labour and in other medical practices, but can be a deadly poison if taken in large quantities. Ruck (in Wasson, *l.c.*) argues that the *kykeon* could induce visions of life and death and of life after death and thereby give eternal tranquillity to the initiate. The aim of the Mysteries was to give "the *privilege* of death" and not *victory* over death. Being face to face with death, it is argued, would neither conquer nor defeat death, but would give the knowledge and certainty that rather than the end of everything, death of the body is the beginning of an entirely new life of the spirit. The passage from one life to another is itself existence. What the Mysteries did was to destroy the fear of death of the body, and thereby gain peace of mind. Wasson *et al.* miss an important point where they mention that Demeter dressed herself in purple colours as a sign of mourning during her search and the absence of Kore. The Greek word used in the original text is "dark," which could be very dark purple, or better very dark grey, but is not "purple" (= lat. *purpura* and gk= *purphura*). In fact black or dark grey is the colour of the *sclerotia* on the ears of grasses infested with ergot. The colour signals the presence of the fungus, since ergot is very dark and becomes black when the spores of the fungus are ready to be shed, hence the name "wheat charcoal" or "wheat cancer" as the disease is popularly known since ancient times.

The recipe for the preparation of the *kykeon* was given by Demeter herself (Homeric Hymn II, 209-210) when she refused wine offered to her on arrival at Keleo's (= Celeo) home. The beverage was prepared with barley flour and mint, here called *glechon* (not *blechon* as in Ruck, in Wasson *et al.*; in this interesting book there are several inaccuracies in the rendering of Greek words and text) diluted in water and no wine added. Infestation with the *ergot* group of fungi specially *Claviceps* spp, is frequent in cultivated cereals and wild grasses, the most common of the latter being *Paspalum distichum,* widely distributed and well known in the past. Ergot could, in early times, have been mixed accidentally in the beverage when pressing barley grains before straining the juice to prepare the *kykeon. Kykeon* was the beverage for the sacred libations during the rites. This could have become a regular part of the preparations for the ritual after noticing the vision-inducing effect of the beverage. Ergotamine is the toxic alkaloid most abundantly produced by the fungus in the infested ears of cereals. The black sclerotia destroy and replace the cereal grains and are present in all the European countries where wheat is grown. Herodotus mentions that in certain areas wheat may grow well but the crops are poor because they are highly infested with the parasite.

Priests of all ancient cultures and religions were reputed ethnobotanists and practitioners of herbal medicine. Knowledgeable *vaids*, anchorites and monks or rustics living with and in nature in both east and west are experts, as were also our grandmothers, of home medicine that relies heavily on plants. Ritualistic libations of prepared intoxicating drinks are common among many people (Iliad 11,634; Odyssey 10, 233-314; Homeric Hymn to Demeter (II, 210). The mixture of the *kykeon* was carefully prepared and could not include grapes' wine, honey, or any other extracts, as opposed to libations with grapes' wine used in other religious rites or profane celebrations in the Graeco-Roman culture. During profane feasts and offerings, grapes' ẉine was usually mixed with water, honey, mint and other aromatic herbs. It was rarely, if ever, drunk pure.

The rituals at Eleusis, specially the procession to Athens and pilgrimage back to Eleusis are the main feature of the Lower Mysteries open to all; they were performed with the aim of participating and supporting spiritually the maintenance and preservation of the fundamental cycles of nature. There was no drinking of the *kykeon* during the celebration of the Lower Mysteries. Similarly *soma* and *haoma* were consumed only during special sacrifices and only by the priestly classes, the brāhmaṇas and the magi respectively. In the east, specific rituals in honour of Lord Viṣṇu are performed for the preservation of seasonal cycles and the maintenance of the integrity and respect for nature, as metaphorically described for instance in the Ṛgvedic Hymn on Frogs (= *maṇḍūka, ṚV* VII; 103. Vannucci 1999).

THE MYSTERIES

The teachings and details of the rites held at Eleusis were kept strictly secret and were memorized. The knowledge of the practicalities for correct cultivation of wheat was given verbally to Triptolemus and there is very little or nothing about this in the Homeric Hymns to Demeter. The general belief was that Demeter taught everything about the cultivation of wheat and other cereals and that she orderd Triptolemus to spread far and wide all details for the cultivation of cereals. Following her order, the young nobleman of Athens departs with a bag full of seeds for his proselytizing mission.

With time Demeter gradually came to be considered *Demeter Thesmophoros* (= legislator or law bearer = law maker) for the simple reason that she teaches how to make and use good healthy bread. By extension she becomes the law giver for what concerns methodical agriculture and the division and care of the land by the new class of people, the peasants. The division of the fields was put in pratice in an orderly and rational manner to ensure that "her rites be correctly performed." Here again the matriarchal aspect of the agrarian culture from which Demeter originally came is obvious and she regulates the property of her offsprings through women power. The *thesmophories* were festivals enacted by women, only married and mature women could participate. There are similar situations and habits in matriarchal societies of south India, but not where the formally patriarchal Indo-European system prevails, like in north India and in ancient Greece and Rome. Implicitly Demeter was requested to regulate community life. The *Thesmophories* thus became the festivals held in honour of the newly proclaimed laws, because "before the cultivation of wheat, mankind moved here and there and was not fixed to the land." The Greek image of "civilization" begins with agriculture and the laws that regulate it in the Greek philosophy of the universal importance of the "*polis*" with its laws and regulations. Nomadic life was considered a primitive existence that had not yet attained the level of a civilised way of life. Even shepherds were not considered as fully civilised because the care of their flocks requires them to migrate and undertake periodic transhumance in search of green pastures at higher altitude. This was an aspect of Greek life well portrayed in the Odyssey when *Odysseus* (= Ulysses) returns to his native Ithaca and is not allowed entry into the palace because of his disguise as a shepherd.

As a digression, it would be interesting to know more of the social aspects of agriculture and about the division of labour among the family members of the ancient Indo-Iranians. Did they follow a matriarchal social system? If so, to what extent?

The Great Mysteries were the esoteric component of Demeter's teachings, based not only on the birth - life - death - birth cycle of living beings, but also on all the cyclic aspects of nature, both material and living. The most important aspect of Demeter's teachings was that the initiation to the mysteries did not request the *mystai* (= mystic, initiated) to **believe** in order to **see.** Understanding was the basic requirement, hence the training by fast, silence, meditation and preparation to receive the secret revelation. Death should be seen and understood as a **privilege** rather than a defeat. This is a striking parallel with the teachings of the Vedic *ṛṣis* who insisted on the need to **see and understand.** Belief should not be blind, it should be based on experience and reason, contrary to the Olympic religion and Semitic and Christian attitude which preach that belief is the basis on which rests philosophy and religion and that only unwavering, blind belief is required of the believer, rather than understanding. The high point of the initiation rites of the Mysteries, was a night-long vigil during which the initiates, according to Pericles, Sophocles and others, would be blessed with the conviction of eventually going to Ades (= Nether world) **consciously**, because "only they will find life there, while others will not." Aristotle, probably himself an *epoptay* (= veteran initiate), said that the initiates were secluded to feel and undergo certain moods, but they were not there to learn. In other words one "feels" an understanding that should be with the entire body and not only with the intellect, as is well known from Raja Yoga teachings and practices. The Atirātra rite, which is part of the Vedic Soma Sacrifice, has some aspects similar to the Great Mysteries of Demeter (*see* Vannucci 1999). Long vigils after days of silence and meditation, fasting, darkness and performing prescribed rites and libations with *soma* or the *kykeon* respectively, would favour enhanced sensitivity and perception of both material and immaterial reality, or "seeing without the use of mortal eyes." The passage from living to dead body is the passage from material to immaterial reality.

Obviously the teachings of Demeter rest on earlier knowledge acquired by "the ancients" so often remembered also by the "seers" who gave us the Vedas. Age-old wisdom is often crystallized as myths. How much transfer of culture, habits, customs and religion between east and west in either direction took place, we cannot tell. Dates are too uncertain at this stage to venture a guess, certainly transfer was not sudden and it would have taken many generations of co-existence for mutual cultural enrichment.

DEMETER — SUMMARY

Homeric Hymn No. II gives in detail the story of the remarkable woman already sanctified when the hymn was put in writing. She instructed Triptolemus (v. 474) to travel far and wide taking with him seeds of wheat and barley and teach people how to cultivate those grasses. Thanks to the many perils she went through, Demeter acquired "magic" powers that enabled her to teach how to perform correctly her rites, "so that you may in the future perform them piously to placate my soul." The word used in Greek is *orgia* (= the word *orgia* originally meant "sacred rites"). Thus was born the sacred rite of methodical agriculture among the Indo-Europeans of the west (details in Vannucci, 1999b). From archaeological and anthropological findings and studies, there is no doubt that the improved varieties of wheat arrived in Attika, Greece, towards the middle of the second millennium BC, brought from Central Asia by knowledgeable people such as Demeter who is not just a symbol; alternately wheat was intentionally brought over by traders and travellers who could perhaps be identified with followers of the teachings of Dionysos, a very ancient god, much older than Demeter. It is also natural that the basic culture of the Indo-Europeans would have identified the Great Nourisher with a feminine figure, a Mother. She occurs also in Phrygia, where she was identified with the ancient goddess Cybele, older than Demeter, since agriculture was practised in Asia much earlier than in Greece. The collective gratitude of mankind is to this day subconsciously expressed by the frequent occurrence of the name Demeter and its derivatives, in both the feminine and masculine forms. In an earlier paper I focused on the type of wheat brought by Demeter and on some aspects of the Eleusinian mysteries. Much more could be said on this myth that more than a myth is a documentary legend of pre-historic facts and is not a phantastic invention. Only a few significant points about the relationships between gods and heroes of east and west will be mentioned here.

There is no doubt that Demeter is an Indo-European name and that she came from the east. She could have been a single person, as the legend tells us, or she could have been the leader and guide of a group of people, expert farmers over which she ruled. Eventually she did rule the farmers of Greece, since she was made the goddess who presided over the ownersip and demarcation of the boundaries of the fields. If this is so, she would have come from a community where matriarchy was the rule or where much of agriculture was in the hands of women, a common situation in the east. It is reasonable to conclude that she was brought, and could not have come alone and by herself, from south or Central Asia, probably Iran or Afghanistan, or even as far as India where those superior varieties of wheat were already cultivated. Archaeology and genetics have shown that at places of present day Iran spontaneous hybridization takes place between cultivated tetraploid varieties (*Triticum* spp.) and wild varieties of wheat (*Triticum tauschii, Aegilops squarrosa*) to produce hexaploid *Triticum aestivum* or bread-type varieties of wheat. These parts of the Fertile Crescent are crossed by the main trade routes from western Asia Minor to present-day Pakistan and India, they run through areas called in ancient times Phrygia, the land of the Medes (now Kurdistan), the lands of the Arya, of the Saka, to mention only a few of the best known tribes, some of which are known to have migrated into India. Details apart it is clear that Demeter would have come from this centre of plant speciation, well known from studies of palaeobotany, palynology, historical ecology and archaeological findings.

Unlike what happened in medieval Europe, ancient Indo-Europeans seldom destroyed or salted the enemy lands, their fields and forests though battles and wars were frequent, for the simple reason that salt was costly and advancing or retreating armies over long distances needed victuals for men and fodder for animals. The Indo-Europeans of east and west maintained during their wars some of the habits of their original culture, for instance warring parties stopped fighting at sunset and if necessary assisted each other in the pious task of burning the dead and retrieving the wounded. Wars were an efficient means for the transfer of material culture and the office of spy, rather than "despized" as in later centuries Europe, was a respected occupation most useful to learn of the progress achieved by neighbours or would-be enemies. However the most efficient means of transfer and diffusion of material culture, knowledge and learning came from traders, pilgrims, enslaved enemies and the common people of the occupied territories. At present we still rely heavily on the information received from original sources verbal, written or figured, or from the traditions of distant cultures and travelogues and we read and interpret signs as far back as we can go, as much as also Homer and Hesiod relied upon when they had only the oral traditional knowledge to guide them.

Whatever her origin, Demeter was undoubtedly a very intelligent woman, a learned teacher and clever magician gifted with a great power of persuasion. Like Dionysos she has to her credit to have lived so far back in time that the memory and the stories of her acts and facts are known throughout her vast domain and were broadcast with new episodes growing at every retelling. Her antiquity is attested by her name, since the very ancient prefix *Da*, meaning mother, could have come from pre-Hellenic languages, or from the Doric language, in which case the name Demeter would be a composite of two words for mother, one in Doric and the other in some pre-Hellenic dialect (*Da* and *mater, mātā* is the wide-spread root-word for mother in the Indo-European languages). In any case, her name expresses the most intimate and perhaps strongest of human sentiments, the attachment and initial total dependence on Mother.

In Ionic and Attic languages Demeter's name can be translated as "Earth Mother, Great Mother, Original root and spring of life," which is not the same as *Ge* (= earth, the land, soil or ground), or *Rhea* (mother of Zeus and wife of *Chronos* = time) the planet Earth. Demeter is stepmother of *Demophont* (= the one who illuminates the people) whom she tried in vain to make bodily immortal. The capital letter Delta in Greek is the same as the feminine triangle, symbol of femininity turned upside down, finally she was indeed the perfect complete woman, so beautiful that she was loved and possessed by Zeus who bowed to her will. Against the will of his brother Ades (= *Aidoneus*) Zeus had to allow his own daughter by Demeter, Kore (= young virgin, girl), later called Persephone, to return to Earth yearly during two seasons, or eight months, before going back to the darkness of Hell to stay with her spouse King Ades (= Pluto), during the four winter months.

In addition to bodily beauty, Demeter had the beauty of a strong willpower to achieve her destiny, her *timai* and to care for her daughter Kore. She had the magic power to cause a terrible drought on Earth, and when she could not find her abducted daughter she deprived men of food and the gods of their offerings. She kept her own ground till when Zeus the father of them all, admitted her to sit with the Olympian gods and crowned Kore now Persephone, Queen of Hades and entitled her to commute at seasonal intervals between Earth and the Nether world. Persephone was finally also admitted to the table of the gods on Olympus, the highest mountain in Greece (2920m high). Demeter was a warrior in her own style; the fury of the betrayed mother, the determination and power of this generous being, the happiness at the restoration of the vegetation on the parched land after the drought that symbolically represents the emergence of Persephone from Hell, were all the many acts which endeared Demeter to men and gods. She failed only in one point, namely her attempt to give immortality to Demophont. This is as it should be because changing fate and the gift of immortality are beyond the power even of Zeus the Father himself. Fate (= *Fatum,* that which has been spoken), cannot be changed. Demeter is above all a human being, therefore different from *Rhea,* born a goddess, or *Ge,* mother of living beings, and therefore also not comparable to Aditi, Mother of Infinity and herself the Infinite. Demeter's attitudes, her happiness and despair, her love and infinite protective tenderness expose the soft corner of a typical human mother. Most of all, Demeter resembles Pṛthvī (*pri* = primitive, primordial), the aboriginal generous earth (= soil) and producer of all wealth.

Demeter[18] could conquer Olympus not because she was perfect, but because like the other Greek gods she had some human frailties which man could understand and forgive, and the Olympians, we must remember, were man-made figures. Her only great mistake, for which she had to make atonement, was the arrogant attempt to impart immortality to the human child Demophont, forgetting that the Olympians themselves would not be able to do so. But, as her very human anger knew no bounds she showed that, as much as she could give nourishment, she could also withdraw it from humans and gods. With these acts she proved the realities of nature and the power of womanhood in all its aspects. Together with Persephone, herself a mother, mother and daughter represent human life on earth and in the nether world.

DIONYSOS AND DEMETER — SUMMARY AND CONCLUSIONS

Dionysos is the one in many and the many in one. Dionysos is the subject of at least three Homeric hymns dedicated to him, no. I, VII and XXVI. He is not mentioned in the Aeneis, which was written many centuries later. The basic teachings from Homer, Hesiod and the Hymns are: 1) Dionysos had three births, one from mother Semele (same root as Russian Zemlya = earth, land), one from the thigh of father Zeus and the third after Hermes put together the pieces of the body of Dionysos torn (or cut) by the vindictive Titans; 2) Dionysos is often remembered and figured as an infant salvaged by Hermes and brought in a winnowing basket to Zeus and to the nymphs who will rear him. He is suckled by a nanny-goat, is educated by Silenus, lives in the company of shepherds and Pan, befriends Centaurs and all real or imaginary creatures of wild nature; 3) he is remembered as an adolescent youth (= the young son of Zeus), and when he was kidnapped by Tyrrenian pirates he performs his first miracles and metamorphoses, changing men into dolphins and himself into a roaring lion, after which he distributes punishments and rewards; 4) Dionysos travelled by sea and probably brought the art of viticulture to Hellas and the experience needed to cultivate the grapevine and make wine. He is symbolically shown arriving in a boat at solemn festivals in his honour like the *trieterides* and he is repeatedly (*Theogonia* 941 *et al.*) characterized as "full of joy," "joy of man."

Dionysos is more than usually respected as "god of vegetation." He is the personification of the entire Nature, of all the Cosmos, he is Demeter's *paredros* (= acolyte), because Demeter is domesticated nature, he is the faithful companion who understands and trusts her. He participates in the Minor Mysteries at Eleusis, which were open to all humans and minor divinities, and follows the yearly procession from Eleusis to Athens and back to Eleusis. However, as far as we can tell, he was not initiated to the Geater Mysteries, perhaps because being more than just the Great God of Nature he is also one of the First Principles (as in Aristotle), and therefore he intrinsically knows all details and secrets and does not need to be initiated.

In the west, from the human point of view Dionysos is man's interpretation of nature. Demeter is the product of human understanding and ingenuity, as far as the power of mankind can go. Dionysos' career is extremely long, probably one of the longest among the western gods of the Indo-Europeans. From being just the violent forces of nature in the early beginnings, he became the *paredros* of Demeter associated to the very best of all fertile nature, giver of the divine drink "wine" (from Gk.(w)inos>*oinos* then Lt. *vinus*) and finally he is the one who takes gentle and *respectful* care of living beings, especially boys and girls, from birth to reproductive age, as well-shown in the poem by Longo (in: Merkelbach, 1988). This poem may well be a figurative description of the Dionysian Mysteries, which are otherwise partially described only in the texts of the tradition of the Orphic Mysteries.

In the east the search went farther. With the growing studies and analyses of various aspects of nature it was inevitable that each aspect, each force and all the energy interchanged among this multitude of forces, be recognized as divine or remain unexplained. All parts of nature, everything is sacred and godly. Everything is in fact sacred, from the very beginning of Vedic times, through the growing complexity of Brāhmaṇism and Hinduism, to present times. It would not be possible to identify any correlate of Demeter or Dionysos among the Vedic or Avestan gods and other deities.

Dionysos is involved with shepherds, herdsmen and other humans, also nymphs, satyrs, maenads, centaurs, theromorphs and deities who do not require assiduous attention by man, except for viticulture and the making of wine, the divine beverage. Demeter is Dionysos' complement and continuity; she is the evolved form, the domesticated nature which is in constant need of care and nurturing. Both names, Dionysos and Demeter and their derivates are currently alive in Europe, while those of the great Olympian gods, are not.

Demeter is the only woman, except for those of the original family and dynasty of Chronos, who is admitted to the selective elite of the Olympian pantheon with full godly honours. The other Greek goddesses were born divine when they were first created by man. Demeter embodies all the attributes of power which she acquired through her own merit, determination and the energy of womanhood, as opposed to the attributes and virtues of the major goddesses, such as *Hera* (= Juno), *Aphrodite* (= Venus), and *Artemis* (= Diana) who did not acquire their *timai* but received it as a grant. She surpasses all in her role of civilizer, teacher and professional agriculturist. She is not only a symbol but also the embodiment of action, she is will-power materialized. Her weapons are the subtle weapons of intelligence, cleverness and know-how. Her name is frequently used as an augural name to this day and as a sign of good omen.

Demeter recalls the personality of Mahādevī, the great Goddess who is imbued with the combined śakti of Sarasvatī, Lakṣmī, Pṛthvī and Kālī. However, unlike Mahādevī, Demeter does not subdue the forces of evil by violence (*Mahiṣāsuramardinī*), but she subdues the will of the Great God Zeus by her cleverness and magical power. However Kālī in her violent aspect is undoubtedly a much more ancient and primitive goddess than Demeter who is the most subtle expression of feminine power in the hedonistic humanism of ancient Greece. It is this humane generosity of Demeter that endeared her to humanity. For this reason she is still alive in the recurring names of Demeter and derivates, in the masculine **and** feminine forms, such as Demetra and Dmitry.

The Homeric Hymn to Demeter (II, 254-274), verse 263 *partim*, can be rendered in loose translation: "Demophont will have eternal privilege (= *timai*) because he climbed on my knees and slept in my arms. In his honour once yearly after the Sun completes his round of the seasons, the sons of the Eleusinians will fight a violent battle among them. I am the Venerable Demeter who more than anyone else offers joy and comfort to gods and men. You will . . . and I will myself teach the [initiation] rite (= *orgia*) so that you may perform it forever to appease my soul." This Demeter declares after she failed to give immortality to child Demophont due to the scene caused by his mother Metaneira. Demeter here recommends and predicts the ritual festival called **The Thrust** (= *balletys*), on which more below, under part III.

Summing up, we may say that the two great nature gods of the Indo-Europeans of the west, Dionysos and Demeter, the Power of Wild Nature and the embodiment of Domesticated Nature, are respectively the rationalisation and gradual understanding of the forces and energy of nature and of the development of man's knowledge and intimacy with those forces. Womanhood, as represented by Demeter, is deified by her own intrinsic merits. Energy and Knowledge, Power and Wisdom are all aspects of reality. Both Dionysos and Demeter are part of reality, material or immaterial, they are alive in the individual and collective sub-consciousness of the western Indo-European heritage specially among the rural people. My own great great grand father, and others before and after him, who were city dwellers of the corporation of engineers and architects, was called Demetrio (masculine form of Demeter in Italian) and frequently supervised the agricultural works on the lands where they had a large *"villa"* (= house) for the enjoyment of all the extended family, where we could spend all our vacations in full freedom. Urban life was for work and study, *real life* was in the country-side. During the general rejoicing at the time of vintage, all children were allowed to press grapes barefooted, like the *amorini* (= baby Eros = "little loved ones") who are singing, dancing, pressing, eating grapes and rejoicing during vintage as painted and carved on innumerable surfaces of vases and sarcophagi of the Etruscans and Graeco-Roman iconography.

As a deified human being, Demeter has as its nearest approximation Mahādevī, the greatest Goddess, Devī, daily invoked and nearest to the heart and mind of all Hindus. The image of the Mother is ever the strongest among men and women. Dionysos has no counterpart in the Hindu religion, but approximate correspondent of some of the different ages of Dionysos can partly be seen in the Vedic Rudra and later in Vedic Viṣṇu. The latest Dionysos integrated in the Orphic philosophy, shows details which recall some basic principles of the brahminical religion.

Finally, the more we analyse the details of the rituals of the Indo-Aryans and of the Indo-Europeans of the west for what concerns the respect and knowledge of nature's cycles, details of particular rites or sacrifices and concepts of metempsychosis as opposed to immortality, the more related they appear to be. More will be given below about the Indo-Iranians.

(D) Gods of the Indo-Europeans of the East

Gods of the Indo-Aryans: Agni, Rudra, Maruts and Vāsus, Varuṇa, Śiva, Indra.

Only a very brief overview will be given here of the most ancient Vedic gods and only some of what refers directly to the subject matter of this book.

Agni (= Fire), is Man's most ancient and first god. Fire is the epitome and embodiment of the concept of God. He is the intermediate link between men and God.

Rudra, the Maruts and the Vāsus. Rudra is the original god of nature; the Maruts are his children, friends and the personification of mild and violent winds and storms. The original eight Vāsus are also the personifications of different aspects of nature. Nature can be very violent though with no apparent cause. Rudra is unexplained, often misunderstood and awe inspiring.

Varuṇa is the evolved knowledge of nature; he is greatly respected for his great magical power and may be understood only to a point, within the limits of man's mental power.

Śiva is the ever-changing and continuously evolving nature and the infinite diversity of the Cosmos. He is the ubiquitous Great God present in all and every action, human or divine.

Indra is the man-made god created as man's own image. Indra is a great leader in battle and giver of material goods (booty), king and god of mankind, in peace and war. Originally Indra may have been the image of man as he saw himself, perhaps the image of the superman he wished to be, man's ideal of Man, an ideal which of course, he could never attain.

The concept of numbers, of order, place and position and numerology were probably the original basic theoretical achievements of the mind of ancient men, Indo-Europeans comprised. They are mentally represented in Vedism by the concept of *ṛta,* the law and order of the universe.

Other gods could be mentioned in this brief introduction. The Hindu Triad where Brahmā and Sarasvatī are the expression of Life and Knowledge; Viṣṇu and Lakṣmī are the Preservers and Wealth of Nature, and Śiva and Pārvatī, the personification of Action and Grace. These concepts are difficult to represent with the means of figurative arts, therefore representations in sculptures or paintings came late and are hieratic, symbolic and conventional, they are never meant to be portraits and do not pretend to have any physical likeness with the subject. They have remained so through the ages. These concepts are better expressed through the means of the performing arts. The variety, meaning and beauty at all levels and all types of Indian performing arts cannot be overestimated. These are also the concepts on which to meditate for the practice and development of spiritual life of laymen, *saṁnyāsī*, *sādhu*s, monks, hermits, anchorites and saints of all faiths. These subjects should be discussed in a context different from the present book. The selection of the gods mentioned above only roughly reflects some aspects of the evolution of the Hindu pantheon, but they are those that might be useful for an attempt to visualise an approximate "comparison" between Hindu and Greek gods.[19]

AGNI AND ATAR

In the Vedas, Lord Agni is common fire as well as the essence or abstract concept of fire. For this reason god Agni was said to be "fireness in fire" (Vannucci 1994). Agni is not regularly personified or figured in the Indian arts but he is omnipresent though usually represented only symbolically. Fire is, however, ever present in daily life and cultic practices. Whatever the understanding and explanation, all cultures throughout the world represented fire in one or other way, in iconography, in prayers, in song, in sculptures and, most important, in the mythology and people's folklore. I have argued earlier that the initial step that made man different from animals is man's ability to make, control and use fire for many purposes, including for worship. Even the most primitive men worship fire and use it with respect, for its luminosity and heat. The use of fire for cooking or roasting food came first but it is equally or more important in agriculture and as the means to harden wooden weapons, such as arrows or lance heads, harpoons, palisades, fences and the like. From respect for its usefulness, great power, purity and purifying capacity, for its beauty and intrinsic nature, devotion to fire is inherent in human nature and therefore had no birth. The living body is warm, it becomes cold after death. The fire god was worshipped as flames in the practice of many faiths, as lighted lamps or candles offered to a deity or the deceased, and as lightning and swamp fire. Fire may become dangerous if the rules of its rites are not obeyed, hence the need to remember, placate and worship Agni daily. Agni, like Kumarbi, was described "headless and footless."

In Vedism Agni (= Fire as God) is the *God first born.* In Zoroastrianism *atar* is the centre of worship and rituals. In the Vedas *Agni* is said to have *"appeared* as headless and footless . . . in the home of Holy Order . . . to fulfil the sacred law of worship" (*R̥V* IV; 1, 11-13). Similar to Zoroastrianism there are, in the practice of the Brāhmaṇical religion, different fires and fire altars, the *ahavaniya* fire being the most sacred. Agni is the god who preserved the seeker after Truth, which is the inner spiritual fire (*R̥V* I; 58,1) and Agni god is different from common man-made material fire (Vannucci 1999). Nowhere else are the Avesta and the *R̥gveda* as close as in their representation, understanding and worship of the Fire God, Atar and Agni respectively, a clear indication of their ancient and common origin. Finally, Fire as Light and Heat is the expression of the potential energy inherent in the material world. Agni is also the expression of the Life Principle which is not easy to define. Fire is the origin and manifestation of life **and** spiritual energy, thought and reason.

Agni is alternately known as the first God, the first principle or in Zoroastrianism, as the son of *"the Wise Lord, the Supreme God, Absolute Knowledge, Wisdom* and *Goodness,"* son of the Creator of all spiritual activities, called by man *"Ahura Mazda."* Among the great ancient civilizations and religions, Zoroastrianism is the one in which fire is most prominent. For them, Fire (= Atar) is the son of the Great Sage Ahura Mazda, the Supreme God. Fire is the link between man and Ahura Mazda. Sacrifice to Atar was meat that was offered while holding a small bunch of consecrated twigs called *barsom* in the other hand (Curtis, 1994). Fire was permanently held ablaze in every home. Atar was closely associated to *Mithra* identified with the Sun-god and still worshipped as *Mitra* in Rome during the first AD centuries. Askarov (1996a, p. 457) traces the earliest beliefs expressed in the Avesta as the cult of fire, in the human settlements in the oases of Transoxiana, east of the R. Amu Darya, at the "turn of the second and first millennia BC." The cult of fire is a marker of the areas where the Avesta ruled, specially in Khorazem, or lower Amu Darya.

Like in Vedic cultic practices, there were three main sacred fires; the holiest of the Zoroastrian fires was the *bahram* which was needed to strengthen the forces of Light and Goodness against the forces of Evil. *Bahram* (= *?Brahman?*) symbolizes Truth. I mentioned above the power of the word Truth among the Indo-Europeans and the concern with its presence and participation at all times in the life of man, woman and family. God *Mithra* grew in importance as it gradually migrated westwards towards the Mediterranean region and finally became **the** god of a semi secret religion that reached its greatest development in AD Rome. The followers met in the *Mithraeum*, frequently underground halls, where only men assembled to worship God Mithra and study the "Oriental" doctrine. *Mithra* represented Purity, Justice and Goodness and was often represented in paintings, bas-reliefs or carvings killing a bull. In a patriarchal society the bull was killed by a male god rather than by the fusion of the *Śakti* of the three Great Goddesses, as in Brāhmaṇism. Mithra or Mitra is alive in the liturgy of the Christian faith as the head-dress worn by bishops and higher prelates during religious ceremonies. The word *mithra* passed into the Greek language as *mitera* (= Lt. *mitra, mitria*) then *mitra* that was the name of the tiara worn by the ancient Persian sovereigns.

Zarathrustra, the founder of Zoroastrianism probably lived or was born in Chorasmia or in Sogdiana in Central Asia south of the Aral Sea. Though very little is known of his life and acts, he is supposed to have lived at about the time when the earliest R̥gvedic hymns were produced elsewhere by the Indo-Aryans. There are many linguistic and other similarities between the *gāthā*s (ancient-most songs of the original Indo-Iranian and Indo-Aryan cultures) of the *R̥gveda* and the Avesta.

Fire appears frequently in most religions, also in the exegesis and practice of the Christian religion, where it appears as tongues of fire, a manifestation of the Holy Spirit, the innate knowledge instilled into Christian saints and holy persons, or when Christ's disciples became imbued with the knowledge and wisdom that was needed for their proselytizing mission. Worship with lighted candles, processions holding lighted torches, offerings to and of ceremonial fire are common in most religions and popular customs at a variety of festivals or gatherings of the community at different occasions.

THE GRAECO-ROMAN TRADITION

Fire in the Graeco-Roman tradition is not a god, it is rather the practical means used to honour and involve the gods in human affairs, including for the smelting of ores and metallurgy, an art in which god Hephaistos (= Vulcanus, of Etruscan origin) is a great expert. Though fire is an important element of the liturgy and religious practices it has only the status of a minor god. Even the sacred fire of the Vestals is only the practical means and handmaid of the cult to Juno. The Vestals were the virgins in charge of keeping the sacred fire of the temple of goddess Vesta always bright and glowing in Rome, it represented and was the safeguard of many of the most noble aspirations and virtues of the Roman Man, whether warrior, law-maker, priest or politician, and of the virtues of the Roman Matron. The most sacred oath of the Roman man was to swear by "bread and salt" and the oath was witnessed and sanctified by fire who watched over its fulfilment. The hearth was the sacred fire of family and State, represented by the ubiquitous acronym S.P.Q.R. (= Senatus Populusque Romanus = The Senate and the People of Rome).

In the Graeco-Roman tradition fire is recognized as extremely important for the survival of mankind and the entire civilization of man. Though fire as a primary god does not exist as such in Greece and Rome, it was a very important entity, always regarded as an indispensable means to some prescribed end. Hephaistus is the god of fire without whom ores cannot be smelted into metals and metals cannot be made into tools, weapons, utensils. But neither Hephaistus is divinized fire, nor fire has the ambition to be an Olympian god. Fire for cooking food and for light and heat is respected and used but not worshipped. Fire is **not** seen as a nature god in the Graeco-Roman world. Natural fires also are ignored by religion and lightning is just one of Zeus' weapons, though the most obvious and frightening. Man-made fires are remembered as guardians, as means for worship or as tools for an end. No spiritual meaning is attached to fire, while god Agni in the east is that which sublimates the material into the immaterial energy or spirit. In the Hindu tradition the mythical Mātariśvan *brought* fire to Bhṛgu (*ṚV* I, 60.1) and instructed Twastar, the divinized or divine skilful artisan, how to use common fire to produce *material forms*. Mātariśvan *does not* *instruct* lord Agni, the god. Prometheus was one of the Titans who fought against Zeus; they were demons who correspond to the later Asura of the Indo-Aryans and the Devas of the Indo-Iranians. He was punished by the Olympian gods for bringing fire to man and was chained to the Caucasus mountains while a vulture feeds perpetually on his ever growing liver, and thereby fire, the god, died with the birth of this myth.

RUDRA, THE MARUTS AND THE VĀSUS

Rudra is the archaic, original nature god of the Indo-Aryans, often violent. Maruts and Vāsus, or only Maruts are also called Rudrīyas.[20]

Rudra is mentioned in the *ṚV* in more than 70 hymns. He is also often indirectly called father of the Maruts, deities of winds and storms, and is remembered as leader and friend of the eight Vāsus who are deities of a variety of natural phenomena. The name Rudra may originally have had the meaning of the colour "red."

Rudra is the ancient "self-dependent god," typically a nature god, impetuous, strong as a bull, healthy and knowledgeable of how to keep good health. His consort is *Pṛśni*, the many coloured earth (= endowed with many original virtues, great competence and capability), according to Sāyaṇa, their sons are the Maruts, and the Vāsus are their friends.

Rudra has a dazzling shape and form; he is armed with thunder, bows and arrows, and maces. He roars like a wild boar and shouts in the high sky. He is invoked as lord of sacrifice (*ṚV* I, 43, 1-9; II, 33, 1-15) who grants health to man and animals, provides balms and medicines and the "best invigorating food." He is the best physician and is prayed to for joy, health and strength, his wrath may be terrible when he is angered.

In *ṚV* V, 42, 11, Rudra is eulogized as "Asura," meaning in very ancient times a being imbued with great magical power and the Maruts are characterized as the "mighty ones generated by the seed of Rudra in Great Mother Prisni, "for man's welfare." The association of Rudra with *Soma* (*ṚV* VI, 74) indicates that at a late stage Rudra was not only the great god of nature, but that his power had grown to admit that under his tutelage medicines and the best food could be prepared also by man. Medicines in this context is a word that includes all nature's gifts from fruits to curative medicines and food for man and his animals. The last of the gifts mentioned, namely *Soma* could refer to agriculture, it is known that primitive agriculture goes back several millennia BC in Asia. In his association with *Soma*, Rudra is invoked to keep sorrow away from mankind, thanks to his loving kindness.

Ancient-most Rudra is described as having braided or matted hair (= *kapardin*, as very ancient men had, in *R̥V* I, 114, 1-11), to be a roaring roarer and also to bring joy, to be the lord of heroes, to have hands full of medicines and of "food that mortals eat." For these reasons men pray to strengthen Rudra's might and pray to spare them and their progeny from his wrath. Rudra is invoked to give 100 years of life to his worshipper and to imbue the worshipper's children with his own personality.

Rudra is further (*R̥V* II, 33, 5) described as the tawny, fair-cheeked god with a gracious hand that brings comfort. Stress is put on the tawny, fair cheek complexion of the god and on his many variable forms, alternately as a slayer of the dangerous beasts of the forest. In *R̥V* VII, 40, 5, Rudra is said to propitiate the many aspects and activities of Viṣṇu from whom "Rudra gained the Rudra strength." Also in a later hymn (*R̥V* I, 72, 4) it is said that the holy ones "revealed the power of Rudra," thereby Rudra is assumed along with Lord Agni among the highest gods. Rudra is absorbed in the personality of Lord Agni, also an original nature god, in *R̥V* II, 1, 6, as the "Asura of mighty heaven." Implicitly, the original nature gods are **one and many**, manifest under different forms. Finally in *R̥V* X, 125, Vāk (= speech personified) is said to travel with Rudras and Vāyus (= winds) who are the retinue of Rudra, which indicates the teaching and training aspects of a mature nature god.

In *R̥V* II, 33 there is also a curious allusion to the "fair complexioned bull" Rudra, who is prayed to for long life, protection from diseases and enemies and to be spared from his anger, the god and the Maruts are here also prayed to "save plants which had been selected by forefather Manu." This appears to be an allusion to a legend according to which Manu kept some seeds which he saved in his vessel at the time of the great deluge. The memory of a great flood (= *pralaya*) is recalled in the Vedas and a deluge of snow and frost (= *praleya*, derived from *pralaya, apud* Pāṇini, ref. Bhargava, 2001, p. 59), is referred to also in the Avesta. Would the memory of the deluge be an input from the story of the widespread flood in Central Asia, or would it be a mere coincidence? Also the tawny, fair complexion of Rudra, and of his later personification as Śiva that can be deduced from several hymns, suggests derivations, imports and exchanges of culture already in the very ancient past, with other Indo-European and other people from Central Asia. Forefather Manu is also credited (*R̥V* I; 112, 16, acc. Sāyaṇa) with having taught man how to sow barley and other grains. Though the verse could be a late interpolation into the ancient oral tradition, it illustrates clearly the evolution from unskilled man to civilized man, the doer, the artisan, the farmer and agriculturist. Most ancient civilizations considered pastoralism a stage prior to the acculturation of man into a civilized community.

There is no sign of Demeter among the Indo-Europeans of the east and some of the attributes of Manu appear to correspond to those of Demeter. This is as it should be, it is the symbolic description of the evolution of man due to the development of agriculture, whichever god presided over the process.

In conclusion Rudra is typically a nature god who exists in its generous and peaceful moods but like Demeter, he can become violent, fearful and destructive if he is not respected by man. He can also become violent for reasons beyond man's understanding. I believe that if we had a verbal description of the proto-Dionysos of the Indo-Europeans of the west, it would be very similar to the R̥gvedic description of Rudra, which is here only briefly summarized. Much more could be said of god Rudra, but the quotes above are sufficient to characterize this most ancient Indo-European nature god of the Indo-Aryans. Inevitably the personality of Rudra recalls that of the pre-Hellenic proto-Dionysan god "Eros Primigenius" or that of "Proterogonos"or "Proteurhythmos," identified as the original nature god or gods and one of Aristotle's "first principles." While the western original nature god is lost in the nebulous past of pre-Hellenic and Greek mythology the howling Rudra has never ceased to exist.[20]

The Maruts, mentioned above as the "*Marutta*," are invoked in their capacity of gods who preside and watch upon the correct implementation of contracts and treatises, as far as Asia Minor and West Asia and as early as the second millennium BC. Rudra among the Indo-Aryans is *manifest* as much or more than the archaic god "Phanes" (= the Manifest) of the very ancient pre-Hellenic Greeks. Rudra is also a leader and friend of all aspects of the dynamism of nature, personalized or not, living and non-living, like storms or the inheritance of genetic characters from parents to offspring (*R̥V* II, 33, 1). Together with Vāk (= word, speech), Rudra travels with the Rudrīyas and the Vāsus. Similarly Lord Viṣṇu will later on go round and round with the Mantras and mature Dionysos will be accompanied by the Horae (= seasons) which are also said to go round and round. These are the rhythms which regulate nature and were recognised and studied during the long process of the acculturation of man.[20]

MARUTS AND VĀSUS

The Maruts are mentioned directly or indirectly in about 200 *R̥V* hymns. They are characterized as *sucayah* (= pure, *R̥V* I, 72, 3), as such they are present with Agni at the *agnicayana* rite, they receive their share of the sacrificial food and thereby become major gods. Originally they are ancient gods of nature, glorious, resplendent in their car and gather glory along their course, they are well armed, possess great strength, they can shake heaven and earth and destroy mountains (*R̥V* I, 37, 12). The Maruts may be beneficial as mild rain, or be highly destructive as violent storms. They are sons of "rain-pouring Rudra" (*R̥V* VI; 56, 3). They are deities of floods and mountains which they fight with sparkling brilliance, some of them are sons of Rodasi (= lightning personified, *R̥V* I, 167, 4) who rides in the Maruts' chariot. Maruts in general are said to be sons of Pr̥śnī and usually represent more earthly phenomena than the heaven-dwelling Rudra, though they are also sometimes said to dwell in the sky or heaven. Maruts are slayers of demons and never grow old (*R̥V* I, 85, 1-2), only in late hymns they are recognized as major gods and their abode is said to be in heaven. The Maruts represent the eternal wish for perennial youth. A large number and variety of attributes (*R̥V* VIII, 20,1-6) are given to the Maruts, including that of physicians who "cast to the ground our sick man's sickness, replace the dislocated limb" and with time they acquire more functions and are called to represent and protect man at a greater variety of occasions. In the second millennium BC they were invoked as gods also by rulers of the Kassite dynasty of Babylon.

Vāsu is the imaginary embodiment of all Vāsus, he is often recalled with the *Rudrīyas* (= descendants of Rudra).

Vāsu (= good, gentle, warm-hearted god) may be an identified personality, or may be used as a collective epithet for all the eight Vāsus. Vāsu is mentioned as having been produced at the original sacrifice of Manu together with Rudras and Ādityas. Manu is identified with Prajāpati in *ṚV* I; 45, 2. The Vāsus, allies of Agni, are evidently very ancient elements and forces of nature admitted and prayed to as protective deities. The Vāsus praise Savitur and among other benefits which they gifted to man, they clear man's path from dangers. They are also capable of discriminating truth from falsehood. They keep man's dwellings safe and keep guard to ward off enemies and curses. For these purposes offerings are made to the Vāsus who possess all wealth. Vāsu's treasure is rich and all Vāsus are eternally young and they can increase man's power (*ṚV* VIII; 21, 8). The Vāsus work with Lord Agni, the universal energy, and are occasionally identified with fire. They evidently represent the elementary forces of nature which man was able to recognize, qualify and then use since pre-historic times. Eventually besides using these forces, man learned to protect himself from them.

Among a large number of nature deities, another, god of winds, Vāyu acquires with time more precise qualifications, attributes and duties; he may be related to the development of the art of navigation. The evolution of ancient nature gods took place at the same time and in tune with man's growing knowledge of nature.

On the other hand, the Greek Olympian gods were static, rigid in the stereotyped majestic glory of a well defined character and function of a State religion planned for political use. The Olympians did not have the flexibility needed to adapt to changes in the environment, to changes in people's behaviour and to the increase of man's knowledge and understanding of nature. The complexity and flexibility of the Vedic gods was one factor that enabled them to evolve alongside with the growth of knowledge, science and techniques that in turn enabled man to adapt to the physical world he had to live in and of which he knew to be a part. Practical knowledge contributed to the development of arts and crafts and lifestyles compatible with the variety of environments where man lived in the east. Gods evolved and new deities came into being. No civilization can survive if it is not compatible with the ecological realities of its domain.

VARUṆA, GOD

The very ancient god Asura Varuṇa is the greatest of the nature gods of the Indo-Aryans, Indo-Europeans of the east. Though both Rudra and Varuṇa are also nature gods, Varuṇa has an entirely different meaning and personality from Rudra and the Rudrīyas. While the latter are mostly personifications of the physical forces of nature, Varuṇa is more subtle, difficult to define or, as described by Dandekar, "his essential personality is somewhat enigmatic." According to Vannucci (1999) he represents among other aspects, also immaterial reality and for this reason he can neither be described in detail nor fully understood. His presence is felt at all times and everywhere, but it is not easy to say exactly how and when he uses his power. Varuṇa is invoked and eulogized under a variety of epithets in about 120 hymns of the *ṚV* alone. First of all and most frequently he is invoked as a god, a magician, an asura with great magical powers who includes and envelopes everything else in his fold, he achieves the purpose of life and existence of man. He is the supreme deity, chief of the world of natural and moral order, king of heaven and earth, punisher of the wicked, he has the power to discover and pardon the sins of sincere penitents, he is the discriminator of truth and falsehood, chief of the lords of natural and moral order, he is founder of society, he is brother of man and has many other attributes. His consort is Vāruṇī who was invited together with Āgneyi, Indrāṇī and other goddesses to drink *soma* at the sacrifice (*ṚV* I; 22, 12 — V; 46, 8 — VII; 34, 22). Varuṇī is mentioned in a matter of fact manner and is not given any special attribute except that of being the consort of the great Āditya Varuṇa.

Dandekar (1997, 1979a, 1979b, 1981) refers repeatedly to the great Asura Varuṇa, the great god with infinite *māyā* (= magical power), meaning something that cannot be readily recognized or understood, the existence of which is attributed to the existence and power of a Supreme Being, itself insufficiently known by man. Following in the footprints of the master, Vannucci (1999) recognizes Varuṇa as one of the greatest gods of Vedic man, one of the ancient-most, the first of the seven Ādityas, sons of Aditi the unbound Mother of Infinity. The concept of Infinity or Infinite is present in the mind of Vedic man since the most ancient times we can reckon with. I would like to point out that the concept of Infinite is logically, but not mathematically, a corollary of the concept or idea of the **cypher zero** that has no value, or all values as a function of its position in relation to other cyphers, **or its position in a number with many cyphers.** Varuṇa is the only Āditya who is not bound and the only one who holds the *pasa* (= fetters, bonds) or "**limitations**" with which he "binds or frees for good or bad human beings and everything else in the cosmos." Everything in the cosmos is therefore limited, or bound by its own nature which emanates from Asura Varuṇa. In Aristotelic language we would say that Varuṇa is the embodiment of the first principle which emerged after the creation of the cosmos.

Hymn *R̥V* X, 129, attributed to *r̥ṣi* Prajāpati Paramestin, states that "at the beginning there was existent or there was non existent (= *sat* or *asat*)," then after considering the steps in the progress of differentiation of the cosmos, the *r̥ṣi*, the sage seer of this hymn, declares: "who knows and who can declare when and where-from comes this creation?." The scientific critical attitude of Vedism is perhaps nowhere else as clearly stated as in *R̥V* X; 129, 7 that reads:

> He, the first origin of this creation, whether he formed it all or did not form it,
>
> Whose eye controls this world in highest heaven, he verily knows it, or perhaps he knows not (transl. Griffith).

It is also said by the same *r̥ṣi* in the same hymn, that at one of the steps in the drama of creation, the power of Warmth (= energy) which had been hidden in darkness, became manifest as Kāma (= desire). This is the same concept that created the *Eros primigenius* or *Eros proterogonos* mentioned above. Kāma is the primordial germ and seed of **Spirit.** This original principle or essence, Kāma, Energy, Desire, Union, Affinity, Life is represented or personified in Vedism by Varuṇa, the only unfettered first son of Aditi, the indescribable, unimaginable "beginning" that extends everywhere at all times. Throughout the Vedas, this "most ancient," "primitive," "original" Power or God is the great Asura Varuṇa, the wise Asura, king of wide dominions (*R̥V* I; 24, 14) who holds the fetters of everything and all principles of the Cosmos. Varuṇa is closely associated with *r̥ta*, the law and order of the universe. He is also associated with *māyā*, the idealised concept of magical power, indefinite and indescribable. Varuṇa imbued with great magical power, inevitably becomes the **lord of immaterial reality**, the **Reality that cannot be perceived by the sense organs of man.** Rudra, the Rudrīyas and other deities of material reality are the governors of what man can see, hear, touch, smell, taste and think, forces which man can represent with the mind and can think about. Man can observe, study, experiment upon and define the laws that govern material reality, he can draw conclusions about the inter-relations of cause and effect of the phenomena which he can perceive through his senses, but there is much more that man cannot sense or explain. There are relations of cause and effect which are only guessed and which escape his reasoning and understanding. Vedic Man confines to the realm of *māyā*, the primordial powers whose effects are tangible and visible but have no easy or obvious explanation or origin. Man's reason however, demonstrates that there is much more that man has not yet, and probably will never be able to, equate with factual knowledge. In Vedism myths are born as a first attempt to explain the multitude of phenomena witnessed by early man. In the Greek tradition of the Olympian gods, myths are mostly disposed of and responsibilities are thrown on the lap of the Olympians and their acolytes.

MYTHS

Myths are self-born creations of man's mind to "explain" the unexplainable. Gods imbued with mysterious powers are created. However, what is interesting from the point of view of the scientist, is the critical attitude of the ancient *r̥ṣis* and most probably also of the *magi*, though at present we do not know enough about their teachings. All that exists in the domain of the *māyā* of Lord Varuṇa is subject to the query: "who knows or maybe knows not"! *Māyā* exists, but "**truth**" (= at present usually called material reality or just "reality") is not easily discovered or in Vedic terms: "uncovered." The perceived reality of *māyā* explains the passionate supplication of *ṛṣi* Vasistha to Varuṇa, his god, the great Asura, begging to help him to **understand**. As mentioned earlier (Vannucci, 1999), Vedic sages considered understanding as man's "*raison d'etre*" and the "scope of their life on earth." The final intention was to have *knowledge* with which to acquire *wisdom* for the benefit of mankind in unison with the world man lives in, and all the cosmos.

The western Dionysos has some traits in common with Rudra. The two gods accept what they see and know, they both use nature in the best ecologically sound way, they both promote evolution and progress for the wise use of nature, such as agriculture or viticulture, they both pay their respects to the natural laws that govern the world. But by no stretch of imagination can Varuṇa be compared to Dionysos, there is no counterpart of Varuṇa in Greek mythology and even Zeus the father, King and god of man and gods, is only a god of material reality.

It is significant that the primordial appearance of the god who would become Dionysos, or nature personified, was *Phanes* the manifest whose acts are obvious, he was accepted and recognized in the restricted sense of some of his unexplained aspects. This Phanes somehow reminds the Great Asura Varuṇa, the immaterial reality difficult to describe and define, the god who can expand the governance of man exactly *because* he understands man's limitations. On the other hand Śiva, the great power of recycling nature, gradually replaces Rudra in all material expressions of a culture evolving into a civilization, but Varuṇa remains ever present alongside with man. Through the study of nature and of the links between causes and effects, Varuṇa helps man to acquire knowledge and understanding of the systems around him, to which man will be forever bound. Varuṇa thus becomes associated with water which is, along with fire as energy, an indispensable element for sustaining **Life.** Varuṇa **Is,** Exists, but does not represent and **is not the embodiment** of "immaterial reality," Rudra **is** the personification **and embodiment** of material reality.

It is clear why Varuṇa is not usually represented in iconography.

ASURA

About the word *asura*. In present day understanding, the name *asura* is used as a synonym of demon. Originally however, and when associated to god Varuṇa, the Ādityas and other very ancient powerful gods or the dual Vedic Mitra-Varuṇa which characterizes an entity or being endowed with unusual behaviour and capable of performing in a manner which cannot be explained or even visualized by man, originally the word asura refers to superhuman beings. Asuras were gifted with great *māyā* and power which could be used for good or evil. Even the ancient sages could not understand fully what *māyā* (= magic power) is, although the "vision" of the sages enabled them to "see" what the eyes of the common man did not see. It is said in *R̥V* I; 151, 4: "Asuras, ancient immortal gods, righteous ones proclaim aloud the Holy Law."

The very ancient myths of Indo-European of the east as well as those of the west describe the rivalry between the powers of Good and those of Evil. Many aeons ago there were long fights between these two groups of superhuman beings, gods and asuras who contended for supremacy. The myths of the Indo-Aryans say that finally the gods had the upper hand while the asuras became the opposers and enemies of the gods, as were the Titans of the Greek myths.

In the myths of the Avesta the names are reversed, but the concept is the same and Ahura (= Asura) Mazda is the highest good while the *Deva* (= Gods) are evil. Summing up, the word Asura among the Indo-Aryans originally refers to primordial natural physical forces later personalized into beings with great magical (= unexplained, unimaginable, unbelievable) power which eventually became powers to be feared. While gods should be respected for their power they should *also* be eulogized. Other very ancient gods are originally also called Asura, amongst others, Indra (*R̥V* I; 54 *et al.*), Dyaus (*R̥V* VI, 131); Savitur (*R̥V* IV, 53, 1 *et al.*); Parjanya (*R̥V* V, 63, 3); Mitra-Varuṇa (*R̥V* V; 63, 6 — *R̥V* X; 177, 1) and other archaic or original deities, such as Agni and Sūryā. However above and beyond everything else, the Absolute Self Existent, the Godhead **IS,** but does not exist to serve man and to grant him favours. **IT** exists to be respected, honoured, cared for and loved.

Some of the epithets given to Varuṇa are: Supreme deity, Discoverer of sin, Forgiver of Sin, Discriminator of Truth and Falsehood, Chief of the Lords of Natural and Moral Order, Punisher of the wicked, Forgiver of the sins of penitents, Founder of human society as the "brother of man" and others.

Asura Varuṇa in Greek terms could be called *Primigenius* (= first generated) or *Proterogonos* (= originally created, one of the *first principles* of Aristotle) while another great nature god, Lord Viṣṇu could be called *Proteurhythmos* (= original true rhythms or cycles). The ancient sages, specially the seven *ṛṣis* and others went into great details in their study of nature, hence the unending growth of knowledge and of the corresponding growth of the Hindu pantheon, the multitude of gods and deities and the sanctity of all nature in its myriad aspects and components, its innumerable myths and legends, its religious tolerance and great advance in the field of experimental and speculative sciences and above all of logics and mathematics. All aspects of tradition tell stories from which we learn some truth.

In conclusion, the scientifically critical attitude of Vedism is evident throughout the Vedas and Vedānta. Whenever an explanation or interpretation of natural phenomena is offered, the door is left open to any other interpretation, explanation or solution that could best fit the observed reality. The door is open to the evolution and development of science and what we now call progress in the knowledge of nature. Since most of the ancient myths represent steps in the understanding of the world in which we live and of man as a biological species, they continue to be alive to this day and will probably remain alive because of their intrinsic intellectual and historical interest, even when not correct from the point of view of experimental science. The scientific attitude led to the proverbial Hindu tolerance, to the avoidance of the rigidity of dogmatic statements and to the Indian acceptance of all religions during the millennia of evolution.

Śiva, continuously evolving nature — Śiva is the Auspicious One. As mentioned above Rudra is, similarly to Dionysos and his retinue, the material, observed reality. The similarity however, does not go further. In fact, the great knowledge of nature as expounded in the Vedas eventually evolved into a philosophical system in which the many various aspects of Rudra differentiated into the personalities of Śiva, Indra and others, all of them absorbed into a comprehensive philosophical system. The basic system of the Hindu religion is often schematically described thus: Brahmā is the Creator of the world of Life, Viṣṇu is the Preserver and Śiva the Destroyer. Śiva would better be described as the recycler of matter and energy in the cosmos. He stepped over and controlled Kala (= Time) standing over whom he performed the furious Tandava dance of Creation. Viṣṇu as the *trivikrama avatāra* encompasses the three worlds, heaven, earth and the world in between them, regulates the seasons and preserves natural cycles, such as astronomical cycles, day and night, the years and species' cycles and metamorphoses like tadpoles into frogs. Needless to say, this common simplification only vaguely corresponds to the full meaning of the gods of the Hindu triad. Śiva is in fact more like the Power, the Competence, and the Great Forces of Nature which produces and reproduces living beings. Śiva is the energy required for the evolution and constant transformation of living and non-living nature everywhere and at all times. Śiva only destroys as a step to and transfer towards creation, as transformation of dead matter into new living matter, from the dead body into the new body, the cycle of life and death of the body and of the spirit, and the geological, hydrographical and geographical changes of the material world. Thus man and other species of living beings are the result of the incessant working of nature rather than the result of specific acts of creation.

In conclusion,[21] as a result of the sages' studies and visions mentioned as "eyes that Soma gives" (*R̥V* I; 139, 2), the great original nature gods Rudra and Varuṇa, one as observed reality and the other as the great magician imbued with *māyā*, grow into a philosophical system inadequately called the Hindu Trinity: Brahmā, Viṣṇu and Śiva. We can also read the Triad as Intellectual activity typical of human beings, man's perception of the visible (= material) and of the invisible (= processes) of nature. The energy to keep the system in motion is provided by Agni which in turn marks the passage from ideas, or basic principles, to the unity of all Creation (*R̥V*; X, 191, last hymn of the *R̥V* Saṁhitā). Even what appears to be static is not so and surely not for a long time and is different at different time scales. Nothing is static forever. The critical constructive attitude and tolerance of Vedism is the secret of the ease shown by Indians to accept and adapt to contemporary theoretical and applied scientific knowledge, developments and innovations. Differently from the stereotyped Olympian gods of the Homeric epics and of the *Theogonia* of Hesiod, the meticulous development of a basic philosophy sufficiently tolerant to admit various viewpoints and contrasting ideas, the ever evolving traditional knowledge of the Vedas and Vedānta continued to live, while the theological system of ancient Greece lived its originally planned role only down to exhaustion. On the other hand the science of the ancient Graeco-Roman ethos and pragmatism survive in the language of modern sciences and philosophies and are the origin of the contemporary western scientific and technical civilization. What should be noticed is the divergent evolution of the basic philosophies and lifestyles of Europe and India.

INDRA

God Indra is the god most frequently invoked in the Vedas. He is also one of the most studied by scholars ancient and modern and for this reason Indra has usually been referred to as the most important of the Hindu gods. Rather than most important, Indra is one of the earliest gods, a leader as would be needed, obeyed and revered by people inclined to migrate and move around. Some of the most authoritative recent studies are those by Dandekar (1997) and by Uma Chakravarty (1997). Vannucci (1999) summarized the knowledge of this most important deified king of the Indo-Aryans, under his aspect of material reality and leader of the Arya tribes of the east. It is significant that in the treaties drafted between the Indo-European Hittite kings and their neighbours, Egyptians and others (see Part I) the following Vedic gods are called to witness: Mitra, frequently associated to Varuṇa in relation to legal testimony in general; Asura Varuṇa and King Indra as spiritual and temporal powers; the Aśvins also called Nasatyas, notably astronomical markers of time, such as day and night, seasons and years. The Aśvins are also learned in periodical practices such as agriculture. Indra is prayed to for victory to obtain abundant cattle and other valuable booty. The gods called to witness the Treaties drawn between the Hittite kings and their opponents are the gods who *represent or are* basic powers needed to create and sustain an organised civilization, they include also the "god of tempests," god of the people ruled by the Indo-Aryan Hittites.

GODS OF THE INDO-IRANIANS

The Avesta was transmitted orally like the Vedas, generation after generation by the *Magi* (= priests) of ancient western Iran during centuries before they were put in writing. The language of the Avesta is "Avestan," which is the language of eastern Iran. The hymns of the Avesta were formulated probably around the beginning of the second millennium BC or earlier. Avestan is very close to archaic Sanskrit and is not fully developed grammatically. According to tradition the first text was written with golden letters on oxhide parchment. It was written in cuneiform script and is dated 1400-1200 BC which is earlier than the advent of Zarathustra who lived around or earlier than 1000 BC. Zarathustra probably lived in Chorasmia or further to the east of northern Iran and south of the Aral Sea.

Prophet Zarathustra is the reputed singer of the *gāthā*, ancient-most hymns of the Avesta. Sanskrit *gāthā*s are mentioned only once in the *R̥V*. They are mentioned as ornaments of the bridal robe and part of the dowry of Sūryā, daughter of the sun god Sūrya. Sanskrit *gāthā*s are also very ancient songs of the Arya tradition, but they are not included in the Vedas as they are regarded to be popular, non religious, profane songs. Though the name is the same and both belong to the archaic tradition, the content of the Avestan and Vedic *gāthā*s is different. The most ancient myths and legends of the Avesta that have come down to us are included in the Yashts, hymns of the Indo-Iranians, dated earlier than the advent of Zarathustra. The original written texts were kept at Istakr, a cultural centre well known down to historical times. They were burnt by order of Alexander after his victory over the Persian Achaemenid king Darius III.

Most probably the complete written text of the Avesta took shape under the rule of the Sassanian dynasty not earlier than the sixth century AD. That version has not survived and what has survived are texts of the first and second centuries AD which are only a fraction of the complete Avesta as compiled in the first centuries of Parthian (174 BC-224 AD) rule in Persia. What we have today is the Avesta as re-written in the thirteenth or fourteenth centuries AD. It was first translated into a modern European language in 1771 by the French traveller Anquétil du Perron. This early rendering of an entirely new original text was inevitably incomplete and is not too reliable. The sacred texts of the Avesta are especially interesting in the context of this book. The Yashts (= hymns) narrate the ancient myths of pre-Zarathustra times. The translation of the Avesta into English by James Darmesteter (first publ. 1887), is to this day probably the best and most authoritaive text of the Avesta in a modern language. It is the text studied for the present work.

AVESTA AND R̥GVEDA

The Avesta and the *R̥gveda* are not only related by language, but most significantly also by the characterization of the gods common to both religions. The groups called Indo-Iranian and Indo-Aryan, who all called themselves Arya, undoubtedly have a common origin and come from the same stock of the very ancient past, when they still lived in the original homeland of the Indo-Europeans. For unknown reasons, the groups respectively called Indo-Arya and Indo-Iranian migrated at different times to different destinations. The Indo-Aryans moved away from their original homeland about the last centuries of the fourth millennium BC and the Indo-Iranians in the early second millennium BC (*fig.* 1). Changes in the traditional culture had taken place in the interval, as evident from the divergent evolution of old and new myths.

The ancient religion of the Indo-Europeans of the east, including both Indo-Iranians and Indo-Aryans is documented in the Vedas and the Avesta. Both were and remained nature religions. The fundamental difference between the two is that among the Indo-Iranians the belief of the over-powering importance of fire, as the means and symbol of the never-ending **fight between Good and Evil**, grew until when worship of fire became the centre and scope of cultic practices. The Indo-Aryans on the other hand preserved the belief in the over-powering importance of *r̥ta*, the **Law and Order that is and sustains** the structure and function of the universe, which is composed of a very large number of entities living in harmony and all considered to be part of the Absolute, the Self-existent. Disaster follows where and when this harmony is disrupted.

One of the most interesting aspects of the technical evolution of the Indo-Iranian civilization is that, in its passionate belief and adoration of fire, engineers, architects and artisans developed ever more elaborate structures and ornamentations for tombs and mausoleums and for the worship of God. Persepolis, religious capital and temple city (521-463 BC) built by the Achaemenid dynasty, is an example of the grandiose architectural, religious and administrative ideal realized to match the infinite majesty of the divine, an ideal and concept beautifully continued by Islamic arts. Conceptually comparable temple cities were developed only much later by the Indo-Aryans. In what is now Iran, the structures for the worship of God and the triumph of Good over Evil started with the building of fire platforms or altars which grew into ziggurats, then Fire temples, tombs and palaces well into AD times. Structures evolved with increasing complexity that eventually matured into well known Persian and Indo-Islamic art. An early example of this is the tomb of Ismail Samanid at Bokhara (907 AD), to mention only one of the early structures of Islamic art, the construction of which required the inventiveness, calculations and skill of architects and engineers and the ability of the artisans who produced more and more intricate designs and details such as the wicker-work-like façade of Ismail Samanid's tomb and eventually the extremely numerous decorations in colours and materials for all types and structures, from hamams to palaces and mosques.

Briefly, the history of Persian architecture begins at the time of the early Indo-European migrations, in the late fourth millennium BC, e.g. tombs at Tepe Gawra, with remains dated 3200 BC. Next to nothing is known about the people who lived there. Later unconditional respect and worship of mountains, fire, life and rivers grew and gradually evolved into Zoroastrianism and worship became finally focused on Atar, fire. The nature of the early gods of the Indo-Aryans is comparable, but they did not find expression in extraordinary architectural structures until very late in AD times. It is indeed a good example of the differentiation of cultures as a function of geography, climates, ecology, neighbourhood, history, and, above all, inspiration.

The Sumerians, inventors of the cuneiform script were also great engineers and architects and great traders. The older clay tablets inscribed with cuneiform script are accounts and inventories of goods. They "arrived in small numbers" in Mesopotamia in the late fourth millennium BC. They were known to have arrived from the sea and spoke a language different from that of the local population. The language was most probably not an Indo-European language. Their original homeland is unknown, though trade with the Harappan civilization is sure. The great cultural contribution of the Sumerians to the world civilizations is the invention of the syllabic phonetic cuneiform script. Thanks to this bench-mark invention, the Indo-Iranians and the Indo-European Medes and people speaking different languages could put on written record historical facts much earlier than the Indo-Aryans. The written text of the *Śruti*, of the *Smṛti* and of the Ītihāsas are late, perhaps not earlier than early AD times, though the facts, legends and myths recorded are many centuries older.

The Indo-Aryan ancient culture was called by modern authors a "pantheistic naturalism," even when not textually described in exactly these terms. This however, is not correct because nature is not worshipped as such, but as the *expression* of the law and order (= *ṛta*) of the Universe and as a *manifestation* of the gods or superhuman powers. For this reason, everything is sacred. Vedism, Brāhmaṇism, Hinduism and Zoroastrianism are all based on a philosophy that endeavours to find the best way to live in tune, peace and harmony with the material and immaterial realities of the world, of human society and of the entire cosmos. The early Indo-Aryan and Indo-Iranian sages sought what we could call an ecologically valid, simple way of living. The Hindu ideal is still mentioned as: "Want not what is not essential for sustaining life." Visitors to India often make the confusion between "a simple way of life" and "a miserable lifestyle." Though undoubtedly there may be poverty, life is not always miserable.

The Indo-Iranian and the Indo-Aryan cultures had in common with Central Asian civilizations important engineering techniques, specially very clever and imaginative systems for water resources saving and management which were needed to obtain and conserve water in dry regions and in areas where rain falls abundantly only during certain seasons and restricted periods. The ancient link canal between R. Tigris and R. Euphrates is an example of hydrological works that were essential for the development of the mesopotamian civilizations. After a common origin, long enough to build and concretize common bases, the myths and arts of the Indo-Iranian and of the Indo-Aryan cultures and civilizations, including engineering and architecture, evolved independently along different paths. This question, however, is beyond the scope of this book and we now return to the ancient past, the proto-, the pre-history and early history of the Indo-Europeans of the east.

ARYAN GODS

The ancient religion and gods of the Indo-Europeans of the east, the Indo-Iranians and the Indo-Aryans (linguistically *Iran* = *Arya*), are documented in various parts of the Avesta and *Ṛgveda* respectively. They clearly indicate common origin but divergent evolution of the two groups. Though both the Indian and the ancient Iranian tradition are nature religions, differences are clear. The Indo-Iranian tradition is alive to date in the religion of the Parsi (= Pharsi, the people and language of the land of Phars in south-western Iran) now residents of India and elsewhere.

In the *ṚV* the *ṛṣis* (= sages) endeavour to "uncover" (= discover, expose, find out) Truth. "Truth is the base that bears the Earth: Sūrya sustains the Sun" (*ṚV* X; 85,1). The *ṛṣis* then rationalised over their findings about Truth to acquire knowledge of the world around us with the purpose of understanding. Understanding should lead to wisdom and to a correct, appropriate lifestyle according to the accepted ethics. All of *ṚV* VII, mainly the Vaśiṣṭh hymns have this predetermined goal in mind. The Śruti are the visions, observations and rationalisations of the *ṛṣis*, believed to arise to consciousness from the divine which exists in each one of us. In the Avesta, the belief in revelation from outside the self, through Prophet Zarathustra, is supreme. Another fundamental difference refers to Agni and Atar. In the *ṚV* Fire (= Agni) is the "first born" while Fire in Zoroastrianism is only the seventh and last element to be created, as reported in the Bundahism (= Creation myth). Only later, after the preachings of Zarathustra and up to present, Atar (= Fire) acquires the central position in the religious beliefs of the Indo-Iranians. However the cultic pactices of the two religions have many significant elements in common, such as the daily worship of fire at home. There is one fire each for priests, warriors and workers among the Indo-Iranians. The important gods and goddesses of the pre-Zarathustra Iranians (probably earlier than eleventh-twelfth centuries BC), were incorporated into Zoroastrianism which is essentially based on the belief of the antagonism between light and darkness, good and evil and the wise Ahura Mazda incessantly opposed by the destructive Angra Manyu. Men are requested to support "Good" against "Evil" and to get involved in the battle for righteousness at all times.

Strictly speaking Zoroastrianism is not a synonym of Mazdeism, as frequently mentioned, because the latter accepts also deities other than Ahura-Mazda.

GODS OF THE INDO-IRANIANS

In brief the earliest ancient gods of the Indo-Iranians are some and the same as ancient Ṛgvedic gods, even if somewhat different in attributes and character.

- Ahura Mazda and Angra Manyu (later = Ahirman) are the antithesis of each other. Ahura Mazda is the Great Sage imbued with absolute Goodness, eternally at odds with the all-evil demon Angra Manyu. Every human being must make a choice between the two, an expression of the full concept of *Liber Arbitrium* accepted by Mazdeism. Ahura Mazda is the Great God of the fully evolved religion of the Indo-Iranians.

- Goddess Ardvi Sura Anahita (= ? Amitābha of *ṚV* V; 53) (Yasht V) is the goddess of all waters on the surface of the earth and she is also goddess of the cosmic ocean, she is the source of all life. "Then came Ardvi Sura Anahita, O Zarathustra. She came down from the stars to earth that Mazda made" (Yasht V, 88). She is worshipped equally by victorious heroes and defeated enemies. They all offer sacrifices to Ardvi Sura Anahita "at the time of sunrise and at sunset" (Yasht V, 91). She is active in the war between Good and Evil.

- God Verethragna corresponds to the Vṛtra-slayer Indra (Yasht XIV). There were many long fights against evil but Verethragna is finally victorious after going through ten successive incarnations during which he had been defeated by evil. In the last incarnation he claims victory as an adult strong boy holding a golden sword. The ten earlier successive incarnations are: wind, bull, horse, camel, boar, young 15-year old boy at the age of entry into adulthood, fast flying bird, wild goat, fighting deer and finally the grown up man. The symbolism is a clear complement of the myth of creation.
- God Mithra (= contract, alliance, treatise, sun-god), obviously represents the long evolution from an earlier primitive culture of the archaic age, into that of a structured civilization, perhaps one with the knowledge of writing. Mithra is very strong and powerful, he never sleeps and he carries a red *copper* mace or club to fight evil. He is the guide of Asha (= Good Order) who, in a way, corresponds to *ṛta*. He punishes the unfair, rewards farmers and is the overlord of ample *prairies.* His festival is celebrated on the occasion of the autumn equinox. Again here the symbolism is clear and can be dated by the mention of the metal, copper and not yet iron, of which the mace is made. Probably in still earlier days the mace or club, would have been of stone or hard wood, but here iron is not mentioned, which indicates the age of the myth. Mithra, an archaic god is the first to arrive on Mount Hara (= the Elburz Mountain chain). He arrives even earlier than the immortal Sun (= during the original "cosmic darkness"). Mithra arrives clothed in gold to settle on the splendid heights from where he looks with a generous eye at the domain of the Aryans (Yasht X, 13). Mithra also has the function of protecting Khvarnah (= Divine Glory) assisted by Apam Napat, God of Water and all waters in general.
- Vāyu is the god of winds, or wind personified. He lives between light and darkness, between the kingdom of Ahura Mazda and that of Angra Manyu. He blows away the evil Spirits. He

is armed with a golden lance and other golden weapons, not Iron.

- Tishtrya is represented by the brightest star, Sirius (= Procyon or Dog Star) and impersonates the rains that fight the she-demon Duzhyairya (= bad harvest) and Apaosha (= drought). Tishtrya (corresponds partly to Vedic Tr̥ta), Yasht VIII, 28 describes his victory over these sorcerer/demons.

The personality of god Tishtrya includes a good description of the hydrological regime of the two main rivers that flow into the Aral Sea, the Sir Darya and the Amu Darya and of the climate of the lands between them, namely Chorasmia including also the plains of the western bank of R. Amu Darya and the land called Sogdiana. The myths tell that there is a sea called Vourukasha, source of all waters, which distributes water among the various lands. On the occasion of his fight with Apaosha, Tishtrya flows towards Vourukasha in the guise of a beautiful white horse with golden ears and golden harness. But the evil Daeva Apaosha, also under disguise of a black horse with frightful markings, follows him. Then "they fight hoof against hoof, O Spitama (= pure, saint) Zarathustra. They fight, the glorious Tishtrya and Daeva Apaosha"(Yasht VIII, 20-22). When Apaosha is winning, Tishtrya steps back away from the Sea Vourukasha and complains: "if men had worshipped me as they should!" Tishtrya is then given the strength of 10 horses, 10 camels, 10 bulls, 10 mountains and 10 rivers (Yasht VIII 24). Finally Zarathustra himself offers a sacrifice to god Tishtrya who can finally flow back towards the Sea on his white horse to engage again his foe in battle. This time "the brilliant and glorious Tishtrya was more powerful than Daeva Apaosha and he is victorious" (Yasht VIII, 28). Also the water cycle is described as the ascent of water vapour from the sea, the formation of clouds carried by winds, then rain or snow that fall on Earth. The hydrologic cycle and the role and regime of rivers are described correctly, as in the Vedas. The observations of nature and the geographic descriptions are correct, though the explanations are still at the phantastic level.

What was probably not just imagination is the statement that the two rivers flow around and encircle the world, then return to the Sea Vourukasha, a none too disparate description of the land south and around the Aral Sea. In the Sea Vourukasha also grew the mother tree of all trees (Yasht XII, 17), called Saena. The fourth month of the Iranian calendar is called Tir from Tishtrya and Tiragan was the festival of rains.

It is interesting to note that the two rivers, the Amu Darya (= Oxus) which has a very long course, and the Sir Darya (= Jaxartes) which is shorter, drain different watersheds of the same chain of mountains, the Pamir, and have different regimes, with alternate floods and droughts at different seasons. There are other similar situations where Twin Rivers have different regimes, notable among them the Tigris-Euphrates system, which is one of the causes of the high fertility and advanced civilizations which flourished in Mesopotamia over a very long period of several millennia.

An important archaic God of the *R̥V* is *Tr̥ta*, also called *Tr̥ta Aptya*, from *ap* (= water, living in water, sprung from or dwelling in the sea or in clouds). Tr̥ta is mentioned 24 times in the *R̥V* alone (including one Valakhilya hymn). Among the most representatives are: *R̥V* VIII, 52; *R̥V* I, 187, 1; *R̥V* II, 34, 14; *R̥V* V, 18, 2; *R̥V* VIII, 47, 13; *R̥V* I, 187, 1; *R̥V* V, 41, 4; *R̥V* IX, 37, 4. Tr̥ta is an ancient god who lives in remote places, such as the birthplace of the Sun (*R̥V* I, 106, 2). He is mentioned in connection with other very ancient gods: Vāyu, Indra, and the Maruts to whom he gives help. He is sometimes identified with Varuṇa who represents the large expanses of heaven. In *R̥V* X, 46, 3, he finds Agni hiding in the clouds disguised as lightning. As Tr̥ta Aptya, as Aptya of the Aptyas he is thanked for invigorating food (= rains needed to raise good crops, specially cereals) and as remover of evils (= dirt, diseases, epidemics) visible or not, lurking against men: "each evil deed (= cause), visible or not, remove from us to Tr̥ta Aptya far away." Water purifies, removes evil dirt and cleanses from diseases. Tr̥ta also refuses to drink *soma*. Like Tishtrya, his heavenly home is on high mountains, the place of sacrifice, he is also at home in springs and in the high reaches of rivers. Clearly the origin of Tr̥ta and Trishtya is the same, though the god has more attributes and a more complex personality in the *R̥V*, which means that he has had a longer stay and performance in the older Vedas than in the Avesta (as we have it). Tr̥ta is used to "wish away" and consign to him any threatening calamity or unpleasantness; and he pervades the three regions: earth, heaven and firmament or sky.

It is clear that Tṛta and Tishtrya were originally one and the same deity of the Indo-Europeans of the East. The personality of the latter has not changed much in the long history of Mazdeism. But it has developed into a many faceted God with growing complexity in the mythology and religion of the Indo-Aryans. This is true for many others if not most aspects of gods of the two religions.

Finally the Avestan Atar is closely associated to Mithra and sides with him in battle. Only few myths about Atar have survived, probably there were not as many as about other gods to begin with. Atar is known to symbolise Truth and his most sacred form is called Bahram (?= Brahmā?). His help is needed to fight the forces of Darkness and Evil. Atar fights against the demon Azhi Dahaka to help Mithra preserve *Khvarnah* (= Divine Glory). Atar has the final victory. After threatening the demon who tried to grasp and carry away Khvarnah, he enters into his body and burns him from inside-out so that the demon may never return to Earth. Thus was Divine Glory saved by Atar (Yasht XIX, 49-51). To the heroic Atar of the early myth follows the later homely Atar: "O Atar, son of Ahura Mazda! You deserve sacrifices and invocations in the homes of men" (Atash Niyayesh, 7, dated after Zarathustra). Traditionally fire was kept alive in every Zoroastrian home of present day Pharsis as well as Hindus. Modern lifestyles inevitably change superficially traditional customs and habits.[21]

God Haoma (= *Soma*) bears the same description and attributes in both Avesta and Vedas. Vannucci (1999c, App. II) discusses the identity of the *soma* plant and offers arguments in favour of the identity between grapes' wine and *soma*.

VENDIDAD II

From the viewpoint of the present book, Vendidad II is specially interesting because it tells the story of the greatest hero of the Iranian mythology. King Yima (corresponds to Vedic Yama) is Justice itself and **the** good shepherd. He lives in the centre of the world, the Airyaneum Vaejah (Curtis 1993) and his empire covers the whole world. Yima ruled an empire where everything was good and he kept his promise: "I will feed and govern and protect your world. While I will be king, there will be neither icy or burning winds [a good description of wind-swept steppes], neither sickness or death" (Vendidad II, 5). Yima kept his promise and over centuries he twice had to expand the world to harbour growing mankind (= migrations?). Then Yima told a lie [= *drug*] and "when he started to use falsehood and untruthful words, *Khvarnah* [= Divine Glory] left him and was seen to fly away disguised as a bird. Then the Great Yima Khshaeta, the good shepherd, was afraid and helpless and he had to face his enemies. He was dejected and thrown to the ground" (Yasht XIX, 34). In the Indian version, Yama became the Lord god of the deceased.

Coming back to the Avestan myth it is evident that it refers to the original homeland from which the Indo-Iranians migrated. Many modern authors based on the Avesta (Vendidad II, 5, 21) consider Chorasmia, to which we should add also Sogdiana, to be the homeland of the ancient Iranians **after** they migrated away from the common Indo-European homeland which was further to the west and north of the Caspian Sea. The close similarity with the ancient-most parts of the Vedas indicate initial common roots and early common migration routes, the detailed description of the Vourukasha Sea which distributes her water to the various lands, the alternate droughts and floods of the rivers represented by Tishtrya, the description of the role of the mountains in the hydrological cycle, the dryness of the river after periods of drought, the fight between Tishtrya (= the flow of waters) with Daeva Apaosha and many other details adjust very closely to the ecological and hydro-geographical system of the Aral Sea and the two main feeder rivers, the Amu Darya and the Sir Darya which come from different watersheds and have alternate seasonal regimes of flood and drought in the lands of Chorasmia and Sogdiana — these details are typical and exclusive of the Indo-Iranian tradition.

The Indo-Iranians evidently brought with them the most archaic myths which they shared with the Indo-Aryans who had left the original homeland before them. They enriched their culture with the specific myths related to the environmental systems of the *Aral Sea*, tributary rivers and steppes. The diversification of mythologies between Indo-Aryans and Indo-Iranians is relatively late and can only have taken place when they reached the plains of R. Gurgan, east of the southern part of the Caspian Sea. Probably the great schism happened when the Indo-Iranians moved eastwards towards

Sogdiana and Chorasmia and the Indo-Aryans split in two groups, one moving eastward and the other westward (*fig.* 1).

The great cultural development of the area south of the Aral Sea, between R. Amu Darya (= R. Oxus) and Syr Darya (= R. Jaxartes) in later centuries, tends to support the theory of a long history of great local civilizations. There are other examples of areas limited by twin rivers with different hydrographical regimes which are important in the history of mankind. Such are the Ural and the Volga that flow into the Caspian Sea, the Don and the Dnieper which flow into the Black Sea, the Gaṅgā/Yamunā pair of rivers and the most ancient and earliest developed, the R. Tigris and R. Euphrates. Alternate regimes of flood and drought at different seasons between the latter mentioned, contributed towards the development of rich continuous agriculture without climatic interruptions in Mesopotamia (= land between rivers). It also favoured the development of extensive and innovative water management practices. R. Rasa (= R. Ranha) was a mythical river, known a long time before the arrival of the Indo-Arya in Punjab. The Rasa therefore could not have been an affluent (= tributary) of the Indus as hypothesized by Kochhar. The story of "R. Rasa" and of "R. Ranha" will be discussed separately.

ṚGVEDIC AND AVESTAN TRADITIONS

There are parallelisms, affinities and identities between the ancient Ṛgvedic and the Avestan lore, but though there is a parallelism, there are no identities and few similarities between the evolution of the cultures into organized civilizations of the Indo-Iranians and Indo-Arya. There are also parallelism but few similarities between the culture and civilizations of the Indo-Europeans of the west, as understood here meaning essentially the Greek and Roman civilizations, and the civilizations of the Indo-Europeans of the east. As everywhere else in archaic societies at the pre-Homeric, pre-Zarathustra and pre-Vedic stages, "reality" did not go beyond that which is perceived by the sense organs. People lived in total dependence of nature and there must have been a ceaseless need to adapt to environmental conditions for nothing more than just survival. It took a long, very long time for man to acquire enough living experience to be able to engage in speculative thinking about the world in which he lived. There was only limited protection to be had from, or control over, nature. As experience and mental faculties evolved it must have become obvious that acquiring more and more knowledge of the static and dynamic environment could facilitate adaptation and would improve chances of survival and reproduction. The dynamism and power of natural forces were the greatest hazards and at the same time offered the best opportunities for better living, such were accurately timed migrations, the great periodical floods of rivers like the Nile and those of Mesopotamia, or those of the Gaṅgā-Yamunā basins, or the use of favourable winds that enabled navigation beyond where oars could take man's crafts. Man learned to retreat to higher levels during predictable floods only to return to the inundated low-lands to practise agriculture in the new fertile alluvial deposits, as in the plains bathed by the Nile and its delta, or the Gaṅgā/Yamunā doab. In addition to agriculture man developed the art of navigation by sea and overland, guided by stars and migrating animals, specially bird migrations, and many other natural signs.

Man could not describe or even guess the origin, causes and effects of the powerful forces of nature, their real nature could not be visualised, certainly they were not understood. Evidently man could only beg for the benign influence of the forces whose effects he saw but could not control. He could only pray that the great unexplained "magical powers" (**ma** of magics is analogous to **mahā** = great and **mā** = mother, the great giver of life and sustenance) would be used for his own benefit. During such proto-historic and pre-historic ancient times, improperly called the time of "primitive religion," myths were born, nurtured and believed by humans, a stage common to all ancient cultures. The word religion however, is not proper, there is no religion at this stage, there are only beliefs. The word **religion** presupposes the existence of a detailed, argumented and clearly thought-out system that links man to the divine. Of such designed systems, there could not have been any during the original stages of mankind and when first instituted they would have been essentially site-specific; hence the existence of sacred mountains, sacred rivers, sacred areas, sacred caves and so on. The proto-history of the Indo-Europeans of east and west must have been basically similar and comparable to that of other groups of humans at the same cultural level all over the world.

The development of articulate language during pre-historic times would have facilitated the development of beliefs in the powers of nature. Beliefs in myths and legends are spontaneous because they are attempts to develop knowledge into understanding and to put on record the evolution, tradition and history of the people. History does not begin only when writing was invented, as usually stated. History is recorded long before writing was invented. It is recorded in the individual and collective memory of people, as we are told by Hesiod (in the *Theogonia*) who makes Mnemosine (= memory), mother of the Muses, a daughter of Zeus begotten at the very beginning of mankind. History begins with teaching and example, with the oral tradition, with songs, dances, games and increasing accuracy of the grammar and syntax of articulated language, capable of giving better teaching and more precise details about everything and anything, specially among people already developed technically, like the ancient Egyptians, the Semites of West Asia and Mesopotamia and the original Indo-European. Religions are formulated when the beliefs of proto-historic times are organized into a system. Many religions were never put in writing and remained forever consigned only to the oral tradition, but nevertheless they were historical forces which could drive pawns. In the early stages the propositions of the oral tradition **are** the tenure of the religion which is strictly or not so strictly observed. The oral tradition among the Indo-Europeans was usually crystallized in poetic form, stereotyped sentences and epithets, songs, poetry, dances "by prescribed steps," for the simple reason that it is easier to memorize knowledge under these forms. T.B. Swaminathan (*in:* Vannucci, 1999) refers to distichs in the Malayalam language of the state of Kerala in India, memorized by carpenters, that give the key to solve Pythagoras' theorem, when needed in their daily work for building structures or furniture of specified dimensions.[19]

The naive, instinctive perception of natural events, including biological phenomena and the communion with nature of countless generations, becomes factual, practical knowledge. It then reaches a degree of understanding such as it becomes possible to systematize the knowledge acquired empirically into concepts widely valid. This was the stage rich in myths of the pre-Vedic, pre-Avestan and pre-Homeric periods which ran a parallel course in east and west, not necessarily at the same chronological age, but at the same cultural stage. There are no similarities between east and west because myths and their late categorization were determined by the different environments in which the knowledge and understanding of nature had developed. In the west, Homer (mainly in the Iliad and the Odyssey and the Homeric hymns) and Hesiod (mainly in the *Theogonia*) produced a system based on reason in which the Olympian gods, immutable and quarrelsome reign supreme. This became the classical Greek religion. In the east the system developed by the sages was based on the observation of nature, its moods, and exceptions. They analysed causes and effects of natural processes. The "vision of the sage, who can see even with closed eyes" (= to see with the mind) was open to discussion, belief or disbelief by individual convictions and experiences. It never was a rigid dogmatic system, differently from developments in Iran when religion was systematized by Zarathustra.[21]

In the pre-historic and historic periods, the philosophic/ religious systems of Indo-European of east and west evolved along divergent paths, separated from each other by environmental, time and historic realities. One of the few fundamental traits common to both was the unshakable importance given to Truth, one result of which is the common Indian reminder: "speak always the truth, but only good truth." To speak falsehood, evil, nasty or bad truth would be an insult towards God; it would be a senseless, ridiculous attempt to fool the Supreme Reality because there is only one **Absolute Truth,** as the myth about Iranian king Yima shows. All other gods are manifestations or personifications of the infinite facets of the Absolute, the Self-Existent God imbued with all knowledge.

The Indo-Aryans and Indo-Iranians who reached Anatolia and west Asia Minor, did not take place as mass displacements of entire populations. Migrants were not numerous and were in many instances represented only or mostly so by the ruling conquerors, the warrior caste, traders and artisans with their women. The mass of the people were local, they were the *demos,* all those who later in Greece were not *citizens* and had no right to vote. Only the ruling classes had the right to vote on all and every matter important for the collective well-being of the *polies.*

Significantly, all the gods mentioned in the treaties drawn between the Indo-Arya and kings of other nations, are the most ancient Vedic gods. This is a proof that the groups of Indo-Aryans who migrated westwards from the plains of R. Gurgan, eastwards of the southern Caspian Sea, were isolated at a very early stage from the Indo-Arya who had migrated towards India. This view coincides with archaeological findings, including dates of migrations of the Indo-Iranians southwards towards the lands of Phars and Elam (southern Iran). It also coincides with the approximate areas and time of the dichotomy between Indo-Iranians and Indo-Aryans for which most important are the datable findings of grey and grey-black pottery. Displacements of the Indo-Arya went beyond Asia Minor, numerous habits, customs and other cultural traits crossed over the Aegean Sea into Greece and Magna Graecia. Such were, for instance, the cult of Demeter and Dionysos (= agriculture, life after death) and many facets of social life, family and funerary customs, matriarchy and patriarchy and warfare, pottery and metal works, the role and importance of women and the child, gestures, habits and some religious traits.

SUMMARY AND CONCLUSIONS

Summing up, the very ancient gods mentioned in the treatises were shared between the Indo-European of the East who later split into Indo-Aryans and Indo-Iranians who migrated southwards from the steppes north of the Black and Caspian Seas in the late fourth and in the early second millennia BC respectively, and settled in the plains of R. Gurgan, off the south-eastern parts of the Caspian Sea. From those plains, the Indo-Arya split into two groups, one migrated eastwards towards India and the other westwards towards Iran and Asia Minor.They all worshipped the same very ancient gods. The Indo-Iranian who migrated from the original Indo-European homeland, had initially the same gods, but their religion later evolved in a different direction when they migrated from the plains of R. Gurgan southwards towards the land of Phars. Their religion evolved into Zoroastrianism.

Homer and Hesiod substituted the healthy nature gods, Demeter and Dionysos and the latter's retinue of nature deities, with the majestic Olympians, but though segregated to a secondary level during the initial stages, nature gods are still alive today. The Olympians survive mainly or only because of their artistic, psychological and social representation and insight. Greek gods are man-made characters who played a very important role in the great drama of the Greek civilization. Indirectly they instigated the debates among philosophers, scientists and artists of classical Greece that were and continue to be eye-openers for present day persons who do not dislike reasoning.[21]

The Vedic gods exist independently of mankind; they are manifestations of the realities of the world man lives in as a participant of nature's vitality. It should be clear that the word *religion* as an organized system is a socio-political issue and *not* a synonym of *"religious spirit"* which is a personal experience. Even in these modern times of growing "needs" and desires, the ancient Hindu recommendation: "want not what is not essential to sustain life" holds its ground. One billion people would not be able to survive in India, if this recommendation was not observed. Anyhow, a "simple life" is healthy.

The Ṛbus, the Aśvins, Rāma, Indra, Kṛṣṇa others and the feats attributed to them are probably adapted from authentic personalities or families that existed in the distant past and are credited with the development of methods and techniques, with acquisition and transfer of knowledge and with the spiritual development of the culture of ancient Indo-Aryans. The most remarkable of these are Rāma and Indra. These primary figures play a fundamental role in the Śruti because they are datable bench-marks of the cultural evolution and development of the Indo-European of the east. They illustrate the means that enabled the Indo-Arya to settle in their new homes, west and east of R. Indus, but not without many wars and battles. Wars raged between the incoming clans of Indo-Aryans and various local people and among different clans of Indo-Aryans among themselves. The duration of the heroic age lasted an untold number of centuries and witnessed the succession of many waves of migrants that gradually expanded all the way south in the Indian peninsula as far as Kanyakumari and Sri Lanka.

Archaeological research is now able to give a date to these ancient movements. For instance much is known about the Indo-Aryans who migrated westwards and came in contact with the Hurrites and other people without past history and no organised culture and civilization. The Hurrites had come down from the mountains into the Dokan valley in northern Iraq as attested by the remains of Hurrite people found at Tell Shimshara (Gibon 1976). The contacts of the western Indo-Aryans with the Hurrites took place around 1800 BC. The Indo-Aryans brought with them the characteristic black polished pottery, the horse, wagons and chariots and the trumpet, remains of which were found in the palaces of kings and noblemen of the kingdom of Mitanni where, as mentioned above, the bulk of the population was Hurrite (Ghirshman 1977) and the higher classes were Indo-Aryans. These changes coincide with the beginning of the "Iron Age" among the western branch of the Indo-Aryans. The excavations at Tepe Hissar, Shah Tepe, Tureng Tepe and others produced datable knowledge of the culture of the Indo-Aryans of the middle and second half of the third millennium BC which is similar to that found in the plains of R. Gurgan, S.E of the Caspian Sea. This culture was introduced in northern Mesopotamia by the ruling class of the kingdom of Mitanni.

Archaeological research also shows that Hurrite pottery earlier than 1800 BC was of the type called Habur ware, with a particular shape and black geometrical designs. The distribution of the Habur ware shows that Hurrites after 1800 BC spread well into the Iranian plateau, from the Mediterranean coast to the Zagros mountains, Kurdistan and Azerbaidjan. The black pottery brought in by the Indo-Aryan ruling class of Mitanni had fluid, rounded designs including birds. It is considered a "luxury" pottery used only by the high class and probably also by the *mariyanni,* the horsemen or mounted warriors "fighting from war chariots." This pottery is absent before and after the dominion of the Mitanni. It is believed that the black polished pottery was imported from R. Gurgan by the ruling Indo-Arya in their western migrations. The presence of this pottery stops suddenly with the last Mitanni king,[22]

Part III

Heroes

To begin with we should agree on what we understand and mean by the word *Hero*. The Greek and Latin word *heros* can be translated as sir, lord, ancestor and is always a term of respect. The cult of heroes is probably derived from the cult of ancestors. The word in present colloquial languages usually refers to valiant, exceptionally brave and courageous men on the battlefield and whenever physical might and special qualities are required. The word comes from Lt. *heros* which designates a man with exceptional personal and leadership qualities and attributes that distinguish him (or her, as a heroine) in a particular manner. The word *vir* and derivates in Latin languages designates men endowed with great virtues, a Great Man. The word *vir* is the abstract noun of the adjective *virile,* as in *virile qualities* and *virtue.* There are heroes in all areas of human activity, in war and peace, at home or abroad, in mental, intellectual, scientific domains, in spirituality and in passive resignation. Rāma is as great a hero in battle as he is a great *Vir* in the exercise of tolerance, justice and kingship. In India the word *mahātma,* a great soul, refers to great spiritually enlightened men. The prefixe *mahā,* like in *mahāvīra* is used to indicate greatness and nobility of purpose and endeavour for the sake of a good cause, a form of heroism.[1]

All archaic cultures go through a "heroic stage" of hero worship. Indo-Aryan and Indo-Iranian people originally shared a number of heroes, myths and legends of the proto- and pre-historic age, respectively the pre-Vedic and Vedic and the pre-Zoroastrian stages. Zoroaster erased the past and created a dualistic religion based on the realities and observations of nature where positive factors are balanced by bad influences and vice versa. Though Zoroaster took this reasoning to the extreme, some traits of the earlier religion survived in the names of deities, natural phenomena and geographic formations, such as Vāyu (= wind) and Mithra (= law, justice), names of rivers and places, like Rs. Ranha and Gurgan and the plains to the south-east of the Caspian Sea. We will not enter into ancient Indo-Iranian mythology here.

In the context of this book the word *hero* is used in its original Graeco-Roman meaning of a man capable of fighting bravely and nobly for an ideal, in battle or otherwise. In the Graeco-Roman and in other mythologies human heroes are frequently the outcome of the love of a god with a woman or more rarely, of a goddess and a human man. Often heroes owe their exceptional endowments and successes to the godly parent who protects and helps them whenever needed, specially in situations of extreme difficulty or great danger.

The word *epic* is derived from the Latin (Lt.) *epicus*, in turn derived from the Greek *epikos* (= song), itself derived from *epos* (= word). The words Epic poetry and Epic poems in Latin and other Latin derived languages designate poetry and long poems that sing the feats, legends and myths related to ancient traditional gods and heroes. On the western world scene, the original model of classical epic poems are the Iliad and the Odyssey of Homer. The Aeneis of Virgil, the late Latin poems of Nonnos, Provençal epics and the late Italian epics of Ariosto and Torquato Tasso and others were all written following the model of the "original" Greek epics.

The *Rāmāyaṇa* and the *Mahābhārata* are usually known as "Indian epics" though they are not composed on the Homeric model and the only similarity with Homer's epics is that they deal with the traditionally known very ancient past describing the feats, myths and legends of gods and heroes. The word "epic" can be used for lack of a better designation though the *Rāmāyaṇa* and the *Mahābhārata* are much more than epic poems in the current use of the word. Under the same reservation, the Shah Namah of Firdusi and other classic works of the Indo-Europeans of the east can be included in the world epic literature. The Shah Namah is partly in poetry and partly in prose. It refers to the heroic age of the history of the Indo-Iranians when they migrated and gradually settled in the lands of what is at present Iran and parts of Afghanistan, from the Arabic Sea and Persian Gulf northwards as far as the lands neighbouring the Aral Sea, Chorasmia and Sogdiana.

Epics and heroic poetry were originally transmitted orally; they are the primordial constituents of the cultural tradition of people sharing common languages and habits. They were sung and later written in the narrative style of the Homeric epics. One of the important aspects of epic poems is that they were one of the main instruments for the formation, growth and development of the language of the people at large and society as a whole. As such, languages are instrumental in the formulation of the concept of state and nation, legislature and government. This is one of the reasons why we find epic poetry at the root of most cultures that evolved into independent civilizations. The rhapsodists, cytharists and aedes of the heroic age usually initiated their songs with the conventional term: "Since when. . . ." The Greek and Latin epics use the same literary technique, such as: "Since when Odyssey left the burning city. . ." and they also use a conventional code of exclusive epithets, stereotypes or patronymics for each character to facilitate both the improvisation of the singer or story teller and the understanding of the audience. Thus Athena is always mentioned as the "glaucopid Athena" (= the blue eyed Athena). These and other fixed poetical mannerisms and code-words continued into historic times and were followed faithfully by Virgil in the Aeneis, although the Greek gods had been renamed with Latin names.

Also the weapons, shield and helmets, bows and arrows in both east and west had distinctive marks, colours and often also individual names for easy recognition on the battle field. Soldier uniforms for open wars could be adopted only when mass conscription of fighters was introduced. Individual soldiers do not count except for their numbers; they are what later would be known as "cannon meat, or flesh for slaughter." Originally famous warriors and heroes were individually known and should be recognized on the battle field for their distinctive features, shape of helmets, shields, swords and colours. Only gods and heroes need be recognized individually. Graeco-Roman gods and heroes were also characterized by conventional epithets, used as one-word codes to make poetry more fluent. Achaeans have long hair, Apollon shoots arrows very far, Hera has large eyes and white arms, Menelaus is fair haired, Athena has blue eyes, and the Cretan Merio has a unique type of mycenean helmet. Herakles, a very ancient hero carried over from the archaic period, is armed with bow and arrows and an exclusive mace. Odysseus preferably fights with spear and sword, Achille's famous round shield made of heavy bronze decorated with golden figures, was made by Hephaistus (= Vulcanus), iron is not mentioned. The Herakles and the discus could be made of stone and were the common weapons of all fighters, the axe could be very large and was usually held with both hands and sharpened on both edges, the handle was made of hard olive tree wood (Od. V 235). Herakles' mace was very heavy and made of solid bronze. Warriors fought on foot, only Stenelus fought from his chariot because he was lame (Aen. II 261).

The picture that emerges after comparing myths, legends, dates, stories, archaeological findings and the oral and written traditions, confirm Renfrew's (1988) overall conclusion that people who spoke Indo-European languages spread westwards from eastern Turkey about 10,000 to 8,000 years ago (= 8,000 to 6,000 BC), the dates should be revised. Nomadic movements were possible thanks to the development of agriculture and animal husbandry. Migrating people would have taken with them specimens of domesticated plants and animals. Apart from dates, Renfrew's conclusions are far more convincing than those to the contrary. The prototype of the classic Greek warrior and hero is the warrior of the Mycenean bronze age culture, fully described by Homer, by Greek and Latin historians, and model of the fighters of the Greek and Roman armies down to the Middle Ages of Europe.[2]

(A) Heroes and Epic Poetry

In this book gods and heroes are classed chronologically rather than religiously. The chronological succession of types and classes of gods and heroes in east and west is comparable, though the sequences happened at different real times. R.N. Dandekar in his introduction to U. Chakravarti's 1997 book on "Indra and other Vedic deities," divides the Vedic gods into: (a) Natural phenomena; (b) Historical figures transformed into gods; and (c) Partial or complete abstractions. Dandekar's division is appropriate to illustrate the historical evolution of the human mind and of modern man's perception of the realities of the material and spiritual worlds that lead to the understanding of the religiosity linked to the concepts of gods and heroes. Gods and heroes are self-generated in the mythical stage (a) of all cultures when reason and wishful thinking evolve from the personal to the community's ecological level. In a second stage (b) great leaders are divinized until when models are no longer needed and abstractions become gods which were earlier difficult to realize mentally. The later stage (c) is the evolved personalized stage of each god.

Most species of mammals have a social life temporarily, seasonally or permanently. Many live in families or groups of families with a leader, usually called the alpha male who is stronger, wiser and most capable. The leader can also be an elder female, often beyond the age of reproduction, as with elephants, baboons and some other species of monkeys or lions. The alpha male is dethroned when a younger male defeats him, the old often toothless lion or wolf then retreats into solitude. A competent leader reigns supreme because he can achieve what others cannot and can take appropriate decisions on how and where to guide the group out of trouble, for instance running away or facing invading enemies, moving away from drought areas or taking shelter from earthquakes or sudden forest fires and other threats or dangers. Some leaders are more successful or more fortunate than others, anecdotes or stories about them build up his reputation as a great man, he becomes powerful, and legends flourish about human or animal leaders, the number of their descendants and the size of the group or herd increases. Some heroes may become gods or gods and heroes at the same time. Maybe at the early cultural stages there is no clear-cut difference between the concepts of *hero* and *god*.[3]

I adopted the division of gods and heroes according to the chronological evolution of the cultures dealt with here to search for corresponding stages of widely distant civilizations having a common ancestry, a common Indo-European background. In general the developmental stages of the cultures of the Indo-Europeans, of east and west are comparable, even if not contemporaneous, the mythical age is followed by geographic and cultural expansionism and a structured religion. The main question addressed here was to find the red threads needed to unravel and compare the traditional stories of different people.

The proto- or pre-historic chronological stages of the cultural development of the Indo-Europeans of the west considered here, the Graeco-Roman world, did not happen at the same absolute chronological time as the proto- and pre-historic time period of the Indo-Europeans of the east. The evolutionary story of the Indo-Europeans of the east started much earlier, as shown in Part I of this study mainly based on archaeological findings. There is, however, a great similarity, though dephased in time, with the succession and development of the traits of other cultures. The succession of cultural periods is similar, the archaic mythical phase is followed by a legendary phase that may be the memory of ancient facts, and this is then followed by a pre-historic and then a historic period. Naturally none of these periods has clear-cut limits and the evolution is a web-like development influenced by geography, climates, and natural events good or bad, availability of raw materials needed for technical improvement, neighbours and cultural transfer and trade with other people, wars or territorial occupation. This is nowhere more evident than in the succession of facts described in the epics of east and west. The study of the Indo-Aryans, the Indo-Iranians and the Graeco-Roman epics shows that they are all based on comparable milestones, but the milestones are spaced differently. The ancient oral tradition was formulated at *different* real-time intervals, but at comparable stages of each cultural development. Stages are comparable vastly *because* all the Indo-European people share the same basic language structure. The structure of the spoken language is both a consequence and cause of the thoughts and logics which are in turn influenced by the environment of the people where the language evolves.

The boundaries between reality, phantasy and magic are ill-defined in the epics. The word *magics* (Lt. = *magia* = G = *mageia*) originally refers to the art of controlling the hidden forces of nature. The Latin word *magus* (Gk = *mago*s = magician) comes from the Persian *magush* and refers to the sacerdotal or priestly class of the Zoroastrian religion. In the western epics, the poets frequently appeal to magics to vouchsafe the participation of gods in human affairs or, in the case of Odysseus or Aeneas and the other classical heroes, to cause or save the god's favorites from trouble. In the western epics, as well as in the Purāṇas and the Indian epics, there are no valid coordinates common to both the divine and the human worlds. The two worlds are separate and different from each other and each must be gauged by its own values. Or, like Dandekar said: "Magics is not mistaken religion, but mistaken science." Magics is an attempt to explain and use what is not yet known or understood or measured in the world of human beings.

On the other hand merits are attained by great heroes through very material acts and facts. Single acts and facts bear comparison between the Indian and the classic Greek and Roman epics. Amongst many instances, one could think of the superhuman expertise in archery performed by Rāma at Sītā's swayaṁvaram and by Odysseus on his return home, the island called Ithaca. The two heroes are able to bend and string the godly bow that no other human could handle and both shoot an arrow correctly at an almost impossible target through a series of rings or at a revolving hanging target.

All the present-day abridged renderings of the epics that may be found in any bookshop include the phantastic episodes which make amusing reading. The popular publications of the epics brought out in both the original and modern languages facilitate the school or college student's task of translation from the original Greek or Latin. But the prose renderings reflect poorly and incompletely the intellectual, historical, poetical, social and otherwise cultural value of the original poems. It is essential to read the entire unexpurgated text of the epics to acquire insight into the deep and often hidden meanings and the value of their teachings.

In Part I above, the archaic or proto- and pre-historic age of the evolution of gods and heroes is referred to as the "early mythical age" which corresponds to the gods of *Dandekar's class* (*a*): divination of natural phenomena. During this period in all cultures, early gods are the natural phenomena *per se* and are seen only later as *manifestations* that may evolve into *personifications* of natural phenomena. Since natural phenomena may be good or bad, such as mild rains or thunderstorms, god and man-made home fire or wild run-away fires, river flow or floods, earthquakes and volcanoes or arable land and mountains, also gods and heroes may be benevolent or fiends. Heroes become the paladins of humankind, but to enable them to fight against the forces of evil they must acquire a semi-divine nature and power. In the heroic age legends are born and develop about the wonderful, super-human achievements of the heroes. For a hero to be really respected and loved and for him to become a paragon for the education of the younger generation, the hero must be one of the locals, knowledgeable of the people's needs, aspirations and competence. Herodotus (I, 92) like other Greeks defines Hellas as **all** lands where Greek people lived, not only in Europe, but also in Asia and Africa. The Romans had a different attitude which proved more successful, they obliged all people to speak Latin even though they were not given Roman citizenship, a privilege that was granted only very late during the Decadence Period. The vast Roman Empire lasted for over five centuries because of its tolerance of the customs, religion, habits and self-rule of the many tribes and nations which they conquered and subjugated, *provided* they recognised the supremacy of Rome and paid the stipulated tributes. All the non-Greek-speaking people who lived in Hellas or Europe or Asia were classed as barbarians, *except* most of those of Asia who were generically called Indians, Persians in later periods or were called by the specific name of the nations or clans to which they belonged. Both the Roman and the Greek civilization incorporated local divinities into their own religion but they did not grant privileges to the people over which they ruled. Because of the elitist tendencies and isolationism of the ruling class of the Greeks and Romans, of the Indo-Iranian, of the Indo-Aryan and of the Sumerians, their heroes are typical of their culture and are not readily comparable to heroes of other cultures. We find similarities of aims among all heroes in general, but the personalities and the means to achieve their goals were never the same, in the heroic age of various ancient cultures. For instance, both Mātariśvan and Prometheus are credited with bringing fire to humankind, but the way they achieved this, the punishment or praise that they received for disobeying the gods and the consequences of their heroic action, are different. The gift of fire to man is one of the fundamental legends of all cultures because it marks the promotion of man into a creature more capable than any other animal. Man could develop his ingenuity and live better and longer only after he learned how to make and control fire. The next big step forward was the invention of agriculture and of the wheel. Man saw God in Fire and perhaps this is how the concept of God, an indescribable entity, the Essence with infinite Power and Knowledge, entered into human minds.

Dandekar's class (*b*) is about the gods who are historical figures transformed into gods. As Dandekar correctly points out ". . . the historical figures transformed into gods belong to the stage when the actual memory of living heroes . . . was still fresh in the community's memory, the record of the details is a pointer to this . . . all ancient mythologies provide parallel histories." Heroes are half gods because of their parentage and also in their own right for having achieved wonders for the benefit of their fellow men. A typical example of this is Indra, a very ancient hero and god of the Indo-Aryan people. Gilgamesh of Sumer, who gained and gifted knowledge to his people, failed at the threshold of being divinized. The most ancient written records of Gilgamesh that have so far been found go as far back as about 2000 BC, however Gilgamesh was never fully deified, he was too real and too spiritually frail to become a god. The great truth that man learned from the story of Gilgamesh, the powerful king of Uruk, is that it is impossible for man to acquire benefits that go against or beyond the laws of the cosmos, the **Vedic Ṛta**, such as was the selfish request of Gilgamesh who demanded immortality for his own body. Having revealed this great truth, Gilgamesh who was a semi-god by birth and because of his intrinsic virtues, like other heroes everywhere, is helped by the gods but is not divinized by man.

Dandekar's class (*c*) are gods who **are** gods by their own nature, in their own right. These are those who are "partial or complete abstractions." On this point emphasis was put in Part II above, and will not be repeated here.

HEROES, WARRIORS AND WEAPONS

A few words on another matter — heroes are not always warriors and warriors are not always heroes. However, there are heroes who are also warriors and warriors who are also heroes. But in the history of mankind, most respected heroes are not warriors, they are supermen, or superwomen in areas other than the battle field, such were the sages. All cultures revere ancestors who become mythical legends due to their great knowledge, wisdom, sainthood or ability in performing specific tasks, or have other important qualities or achievements for which mankind is grateful, they are developers and inventors of special techniques, such as the smelting of ores and the metallurgy of copper, iron and other metals and their alloys. This varies with availability of raw materials and technical details of manufacture and differentiates one culture from others.[4] Originally the heroes of the Indo-European of east and west as described in the epics were warriors endowed with great or superhuman bravery and strength. Such were the warrior-heroes of the Graeco-Roman epics, the Indian epics, the medieval Provençal (southern France) epics, the "Roman de Roland" (Romance of Roland, paladin who fought for Charlemagne and died in the battle of Roncesvalles in 778 AD) and the "Roman de la Rose" (Romance of the Rose, also Provençal), or the heroes of the Italian Renaissance epic poetry. Many mythical heroes of the ancient heroic periods were warriors **and** sages because the two attributes should be united in a single heroic personality to promote balanced development of the growing culture and burgeoning civilization. They could be *purohits* at the courts of Indian kings and rajas who survived until recent times, such were in the heroic ages the wizards, magi, leaders who had also fighting weapons such as double axes, bows and arrows, lances and maces, but above all had faith and conviction in the righteousness of their cause. They had the willpower to lead and be an example to their people. Such were Moses, Priamus king of Troy, Grand-sire Bhīṣma, or Kṛṣṇa. There were practically no mythical super-human heroes in Roman culture because Roman culture was newly born and jumped over the mythical phase. Rome had to borrow Troyan Aeneas, son of goddess Aphrodite as its ancestor and the Etruscan Numa Pompilius whose counsellor was a nymph called Egeria (a local Italic name), as its first king. These semi-gods were the Roman links with nature and the superhuman levels of the mind.

The oldest and traditional weapon of Graeco-Roman and Indian heroes is the bow and arrows and the mace. Typically the arc of the greatest heroes was god-given. The bow of the Troyan Pāndaros, leader of the Indo-European Lycians was gifted by Apollon (Il. II 826), the great Philoctetes' bow had been gifted to the archaic hero Herakles while the story of the divine origin of the bow of Rāma is well known. Heroes do not discard material weapons but above all they show the effectiveness of the use of intelligence, wisdom and justice. Athena is the goddess of reasoned war; Mars is the god of brutal war. The vicissitudes of life often demand more courage and willpower when off-battle and with no weapons in hand. Kṛṣṇa served better as a charioteer at Kurukṣetra than as a diplomat performing his role of prince and warrior. Such were the teachings of Bhīṣma lying on the bed of arrows awaiting death of the body. One of the greatest teachings of great warrior-sages is the courage to face victory and defeat with an even mind; it is only with this state of mind that cultures can evolve towards mature stages. The personalities of Rāma and Indra are significant examples of different types of heroes.

Rāma and *Mara* are nouns that designate *also* abstract heroes; the name of each is an inversion of the syllables of the name of the other. Two facets of a complex being, one positive and the other negative, an aspect of the wise god Rāma seldom mentioned or remembered. The names Rāma and Mara (cognate of the root-word *mṛti* = death) are known from the most ancient cultures and civilizations, including the Egyptian and Chaldean. One name indicates excellence in maximum ethical life and the other maximum absence of life and absolute indifference to ethical behaviour. Modern students of the esoteric cults of the ancient past noticed the presence of heroes with these names in secret cults of the eastern Mediterranean, Asia Minor and Central Asia. Rāma is the prototype of a higher human being, a figure superior to all others, excellent in all fields of activity, knowledge and wisdom, a great archer, a noble warrior, both a hero and a god of the Indo-Arya lore, the perfect prince, leader, son and husband, giver of justice, ever victorious in the destruction of evil. Mara is the exact opposite of prince Rāma and as such Mara is engulfed in dark, cold, hidden secrecy, most rarely mentioned and when mentioned, it is only with great precaution and circumspection. Mara plays an important role in the early life of the Buddha during and after enlightenment.

Rāma in human form and as an *avatāra* of Viṣṇu, proved his determination and final victory and valour in his long fight against Rāvaṇa. Rāma epitomizes the victory of Good over Evil. He was the prototype of the perfect ruler and his name became the traditional name of the Buddhist ruling dynasty of Thailand, amongst other historical rulers of other countries. All the details of the story of Rāma are epilogues of the drive of man as a species, towards perfection. The years spent in the forest are a reminder and proof of the need to return to nature, to man's primary nature, to aknowledge the powers from which no living being can escape. Rāma is both Hero and God incarnate as an *avatāra* of Viṣṇu.

Differently from Rāma, Indra the great leader of the Arya clans, the hero warrior, has temporal rather than spiritual power, he fights for pride and conquest, for himself and for his people. He is king, a powerful king and is also called a god, but a very human god with all the good attributes of man. Indra fits well in Dandekar's class two: historical figures transformed into gods.

The personality of Indra was recently discussed in a scholarly manner by Chakravarty (1997) and briefly by Vannucci (1999). Quoting from Chakravarty, U. (*l.c*):" Indra the powerful leader of his nomadic Arya followers was a culture hero. Like many culture heroes, like Kṛṣṇa, Jesus Christ, etc. his birth was abnormal. He was born from his mother's side and did not follow the usual path. . . . He was a saviour of his people. A saviour god is normally a solar god. Indra was solarized and there lies dignity in being solarized. . . . Comparatively only a very small number of *ṚV* hymns depict Indra as the highest god whereas the majority of them speak about his martial feats. . . . Unfortunately the most glorious phase of Indra's mythology was a temporary one. . . . Indra in the post-vedic age, in the epics and in Buddhist literature is shorn of his glamour, he is then a colourless titular head of the pantheon yielding place to some other deities — Viṣṇu or Śiva — whose service was felt more urgently by the people of the time and whose prime occupation now turned to agriculture." This short description of Indra as an ancient god, is sufficient to show him in the garb of paladin and leader of his followers, rather than a distant god. Like everything else, the personality of Indra evolves with time.

Many centuries later Espinoza (= Spinoza, 1632-1677 AD, Netherlands) said: *Aequam memento rebus in arduis servare mentem* (= Remember to keep an even [tranquil, levelled, equal] mind in difficult times), an injunction followed by Rāma but not by Indra. Many great heroes on the battle field regretted having been warriors, in the course of time they gave greater importance to moral justice and spiritual valour, as the conversion of good King Ashoka of Magadha shows (died 232 BC).

GRAECO-ROMAN CULTURE AND CIVILIZATION

In classical Greek the word *hero* designates men to whom mankind, specifically the Greeks and the Romans, owed very much, figures to whom everybody was greatly indebted. The classical hero did not benefit himself from his heroic acts and some had to be purified or punished for the sins committed while performing dire acts necessary to achieve the noble feat imposed on them by destiny. Herakles had to be purified prior to initiation to be admitted in the Eleusynian Mysteries of goddess Demeter. Mātaṛśvan and Prometheus had to bear the consequences of their heroic act of bringing fire to earth which elevated mankind almost to the level of the gods. Zeus and Indra acquired their kingship and divine nature by virtue of their exceptional feats. Divinity was attributed to them by man because a tangible personality who behaved in the past as a human hero is far more accessible to the mind of individual men or women than a great philosophical or saintly hero or god whose concepts and acts are sometimes difficult to understand.

In the Graeco-Roman tradition heroes are seldom deified. The sacred and the profane were kept separate and many conditions had to be fulfilled before man or woman was called god or goddess. This could only happen in the Heroic Age, when the difference between tangible and intangible reality was not yet clear in man's mind, deification was formally codified late, by Homer and Hesiod who could draw a system from the rich mythical pre-historic tradition which enabled them to plan the epics and the *Theogonia*. Demeter herself became a goddess only because of her gift to mankind, the teaching of methodical agriculture. Prometheus was never divinized; on the contrary he was punished for his daring act of stealing fire from the gods to bring it down to man. Human heroes were elevated only very late to the stature of gods and only during decadence periods, such was Nero, the "divine" emperor of Rome, and the deification of outstanding personalities occurred only too often for political reasons and for the political needs of the priestly class. This was also the origin of the divinity of the ancient pharaohs of Egypt and when Pharaoh Akhenaton (1375-1358 BC) the religious reformer changed the rules, he was carefully but determinately abandoned by the priestly orders who withdrew their support to the new human "god." The loss of prestige of Alexander the Great was partly due to his inflated ego and declaring himself a human god, his downfall was avoided only by his premature death. The century when the Homeric poems and the *Theogonia* were written down marks a hiatus in the development of Greek culture. Homer and Hesiod had the determination and far looking approach to declare that the real and true past was the foundation over which the new religion had to be built. Homer and Hesiod were the heralds who closed one era and opened another. These developments in Greece coincided with the time of the foundation of Rome. Like Mrs. Ponza of Pirandello's play mentioned above, Homer and Hesiod had the courage to declare, paraphrasing Mrs. Ponza, that "This is so. This is how truth speaks by the voice of the Muses and we are those who are believed."

As the Greek gods and heroes were adopted and became acclimatised in Rome, the concept of hero was influenced by the Roman praxis that made of Rome the greatest long-living state in BC and early AD times. Roman heroes were practical and used their valour for specified ends. The decadence of the Roman Empire began when the courage of man was no longer used *exclusively* for serving faithfully the civil and military powers of the State, but was used also for one's individual glory. From this point of view Caius Julius Caesar, the great Roman military leader and hero, marks the beginning of the end for which he paid with his life. He was assassinated in the year 44 BC because of his inflated ego. Though the greatest Roman emperors were Caesar's successors who came, most of them, from the same lineage, the *gens Julia,* and though the Roman Empire continued to expand its frontiers after his death, there was no longer, exception made for the first few enlightened emperors, an ideal higher than the individual ego to keep the State intact as a coexistent whole, a nation worth its name. The Great Caius Julius Caesar is responsible for having changed the figure of the altruistic hero into that of a selfish inflated hero. Centuries later history repeated itself with the story of the inflated ego of Napoleon Bonaparte.

The Greek cultural tradition begins early in Greece[5] but Rome was founded late (754 BC), the Roman civilization was structured on the basis of the Etruscan civilization and of the primitive cultures of the ancient Italic people. There is no Roman "heroic" age as such. Rome inherited the heroic, pre-historic culture from Greece and incorporated little of the poorly known legends of the early Italic people. The very ancient proto-historic and pre-historic culture and tradition of the Italian peninsula do not belong to the Greek cultural tradition, and Rome itself was founded by a band of uncouth young men in need of land and women to make their own. Romulus and Remus, the legendary twin founders of Rome and their band, can best be characterized with the ancient Indo-European word *maryanni*. The Latin alphabet was derived from the Greek alphabet but had initially only 14 letters. Learning followed mostly the Greek cultural tradition and Horace (68-8 BC) was correct when he wrote: *Graecia capta ferum captorem cepit* (= vanquished Greece conquered her rough, wild conquerors). Greece was made a Roman Province in the second century BC. Greek learned men, philosophers, meaning also scientists, many of them coming from the Greek *polies* or colonies scattered over the Mediterranean and West Asia worlds, were engaged as tutors and teachers by the rich patrician families. Though they had the civil rank and name of "slaves" the tutors had an honoured position and a princely lifestyle in the home of their patrons. Rome's cultural tradition already since the days of the Republic suffered the onslaught of almost uninterrupted barbarian invasions, internal unrest and amongst the most devastating, from the literary point of view, the biased writings and works of the converts to Christianity during the last centuries of Imperial Rome that ended with the descent of the Longobards in Italy and the fall of the West Roman Empire in the year 476 AD.

Fortunately the epics, including Virgil's Aeneis, the writings of Homer and Hesiod, of the historians and of the dramatists, of the scientists and much of the philosophical writings of Greeks and Romans have come down to us almost intact thanks to the patient work of the learned men of the Library and Museum of Alexandria of Egypt founded by Alexander the Great, and of European medieval monks and scribes, to mention only the most relevant.

The ancient tradition of the Indo-Aryans and of the Indo-Iranians was preserved orally and in writing by the learned men of both cultures. The present book is based on the original sources and texts, only main points of similarity and dissimilarity are mentioned here.

EPIC POETRY

The latin word *epic* comes from Greek *epikos* (= *epicus*) that is derived from *epos* (= word). Epic poetry therefore literally means the word [= story] about the heroes. The word poetry comes from Lt. *poesis*, from the Gk. *poieo* (= I create). Ancient epic poetry was considered to be created by the *rhapsodists* and *cytharists* who sung with their *cithara* mostly about the heroes while the *aedes* sung about the gods. The two poetries were intertwined and there could not be a strict division of attributes or duties between aedes and rhapsodists, because gods and heroes interacted and could be one or the other at different times.

Epic poetry is centered on the acts and the glorification, rarely also on the condemnation, of heroes. The heroes may be gods, semi-divine, human-like or theriomorphic creatures, or may be men or women. Children as a whole, or heroic children in particular, are rarely present in the Homeric epics, they must be inferred indirectly. Heroes are usually under the personal protection of some god or goddess. Heroines are not warriors but are nevertheless endowed with great courage, a basic feature of heroes, their fathers, husbands and brothers from whose example they draw their own power, fortitude, faithfulness and virtue. Such were Draupadī or Penelope. Epics are poems of varying length that sing the acts and facts of legendary heroes who may become traditional national heroes or symbols because they are involved in vicissitudes, wars or other episodes defined in time that contributed to the formation of their nation, like the Pāṇḍava brothers or Ulysses. The folklore of all people is to a great extent based on epical, heroic stories which are milestones in the evolution of that particular civilization. We are not concerned here so much with the history or the stories themselves as with the details of the behaviour and gestures of the people that may throw some light on the causes or origin of similarities and differences between Indo-Europeans of east and west.

In the west the Homeric poems are considered to be the original model of epic poetry followed by all later poets. Scholars, however, discuss whether the blind singer Homer really existed as a man and whether it was the same person who sung both the Iliad and the Odyssey. After reading the full texts in immediate succession and checking repeatedly on the original Greek verses, it seems clear that one poet composed the two epics and that they were written at about the same historical time. It is also quite clear that the Iliad and the Odyssey, as well as the *Theogonia* by Hesiod were carefully planned and sung on a blueprint that obviously availed itself of a rich pre-existent oral tradition. Whether Homer was blind or not, whether he was born on the island of Khyos or elsewhere, the discussion is immaterial and futile.

The basic importance of reading the complete texts of the Iliad and of the Odyssey for understanding the culture and facts of ancient ages remains unaltered over the centuries. We respect and admire "Homer" for his knowledge and for putting in writing the songs of the *aedi* and of the *rhapsodists* and much more. These are priceless windows opened on the very ancient European and Mediterranean past, they formed the bases and inspired the development of the Hellenic world and Hellenism. Homer and Hesiod gave an identity to the Greek people, and the basic principles of the Graeco-Roman civilizations survive to this day in the western world.

This also is not the place to discuss subjects such as, which is older, the *Mahābhārata* or the *Rāmāyaṇa*, or enter into endless discussions on the innumerable aspects, factual, fictional, educational, devotional or epistemological and others of the Indian epics. I will concentrate only on a few selected aspects which bear comparison with corresponding features of Homeric and other western gods and heroes as we know them from the ancient oral and written traditions.

Differently from the Indo-Arya virtually unbroken tradition, oral and written, the Indo-Iranian material, cultural and religious, oral and written traditions, have had some deep-rooted rearrangements. First the advent of Zardosht (= Zoroaster) caused a breach in culture by stating the preponderance of Atar, the fire god and emphasizing selected definitions of ethical and philosophical aspects different from those of the ancient tradition. Existence came to be seen as the unending struggle between the forces of good, represented by the "All-Good Ahura Mazda" and the forces of All Evil, represented by Ahirman. In the fourth century BC the second breach in the ancestral tradition was brought about by the warring frenzy of Alexander the Macedonian who ordered the destruction of the written texts of the Avesta and of the Gāthās. The third breach in tradition was radical in the sense that an entirely new culture and religion took place with the Islamisation of Iran. We are concerned here only with the tradition of the heroic times up to and as far as the wars of conquest of the Persian Emperors of the Achaemenid dynasty. Scattered archaeological findings in present day Iran dated earlier than the *Habur ware*,[4] suggest that the ancient Indo-Iranian people who travelled west and southwards over the Iranian plateau were probably nomadic people and surely not very numerous.

What we know at present of the Heroic age of ancient Persia, or Phars, or Iran and of the development of the cultures of the Iranian Plateau, is mainly what we have from archaeology, from the Shah-Namah of Firdusi (? 940-? 1020 AD), from what has come down to us of the Avesta and the Gāthās, and what was written by the Greek and Roman historians. The story of Jesus of Nazareth and the description of the visit of the three Wise Men to the newborn infant, is direct evidence of the high esteem in which was held the wisdom of the Magi, the priestly class of the ancient Medes, incorporated into the Persian culture at an early stage. The Concilium of Florence, begun in 1439 and drawn over more than ten years, also brings evidence of the influence of ancient Mazdeism on the Church of Rome, heir to the Roman Empire, and inherited by the Oriental Christian Churches.

Many authors compared the epics of the Graeco-Roman tradition with the Shah-Namah pointing out similarities and differences. In fact also both the Iliad and the Odyssey had earlier described facts that happened a long time prior to being put in writing and noted that much had been added to the original stories and myths. Comparably to the Indian and Greek epics, the Shah-Namah also describes wars waged between different Indo-European clans as well as battles against local, non Indo-European people for the supremacy over land and sea.

The *Shah-Namah* by Abdul Qasim, called Firdusi, makes very interesting reading and is more than just a historical rendering of the ancient Iranian people and kings. The Shah Namah is well-known, well-read and extensively commented. The contents of this "epic" have been widely studied. There is clear twining between the Indo-Iranian and Indo-Arya traditions and culture which are evident in the close relationship between the Gāthās, the Yashts, the pre-Zoroastrian and Zoroastrian tradition with the pre-Vedic and Vedic culture and tradition. The Indo-Iranian literary tradition is much closer to the Indo-Aryan than to any other Indo-European tradition. Among late Indo-European cultures, the Shah Namah, written at the same historical period as the Provençal literature mentioned above, has more affinity with the Italian medieval literature than with the Graeco-Roman tradition.

(B) Iliad, Odyssey, Aeneis

Invasions, migrations and mixing with different Indo-European clans and with non-Indo-European autochthonous Mediterranean people, created the rich and powerful Greek culture which owes much to those varied sources (Menghi 2003). The Iliad and the Odyssey taken together have 27, 803 verses in 24 books each.

The scene of the Iliad is from first to last verse the plains and sea in front of the besieged city of Troy. The scene of the Odyssey is the Mediterranean Sea, some of its islands, harbours and landing places and the ten-year-long return voyage of Odysseus (= Ulysses) back home after the destruction of Troy. The time when the facts described in the Homeric epics took place is about the late twelfth century BC. The scene of Virgil's Aeneis, is the route followed by Aeneas from the day when he escaped and sailed away from the pillaged and burning city of Troy with his old father Anchises on his shoulders and holding his son by the hand after having lost his beloved wife in the confusion of the burning city, and his arrival on the western shores of Central Italy, where he is well received by the Etruscans. Like Ulysses, Aeneas is an idealised historic figure who underwent many trying experiences on his long voyage by sea. Virgil, the poet author of the Aeneis, was inspired and encouraged by Augustus who was then aiming at becoming the first Emperor of Rome. The divine origin of Rome and the equally divine ancestry of the *gens*

Julia to which Augustus belonged, had to be disclosed and proved. Aeneas was thus declared son of goddess Aphrodite (= Venus). The Aeneis was transmitted in writing, not orally, but was never completely finalised, due to the demise of Virgil in the year 19 BC, followed by emperor Augustus' death (14 AD).

Heroes of the Iliad arrive on the battle field on their two horse chariots but fight on foot. They often fight in their own interest because of wrath or revenge, rather than in the interest of the war waged by the Acheans (= Greeks) against Troy (= Ilio). There is not much of an army, or navy as we understand the word, nor is there much of organized battle or war strategy among the attacking Greeks or the defending Trojans. The society is still that of free and equal warriors and rulers of cities, already evolved and differentiated to a point. Agamennon, king of Mycenae and brother of Menelaus, king of Sparta and husband of the kidnapped/runaway Helen, is the overall chief, or leader, but his authority is very limited. All decisions of the Greeks are taken by the Assembly of Kings, each one of them leader of a small group of warriors coming from various small "kingdoms." There is no similarity with the well-planned and organized wars and battles of the Indo-Aryans of the second millennium BC of which there are historical records, as mentioned above in Part I. The princes, kings and warriors are heroes on the battle field; they are martial heroes who follow the rule of individual strength and ability.

The declared cause of the war was that prince Paris of Troy kidnapped the not-unwilling Helen, wife of Menelaus, king of Sparta, and brother of Agamennon. Paris was much less than a hero on the battle field and he was the indirect cause of the death of his elder brother Hector who tried to save the honour of the ruling family and of the city. Hector (Gk = *Ectoros*), brother of the cowardly Paris, was defeated by Achilles and his body was outraged to avenge the slaughter of Achilles' friend Patroklos by Hector. The sense of honour and duty of the individual personalities varied from one hero to another and the Olympic gods sided with their favourites, irrespective of ethical codes, of which there were few. In fact there is not much moral concern or judgement of individual behaviour in the Homeric poems. There is no strict code of conduct valid for all the fighters and there is no individual right or wrong, usually no praise or condemnation of the acts; discipline was a rare word seldom used by the Greeks.

The battle scenes themselves are a great confusion, usually each man fending for himself. The Iliad is rich with gory details of bodies cut to pieces, busted skulls, bloody brains and entrails dropping to the ground. Duels are brutal encounters between the strongest. On the whole, however, because of some key episodes describing acts of friendship, honesty, honour and bravery and above all because of intertwined stories, the Iliad is informative and relates acts and doings of a multitude of people. It is a most interesting epic poem still worth reading in full nowadays. The frame story and the details of the ten-year-long siege and war show the cultural background and illustrates the way of life in that part of the world three thousand years ago.

The Odyssey describes the return of king Odysseus (= Ulysses) to his native island of Ithaca after the arson of Troy. The return travel took ten years, all the ships of his fleet and all his companions were lost or dead and he was himself saved only by chance and divine will. The Odyssey describes indirectly the discoveries and accomplishments of the expansion of the Greek people over the Mediterranean and beyond, east and west of the Greek peninsula. It is a useful source of information on the geographic and mythical knowledge and customs of the Greeks of the eighth century BC when the poem was written, and of the last centuries of the second millennium BC, which is the time when the facts described took place.

The Iliad and the Odyssey are a purposeful synthesis of the epic songs and oral tradition of ancient heroes and gods that the rhapsodists and aedes sung to kings and warriors of the many small states of the Mycenean world. The Iliad knits together into a consistent whole the traditional lore, customs and habits of the past Mycenean and Greek heroic ages prior to the Doric "invasion," when there was for the first time a drive to unite all the Greek people into a nation which at that time was called tentatively the "Achean League." With the passage of time, this proved to be a leaking ship with holes blocked only occasionally as the need for concerted efforts arose. Much later, in the sixth century BC the Greek League, motivated by the threatening approaches of the great Persian army of King

Xerxes (519?-465 BC), was successful in joining most of the scattered forces of Greece to face the common enemy.

The Iliad and Odyssey are jointly called the "Homeric epics" though they may be the work of two different poets. The language used was a form of ancient Greek and the facts described are from the late period of the Mycenean civilization, fifteenth to twelfth century BC. The Doric tribes coming from continental Europe, most probably Thracia put an end to the Mycenean culture not yet fully organised politically in the twelfth or eleventh century BC. Mycaene was a city in the Argolid peninsula of the central part of the Peloponnesus, at about lat. 37° N. The Homeric epics were formulated and put in writing at least five to six centuries **after** the facts described in the poems took place. Many important descriptions, like that of the weapons used, of the social structure in peace and war, of individual habits, of details of ships, fights and many others are lumped together irrespective of chronological sequence and evolution of culture. The descriptions cover the period from the height of the Mycenean culture to the evolved Greek culture of the eighth-seventh centuries BC, when Homer formulated the poems that were perhaps written down by someone else, since Homer was said to be blind. The culture level described is that of the Bronze Age. There is no mention of iron; even the detailed description of Achille's shield does not mention iron. Mycenean helmets were made of leather, covered with felt and with dense rows of male pig or boar's tusks fixed on the surface. Bows and arrows, maces, lances and javelins continued to be the main offensive weapons, while shields and armours are still made of heavy bronze, including swords, daggers and double axes. In the Mycenean age, gold was cheaper than iron and warriors' armour and shield were enriched with gold, a marked difference from the description in the Aeneis, where iron and steel were the rule of the armament of the warriors because gold had become a precious metal brought from Asia.[5]

The Greek epics are the prototype of what is usually called "epics" or "epical poetry" in the learned world at present. The Indian "epics" are represented by the *Rāmāyaṇa* and the *Mahābhārata*, though they have characteristics of their own that show a great difference between Indo-Europeans of east and late Indo-Europeans of west. The Indian epics are more than just epical poems; they include history, geography, genealogies, science, specially astronomy and numerology, religion and philosophy. Interpolations of various lengths introduced at different and unspecified times are frequent. For these reasons and because the "old" was never discarded when new wisdom was added, the Indian epics are much longer and convey more information about the cultural past of India than the Greek epics about the cultural past of the Mediterranean world.

THE ILIAD

The title of the poem indicates the paramount importance of the destruction of Troy for the Hellenization of the Troade area of Asia Minor. The *"demos"* (= the mass of the people, the people) of Troy was a mixture of many people of different *"lineages"* (Il. II 804). The rich city of Troy was a strategic competitor of Mycenean Greece.[6]

The Iliad is centered on the Trojan War but the core subject is the interaction of gods and man during the Heroic Age of Greece, as well as the story of the siege and destruction of the ancient city of Ilio. The Iliad is also the story of Achilles, son of Tethys, a goddess of the sea, and of Pelaeus, grandson of Zeus. The 24 books of the Iliad are written in typical epic style of classical Greek. The poem is carefully planned, uses various literary modes and techniques, including flash-back episodes, dialogues, similarities, contrasts and surprise actions. The scene is the plains of Asia Minor facing the Aegean Sea where the city of Troy was built at the entrance of the Straits of Dardanelles. The Achaean League was successful in uniting temporarily the many Greek city-states and people for a single purpose. The pretext for the war between Greeks and Trojans was the abduction of Helen, wife of Menelaus king of Sparta, by Paris prince of Troy (= Ilio). The city of Troy was ideally located to dominate the maritime route that links the Mediterranean to the Black Sea through the Straits of the Dardanelles, the Ellespont, (Il. XII 30, = Sea of Marmara) and the Bosphorus, going from west to east. The siege of Troy lasted ten years at the end of which the city was taken by deceit, plundered and burned. Archaeological evidence confirms that a city was burned towards the end of the second half of the twelfth century BC at the traditional site described as the place where the city of Troy stood. Archaeologically identified and dated remains of Troy are those found at levels VI and VII. Archaeological evidence also shows that levels I to V contain the remains of earlier cities about which there is not much knowledge. Earliest occupation probably goes as far back as the middle of the third millennium BC or earlier, according to tradition confirmed by recent studies.

The migration of people usually known as the "Doric invasion" of Greece coincided with the end of the Mycenean civilization and marked the return to earlier, less elaborate living styles. The Iliad gives many details of the culture of the cities and people which formed the Achaean League and of the Indo-European ruling class of Troy. From a historical point of view it is clear that the position of Troy was strategically important as it could control and levy duties of transit on people, goods and ships plying the only waterway linking the Aegean to the Black Sea, where there was active trade between Mediterranean people and the flourishing Indo-European settlements on the littoral zone of the Black Sea. There was interest in achieving supremacy over the area, especially at a time when the Greeks aimed at becoming a great nation and state. The abduction of Helen, wife of Menelaus of Sparta and the recovery of the princess are evidently only a pretext for the war, the siege, the plunder and the arson of Troy, though we are told that Menelaus succeeded in taking back to Sparta his beautiful wife Helen, an important political accomplishment. From the beginning of the last millennium BC the Greeks extended their zone of influence also westwards. By the sixth century they had reached Sicily, the west coast of Italy, Nice, Massilia and Emporia on the southern shores of present day France and Spain, and eastwards all around the Black Sea. There were only three Greek cities on the North African coast: Barca, Cyrene and Apollonia. The Greek peninsula was colonized by Greek people as well as the island of Crete and the western shores of West Asia and Asia Minor facing the Aegean Sea. The Greek colonies were surrounded by Iberians in the Iberian Peninsula, by Celts in what is now France, by Italics and Etruscans in Italy and Illirians to the north of Macedonia. The Greek people expanded and traded with people living around the Black Sea, while most of north Africa, Palestine and Phoenicia were already occupied and under the sphere of influence of the Egyptians and of Phoenicians and other Semitic people.

The frame story of the Iliad is the recovery of runaway princess Helen and the destruction of Troy as an act of revenge for the offense made to the honour of the rulers of the Mycenean dynasties. Within the leading story, a large number of family genealogies of both Greeks and Trojans are given in detail, as well as descriptions of armours, funerary customs, food, battles, the city itself and the participating countries or city states. Attributes and family history of the warriors of the attacking Greeks as well as their contribution to the war in terms of ships and men are given in detail, they offer significant information for visualizing customs and habits of the people of that period. The meaning of the poem can be fully appreciated only by reading and re-reading the full text to understand the teachings or interpret the descriptions of the scenery, of the characters of the play and of the lifestyle of the people. The original Greek text often has to be resorted to for understanding and clarifying doubts in the translations.

Interestingly the Iliad ends with the description of the funeral rites and the entombment of Hector, killed by Achilles. In the Mycenean age, and later, burning of heroes and kings was the rule, while common men were usually buried. The escape from burning Troy and the long troubled journey by sea back to Ithaca narrated in detail by Odysseus (= Ulysses) to Alcinoo, king of the Phaeaces (different from Phoenicians, Aen. VI, note by La Penna, 2002) on his way back to the island of Ithaca are described in the Odyssey. The destruction of Troy is narrated also in the Aenaeis, by Aeneas son of goddess Aphrodite and Anchises, a nobleman of Troy. The narration is given, according to Virgil, by Aeneas to Dido, queen of Carthago, a Phoenician colony on the southern shores of the Mediteranean, present day Tunisia.[6]

Obviously the Iliad is complex and detailed; it includes many of the legends and myths of the heroic age on which it is based. From the heights of mount Olympus or from the battle field itself, the Greek gods are always present, they fight for their protegees and because there are some gods on either side, the gods and goddesses also fight amongst themselves some not very godly fights. Obviously the real meaning of the Iliad is beyond the abduction of Helen which is but an episode for a purpose. The poem signifies that long works of diplomacy in peace and war were needed and were carried out to establish the supremacy of the Greeks, set the bases and introduce Hellenism as a culture and way of life over Asia Minor, the Black Sea, the Aegean and the Mediterranean Sea at large, except Egypt and some Phoenician colonies west of the Greek peninsula. About battles, the Iliad does not mention the *tuba*, or trumpet that was already known to the Indo-Aryans of Asia Minor since the second millennium BC. However it describes Patroklos as a "cavalier = horseman" and "fighting on horse back" or as overthrowing horsemen.[7]

The Iliad represents the growth of various cultural units, the Greek *polies* which were still considering whether to merge into one nation or not. Political unity was not achieved but the concept of Hellas and Hellenism was born and deployed its wings over much of the ancient world prior to the rise of the Roman Empire. The concept of Hellas was admirable but it did not materialise politically into a single great nation though the spirit lived in the future for many centuries, upheld by its own vigour and by Rome as a republic. Homer produced the seed of the typical culture of Hellas and of the ideal concept and philosophy that grew and developed in what became known as Hellenism. The reasons why it did not materialise into a single strong nation are many and are not to be analysed here. One reason however could be mentioned, this is that the Greek learned persons were individualistic orators, philosophers, scientists, dramatists, artists, also politicians while the concept of the *polis* put more emphasis on the city itself rather than on building a coalition of cities or on satisfying individualistic egos even if justified. Though the Achaean and later Greek leagues did not live long politically, the most valuable aspects of Greek culture still survives in many ways to this day. Hellenism and the Hellenic world as a symbol of ancient western culture were never defeated.

It is to a large extent due to the lack of political union and single dominance, to extreme liberalism, individualism and independent evolution and creative power of each unit and each person that the West owes so much to the ancient Greek world in the field of sciences, arts and all branches of philosophy. Each individual, each city, each island, never mind how small, each and every *polis* or single man had the opportunity and was able to offer the best of itself.

Every single valuable contribution in whatever field was recorded and kept alive by the disciples of great masters and was enriched with ever-new knowledge. The last verse of the Iliad reads: "Thus was honoured the tomb of Hector, *horse trainer*": to be a great horse trainer may be as valuable and praiseworthy as being an honourable warrior and prince. Each one of us should be great in his own field, whatever the field in which he excels, as a hero, horse trainer or both. So was also prince Rāma, great as a prince and king, as an archer and warrior, as a hermit and thoughtful husband and as a ruler and politician. To the name of Rāma should be added so many others, beginning with brother Lakṣmaṇa, the epitome of faithfulness. There are many similarities between Hellenism and ancient India in the basic philosophy of the art of living, knowledge, understanding *and wisdom* as different from mere erudition. The purpose of the Iliad was to support and advise on the need to establish the supremacy of Hellas over a vast area in the Mediterranean and Asia, on whose products Greece was dependent. The latter were mainly metals such as gold, silver, copper, iron and steel (= *ferrum candidum*= white iron). The Iliad showed that the Achaeans were stronger, more skilled, capable and cunning than the rich Troyans. In the Mycenean age, iron was rare, however iron is repeatedly mentioned in the Iliad (IV 123; VII 141, 473; XVIII 34; XXIII) where it is said that iron was given as a prize in XXIII 826, 850. Homer also mentions steel as requiring much toil to be produced, his very picturesque naming of steel is: "tiring iron" (Il. X 379 *et al.*) because iron had become common during his time, although it was yet relatively unknown and not used at the time when the facts described in the Iliad and Odyssey took place.[8]

In conclusion, the Iliad of Homer was successful in bringing together myths and legends of the heroic past that were floating around in the Greek world. The frame of this anthological poem is the pre-historic war between two clans of Indo-Europeans of west as defined here, those of Greece and those of Asia Minor, and the alliances of either with autochthonous people. The cultural development that took place beween the time when the facts described in the poem and their record in Homer's epics, was the invention of the alphabet and development of a phonetic script in the eighth century BC, which the Greek owed mainly to the Phoenicians. On the other hand the development of a written language increased the schism between the Greek, later also the Romans, and the "barbarians" who neither spoke nor wrote the language of the learned Greeks and Romans.

THE ODYSSEY

The Odyssey is centered on various Mediterranean people and introduces the idea of Hellas as a great nation through the integration of different people and cultures. Except for the language, which is ancient Greek, and for the script which is the same as that of the Iliad and is adapted from the Phoenician script with inputs from other sources, the Odyssey differs from the Iliad in purpose and general plan. I see no need to presume that there were two different poets of the aedic tradition who were authors of the Homeric poems. Both the epics were developed on a well structured and completed plan, with a scope. Like the Iliad, the Odyssey is written, and was sung, in hexameter poetry.

Odysseus (= Ulysses) is said to have contributed 12 ships fully equipped to the Trojan War (Il. II 637; Od. IX 139). He was an ancient figure of Greek mythology. "Odysseus" and "Achilles" are names known to be more ancient than the Greek language. In the epic, Odysseus appears as a composite of several persons or perhaps he represents the many incarnations of a single one, similar to the composite figures of Dionysos and Herkules, who became gods very late in their long careers. Odysseus is the king of the small island called Ithaca, off the western coast of peninsular Greece, in the Ionian Sea. Evidently the adventurous Odysseus, as a prince and warrior symbolizes the early Greek expansionism. He is a multiform hero, a vigorous fighter, a wise prince, an able and cunning man, son of king Laertes of Ithaca. Above all Odysseus is shrewd and crafty. The treacherous plan of introducing armed warriors hidden inside a gigantic hollow wooden horse into besieged Troy was his and it was his shrewdness that saved him from all the perils he went through that cost the life of all his companions and the loss of all his ships with the booty taken from Troy. Current or newly invented technical details that were already developed in Homer's time can be seen in the story of building of the "Trojan horse" under the guidance of Ulysses. The gigantic structure was truly a siege machine, as were later used by Romans and during the Middle Ages, in fact part of the walls of Troy had to be destroyed to introduce the towering horse into the city.[9]

As much as the scene of the Iliad is geographically static, namely the plains of Ilio in the region called Troade, the Odyssey covers much of the Mediterranean world as known to Homer. There is a large number of characters in the Iliad while the Odyssey is centered on Odysseus. The poem covers a period of ten years during which the hero navigates by oars and sails bound to Ithaca and has many adventures on the way. Due to the enmity of Poseidon (= Neptune), Odysseus underwent many painful and difficult situations from which he could extricate himself only due to his intelligence, experience, physical strength, endurance and above all the protection of gods other than Poseidon. One by one he loses his ships and his followers until when he is thrown off by the waves of the sea, naked and almost dead on the shores of the island of the Feacians (= Phokeians) called Skeria, where he is assisted by the local king Alcinoo, his family and people. Finally he is taken by a Feacian magical ship to Ithaca, where he is left on the shore, asleep and covered with precious gifts.[10]

Literarily the well drawn plan of the poem is simple and linear, though there are flash-backs and secondary stories interwoven into the main one, as in the Iliad. The language, the script and the style are the same as those of the Iliad. Both the Iliad and the Odyssey are based on ancient legends of the heroic and earlier ages, many of the acts and facts described can be archaeologically dated. The arson of Troy and the writing of the poems are chronological benchmarks to assess the development of the cultures bordering the Aegean Sea.

The Iliad begins with a crucial episode of the tenth year of the siege of Troy and the poem covers the last six to eight weeks of the war. The Iliad ends with the defeat and killing of Hector by Achilles and the description of the last rites and honours due to the great warrior prince. The Iliad closes prior to the introduction into Troy of the wooden horse with the Greek warriors hidden inside. The story of the last days of the Troyan war, the episode of the horse, the battle and the arson of Troy, the death of old king Priam and his family and the ten years of Ulysses' wanderings from islands to shores are not described in the Iliad, but in the Odyssey, where Ulysses recounts his travels at a banquet given in his honour by Alcinoo, king of the Phaeces, who enquires about his guest's identity. More than half of the legendary places and people mentioned can be geographically and culturally identified, though most of them are described partially enveloped in magical phantasy. Finally, Ulysses is reinstated in his island, with his faithful wife Penelope and his valiant son Telemacus at his side in his palace, after he overcomes and kills the Procians who had unsuccessfully wooed Penelope's hand during his absence.

The original idea of the hollow wooden horse was given by the ever imaginative Odysseus who also helped building it. The ten years of wanderings and sufferings inflicted on him were a punishment for such a base behaviour, unworthy of a noble Greek king and warrior, as well as the curse inflicted on him by Poseidon who resented Odysseus' killing of his own son Polyphemus, the gigantic Cyclop with a single eye in the middle of the forehead.

Some of the places mentioned are easily identifiable geographically or are natural phenomena, such as the description of the Straits of Messina, between Sicily and Italy where two monsters, Scylla and Charybdis, one on each side of the waterway, sucked up and swallowed ships, engulfed them in monstrous whirlpools and devoured the drowning mariners (also in Aen, III 560). This is actually an accurate description of the whirlpool and high waves that are formed every three hours regularly, a phenomenon caused by the different timings of the tidal wave in the Thyrrenian Sea north of the Straits and the Ionian Sea south of it. Tides in the Mediterranean Sea are normally of small amplitude, about half a metre, rarely reaching a metre in height; however the whirlpool and high waves are specially strong in the Straits or during storms and high winds. Local people knew and still observe correctly the best or alternately forbidden timings to sail or row across the straits. The monsters are of course phantasy that adds dynamism to the story that otherwise correctly renders a natural phenomenon and is easily located geographically and tides-wise.

Similarly to the Iliad, the Odyssey follows a well studied plan and describes the gradual expansion of the Hellenic culture towards the central and western Mediterranean. Significantly the earliest important Greek colonies were in the lands bordering the Ionian and Adriatic Seas that were collectively called *Magna Graecia* (= Great Greece). Syracusa was the first of the important *polies* on the eastern coast of Sicily, Massilia founded by the Feacians in the Gulf of Lion (southern France) and many others were founded at about the same period, the eighth to seventh century BC. Most colonies followed the same pattern, but this could not have happened if the classical Greek civilization had not been preceded by the primitive cultures of autochthonous people. The pre-Greek Mediterraneans who lived in the region had ample contacts and trade among themselves and with the advanced cultures of the Egyptians and Semitic people.

The founding of Rome in the eighth century BC coincides with the time when Homer and Hesiod were shaping the new religion of Hellas, the epic poems were written and the Greek colonies were founded and flourished.

Compared to the Iliad, the Odyssey is at a different level of phantasy, more down-to-earth than the Iliad. Even Circe who had magical powers and was able to transform some of Odysseus' companions into animals, is just a beautiful woman with human instincts. Or the Cyclop Polyphemus, a son of Poseidon (= Neptune) killed by the human hero Odysseus, cannot be saved by his three eyes and gigantic size and strength; the Sirens (= mermaids, half beautiful girls and half fish) of the Straits of Messina (= the she-monster Scylla) and others, were all easily fooled by Odysseus, a man and not a god, not endowed with magical powers. Finally even Poseidon, Odysseus' major enemy, abandons all hopes of defeating the crafty hero and allows the Feacians to take him safely back to his island where he wins the last victory over the *Procians* (= suitors) who were robbing him of land, fortune, son and were trying to win his wife Penelope. Odysseus defeats them by a great feat of archery (Od. XXI), the final feat of Odysseus which is almost within the possibility of a human hero. The great archery feat of Odysseus is comparable almost step by step to the great feat of archery performed by prince Rāma at Sītā's swayaṁvaram. Odysseus is one of the last Indo-European human heroes of the heroic age of Greece.

By all standards the ruling class of Troy belonged to the groups of Indo-Aryans settled in north-western Asia Minor who had come centuries earlier from the eastern lands around the Caspian Sea. At this stage it is important to note that there is almost no mention of the "people" (= *demos*) at large in either the Iliad or the Odyssey, it almost seems that there were no people in Troy and surroundings other than kings, princes, warriors and slaves.

The purpose of the Odyssey was not only to illustrate geographic expansion, it was evidently produced also to show where and what goods or raw materials could be found that were not available at home, a universal limiting difficulty for small or island nations.

The Iliad and Odyssey together gave an identity to Greece, cultural rather than political. Hellenism was born and over the centuries many authors repeated: "we owe everything to Homer." Hesiod codified Homer's gigantic work with the *Theogonia*, and other writings. The heroic age of Greece was sealed with a golden key and the echo of its culture survives to-date. Practically many of the ancient Greek colonies are still now flowering cities that have had a long history of trade and cultural success. The epics are also a useful introduction for the knowledge of lifestyles, habits and customs of the Indo-Europeans of that age.[11]

Differently from the Homeric poems, the Aeneis of Virgil marks the end of the first seven/eight centuries of the life of Rome, firstly ruled by kings, later a republic, finally an empire too great to survive indefinitely, as hoped and planned by Emperor Augustus.

Rome was founded by Romulus and Remus at about the time Homer's poems and Hesiod's *Theogonia* were written, in the middle eighth century BC. Romulus was a putative descendant of Aeneas, the Trojan hero son of Aphrodite (= Venus), who fled from Troy carrying his old father Anchises on his shoulders after the destruction of Ilio (= Troy). Since its inception Rome had close ties with the descendants of Trojan Greeks following the diaspora of the warriors and of the people who survived the killings and the arson of their city. This is the basic story of the Aeneis. Many Trojans found refuge in Italy as mentioned by Virgil who says in the Aeneis (I, 242) about Antenor, the Trojan hero who founded the city of Padova on the Adriatic Sea coast, that he found *certa domus* (= a safe home, or safe haven) in Italy. Repeatedly (in Aeneis, books IV 85-89; VI 4-10; XI 116-141) we find in the three poems instructions on how to select appropriate sites for establishing new colonies.

THE AENEIS

The Aeneis of Virgil was written to eulogize the newly acclaimed First Emperor of Rome, Caesar Octavianus Augustus (63 BC-14 AD) and the *gens Julia* to which Caesar and Augustus belonged. It is meant to be a historical poem, though tendentious phantasy often mixes with historical accuracy.

The Aeneis is a poem in twelve books written in Latin hexameters, in the last century BC by P. Vergilius Maronis (70-19 BC), seven centuries after Homer composed the Iliad and the Odyssey. Vergilius (= Virgil or Vergil) is considered one of the greatest Latin poets, friend of Augustus, a relative and adopted son of Julius Caesar who was Virgil's patron. The Aeneis is a purposeful mixture of history and legends aiming at giving a divine origin to Rome founded, by modern calculations, in 754 BC (traditionally founded 752/751 or 751/750 BC, according to Marcus P. Cato the Censor, lived 234-149 BC). The historical background of the Aeneis is the Greek, including the Trojan colonization of the Latium region of Italy and the birth of Rome as a city. The legendary story given in the poem, is the divine origin of Aeneas, son of goddess Venus (= Aphrodite) and Anchises, a Trojan nobleman. According to other legends that reflect the most probable historic truth, Aeneas is a linear descendant of the first Trojan immigrants to peninsular Italy. Aeneas participated with Herakles, so says the legend, towards the settlement of the Trojans in their new territories in Italy after the arson of Ilio (= Troy). After the destruction of Troy, the people dispersed all over the Mediterranean Sea, a movement called the diaspora (= dispersion) of the Trojans. According to Greek historians, the arson of Troy occurred in 1184 BC. Traditional ancient sources said that the "kingdom of Troy" lived for 2800 years that would push the first settlement in the Troade region back to the third or fourth millennium BC, a date only approximately confirmed by archaeological findings of the ancient-most city-remains that are at the bottom level of the site where the city of Troy stood. The city of Troy sung in the epic poems corresponds to archaeological levels VI-VII. It is immaterial to ponder whether the date given is correct or not. The meaning is just that Troy was founded far back in the nebulous undated past by a man called Dardanus, ancestor of the kings of Troy and son of Zeus. The last of the lineage of the Dardanids was Priam who perished during the sack of Troy.[12]

Five or six centuries elapsed from the destruction of Troy to the foundation of Rome, hence the need of fusing legend and history to declare the divine will to establish a new city and nation "destined to rule the world with Justice and Peace." After the foundation of the new city on the banks of river "Ruman" (the name was later changed to "Tiber"), there was an initial period of rule by the legendary Seven Kings, the first four were Etruscans. In Aen. IX 325, Virgil mentions the various people of the original city of Rome. The Ramnenses (from the name of river Ruman), were said to be the direct descendents of Romulus and his companions. The rule of the kings was followed by the Republic of Rome that lived for about seven centuries before being replaced by the Empire. The core purpose of the Aeneis is to enhance the glory of Rome as a nation and the role played by the "Divine Augustus" to usher in a new era. Rome had all the elements necessary to become a great nation; it had lands, people, independence and self-determination. The fall came when it lost its primordial character of self-determination. The fall of the Roman Empire of the west is dated 476 AD.

Virgil was a great poet of nature who sang the *divini gloria ruris* (= divine glory of the open fields, the country-side, the rural land, *Georgicae* I, 168), the glory of life in nature, beautifully expressed also in his "Bucolics" (*boukolos* = shepherd). The need of the hour, however, was to produce an epic poem to bolster the new Era of Rome, the passage from the Republic (= *res publica* = the public thing, the State, the common domain), which was ruled by the "*Senatus populusque Romanus*" (S.P.Q.R. = the Senate and the People of Rome), to the rule of an Emperor. The Roman Empire would create the era of the "*Pax Romana*" (= Roman Peace). Emperor Augustus received ambassadors from all the known world, including twice from India, in the years between 2 and 19 AD. Trade with India was active and words relating to *India* and *Indus* are not uncommon.

Pointedly the Aeneis commemorates the political change from Republic to Empire. The centre piece of the poem is a political panegyric of Augustus (Aen. VI 756-886) formulated with the intention of infusing unshakable faith in the future of Rome represented by Augustus, himself descendant of the "pious Aeneas." The new Imperial regime was to be seen as the crowning glory for the security of Great Rome, no longer just a city, but a successful nation with distant frontiers, successful achievements and noble endeavours, from politics and jurisprudence that are the arts of ruling, to engineering, architecture, learning and teaching that are the arts of living. The panegyric contains the stated article of faith that became famous (Aen. VI 823): *vincet amor patriae laudumque immensa cupido* (= the love of the home country conquers [or: will win]; [*patria*, a term which includes also philosophy, religion, the objects of the cult and liturgy specific and typical of a nation]. An alternate translation could be: the love of the nation as well as an immense urge for praise will win. The general subject of the Aeneis is the adventures of Aeneas from the day he departs from plundered Troy to the time when he finally settles in Italy.

The *Pax Romana* was eventually lost and the Empire broke down in 476 AD, essentially because the high level ethical code of conduct of the men and women of the *Res publica* (= Republic) was lost during the late days of the empire under all sorts of richness and corruptions and also because of the unmanageable size of the Roman dominions. Due to Virgil's own tendency of a singer/poet of nature, the Aeneis, though an epic poem describing battles and violence includes also much lyricism. The lyricism of Virgil shines with full pathos in the scene describing the meeting of Aeneas with the soul of his defunct wife Creusa (II 771-794) who was lost in the confusion during the escape of the family from Troy. When he finds the shadow of her ghost enlarged (Aen. II 790) against the background of the moving flames of the great fire of the nether world, he desperately tries to hold her, but though he sees, talks and listens to his beloved wife (Aen. II 790-795) "thrice I tried in vain to hold the image which escaped from my hands like a light breeze and a vanishing dream . . ." (= *par levibus ventis volucrique simillima somno*). This scene is taken directly from the Odyssey where the hero is allowed to have a relatively long meeting with his mother in Ades. Great epical heroes are exceptionally allowed to visit Ades, the nether world. Virgil faithfully acknowledges repeatedly his debt to Homer, the "greatest master of all times."

Gruesome, bloody descriptions of killings, revenge and vandalism are fewer and shorter in the Aeneis than in the Iliad and the Odyssey, not a small feat to the credit of Virgil, considering that the poet follows the model left by the Master almost step by step. Virgil however does not forget that Aeneas will eventually have to be purified and redeemed because of his blood-tainted hands, before he is allowed to sacrifice again to the gods. The poem is written in the style of Greek epic poems, as Virgil praises himself for having received the inspiration from the Muses *through* Homer.

The scene of the Aeneis is the eastern Mediterranean and the wanderings of Aeneas. His father Anchises carries in his hands the *Penates*, family and city deities whom the legend says were those which became the household deities of Romans and Rome. Much of the historical significance of the Aeneis lies in the accurate geographic descriptions of many places, the genealogies of heroes, families and illustrious men and women, the many temples to Aphrodite (= Venus) visited by Aeneas, the descriptions of the scattering of Trojan and Greek people all over the Hellenic world, the battles and difficulties encountered for the settlement of the new immigrants in the Latium and the description of habits, customs, rites and ethics of ancient and contemporary times. To us, the Aeneis has the added value of showing the changes, progresses or regresses that may be, that took place in the culture and knowledge of Rome after the eighth century BC when the Homeric epics were written based on traditional lore, knowledge and morals. The Romanisation of Greek Gods took place during this period, it was evidently needed to give an identity to the city of Rome and to the new forms of government: the Republic first, then the Empire, in a manner corresponding to the identity given to Hellas by Homer and Hesiod. The old Greek Gods in new attire, Romanized in their names and character, together with ancient local Italic gods added to the Greek pantheon became the guardians and guarantors of the new form of government, the *Res publica*. The genuine Roman invention called *Republica* has its counterpart in some forms of government of ancient Indo-Europeans among which were a few clans, such as the Śākya kingdom in India into which was born Siddhārtha Gautama who became the Buddha.

The essence and ideals of Rome as a civilization were different from those of Greece since the first day of ploughing the perimeter of the square area that would become the city of Rome. Greece had emphasized the importance of numbers, measures, all the arts, abstract knowledge and politics. Rome applied Greek science (= *philosophia* = philosophy, knowledge) rather than Greek politics to nation building and to all the practical aspects that had to be developed to build and control the extensive Roman domains, including the martial arts and engineering. Heir to the Greek civilization, Rome survived for centuries mainly thanks to the Jurisprudence it developed and applied. Jurisprudence is the philosophy, reason and justification that support *The Law.* Roman Legislation was inflexible and applied inexorably. The practical attitude of Rome was different from the principles and ideals of the autarchic attitude of the Greek *polies*. Virgil in the Aeneis (Aen. VII 203) repeats the famous sentence of Senocrates, a disciple of Plato and head of the "Accademia" after Plato's death, who replied to those who enquired what would be the results of his teachings: "They [his disciples] should do **spontaneously** by their own will-power, what others are **obliged** to do by the law."

The Aeneis describes the Greek colonization of the Latium and other regions of Italy and the association with the Etruscans soon after and since the diaspora of the Trojans. Culturally the Aeneis covers the historic/cultural gap between the Doric invasion of Greece and the writing of the Greek epics in the eighth century BC. The assimilation of pre-Roman indigenous gods as well as the Romanisation of Greek gods that took place after Homer was needed to give an identity to the new city and its ambitions. Aeneas was recognised as the remote ancestor of the baby twins suckled by a she-wolf, though later both Romulus and Remus were declared descendants of god Mars who, according to Virgil, would have been the father of Aeneas, rather than the mortal man Anchises.

In the Aeneis the historical perspective tends to be accurate, and would-be "historic" facts are often referred to as "legends and myths of the ancient oral tradition." There are many literary and traditional influences on Virgil but there are also many philosophic discussions, specially important those on Fate and Destiny. Virgil like Homer, purposefully or naively mixes up contemporary with ancient features, such as the use of war and siege machinery that were invented and used by Romans, but are mentioned as being used during the siege of Troy, one thousand years before they were actually fabricated. The mixing of cultural traits of different ages is a feature common to most epic poems.

Virgil insists that Aeneas fulfils a historical duty imposed on him by Destiny. In fact it is historically recorded that there was much influence and mixture of Trojans with Etruscans and of these with Romans, specially in the early age of the seven kings of Rome, when Etruscans had already reached a high cultural level while Romans were still a rustic assemblage of various people who initially had to rob their neighbours' women to start their families and populate the new city, an incident known as the "Rape of the Sabine women," an episode that epitomizes many skirmishes and battles that Romans waged in the early years to strengthen their position locally. The Aeneis celebrates the birth of a new era and the evolution of the Graeco-Roman civilization. The Roman republic under the acronym SPQR (= *Senatus Populus Que Romanus* = the Senate and the People of Rome) was successful in what the Greeks had failed, building of a strong nation based on a well defined culture developed intellectually and technically. Roman praxis and strict enforcement of the law were its strength.

Following the mixture of cultures, we find in Etruria, then in Rome, growing and increasing cultural richness and diversification. The symbiosis of cultures of different origins promoted the creation of a vigorous and revitalised culture, the new Roman civilization. As mentioned above, a similar fact happened earlier in the acculturation of the Hurrites following the cultural inputs of the Indo-Aryan Mitanni and Hittite dynasties that ruled from the seventeenth century BC onwards in what are now parts of western Iran and Anatolia. The development of the Roman civilization occurred late enough in the history of the Mediterranean cultures to bypass the heroic and pre-historic cultural periods and enter directly into history.[10]

In the Aeneis as compared to the Homeric poems, there is more ethics and concern with proper behaviour, more propriety, sometimes even bitterness over a long sought-after victory that had caused deaths and sorrow to the defeated. There is more honour and there are debates about loyalties in conflict, more concern with the law, individual authorities and philosophy as well as more hope in new values, more belief in positive prophecies, more civility and much more concern with godly gods, rather than humanized gods participating in battles to ensure victory for their protegees. The gods of the Aeneis are more refined and civil than Homer's gods; they do not behave like uncouth human beings and cannot be wounded by human weapons, differently from what happens in the Homeric epics. They do not lack in godly behaviour and they participate physically in the free for all battles and fights only rarely. From the point of view of the present study, the Aeneis is particularly interesting as a source of information on the practical and technical progress achieved in the seven centuries between the Homeric epics and the last century BC. Places and times are described more accurately as well as the customs and history of the various people encountered during the migration from Asia Minor to Italy. The description of the tempest that strikes the little fleet of 12 ships of Aeneas escaping from Troy is realistic and testifies to the story about a tempest that poet Virgil had suffered aboard a ship during one of his travels.

The Aeneis is an epic/historic/political poem written by a learned poet in well documented historic times. Virgil was the companion of a learned emperor and of other learned men of his times. He was born in Mantova (northern Italy) and was made a Roman citizen by Augustus only after he became famous as a poet. The Aeneis is a fully developed poem that benefited from debates held among the many poets, philosophers and historians who thrived in the golden age of Augustus. Some passages and verses of the Aeneis remained unfinished, probably due to the premature death of Virgilius (19 BC, in Brindisi) who was later entombed in his favourite city of Neapolis (= Naples).

Virgil renders successfully the fusion of the ancient myths of the Italic heroic age with the legends of the Greek culture. At the same time he also relies heavily on the writers, poets and historians who preceded him or were his contemporaries, specially those proficient in the Greek and Latin oral tradition and written history. The invention of a script for the Greek language and the use of an exclusive script for Latin were at the origin of recorded history of the Roman civilization in the present understanding of the word. One of the merits of Virgil was to recognize the importance of the oral tradition, of myths and legends which play a significant cultural role in all civilizations and are often the only window open on their past.

GRAECO-ROMAN EPICS — SUMMARY

The descriptions found in the three epics illustrate the evolution of the material aspects of the culture of the ancient Greeks and Romans. Shields, helmets, swords, daggers, spear points and other arms were still made of heavy bronze in the Mycenean age when gold was freely used to beautify the armaments, even shields to be used in battle were decorated with gold until when iron displaced bronze. Initially gold was cheaper than iron, until when discovery of abundant iron ore in Italy, first from the island of Elba, turned iron into the most commonly used metal. The use of the horse in parades and battle was the rule, but the charioteers were not always succcesful in manoeuvering the two horses that drew the *biga* (= two-horse war chariot) forcing the warrior to leave the chariot and fight on foot. Fighting from horseback became common under Philip and Alexander the Great and current in Rome where horse breeding was a highly developed art. Racing came late and the *quadriga*, a chariot with four horses harnessed in a single front row came in use mainly for races, in the circuses or military parades. Stirrups were unknown; they were used and introduced in Europe much later by invading Mongol hordes. The trumpet (Lt. = *tuba*) was imported from Asia and was an indispensable element of the Graeco-Roman military, as it had been much earlier at the time of the Indo-Aryan Mitanni kings. The curved or looped trumpet was an Etruscan development, as was also the stone arc and stone arched bridges and sewerage system, later perfected by Roman engineers. Darius III of the great Achaemenid dynasty of Persian kings was the first who crossed dry-foot over to Europe from Asia Minor in 480 BC on bridges made over floats and boats, in the same manner as Alexander and other leaders crossed rivers with their armies. The hollow wooden horse where Greek soldiers were hidden (Aen. II 235), with its height and fortifications, was an imaginary mobile assault tower, but assault machinery was developed only much later by the Romans. The wooden horse had served its purpose; parts of the city walls had to be demolished to introduce the heavy machine into Troy. The development of war tactics, strategy and logistics, were some of the great practical improvements made during the time of the Roman Republic, they were as stringent as the enforcement of the law and the creation of detailed jurisprudence. Much engineering was developed by Rome, specially in the fields of urbanistics, hydraulics, sewerage, road building, water resources conservation and utilisation and architecture which was essentially based on the pure Roman arc (= maximum width equal to twice maximum height at the middle of the arc, in other words, width equal to the diameter and height equal to the radius of the full circle of which the perfect arc is the hemicircle), was originally an Etruscan invention. The art of sculpture was inherited from Greece, mosaics and painting was highly developed specially for interior decoration of the houses of the Roman patricians. The most ancient Greek and Roman statues were made of wood. The *Panthaeon* of Rome (= temple of all gods) is still standing and is still the largest dome ever built, with a maximum diameter of 43.30 metres. Second in size is the dome of S. Peter in Rome, with 42.52 metres and third, the dome of the cathedral of Florence with 41.47 metres diameter at the base.

It is well known from the decipherment of ancient texts written in Linear B script, used in Crete and in the Peloponnesus since the second half of the second millennium BC, that the Mycenean and Greek cultures were at different levels of development and were different from each other. The Mycenean culture was very rich, it had a complex political, administrative and military structure, the people were divided in numerous classes according to their professional specialisation and activities while at the same period in time, division of labour and professional specialisation were just beginning to take shape in Greece that was still a pastoral society with only rudimentary agriculture and was not yet organized into a State. After the Doric invasion that took place towards the end of the second millennium BC, the rich Mycenean culture declined and there was a return to village life.

The Greek colonisation of the eighth century BC Latium started with the mythical ancestor Evandrus, a local chieftain and shepherd who had been a king in Arcadia, Greece, "in ancient times." After coming to Latium, Evandrus (or Evander) had built a city whose gods were enshrined in temples on the hill called *Pallantheum* (later = *Palatinus*) one of the Seven Hills of Rome, he is reputed to have given to Rome its language and alphabet (Aen. VIII 50).

Considered from the perspective of this book, there are many details in the Graeco-Roman epics worth mentioning because they illustrate the cultural evolution that took place in the Mediterranean civilizations from the age described in the Iliad and Odyssey, up to the beginning of the Christian era. The culture that followed the period when Homer lived and Rome was founded marks the establishment of the solid foundations of the Roman culture, its vigour and inbuilt strength. The last century BC was marked by the civil wars in Rome, by the end of the Roman *Res-publica* and by the birth of the Roman Empire. Virgil was convinced that he was writing to usher in a new age, what happened instead is that he closed with a golden key a great era of nation building and epic literary past. After Virgil no really great epic poems were written in the classic Graeco-Roman world, literature developed along different avenues. Among the epic poems written before the fall of Rome, the best known is the "Dionysiacs" of Nonnos that is no way comparable to the classics. Much later the Provençal epics of southern France and the Italian epics of Ariosto and Tasso tried to imitate the great classics, but they fall short of the epic value of the early European or Indian masterpieces.

I have no competence to discuss Indo-Iranian epic poetry. Quoting from Ghirshman (1977, p. 76, *transl.mine*) "An important role . . . in the cultural manifestations of the Iranian people is that of the epic poetry whose origin is . . . eastern Iran . . . which is a rich literary rendering of epical subjects and their adaptation to historical figures."

(C) The Thrust, Bagao and Balletys

Most Homeric hymns are in hexameters but they are not arranged as a single poem and therefore are not considered to be an epic poem.They probably were not written by Homer and the word *Homeric* should be considered an adjective of praise, rather than one of authorship. On the whole they are what remains of an ancient, probably much longer collection of hymns made by unknown author or authors and addressed to various deities and heroes of ancient Greece. Hymn II is one of the longest with 495 verses. It is considered by Mylonas (1961) to be the most authoritative source concerning the Eleusinian mysteries of goddess Demeter. It is undoubtedly the oldest text on the origin of the cult of Demeter that has survived down to present days. Vannucci (1999b) discussed the contribution made by the goddess to the development of the Greek civilization. Above and beyond the important introduction of hexaploid wheat in *Attika* (= Attica), the most meaningful and efficient contribution made by goddess Demeter was the teaching of methodical agriculture, already well developed in Central Asia, where she came from. Transfer amongst ancient civilizations of techniques invented by applied science and moved around by trade, were the crux that put in motion and nurtured their accelerated growth and development, from the fourth and third millennia BC onwards.

The remarkable parallelism between east and west Indo-European traits is here focused on lines 265-267 of the hymn to Demeter (Hymn II) which refers to a game called *Balletys* in Greek (= the Thrust) and a contemporary "game" called *Bagao* which takes place in village Devīdhura near Lohagat in Kumaon, Uttaranchal State of India, in the month of August on the day of Rakṣābandhan.

Rakṣābandhan is a relatively recent festive occasion that is most seriously observed in North India. The little ceremony consists essentially in tying a string on the wrist of a respected elder as a sign of friendship, respect and as an unspoken request for protection. The elder rewards the younger with blessings and a small amount of money, preferably just a coin or two, and sweets. This custom is the survival of a gesture that became institutionalised some centuries ago when young Hindu girls tied a coloured thread on the wrist of a Muslim older man who thereby became her "brother," responsible for her safety. Hindu ladies were also known to tie the thread on adult men with the same meaning as well as a request of protection. The ceremony has no strict rules attached, it can happen at any time during the day, there is no formality, it is short but meaningful and somewhat emotional, sweets are distributed to children and neighbours. At present it is not limited to youth or young girls and boys. Often a young servant or other children tie the string on the wrist of the mistress or master of the household and neighbours rejoice going around with trays full of sweets to be distributed to children and friends.

At village Devīdhura in the month of August a game called *Bagao* is preceded by the voluntary participation of young men who retire for fast and worship in the temple of *Devī*. It is a special spiritual retreat when the boys keep fast, purity and abstinence and restraint from certain foods. There are also other rules which must be strictly observed. Each boy takes individual offerings to the temple and on the last day they are divided in two groups, each group offers seven goats and one buffalo to *Devī*. The temple is a permanent structure, it has a small entrance door, and everybody and everything must go through that entrance. One has to bow low to be able to enter, as one would have to do to enter into the womb of mother Earth: an act of obeisance, respect and an imploration for initiation into the archaic mysteries of the divine.

At the end of the preparatory period the boys who stayed in the temple fasting and worshipping come out in the open, then two groups face each other and pick up stones which are said to appear spontaneously on the premises. On the day of *Bagao* a boy or a girl more often a girl is taken in a *dhola* and he or she falls in a trance. Then every single boy of each group facing the other group throws stones at every boy of the other group, but usually nobody gets hurt, only occasionally someone is slightly hurt or wounded. When this happens the boy is taken care of, the leaf of a local plant is rubbed on the wound that heals quickly.

I never witnessed the game personally as I never was in the district at the right time, the description I received does not go much further except for saying that the person in charge of organising and overseeing the play of the ritual game, is normally a venerable member of a *Pande* lineage from Almora. What I know so far is that the two rites, the *Bagao* of Kumaon and the *Balletys* of ancient Greece follow the same steps and ritual, including periods of fast, study, ablutions, libations, worship and meditation. The final game of the thrust of stones is performed under the same rules and has the same intention in east and west: ensure protection to youth upon entering maturity, hence admission only through the narrow opening, when the boy is presumably apt to receive the initiation to *Devī*. The goddess is a Mother in either case, east and west she is the one who nourishes. "*Devī*" Demeter was revered because she was the one that ensured regular supply of food by teaching methodical agriculture to the Greek people.

Homeric Hymn II 265-267 addressed to Demeter reads:" . . . yearly in his [Demophont's] memory (= honour) when the year completes its cycle through the seasons, the sons of the Eleusinian people will forever engage in a violent fight. . . ." When she spoke thus, Demeter was under disguise as the old nurse of king Keleos and queen Metaneira of Athens, in the middle of the second millennium BC. According to legend Demeter had disguised herself as an old woman after her daughter, the maiden Kore had been abducted by the wicked Aidoneus, king of Hades the netherwold. Demeter found refuge with the then king and queen of Athens in whose palace she was bringing up their youngest son Demophont. Suddenly one night queen Metaneira surprised Demeter while she was keeping the young boy in the fire (or under the fire's ashes). Metaneira shouted loudly and called an alarm, giving no time to Demeter to explain that she was a goddess and her treatment would ensure eternal youth and immortality to the child dearly loved by the two of them, mother and nurse. When the sortilege was broken by Metaneira's cries, Demeter cursed the faithlessness, distrust and stupidity of the human race and resumed her own true image of a most beautiful woman. However the motherly side of goddess Demeter prevailed, she remembered that "the child slept in my arms and climbed on my lap . . . therefore the sons of the Eleusinian people will fight a wild fight between them to remember Demeter who offers joy and comfort to mortals and to immortal gods" and this is how the young participants will not gain immortality, an impossibility declared by Fate, but will be protected by invulnerability to a certain degree. They do not get seriously hurt; this is as far as the protection of *Devī* can go, within the realities of nature and the traditional naturalistic principles of matriarchy.

Herodotus (IV, 180) also mentions that the people called Maklies and the Auseys [of Libia] celebrate an "unusual festival in honour of Athena during which young girls are divided in two groups and fight each other with stones and sticks, *according to rites ordained by pre-Hellenic ancestors to* honour the indigenous goddess whom we call Athena." Herodotus further adds that "they call false virgins the girls who die as a consequence of the wounds received."

Contemporary authors produced various learned interpretations of the rite, though some mentioned that it is "very strange" that the privilege granted by Demeter recommended a fight, because Demeter was the nourisher, they say, she should recommend peace and not war. This is a useless misconception or a wrong interpretation, whatever we wish to call it. The episode of Demophont is short but most significant in a hymn that is rich in meanings and teachings. Nobody can give immortality to humans, not even gods, because nothing can go against the laws of nature or the cosmos (*ṛta*). Nature, however, or the nature gods can offer all sorts of protection, if only we learn to understand their hidden language. Protection of the body has many different aspects; Āyurveda's principles are based on this type of knowledge.

Relating what goes on in India to what happened in ancient Greece, we find that games similar to the "Thrust" (= *Balletys*) were practised in several places of the world where they may be part of initiation or purification ceremonies and rites or, like at Devīdhura and Eleusis, the performance of the rite has the purpose of strengthening self-respect and self-reliance, physical fitness, truthfulness, unfailing faith in the power of the Godhead and steadfastness to conquer the fear of death of the body. Intimacy and love for the protecting and helping *Devī* are knitted tightly as the knots of a thread. Participants in a state of trance or fast may have visions about present and future, they pass through trying purification tests, they are not promised immortality but they develop a strong desire to deserve a wholesome future, including a good body, shielded as they are by *Devī*, whatever her given name, presence and origin. The greatest gift is to conquer the fear of death of the body.

The practice of auto-flagellation is indicative of the need of cleansing oneself from the scourge inflicted by offended gods or by one's own actions. From the point of view of these "games" in India and Greece, bloody flagellation is substituted by a very youthful and human game accomplished in a lighter vein inspired by the trust in *Devī* Demeter. The game is called *balletys* or *bagao*, but whatever the name, the great majority of boys who participate in the game at Eleusis or Devīdhura are fortified by trust and respect for the master, they acquire a clear conscience and fortitude. Everybody performs better when well guided (Vannucci 1999).

Purification by blood, whether one's own blood or that of sacrificial animals, or purification by water are and were practised everywhere at different times in the entire world. Purification is the means to free one from feelings of guilt, sin or defilement of the body, conscience, soul and spirit when someone who correctly or not feels guilty of some bad action. With motherly love Demeter decides that the children of Eleusis should not be burdened by the faithlessness of Metaneira and by the curse that she inflicted on her, she loves them as she had loved Demophont. And because she cannot give them immortality, she gives them the capacity to earn their own will-power, freedom and independence. The boys playing the *Bagao* at Devīdhura or elsewhere feel that *Devī* is near and dear to them as they are to her. Demeter, a goddess herself, promised continuous assistance to attain the benefits of bodily death without fear, she is no longer worshipped under this name in the west, but many festivals and religious blessings that commemorate and bless agricultural practices, can be traced back to the Eleusinian and Orphic mysteries. They promise and ensure respectful and warm intimacy with the deities and ultimately with the Godhead.

Was the practice of the game a transfer of culture or was it developed independently, based on common roots? As mentioned earlier (Vannucci 1999b) we have an approximate acceptable date for the arrival of Demeter "from the east" to Athens, we also have tentative dates for the migrations of the Indo-Arya towards the Indian sub-continent. They are the two extreme poles of a geographic continuum. Absolute chronology is at present almost impossible to define; it is therefore safer to say that if there was no transfer of culture, there was survival of ancient myths, legends and beliefs in basic principles and human aspirations at either end of that cultural world. In other words, if not direct transfer of culture, there was a most remarkable convergence of the survival of archaic traditional practices among the Indo-Europeans of east and west.

The parallels between the Bagao of India and the Balletys of Greece are so close in spite of an entirely different setting and scenery, that it is impossible to avoid the conclusion that the two "games" have the same root in some proto-historic event or belief of the Indo-Europeans. Probably we could find here several events linked to the birth and development of agricultural practices. One is tempted to identify the common root in the culture of the Indo-Aryans living in the plains of R. Gurgan south-east of the Caspian Sea, **before** they split in two groups, one going eastwards towards India and the other westwards towards Asia Minor and Greece. Approximate datings are supportive of this hypothesis. The roots of the rite could be even more ancient, they could be as old as the most ancient Indo-European culture, earlier than the first migrations. The widespread occurrence of practices somewhat similar to the present day Bagao of India among Indo-Europeans who migrated to Europe over the route north of the Black Sea, suggests that similar rites started very early, already among primitive clans of the Indo-Europeans, perhaps as a test of virility of the young boys when they reach bodily maturity. In this context, dates and absolute chronology are immaterial. What **is meaningful** is that the idea and the materialisation of the idea into a participatory rite in honour and communion with *Devī* survived for a very long time since the origin of the myth. In this case, agriculture and the gratitude to **The One** who taught how to observe and manage the production of "food made by the Gods" (the rite of *annāpraśana*), whoever that **One** was, the myth gives the key for understanding the deep meaning of "games" superficially described as "strange" by many authors. There are no cultural traits anywhere in the human world that do not have a kernel of truth, often disguised as a superstition or legend under the word "habit." The other side of the coin is that insignificant or useless customs or habits are usually selectively discarded.

In the cycle of myths related to Osiris, the major god of ancient Egypt, there is a short story that tells how Isis disguised as an old woman (corresponds to Demeter) is met by the queen of Byblos who sees the crying woman seated next to a fountain.[10] The queen takes the old woman into the palace as her servant and finally makes her the nurse of her son. Isis in disguise did not suckle the baby but gave him the tip of her fingers to suck, finally one night she *"burned the mortal portion"* of the child, but when the queen saw her baby in the fire, she shouted and the spell was broken. Isis flew away disguised as a swallow; she was very angry and caused the waters of the river to dry off. This story is told both in ancient Egyptian terms (names of the gods) and in its Hellenized (Greek name of the gods) form, revealing its survival and the introduction into Egyptian mythology as late as the age of the Greek pharaohs, the Ptolomies. It is however a sure sign that "Hellenisation" of the myth of Demeter became current in Egypt during the Hellenistic period, after the conquest of Egypt by Alexander in 332 BC. It is a typical example of transfer of cultures and adaptation of alien myths following the acculturation introduced by the supremacy of a new culture (ref. Brunner-Traut, E. Italian transl: Favole e Miti dell'antico Egitto. German original, publ. 1963, Munchen. Orig. title: Altagyptische Marchen, Mythen und andere wolkstumliche Erzhalungen). The original myth of Demeter is undoubtedly many centuries older, it is more detailed and complete, bears an approximate date and place of origin, mentions names known historically at least one thousand years earlier than the Isis myth. The transfer of culture between Egypt and Greece is surely as ancient as the last millennium BC but may have been as old as the Mycenean age.

The game called Balletys is widely known. The thrust of one or more stones is a game played annually during a folk festival in Croatia as well as places in Greece where two groups face each other taking much care not to hurt the others. In northern Spain, the game is still now played in a village on R. Ebrus. Throughout the Himalayas groups of boys and girls face each other singing defiant songs and moving against each other in a row, rather than throwing stones at each other, at various festive occasions. Similar habits are found also in many ancient agricultural communities the world over, or on high mountains where singing and dancing are ritual occupations during harvest and are useful for keeping warm during the long, cold winter nights. Of course most of the contemporary singing and dancing between groups of boys and girls in the Indian Himalayas is not to be related to Demeter's curse, it is just a convergence of habits and customs caused by ecological and climatic imperatives.

(D) Herakles and Other Ancient Greek Heroes

Herakles (= glory of Hera, beloved by Hera, Juno for the Romans) the strongest man ever, was begotten by Zeus on Alcmena, the pious wife of Amphytrion, king of the city of Thebes in Greece, not the Egyptian homonymous city. Zeus disguised himself as Alcmena's husband to be able to lie for a long time with the woman who was destined to be the mother of the powerful hero who alone could become the all-times-champion of gods and men. Sun and moon stood still as the union of Zeus with deceived Alcmena, who believed to be lying with her husband Amphytrion, lasted three days and nights. Such a long time was needed to produce the most powerful and famous Greek hero who travelled the "infinite lands and seas," from the Atlantic Ocean to Anatolia and further as far as peninsular India and the eastern shores of the Black Sea. Herakles was the hero of great feats, immense strength and incredible achievements. Herakles is an integration of the anonymous heroes of the very ancient times, his feats cover the entire world known to the Greeks. None of the later heroes, such as Geryon or the athenian Theseus have as wide a geographic and time expansion as Herakles alone had. In the *Theogonia* and in Herodotus (IV 9-10) the Scyths are said to be the descendants of the sons of Herakles and Ekidna, one of the Gorgons. The Scyths were a nomadic tribe of Indo-Europeans who arrived from the Eurasian steppes moving around the Black Sea. They reached the lands on the margin of the Black Sea and north of Crimea, around the eighth century BC. Herakles like his father Zeus, sired many offsprings from several women and semi goddesses.

Herakles is repeatedly mentioned in the epics. He is mentioned in the Iliad, a poem centered on the relationships between gods, heroes and men; he is also mentioned in the Odyssey, a poem centered on the geographic expansion of Hellas and of the Hellenic culture, and is at the same time a panegyric of heroes past and present. From the Odyssey we learn that Herakles gave to Odysseus (= Ulysses) the great unbreakable bow of the great archer Euritos. The *Theogonia* (vv. 286-289) tells how Herakles the "strong," the "lion-hearted" killed Geryon in a fight, while Homeric hymns XV, XVI, XVII respectively dedcated to Herakles, Asclepius and the twin Dioscuri, Castor and Polydeuces (= Pollux), refer to characters variously called heroes or gods at different places and times. The great number of conquests and victories attributed to Herakles could not have been done in a single life time, the myths and legends evidently summarise achievements of a host of heroes integrated in the figure best known, that of Herakles who left behind him an entire lineage of descendants, the "Heraklides." Herakles' weapons are the bow and arrows and the mace that he made from the hard wood of an olive tree that he pulled out bare handed from the soil.

The Herakles currently best-known is the last embodiment of several characters whose story and feats are told since the very ancient past. Herakles and Dionysos are personified aspects of the material and immaterial forms and features of mother nature created by early man to encourage men, women and children to struggle and overcome the difficulties that each one will inevitably find on his/her path during the arduous travel throughout life on Earth. Heroes are most important as examples and masters, but even more as comforters to hearten the tired, disillusioned and disheartened. Herakles like Dionysos of the popular tradition must have been preceded by un-named awful creatures or wild forces best known from the results of their acts. With the evolution of cultures, the "beings" acquired name and personality; they are often classed as demons or creatures with dual personality.

Considering history and geographic occurrences it is clear that Herakles' career over many centuries of great feats and brutal power is the other side of the coin where the face is Dionysos who progresses along an acculturation and civilising path. The earliest myths are the most phantastic dreams and nightmares as could only occur in the primitive mind of early man who could not understand or explain natural phenomena and feared the supernatural monsters created by his own imagination. Phantasy and imagination again enter into stories created during decadence periods of all cultures; they are an attempt to uphold the morale of the ruling and the ruled. Having been promoted from manhood to godhood, both Dionysos and Herakles are finally accepted among the Olympians — Dionysos because of his intelligent services and inherent understanding of the world around him; Herakles because of his parenthood and material services though he was not always morally correct. Finally late Herakles (Herakles) is initiated to the mysteries and enters Olympus thanks to his marriage to Hebe, daughter of Zeus and the personification of youth, being herself eternally young and beautiful.

The creatures killed by Herakles, beginning with the strangling of the two serpents sent by jealous Hera to the baby's cradle, were at the initial stage of the myth just small animals that at every re-telling became bigger and bigger until they reached sizes much larger-than-normal monsters, ever more difficult to kill or subdue, such as the Hydra of Lerna. Finally Herakles carried out single handed superhuman material works at the service of his elder half-brother king Eurystheus, whom he had to serve throughout life — these were the famous twelve labours of Herakles.

There are, as for Dionysos in the Mediterranean region, on the European coasts of the Atlantic Ocean and around the Black Sea and Asia Minor, many places that claim to be Herakles' birth-place or the site where he performed one of his many outstanding feats. Similarly to Dionysos', Herakles' career and stories cover a very long period and are spread over land and sea. There are good reasons to believe that there is a core of historical truth in most legends that tell about Dionysos and Herakles, who both went at some unspecified point in time as far as the geographic part of Asia that we now call India. As befits Greek heroes, both Dionysos and Herakles visited Hades, Dionysos retrieved his mother and Ulysses meets Heracle's "shadow," not his ghost because by that time Herakles was already on the Olympus.

One of the feats of Herakles related to the present study was the destruction of a precursor city of the Homeric Troy as vengeance against Poseidon (= Neptune, Iliad XXI, 442-455) who had failed to give him his immortal horses as promised wages for his services. When Troy was finally destroyed at the end of the Trojan War Herakles had been dead or deified since a long time. For this reason Herakles returns to Troy only as a ghost and takes no part in the war. He was met in Hades by Ulysses (Od. XI, 267, 601-629; XXI, 26-30 et al.). Herakles was always a single fighter, never a sworn or constituted warrior. One of his most significant feats is the killing of Ifitos, son of Euritos and the gift to Odysseus (= Ulysses) of Ifitos' unbreakable and very heavy bow. Odysseus uses this bow and arrows to exterminate the Procians on his return to Ithaca. The attributes of Herakles are the mace, the bow and arrows and he is covered with the pelt of the terrible "Lion of Lerna" that he had killed as the first of the twelve labours.

Herakles was the founder of the Olympian Games. The first took place in 776 BC in the sanctuary of Zeus at Olympia in the Peloponnesus; it lasted five days. During the games, prominence was given to horses and human fitness, essential Indo-European characteristics. The first day was spent with the swearing in of the athletes, the second was taken by horse and quadriga races. Saddles, stirrups and spurs were unknown. Other athletic games (= sports) followed from the third day onwards. Sports and religion were closely interwoven. In several Greek cities special recurrent festivals were celebrated to honour Herakles, the great hero who was said to have participated in two important expeditions of the expansionist movement, the travel of the Argonauts to conquer the Golden Fleece and the hunt of the Kalidonian boar.

Herakles is the most universal of all the Greek heroes; he is certainly not refined and may stoop down to infamous acts if necessary to achieve the ends commandeered to him. One of his worse acts was the killing of the learned centaur Keiron, for which he had to perform strict penance before his initiation to the mysteries of Eleusis. He is the best known of the many Greek heroes because of his fame and incredible strength and achievements, his daring courage, prowess and great might. If a far fetched approximation of Herakles to an Indian hero could be attempted, it would be Bhim, the incredibly strong among the Pāṇḍava brothers.

Many other Greek heroes achieved great feats, but they will not be mentioned here, though many are significant in the context of this book. Differently from Herakles other heroes were not necessarily universal heroes of all Hellas, they were comparably restricted geographically. Theseus the Athenian was son of Aegeus, an ancient hero who is a symbol of the ascendancy of Greece over Crete. The Aegean Sea is named in his honour. Theseus (Il.I 265) killed the

Minotaur, bull-headed son of Zeus and Pasiphae, queen of Crete. The Minotaur was kept in the centre of the famous labyrinth of Crete, where king Minos, son of Zeus and Europa, had hidden the monster. Theseus found his way in the labyrinth by unwinding the red thread given to him by his beloved Ariadne, daughter of King Minos, whom he later abandoned (Il. XVIII 592). Ariadne (akin to *Āraṇyāni*) was then saved by Dionysos, she became a goddess of nature, and the oak was particularly sacred to her. Another famous hero was Jason (= healer) who guided the Argonauts to the conquest of the Golden Fleece. Perseus (= destroyer) saved Andromeda and decapitated the Gorgon called Medusa who had serpents instead of hair on her head and whose glaring eyes petrified whoever would dare look at her, specially her enemies.[12]

Mythological Herakles belongs to the lineage of Perseus son of Nestor. There are numerous other Greek heroes most of them directly or indirectly historical or pre-historical figures. Herakles is the ideological syncretism of the powerful fighters of the very ancient Mediterranean world. These and other heroes eventually enriched the mythology of Hellas and the culture of ancient Greece, itself fertilized by interaction with neighbouring Indo-European and non-Indo-European cultures.

(E) Heroes and Epics of the Indo-Aryans

It would be superfluous to write about the Indian epics in a book published in India. The *Rāmāyaṇa* and the *Mahābhārata* are part of everyday Indian life and are well known. Within the frame of this study, only a few comments should be made.

The Indian epics, specially the *Rāmāyaṇa*, are mainly devoted to the teaching of Hindu *dharma*, an echo of the pre-history of the Indo-Aryans, and of the geographic expansion of waves of migrating Indo-Europeans who arrived "in the land of the seven rivers" from the region north and west beyond the Indus hydrological system. Details of proper behaviour of individuals and families, administrative and political duties and rights are always at the forefront of descriptions, discussions, examples and recommendations. Hindu *dharma* is then personalised as the ideal for men, women and children of all ages and communities. The central theme or frame of the *Rāmāyaṇa* is the story of Rāma and his consort Sītā. The poem covers Sītā's swayaṁvaram (i.e., choosing a husband oneself), the marriage, the life and intrigues at princely courts, the life of the couple in the forest which is the symbolism of the return to nature, the abduction of Sītā the ideal woman and glory of womanhood, and related stories. Rāma, the ideal ruler and Sītā, the ideal woman, were royal prince and princess hence much of the background is specifically related to Kṣatriya *dharma*. The *Rāmāyaṇa* teaches that righteousness will always prevail over wrong, good prevails over wicked. Rāma was so fair and just that even animals, bears, monkeys, the bird Jaṭāyū and others helped him to retrieve pure and faithful Sītā after she was forcibly kidnapped by evil Rāvaṇa. The understanding with nature was complete. On the other hand and completely opposite to this trend, is the faithlessness of Helen and of Paris whose story is only the pretext to justify the war for military and political supremacy waged by the Achaeans against the Trojans.

There is one important aspect of similarity between the *Mahābhārata* and the western Indo-European epics, this is the internal jealousies and fights among the various clans of Indo-Europeans that has been the scourge of all the Indo-Europeans since ever. It is repeatedly discussed in the Indian epics, the Purāṇas, Itihāsas and ancient literary sources as the bellicosity of the "kṣatriya race."

There are only few similarities between the Greek, Latin and Neolatin language heroes and epics on one side, and the Indian heroes and epics on the other, except for the persistence of some very ancient cultural roots in both east and west traditions. The western epics were planned before they were put in writing, the eastern epics had most probably never been planned to be written and reproduced in the modern sense of the word (= *published* is a notion that did not exist in ancient times) and when they were finally incorporated and named as major productions of the "Indian" mind, they had already undergone a long series of interpolations, additions and deletions in both the oral and the written forms. Inevitably minor or major changes were introduced in the great epics during the long centuries of popular and learned but not necessarily written traditions. Nevertheless all poems that can be classed as epics in the east as well as in the west, reflect the stories and history of the people they talk about, their customs and habits and the cultural evolution that led to what we recognize as the ancient civilizations of which we are heirs.[11]

The great art and science of recording and "publishing" learned texts was codified and widely practised with the founding by Alexander the Great of the Museum and the Library of Alexandria in Egypt (Casson, 2001; McLeod, 2000).

The main similarity that enables us to classify ancient poems as epics, is perhaps the presence of different sorts of heroes in both east and west. The parallelisms are not one to one at the level of single heroes, they refer mainly to the concept of hero or what makes a human character a Hero. The basic connotations of the "heroic" period of civilizations are those of an age when specially gifted men were able to improve living conditions and chances of survival and thereby improve life expectancy, reduce infantile mortality, achieve better nourishment for all through cooperation and division of labour. As a consequence, the general set-up of "heroic ages" is everywhere similar, even comparable. Undoubtedly the main purpose of the ancient epics is to remember and give due recognition to the great men and women of the past, imaginary or real. Symbols are produced and examples are available to be used as reminders and models to help mould the character of the new generations.

Greek epic poetry was closely followed by the forceful poetry and prose of the Greek dramatists, the most notable are the tragedies by the great masters Aeschylus, Euripides, Sophocles, to quote only a few of the greatest, and was followed by the major schools of "philosophers," including those who would now be called scientists.

The tragedies and comedies written by Greeks as special dramas to be represented by masked actors had in India their counterparts in episodes described in detail in the epics and other literary texts, sung by story tellers, probably had not initially been intended to be special self-contained performances to be given by human actors, nor was the name of single authors mentioned. The episodes were in the course of time put in mime, music or dance and performed by puppets or human beings in an astonishing variety of different moods and arts, in many different languages and dialects and at different levels of sophistication. The development of every imaginable possible mode of the performing arts in India, both lay and religious, has no parallel anywhere in the world. Performances were held in specially built stages in the open, not infrequently built on the occasion of village celebrations or recurrent fairs or special days, as is still done at present. Only later performances were held in temples as acts of devotion to the deity. Typical and exclusive Indian forms of music or performing arts are amongst the most excellent and meaningful, such are bhāratanātyam or kathakalī, north Indian style or south Indian Carnātic style music amongst many others.

Ancient Greece, and later Rome, developed spectacular theatres, the famous amphitheatres for performance of theatrical plays. The most beautiful was deemed to be the amphitheatre at Ephesus that could seat twenty four thousand persons, and the one at Epidaurus, famous for its perfect acoustics, and the amphitheatre of Dodona, excavated behind the hill where the acropolis of Athens stood. Many of the Greek and Roman theatres survived intact or almost so up to present days. Circuses and theatres were among the first structures built by the Romans when they planned new cities. Music and artistic representations are the best means to remember and honour the great men of the past, their genealogy, their achievements and the contributions they made to the spiritual evolution of the people, aided by the gods. "Gods" are sometimes just idealised techniques or methods. Wine making became a symbol if not a synonym of Dionysos when his name became *Bacchus* in Rome, and *Iacchos* was his esoteric name. Demeter became a goddess because she taught Triptolemus how to grow wheat. Dionysos and Demeter were not deified because they brought the grapes vine or hexaploid wheat to Greece, but they were deified because they instructed "their people" on the appropriate agricultural techniques and methods to make wine and specially nourishing bread. Before being deified they were heroes and they were deified *because* they were heroes, *because* of their teachings and *because* they deserved to become models and idols for others. They were entitled to be deified by humans.

Philosophers, sages, masters, ācāryas, teachers, learned and wise men in general are special types of heroes who enjoy the reputation of being the guides who promote cultural development, including religion, and are the decisive factors for the establishment of civilizations that have a longer duration, and a more rational and wiser culture. We could perhaps mention here just two names taken from the epics, Droṇācārya among very many others in the east and perhaps Tiresias or the Centaur Nestor in the west, or Socrates, Plato and Ādi Śaṅkara of Kāladi. Incidentally it should be remembered that the legendary Centaurs, exceptional creatures, half man and half horse, are typically the Indo-European concept of the fusion of the two most important Indo-European heroic mortal creatures: man and horse.

In east and west facts and imagination are combined more as we go backwards in time into pre-history and proto-history. Mazumdar (1988) points out that the *Mahābhārata* is a sociological history of our ancestors. To this we should add the *Rāmāyaṇa*. Among the best reported examples of Indian heroes are the Pāṇḍava brothers and the Kaurava princes. The dissimilarity between east and west is nowhere as evident as when comparing apparently "similar" episodes, while the core meanings and teachings are entirely different. The most striking is of course the frequent though absurd comparison made between the "abduction" of Helen of Sparta by prince Paris of Troy with the abduction of Rāma's Sītā by Rāvaṇa. Any number of examples could be quoted.

Polyandry and polygamy occurred in east and west, but they are judged under totally different perspectives. Practices quoted under the same name, may have different origin, explanation or purpose. Draupadī was married to the five Pāṇḍava brothers due to a promise made lightly by one of the brothers. A promise is a vow that can never be broken, especially if made to the mother. Polyandry is a socio-ecological necessity in the harsh environment of the Himalayas, in this case the high reaches of the Beās River where the brothers were in exile together with their mother, and thus the promise was fulfilled and sanctified. On the other hand, in the mild climate of the Mediterranean region there was not more than one or perhaps two ancient Greek goddesses or heroines who refrained from knowing men or gods other than their husbands. Most Olympian goddesses succumbed willingly to Zeus' or other gods' or mens' pressure, and behaved according to their wishes rather than to the recommended rules. Other contrasting examples could be drawn about the polygamous and polyandric practices in east and west.

There are innumerable examples among the Indo-Aryans of the east, of adherence to the strict code of conduct to be observed by family and clan members. These were necessary to ensure the cohesion and survival of small groups living in isolation from other groups or families of the same or other people. Habits and customs inevitably change and become adapted to new and different environmental conditions. Initial handicaps arose because migrating people were few in numbers compared to large groups of autochthonous people, there was a high mortality among adult men and young children due to displacements, migrations, adaptations to new living conditions, climatic and agricultural failures or rivalries, vengeance, fights for ownership of lands and mines, jealousies. The consequences resulted in isolation of entire lineages, such as the *gotra,* the imperative need to create rules that would ensure increased natality, such as the practice of levirate, as well as rules to avoid inbreeding or alternatively promote exogamy. These practices were well known to the pastoral societies that had migrated over different landscapes and mountains before settling in the Hindukush or Himalayas. Casteism was a necessity to keep the many groups socially united though scattered over distant horizons. New family ties and honour adhered to strict rules, even if otherwise condemned as incorrect. We could also remember that Bhīma took a vow to break Duryodhana's thigh after the latter maliciously tried to oblige Draupadī to sit on it. Bhīma vowed to kill all the Kauravas and had to be restrained by Yudhiṣṭhira. Though Yudhiṣṭhira had himself fallen into a grave sin, he was duly obeyed by his younger brother. On the other hand in the west, Paris did not show much respect to his honest, brave elder brother Hector and he was the cause of Hector's death at the hands of Achilles. The Indo-Aryans of India were strictly obliged by tradition to respect and obey their elders and to uphold by all means the purity and honour of their women. Even after the Great Bhārata war was over, Aśvatthāmā's life was spared, though he had fought on the enemy's side, only because he was the son of the great ācārya Droṇa. But no Troyan was ever pardoned, after the Achaean Greeks treacherously entered, sacked and burned their city. However, descriptions of bloody killings on the battle field are to be found in epics of both east and west. The Indo-Europeans in general are violent people.

The concepts of ethical behaviour, gratitude and fidelity vary between east and west. In the east, throughout the Indian epical poetry, the Purāṇas and traditional folklore, the basic code of behaviour and individual *dharma* varies according to his or her status, caste and duties towards gods and men. Undoubtedly, however the Great Bhārata War, Rāma's wanderings and his war against the bad Rāvaṇa were not moved only for the sake of righteousness and piety. Conquest of land and riches were the strongest incentives to expansion, as evident in the *Ṛgveda* from the frequent invocation to Indra with requests for rich gains in war. Wars were moved by selfish interests in east as much as in the west. Wars were fought for land ownership, for power, for plunder and material gains and for facilities and opportunities for trade. Men would be men everywhere.

The most common mistake made by western writers is to equate the abduction of Sītā to the so-called "abduction" of Helen of Sparta. Helen followed prince Paris willingly; she abandoned husband, home and children, the greatest sins that women can commit. Mother Sītā was forcibly taken away and she never agreed to Rāvaṇa's advances. The core of the question is "when" and "how" the *Rāmāyaṇa* differs from the Iliad, since the original cause of the Trojan war and of Rāma's war against Rāvaṇa are *apparently* comparable. The differences are contained in two essential questions, first, the attributes and personal traits of the two princes and princesses are entirely different, and second, the nature of the wars waged "by them" or "for them" is also widely opposed.

First and second, the personal and ethical differences reside in the behaviour of the heroes, the nature of the supporters of the wars as well as of the scene where the battles took place. The story of the Iliad is that handsome prince Paris of Troy visited king Menelaus of Sparta who, after receiving the visiting would-be-hero had to travel somewhere. It should be noted that in east and west, visitors and guests should be received and welcomed with all honours and respect; in the east guests are even equated to a "god." On the other hand the visitor or unexpected guest should first of all introduce himself, giving name, place of birth and parentage. During his absence, Menelau's wife Helen and Paris fell in love and she decided to leave home and family and follow Paris back to Troy, Paris' home. On the way to Troy they stopped at several places, visiting other princes. They delayed the return to Troy because they were embarassed about what they had done and feared that they would not be welcomed upon arrival. The weak, cowardly Paris was no match for the Achaean heroes during the Troyan war, it was his elder brother Hector who paid with his life to clear the honour of the family and of the city. During and after the sack of Troy, Helen approached her husband Menelaus though she was held in bonds because of her fault, and with all the feminine tricks that she had *learnt from goddess Aphrodite,* she seduced Menelaus. Thus prince Menelaus returned to Sparta covered with glory, with the abducted wife he had "re-conquered" and with his rich share of the loot of the city, slaves, gold and precious objects taken during the sack of Troy.

On the other hand the story of Sītā's forceful and treacherous abduction by Rāvaṇa, a great expert in magical arts and under disguise of a *sādhu*, is well known. So is also the description of Sītā's captivity and misery for the safeguard of chastity and loyalty to her husband Rāma. The joyful return of Rāma and Sītā to Ayodhyā, her trial by Agni and innumerable other details are a proof of the differences between pure and dutiful Rāma and Sītā on one side and the not-so-correct Helen and Paris on the other. The two couples are at entirely different levels of culture and correct behaviour. One couple brings prosperity and happiness, the other only war, destruction and sufferings. Finally Rāma the ideal prince, throughout the many perils of his public life, sternly stood by his duties, his kṣatriya *dharma* as a king. Whenever he had to take a decision, he opted first and foremost for the benefit of the people over which he ruled. Rāma always put the interests of the community above his own, even at the cost of being unfair to his family. Sītā quietly agreed with Rāma's judgements and decisions, though she had to undergo the greatest sufferings, having been banned from Ayodhyā because of vile calumny. The irresponsible and cowardly behaviour of Paris and Helen was exactly the opposite of Rāma and Sītā's conscientious, stately and generous behaviour.

The wars that followed the two "episodes of kidnapping" are also entirely different. The Trojan war was planned in detail; it was the tentative plan to unite the various Indo-European clans of the west who had migrated into the Aegean islands and further west into peninsular Greece and surroundings. There was a nominal chief of the "Achaeans," Agamennon king of Mycenae and elder brother of Menelaus, there was also an assembly of princes and kings who had the task of agreeing on joint stategies, rules and martial operations. Though most princes had contributed ships and men to the enterprise, there were also much independent and individual actions, quarrels, fights, also changes of agreed cooperation that involved the participation of Olympian gods and goddesses and minor deities.

The *Rāmāyaṇa* is the war waged by a single man Rāma, temporary in exile, constantly backed by faithful younger brother Lakṣmaṇa. The *Rāmāyaṇa* sings the feats of a great man, more than just a hero. Significantly Rāma's war was a single man's fight, the fight of honour against disrepute and treason, the war of a prince supported by the mass of common people who recognised him as a superior exemplar. These were the "bush-men" (= the *vānara*, forest people), represented in the poem by monkeys which include Hanuman, the epitome of faithfulness, and the wisest among animals, while the bears are representatives of all "intelligent" nature. It was Rāma's righteousness that ensured the unfailing help and faithfulness of his nearest friends, beginning with Lakṣmaṇa and Hanuman, and attained victory over Rāvaṇa, a great magician.

The Sugriva episode of the *Rāmāyaṇa* has been much discussed from all points of view, especially whether it was morally correct to shoot a deadly arrow from a hidden position at an unfaithful ally, though for a noble cause, so as to benefit a faithful friend. There will be no end to the question of correct attitudes to be taken under situations of contrasting loyalties. Here again, there is no single valid answer to the problem. Nothing can undo the Gordian knot of loyalties in conflict. Whatever the decision taken, it will be subject to criticisms, praises or condemnation, it will be right or wrong depending on the point of view. Each problem must be analysed separately from any other. The ruler must have the courage to take a decision, knowing full well that he will be both criticized and praised. Courage is needed to face reality and accept responsibilities; courage is needed to uphlod ethical and moral behaviour even when the decisions taken seem to be biased. In contrast, avoiding responsibilities is the cowardly attitude of weaklings that more often than not will cause disasters.

The difficulty in making choices and taking decisions lies in that there never is anything "absolutely" right or "absolutely" wrong, good or bad. Each case is different from any other and the human mind will never be able to evaluate fully all the factors past, present and future which are, or were, or will be inevitably linked to that particular situation. It will never be possible to make every single person happy with any or all decisions. When trying to solve the problems of loyalties in conflict we are faced with the absurd situation that the future influences the present.

The frequently mentioned sentence "the end justifies the means," a hurried and mistaken quote from the treaty by Machiavelli (1469-1527) called *"Il Principe"* (= The Prince) refers exactly to the problem of loyalties in conflict, proper behaviour and action. Sometimes wrong and even awful decisions must be taken for the benefit of the future of the same or other people under the same or comparable situations.

About the epics of the Indo-Iranians, I will not enter into discussion of the Shah Namah, except for saying that Firdusi (? 940-1021? AD) is more of a historian than an epic poet. Much of the Shah Namah is in prose. Mythology is critically discussed and tradition is respected throughout. Traditional situations and accounts cannot be excluded from the description of facts that happened in proto- and pre-historic ages of ancient Iran, or any other culture, nor can ancient facts and acts be judged centuries later.

Modern authors tend to find similarities between east and west where there is only superficial resemblance and they tend to disregard more profound and difficult-to-interpret real common ground, often anchored in the very ancient past under different social and environmental situations.

(F) Ancient Indo-European Heroic Traits

Details of behaviour, simple colloquialisms, gestures, daily individual and family life, social and political behaviour, habits and customs are the best evidence of common roots of Indo-Europeans of east and west. Only a few of the the many traits common to the Indo-European civilizations of east and west, many of them taken from the epics, are summarized below under two categories; (1) Influence of non Indo-European cultures on the Graeco-Roman civilizations; and (2) Ancient Indo-European characteristics common to the Indo-European of east and Graeco-Roman civilizations. The Indo-European of east considered here are almost exclusively the Indo-Aryans.

The cultural evolution of the Indo-European of east and west which is the object of the present study was recorded in the east mainly as the oral tradition, as rhythmic poetry and other musical forms, in the use of string (ex. the cithara = Lt. and Gk *kithara*) and above all vocal music and percussion instruments, as well as different forms of performing, engineering and architectural arts and story telling and folklore. In ancient India there was not much recording of chronological order, except for memorising genealogies, and it is sometimes difficult to relate facts to their place in real time. The Bhṛgu Saṁhitā are one of the notable exceptions on which no comments can be made here. In the west at relatively early stages of cultural evolution, myths, legends and history were recorded in writing, using scripts invented by people of non Indo-European extraction. Vedic man memorized the lengthy sacred texts called Veda that express knowledge and wisdom in synthetic sentences, paraphrases, proverbs, analogues, riddles, stories and a variety of memory aides known from the oral transmission in prose or poetry. Additional explanations and details were given in the Vedānta as formal or informal teachings to disciples, and much of tradition for practical uses was not put in *nagari* or other forms of script, they are mostly lost to westerners used to believe only in the written word, though often biased or even treacherous. The oral tradition is richer than the written tradition, it includes **also** the texts produced and memorized after the use of writing had already been accepted, but it may prove to be difficult not only to place facts in their relative perspective but also to find the relationships with what happened elsewhere in absolute time and chronological sequence. Even cross references between the two great epics, the *Mahābhārata* and the *Rāmāyaṇa* are difficult to establish. These are some of the major reasons, besides geographic distance, why the Graeco-Roman civilization was better and sooner known than the Indian civilization in the contemporary western world.

1) INFLUENCE OF NON INDO-EUROPEAN CULTURES AND THE LATE GRAECO-ROMAN CIVILIZATION — SOME EXAMPLES

a) Typically the Indo-European prayed with joint palms, as stated in ancient texts and iconography in east and west and in the tradition of the dominant Indo-European cultures of the world. However, we find in the Aeneis, but **not** in the Iliad and the Odyssey, that prayers and invocations to the gods are sometimes offered with the palms of the hands turned upwards towards heaven, towards the stars or to the waters of the sky, when the supplication is addressed to them. Aeneas, when in Carthago, a Phoenician (= Semitic) colony, prays "with both palms turned towards the stars" (Aen. I 3; Aen. IV 204); Anchises, father of Aeneas also prays in this pose (Aen. II 687, III 263 *et al*), others were Turnus, king of the Rutuli, ancient non-Indo-European Italic people (Aen.IX 17; X 523, 566) and others of North Africa like Iarba, king of Numidia (Aen. X 666) (modern Algeria). Interestingly Priam, the old king of defeated Troy, is shown in a temple to Juno (= Hera) made in Carthago many centuries *after* the arson of Troy (Aen X 666), with "both palms turned towards the stars." This does not mean that Priam, the Indo-European king of Troy prayed in this way, it only means that the Semitic people of Carthago prayed in this manner when the temple was made by Semitic architects and artisans. These are only a few examples that indicate the shifting from one posture for praying to another, with changes of the culture from the heroic and Homeric age to the late centuries BC under the influence of non-Indo-European cultures. The latter mentioned cultures displaced some of the ancient Indo-European traits of the Mediterranean population of Indo-

European extraction. Indo-European of the east and later Indo-European of Europe pray with joint palms.

b) In the Aeneis it is repeatedly stated that Dardanus, reputed son of Zeus, was the ancestor of the Dardanids. He had gone to the shores of north-west Asia Minor during his extensive wanderings "far and wide in ancient times." In the Aeneis it is also said that he went there from Italy, an impossible and not verifiable assumption. Another probably correct legend does not make Dardanus a traveller from Italy though it confirms that Dardanus founded Dardania, the first city of mortal men in the plains in front of the "sacred mount Ida [near Troy] rich in water," much earlier than "sacred Ilio." Dardanus' son Erictonios was said to be the richest of mortal men, he had three thousand mares with healthy colts. The first twelve mares had been impregnated by *Borea* (= northern wind). Erictonios was the ancestor of the Trojan lineage (Iliad XX 215-245) of rulers (= kings) and *Odysseus*, son of Anchises, was the last of the family. Dardanus had been the ancestor of later Trojan lords, hence the name of the strait of the Dardanelles on the sea route between the Aegean and the Black Sea, through the Ellespont and the Bosphorus. This most important waterway was under the tutelage or control of the people where "the rich city" of Troy eventually grew. The control of the straits was the main source of the wealth of Troy. The city was placed at a nodal point of the extensive web of trade routes of Asia and was the "jumping point" to Europe. I may refer to some curious observations I made about the *"Dards,"* nomads in the Himalayas. They have features very similar to those of the ancient Greeks as shown on Greek statuary and iconography, as well as other traits such as the way the women part their hair and put flowers in them, or the designs of the textiles of their clothes, besides other features and habits that appear to be reminiscent of ancient Greeks. Many designs of local textiles of high Gahrwal, the area earlier known as Dardistan and others in the Himalayas, lower Karakorum and Hindukush range of mountains are simple borders usually called "Greek design." The origin of Dardanus and that of the Etruscans is not yet known for sure. Most authors agree that the Etruscans were not Indo-European people, but their language is still poorly known. Quoting from Harmatta (1992), Dardic and the Kafiri (= Nuristani) idioms became isolated from the 'Indian' ones before the rising of prakritism [middle second millennium BC] that have their roots in ancient Indo-European languages.[12]

c) Children of the Indo-Europeans are given an important role in the life of the community, differently from non-Indo-European cultures, Egyptian and Semitic where children are seldom mentioned and often altogether ignored, forgotten or even killed.

d) The Phoenicians already had an advanced culture when the Indo-Europeans of the east arrived in western Asia. They contributed the basic phonetic script, many different types of glass, the technique for the preparation and use of the beautiful deep red dye "*purpura*" (= Lt. *purpura,* Gr. = *porphyra*) extracted from marine gastropod molluscs of the family Muricidae, genera *Murex, Thais, Purpura, Concholepas* and other related genera of marine snails. They knew how to rear the snail and how to dye the threads before weaving the cloth and without killing the animal. The dye, now called *muricine,* chemically classed: 6,6'-di-bromoindacotin (DBI) was known as "royal porpora." It was used to dye the border of the *toga* and other luxury robes of high class Greek and Roman citizens. The width of the *purpura* border proclaimed the status and official position of the wearer. Only patricians of high ranks could bear the title of "togated Roman." The Greek, Etruscan and Roman alphabet and other scripts are partly derived from the Phoenician, but the early Roman alphabet had only 14 letters when Greek already had 24. Among the Indo-Europeans of the east there were, and still are, suggestive details in dress, individual marks and make-up, habits and behaviour typical of the social position, profession and level of men and women and their place in the community. All communities or societies have distinctive marks, but most unfortunately not many have survived the iconoclastic "culture" of the twentieth century. The twentyfirst century is now fast homogenizing the world into a bleak common grey culture, the colour of dirt and destruction, with exceptional peaks in different directions, marked by a desperate escapism hidden under a variety of face-masks painted with all shades and colours from joyous to atrocious. The Greeks and Romans were quick in learning better techniques from other people but were unfortunate when they tried to copy some of their customs and abandon the austere habits of their forefathers.

e) The Phoenicians were Semitic people who developed the art of navigation at sea, as the Arabs developed first the art of navigation on land and only later the art of navigation at sea, could engage in the transport of people and goods far and near. In the Mediterranean Sea the Phoenicians were the first able mariners and produced sea-worthy ships. The Indo-Aryan and the Indo-Iranian cultures had developed inland and it must have taken several generations before they acquired the art that enabled them to navigate the length and breadth of the Mediterranean and Black Seas with enough confidence to go even beyond the Pillars of Herakles. The "Pillars of Herakles" is the term usually used for the Straits of Gibraltar, but there are other "pillars" so named at different places on the Atlantic coast of Europe. "Pillars" are land marks serving the same purpose as later times "light houses," for the orientation of pilots at sea. Pilots take their bearings from individually described "pillars" or light houses. They were called pillars because high rise mountains or rocky formations and promontories on the coast can be seen from great distances. Ship building was also learnt from Semitic people, mainly the Phoenicians and their colonies and from the ancient Thyrrenians (= Etruscans who were reputed to be good sailors and pirates) or Pelasgians (= from Crete?). The *Cretan* Pelasgoi sided with Troy; they contributed 12 ships with crew. The men at oars also served on land as soldiers, artisans, labourers and servants during the siege of Troy (Od. IX 139; Il. II 637). Ship building and navigation were still in their infancy in Greece in the last centuries of the second millennium BC. The Greeks and later the Romans were indebted to the pre-existing Mediterranean cultures for their maritime development. Significantly the Greek won the wars over the Indo-European Persian kings only after acquiring maritime and seamanship expertise and only after they had been defeated on land by the higher strategy and numbers of the land army of the Great Xerxes. The Achaemenid Persians extended the war overland by taking the army to Europe across the straits over a pontoon of boats and barges made during the reign of Darius III.

f) The association of pre-Roman Greek gods with ancient Italic gods in temples on Capitol hill (= *Capitolium*) started in the very early stages of the building of the city of Rome, or earlier. Names of Italian places, gods and heroes are earlier than the first introduction of Greek culture, many are not Indo-European names.

g) The fig and the olive were typical basic food items in Anatolia, Asia Minor, the Aegean islands and mainland Greece since pre-historic times. Very soon a small branch of the olive tree became the symbol of Peace in Rome. In the agora of Athens there was a "sacred fig tree." Also the grape vine was probably known for its fruits and for making wine also in Greece since ancient times. McGovern (2003) shows rather convincingly that the wild ancestor of wine grapes, *Vitis vinifera* L. subsp. *sylvestris* was probably natural and widespread over the entire Mediterranean basin and beyond, *Vitis vinifera vinifera* is the domesticated sub-species that was widespread from Egypt to Mesopotamia. Wine was produced in north-western Iran at Hajji Firuz Tepe already in 5400-5000 BC (McGovern 2003). Probably the knowledge, method and techniques of how to make wine from grapes was learned by the early Indo-Europeans of Greece from other Mediterranean people, perhaps the Semites of western Asia. In my opinion the often repeated expression "Dionysos brought grapes and wine to Greece," as it appears in the epics and later Greek and Latin literature, is a code-word or pre-fabricated expression meaning that Dionysos brought *the arts* of viticulture (= grapes cultivation) and of viniculture (= making of wine) to Greece, as Demeter brought *the art* of proper cultivation of cereals specially bread wheat, though *wild grapes* and *durum wheat* respectively existed in Greece before the advent of Dionysos or Demeter. The character known to us as Dionysos is the last of a series of personifications of the wild aspects of nature that was preceded by one or many unnamed mythical and semi-mythical characters. What the last character known as Dionysos brought, were advanced techniques and methods, in other words, he brought the art of making *good* wine. Good bread and good wine were credited with providing the good physical performance of Greeks, Romans and Persians (= Iranians), but Dionysos was not an innovator, as clearly stated in the ancient texts. Also Demeter did not "invent" fluffy or hexaploid wheat bread, she brought the teachings with her and introduced the art of agriculture. There was wheat (tetraploid varieties of wheat= *durum* wheat) in Greece before the advent of Demeter, but improved varieties of cereals as well as methodical agriculture were an innovation brought to Attika by Demeter (Vannucci, 1999b). The role of Dionysos and Demeter is not so much what they did or brought, even more important were the teachings and practical demonstrations on how to use and what the techniques to achieve prefixed agricultural goals were. In other words, both characters were significant forces for the acculturation of the Indo-Europeans of the west in the lands of the Mediterranean basin.

h) The ancient Italic god *Janus bifrons* (= Janus with two faces), looking towards either property along a common boundary had a temple on Capitol hill the doors of which were always kept open, except when the Romans moved to war. During war time the Consul closed the doors of the temple, no exchanges in property matters were allowed while the Republic was totally engaged in guarding its internal safety and distant conquests. The legal demarcation of agricultural land property entrusted to Demeter indicates the fundamental importance given to agriculture and to the equitable distribution of land among various families whose activities had to be checked by law when methodical and productive agriculture became more and more important to feed a growing urban population. For these reasons goddess Demeter, called Cerere in Rome (= from *Cerere, cereales*, cereals), acquired vital importance in the Roman civil world, she was called to supervise the distribution of rural lands and settle inevitable disputes. The principles of Roman legislation and jurisprudence still survive in the modern western world. However rhetoric, the art of persuasion and logics was born in Athens. Much more could be added on the topic of mutual influence between different cultures and civilizations in ancient times; the above is sufficient to illustrate a few representative issues.

2) ANCIENT INDO-EUROPEAN CHARACTERISTICS COMMON TO THE INDO-EUROPEANS OF EAST AND WEST — SOME EXAMPLES

a) The gory description of battle scenes. Great similarity between all Indo-European warriors and their defensive and offensive armament. Weapons follow a straight development, such as the Stone-Age double axe held with both hands that was initially made of stone and passed through all stages of improvement, including bronze and iron and was still used under the Roman empire, made of iron and called *labrys*.

b) Funeral and other rites, also in Iliad, books XXII and XXIII. Fighting stopped at night when both sides took care of the dead bodies; the battle field was lighted by the funeral pyres, as described also in the *Mahābhārata*. In very ancient Ṛgvedic and Greek times, both burial and cremation of dead bodies took place. Descriptions of procedures are about the same in east and west. Amongst others, such are the careful process of preparing the body to be consigned to fire, building of sacrificial altars and pyres, women and men loosening their hair, funeral chants and offerings, cups full of boiling milk and large vessels full of consecrated blood and other offerings, the cutting of the long hair of the Achaean men, the last funeral games and feasts in honour of the deceased to remember him and give him moral support on his journey to the nether world, and others details. Many of these customs are also meant to make sure that the deceased will not return to this world to trouble the living, and many more are openly or quietly still practised nowadays in the west. Many ancient customs, habits or "idiosyncrasies" are at present called superstitions. The ritual burning of dead bodies, specially of the heroes who were cremated together with their weapons, was a relatively recent development rendered necessary when there was a large amount of dead bodies on the fields; so many were the fires in the night following the battle at Kurukshetra. In early periods or if there were small numbers of dead heroes, the bodies were entombed. The typical Indo-European weapon was the double axe (= *labrys*), it was used also during Roman times. For rituals and festive occasions, when wine was not available for libations to the gods or for sprinkling the sacrificial offerings already placed on fire, pure water could be used for libations, for sprinkling or as offering to the gods (Od. XII, 1 *et al.*). Cutting or shaving the hair is still now a symbol of mourning. Cutting off nose and ears to humiliate the captured enemy, was common. Many of these customs and others are still alive at present. There is a hint at human sacrifices in Il. XXIII 23, where Achilles promises to behead twelve young Trojans at Patroklos' funeral pyre. Gradually daily habits and customs had to be attuned to the different environments where the Indo-Europeans found themselves and the experience of earlier inhabitants had to be learned and applied by the newcomers.

c) The many marks of respect given to god, elders and women who are the feeders and stronghold of the family's physics and morale. Mention of an elder, the master or of any other responsible or higher-up person by name was inadequate lack of respect and propriety. During rituals the name of the invoked god was not mentioned directly (Aen. IV 577, often the god was literally addressed as: *quisquis* es = whichever you may be) perhaps to avoid making a mistake in naming the god or because the invoked god should remain anonymous. In India and in Italy the habit still prevails to address respected persons by their social or professional designation. In India only children are called by name, gods are addressed in the second person (= *tu*). Among the Indo-Europeans of east, human adults, even husband and wife even now address each other by title or nickname, never by name. In Latin languages, elder members of the family and of the society are addressed by the place they have in the hierarchy, such as grandfather or grandmother, uncle, aunt, governor, Mr., Mrs., doctor and so on. Indian languages are the most detailed in giving specific designations, specially to all the members of the extended family. Aeneas carries his old father "on his shoulders *after* bending the neck" while the elder carries the home gods who, we are told, will become the *Penates* (Aen. II) of Rome. Aeneas could not carry the gods because his hands were soiled with the blood of fighting warriors and would remain so "until when I will be able to wash in clean current water" (Aen II). In India the usual daily family and elaborate and strict social code of conduct is ancient and engraved in the language and collective memory of the people, children grow with it as they learn to speak.

d) The mother is all important and may be a reminder of the entirely dependent child when it approaches the mother and climbs on her knees, ". . . mother I am hungry, thirsty, I want to go out to play, I want . . . I need . . . I." The helpless, the desperate, the dying always invoke the mother. In India the gesture of pressing the knees is common to this day on many occasions, such as an invitation addressed to the honoured guest to enter into the inner quarters on his first visit to the new home and bless it with his presence. Pressing the knees, touching the feet requesting a favour and protection are common, though with slightly different meaning. Demeter remembered that child Demophont "climbed all over my lap and knees." The mark of respect by touching the feet of the honourable person or deity has its equivalent with present Roman Catholics touching the feet of the image or statue which they revere. Famous among these is the old statue of St. Peter in the Basilica built in his memory in Rome whose big toe is worn down from the innumerable strokes and touchings of faithful fingers. The statue of the seated saint is placed high and out of reach of the pilgrims who "hug" the toe instead of the knees. It is common in east and west for grandmothers or other elders to kiss the head and the eyes of children and grandchildren (Od. XIX 348-502), a gesture of protection and silent blessing. In the Greek epics more rarely the gesture of touching the knees is followed in quick succession by "touching the chin" of the elder. The explanation of this gesture can only be interpreted as a request for protection also by word and speech. Elder, learned or influential Greek men were bearded, differently from clean-shaven Romans and Indians.

e) The importance given to the horse is a typical characteristic of the Indo-Europeans everywhere. The "noble animal" is still cared for as a good friend, as if every single person remembered that so much of their cultural evolution was due to the domestication of the horse and the development of the wheel. One Kikkuli, a famous Mitanni horse-trainer was requested by the Hittite rulers to draft a very detailed treatise teaching the training and care of horses. Special attention was given to the horse's food, technical terms, numbers, distances; geometric figures like the circle are given in Hittite language. The Trojans were famous as horse breeders (XX 180; XXII 161, 182). The centaurs had human head, torso, arms and stomach, while front legs and the rest of the body were equine. The "fusion" of man with horse is well known to whoever has done much horse riding, it would be impossible to travel long distance or fight in battle if horseman and horse had not learned to have the same reactions at the right time and opportunity. Centaurs in Greek mythology fought with bow and arrows since they were as ancient as the most ancient heroes and their characteristic weapon. The centaur Keiron (= Cheiron) was famous for his knowledge, specially of medicinal plants. The centaurs were good teachers, wise and learned from wisdom stored in their memory over countless generations, but wise minds were then few in numbers, and are even more so at present! During cold winter days it is common in India to see cart drivers rubbing vigorously with their forearms and elbows their horse's necks all the way down to the front and back to warm up the animal and themselves before beginning the day's toil or during some pause in the daily routine. Cows, bulls and bullocks, goats, sheep, pigs and dogs are some of the other important domesticated animals who became family members of the Indo-Europeans of east and west, a sure sign of their geographic common origin and use. *The development of agriculture would not have been possible if the symbiosis of man and horse, and the cow and her family had not already taken place.*

f) Before the foundation of Rome and during most of the republican age, lifestyles among the Italic people and the early Romans were simple. Pastoralism was wide-spread and agriculture was at an early stage of development, similar to that of the very early stages of the Indo-Europeans of east. Legends tell us that the twin brothers who founded Rome had been suckled by a she-wolf. The common food in addition to bread were olives, figs, some cereals other than hexaploid wheat, barley was probably the first cereal species domesticated by man, there was also game, milk and derivates. In addition to animal skins, wool was the main raw substance to make cloth and garments. The main inputs for the original growth of the cultures of the Indo-European people was the invention of the wheel and training of the horse for work in times of peace or war, for traction and riding. The horse arrived in Europe already fully grown and domesticated. Agriculture, also horticulture, became specialized valuable arts introduced from Central Asia that contributed to the development of the Graeco-Roman culture. At the very early stage, when Indo-Europeans still lived in their original homeland, the horse was small and was reared mainly to be butchered for its meat. The great leap forward of the culture of the Indo-Europeans of west and east was the development of a phonetic script. About agriculture it should be remembered that olives, figs, grapes, cereals and other seeds or fruits can be preserved over the long winter months after sun-drying in hot and dry summer climates.

g) Similarly to the Indo-European, the main religion among the early pre-Indo-European people of west was based on the worship of nature deities and heroes. Local deities were Sylvanus, Pan and the fauns, nymphs, heroes. Bacchus (= Dionysos) represented by the grape vine and wine must have appeared very early on the scene (McGovern 2003). Dionysos became an important item of the developed culture of Greeks and Romans, no longer just an item in the liturgy of the early nature cults. Originally, before Pisistratus introduced Dionysos into Athens to organise the festivals, Dionysos was a simple god of wild nature. Wine probably became an element of the rites of mysterious cults specially the Orphic mysteries. Wine was an important element of the religious and social ceremonies and was never drunk pure, it was diluted with water, honey was added and it could be laced with aromatic herbs, spices, and even intoxicating substances, according to the occasion. Mixing was usually done at the moment of the ceremonial or festive libation. Wine was drunk before going into battle to boost the morale and invigorate soldiers, a practice followed well into the nineteenth century in Europe, when instead of wine strong distilled drinks with high alcoholic content were distributed to the men sometimes with admixture of other substances, such as pepper in small quantities, to boost their bravery. Even after wine became popular, its sacredness was remembered and most probably grapes' wine is the descendant or ancestor of the ancient Indo-Aryan *soma* and Indo-Iranian *haoma*. Vedic *soma* may have been grapes' wine mixed with water and other substances (extracts of *Ephedra, Cannabis, Papaver,* others?). Grapes' wine was not produced over all the regions occupied by Indo-European people, in many areas wine had to be imported and when this could not be done, other plant juices were used as substitutes. From internal evidence of late Indian texts it is known that the name *soma* was given to more than one species of plants. Some of these habits and customs are linked to local environmental conditions of life in the plains, mountains or forests, and to the availability of the desired plants, they survived into the Christian age, some are still practised and called "superstitions" or are used to cure different ailments.

h) The plough and other agricultural implements did not change much over the past centuries. The exact time when the horse was introduced in Italy is not known for sure. It was already domesticated when it arrived there and it was harnessed the same way as the bullock-drawn plough was fastened to the beam. Later in Rome Thracian horses were reputed to be the best for war.

i) The ancient habit of placing large stones as markers of field boundaries persisted until late AD ages. At present rows of trees, walls or "mile stones" as used by Romans are still the rule. The pre-historic "protective" and erect large stones, or boulders the menhirs of Europe, may have originally been threatening phallic symbols meaning: *keep out*!

j) Aeneis III 83 reads: "let us join our right hands and let us enter under our roof," a form of greeting with the value of a promise. Greetings could be almost as meaningful as an oath or a sermon. This is a very close approximation to *ṚV* X, 191, 1-4.

k) Jupiter (= Zeus) (Aen. IX 631) is described as shaking his head sideways as an order, or a sign of assent or a personal way of saying **yes**, as present day in India. A shaking to the right side was considered favourable and one to the left, unfavourable. Details of the sacrifice of a bull to Apollo (Aen. III 370) and of other sacrifices, such as undoing the knot that fastens the sacred bands of the performer of the sacrifice have corresponding gestures at present. As a sign of respect we see both men and women covering their heads (Aen. III 405). However the Greek offered sacrifices with uncovered head, while the Romans covered theirs with the loose end of the toga that corresponds to the *pallu* of the sari. The Greeks had long hair and long beards, the Romans kept short hair and were clean-shaven, probably for hygiene and a consequence of the wide-spread use of iron and steel that could be sharpened into sharp cutting edges. The most praised gift that Alexander the Great received in India was *"ferrum candidum"* (= steel). Alexander was clean shaved while his father Philip II of Macedonia was bearded. Many of the soldiers of Alexander's army adopted the habit of shaving off the beard.

m) One of the most significant gestures several times repeated in the epics (Iliad I 407, XXI 65) is "to hug the knees," meaning to hold or press sideway with both hands the joint knees of a person in a higher position, to plead for a grace, to implore for compassion (Aen. III 607 *et al.*), mercy or protection. This attitude is a form of speechless imploration typical of the Indo-Europeans of the east since very ancient times and still in common use. Old king Priam hugs the knees of the younger Achilles imploring for the return of the desecrated corpse of his valiant son Hector. Thetis, Achille's mother hugs Zeus' knees (Il. VIII 369-406). The magician Kirke, daughter of the Sun and of Perse daughter of the Ocean, (Od. VI 311; Od. VII 142, 146 Od. X 323) hugs Odysseus' knees. The same gesture in the Aeneis follows diligently the canons of the older Homeric epics. The same gesture with the same purpose or meaning or just pleading for blessings is still current in India at very important occasions. To hold the knees also binds the elder or patron to make sure that the person begging for mercy cannot be further beaten by others or otherwise punished again for the same mistake, sin or bad action. The gesture ensures tutelage and protection but is never an act of servility. It is a sincere welcome to a beloved elder and means: "enter and bless this house, it is your house. Enter and be one with me."

n) We find in Rome purification rites by fumes of burning sulphur, by water (Il. XVI 563; Aen. II 6) and by fire, since the most ancient times and in India at present. Sacred plants were attached to sacred places, among the most common were laurel, myrtle, olive, ivy (Aen. II 249, *et al.*) and all temples had a *cella* or *sanctum sanctorum* (= sacred-most of the sacred) the innermost, protected and protecting part of the temple, as in Hindu temples. The symbolism, meaning, story and usefulness of trees and other plants in India is well known, from the *ashwattha* tree and beyond. The deity of a shrine or temple may be a tree, fire, a spring, a cave or something else and the sanctity of the place need not be inspired or linked to a man-made idol.

o) Fire, as well as the Sun, though not gods, were revered in Rome as the sacred symbol of life. The Vestals were the sacred virgins who guarded the home fire of the State altar of Juno on the circular hill temple on the Capitol, guarded by the geese sacred to the goddess. Ritual purification by fire of people, temples, homes, spaces, animals or things continued for many centuries. Agni (= Fire) is the "first god" in the east. Many of the ancient-most temples in Kerala are built on a circular plan, like very ancient Christian temples or churches that had the main altar instead of fire, in the centre. The red colour is an attribute of divinity. The ancient Indo-European root *pur* or *pyr* indicates fire. *Pur* or *pewe* is given in Indo-European etymological dictionaries as akin to the Indo-European *pewe* or *py*, meaning "to purify." In Lt. and Grk. the root *pyr* = fire, pure, means to purify, because fire is the purifier par excellence, it safeguards purity and preserves from contamination, desecration or spoilage. Pyromaniacs are mentally sick people fixed on starting fires.

p) Prostration is the form of utmost respect and submission to ancestors, priests, gods and prophets or their representatives, like when facing the Cuman Sybilla (Aen. III 93 *et al.*) or other prophets of the Greeks and Romans and the gods of all faiths.

q) Astrology and divination as a prophecy is common in the Graeco-Roman epics and classical age, the art was greatly developed by the Etruscans even before the birth of Rome. The priests knowledgeable about prophecies were the *augures* who used different techniques including astrology, to reply to the questions addressed to them. From this art were derived many superstitions of Romans, Italians and other people with Indo-European ancestry, most of them still alive today, though often in a disguised manner. One of the most famous prophets was the Cuman Sibylla, priestess of Apollo, gifted with the power of vaticination (= divination, prediction of the future). Apollo had gifted the Sybilla with a very long life, but not immortality or ageing. Divination is different from magics. Magics is as common in Greek epics as in the Indian epics and folklores of all people.

r) Archery was the ancestral excellent art of the heroes. Rāma's double bow has a very close parallel in the bow of Philottetes that was given to Odysseus, a deserving hero who alone was able to bend and string it. Both Rāma's and Philottetes hows were gifted or made by a god and the string was made from the tendon of sacrificed animals. The feats achieved by Rāma, Odyssey, Herakles (Gk. = Herakles) reveal the superhuman, unique god-given power of the deserving heroes. Bow and arrows is the traditional weapon of ancient hunters and warriors in east and west. In the poem (Od. VIII 224-229) Odysseus boasts to be "stronger than present day mortal men on Earth who eat bread . . . he does not wish to compare himself to ancient heroes . . . such as Herakles or Eurytous who challenged with bow and arrow even the immortal gods." These and others are models and examples carried over from the heroic proto-historic age into pre-historic and historic culturally evolved civilizations.

s) The Horae (= hours, seasons) are the goddesses who mark the seasons and the progress of time, like the *mantra*s in ancient Vedic lore (Vannucci 1999). They are regular followers of Dionysos and Viṣṇu respectively.

t) There are many common legends related to natural phenomena that reflect the eagerness to know and understand, one of the basic characteristics of the human mind. When no plausible explanation was found, myths were created to satisfy the inborn curiosity of humans.

u) The rituals of *Anna Perenna* in Rome and of *annāpraśna* in India. The myth of "*anna*" may have been inherited by Rome from very ancient times. Ovid (43 BC-18 AD) writes in the *Fasti* (= feasts, celebrations, commemorations, in 3, 522-540) that Anna, sister of queen Dido of Carthago, escaped from that city after the queen committed suicide in despair for being abandoned by Aeneas, the Troyan hero who was on his way to Italy after the destruction of Troy. Anna took refuge in the Latium region where Rome eventually was founded. In the history of Rome, Anna reappears as an old woman who fed the plebe when the hungry people were camping on the "Sacred Mountain" outside Rome. We would call it a strike against the injustices suffered by the common people at the hands of the Roman patricians. At the time of the strike Anna prepared daily hot breads (= *roti*) to be distributed to the needy people. A statue was made in her honour and the word "*perenna*" (= *per annum,* perennial, throughout the year) was added to the name *Anna,* the food giver. A feast was held yearly in Rome on the *ides* of March (= 15 March), approximately the day of the spring equinox, to honour *Anna Perenna.* She became the local deity who ensured that food for the people (= *demos*) would always be available. Ceres, Roman goddess of cereals, agriculture and good fortune, was also called *Annona* (= the big annual, the year round, circular movement such as the seasonal cycles and astral movements). The priests of goddess *Ceres Annona* were plebeian magistrates called *edili* whose function was to take all measures necessary for the equitable distribution of grain to the Roman plebe and all the *demos*. On the other hand, the rite of *annaprasana* in India is celebrated when the child is first fed with solid and salty food, in this case boiled rice. This is first done at about six months of age of the baby when mother's milk is not enough for the growing needs of the infant. At the time of weaning it is declared that the child will from now on be fed by "food made by the gods" (= food from good mother earth, nature's food) and blessings are given for this food never to fail. The infant is no longer in the exclusive care of the mother nor is it any longer entirely dependent on mother's milk; he acquires also the protection of the gods as he can now eat food grown naturally. The very ancient Indo-European prefix *an* indicates movement (= around, circular movement, rhythms), such as the day/night rhythm and the seasonal movements, the circular dance (= life) of celestial bodies, food for body and spirit is needed the year round. Singing to the gods was and remains common (Il. I 472; Il. XI 631). The word anna in Sanskrit has also been understood as "vital essence of the cosmos" and *annapūrṇā* has been interpreted as the "goddess of food which is always full." anna, Annapraśna and Aṇṇā Perenna all have the inherent meaning of "sacred food," the material and immaterial nourishment of humans in east and west. Barley (= *sacred barley*) was domesticated before wheat, it is used as an offering to gods in preference to wheat to this day, the offering of barley is more often made by women. Grains of *barley* were thrown in the sacred sacrificial fire (Il. I 449; II 384). Wheat became a partial substitute of barley because it can produce more in weight of harvested grain than barley, for the same area of tilled field. Washing of hands is a must before praying. Circumambulation for praise or devotion to elders or gods is correctly done turning to the right (Il.I 597). Handicapped persons cannot become priests, prophetesses or other consecrated persons; they become field workers or hunters. Aquaculture of molluscs and fish and horticulture were developed only late in BC times.

v) The Indo-Europeans were and always remained a strictly patriarchal society. But the mistress of the house was the mother who ruled over the life of the family, servants and animals (*Ṛ̥V* X, 85). The family was the unit of the Indo-European group or clan to which it belonged and the general concern was turned towards the child who is pure, needs to be instructed in all matters of its future life and is the hope of the days to come. Cato the Censor (234-149 BC) said that the *"Pater familias"* (= the father or head of the family) is he who is a good shepherd and ploughs well the [family] fields." Family and society were ruled by strict regulations and duties of every component of the society, every individual. In India it is inbuilt in the concept of *dharma,* a term without a perfect or complete correlate word in the west, as is also the key role of the mother which is well defined in *Ṛ̥V* X; 85.

w) Dowry (Il. XIII 382; Od. VI 159) as a gift to the daughter being "married off" into another family comes with blessings and wishes of a happy married life, welfare and good fortune. It has survived in the entire Indo-European world and was originally, and still should be taken as a safeguard for the future of the mother and her offsprings, if the husband and father would no longer be able to fulfil his duties or would pass away.

x) The guest is sacred and should be received with all honours. The guest may even give orders in the house of his *Amphitryon,* the perfect host. The name recalls the myth about the birth of Herakles, son of Zeus and Alcmena, who was married to Amphitrion who in obeisance to Zeus and respect to Alcmena who received Zeus in her bed believing him to be her husband, never complained of what had happened. Equally sacred is a given promise and telling a lie or falsehood can never be pardoned. Exceptionally only strict penances can help cancel this type of offensive behaviour.

y) A common gesture of great sorrow or mourning in east and west alike is to beat one's own thighs as an act of mourning, despair or giving up all hopes. Ares (= Mars) beats both thighs with the palm of his hands (Il. XV 113) after the death of his son Askālaphos.

z) In the Odyssey more than in the Iliad, details are given about the cult of the gods. Telemacus, son of Odysseus, before leaving

> Ithaca in search of his father, offers prayers and libations to the gods, women offer barley, dances are performed in honour of the gods (Od. II 432; Od. IV 760; Od. VIII 261) and the *Telemakia*, the book that sings about Telemacus traveling around the Mediterranean Sea in search of his father Odysseus, gives testimony of routes and trade, such as the use of Arabic incense in Greece, to mention only one.

Indo-Aryans and Indo-Iranians acquired divergent types of dressing. The Indo-Aryan men were often naked and both men and women covered themselves with unstitched long pieces of cloth, a style still alive in India where the traditional clothing is the "sari" of women and monks. The Indo-Iranians developed elaborate stitched clothing since very early days. This is an important trait indicative of the Indo-Aryan origin and cultural input in the Graeco-Roman world.

Many more examples could be added but those mentioned above give a general picture of the close affinities or identities of the life style and code of behaviour of the Indo-Europeans of east and west at comparable stages of cultural evolution.[1, 2]

LATE INDO-EUROPEAN EPICS, AD AGE DIONYSIACS AND THE SHAH NAMAH

The *Dionysiacs* (= the acts of Dionysos) by Nonnos of Panopolis was written around the fifth century AD. Very little is known about the life of Nonnos except for the name of his birthplace: Panopolis, a city about 200 kms downstream of Thebes on River Nile in Egypt. The poem in 48 books, has the combined number of books as the Iliad and the Odyssey. Nonnos follows Homer the Master, but is left far behind in every aspect, though the intention was to glorify Dionysos and his Asian expedition "to civilise the barbarians." Interestingly, even at such a late day Nonnos defined as "Indians" all the people from Asia Minor and Central Asia to as far east as R. Ganges. Nonnos reinterprets and uses the ancient myths to develop a new epic poem based on a well known repertoire of common myths and legends from the Greek heroic age enriched by his own phantasy and that of an untold number of aedes and cytarists who could not escape glorifying and beautifying old stories with new episodes to satisfy the whims and curiosity of their audience. The poem is clearly written by a mind holding an impressionist pen.

Differently from the Dionysiacs, the Shah Namah was not forgotten by following learned people of Asia. There is nothing new that could be said here about the learned scholar Firdusi and his *Shah Namah*, a historical/mythological treatise in Iranian prose and poetry of the tenth century AD, with interpolated poems of great dramatic and lyrical beauty. The Shah Namah is the nearest approximation to a "traditional" text in the Greek-Homeric sense, intended to be a truthful historic rendering of the kings of Persia from the heroic age to Firdusi's time. Firdusi deserves special attention for his great and devoted work which well deserves to be considered a remarkable epic about the ancient Indo-Iranian people.

SUMMARY AND CONCLUSIONS

There are other epic poems in the Graeco-Roman literature; we are not concerned with them here. The three mentioned cover the trend of developments of the last millennium BC. We are also not concerned here with Indo-European people of other parts of Europe or their culture and literature.

The three epics considered here are the Iliad, the Odyssey and the Aeneis. The Iliad is focused on the Mycenean culture and civilization that flourished in the second half of the second millennium BC and in the beginning of the formation of Hellas, or Greece as a concept and nation. The Odyssey is focused on the Greek civilization of the Aegean Sea and on the Hellenic cultural expansion throughout the Mediterranean world and beyond. The Aeneis is focused on the story of the foundation and development of Rome as a nation and State and on the hegemony of Rome in Europe and West Asia. The three poems taken together eulogize the three ages of the development of the Graeco-Roman world: the heroic pre-historic period (the Mycenean culture); the culturally dominant period (the classic Greek civilization); and the military/legislative/political hegemony of Rome. Geographically the coverage goes from the Gaṅgā-Brahmaputra delta in the east to the columns of Herakles and beyond in the west. The age is from the fourth millennium BC and perhaps earlier, to the decease of the first emperor of Rome,

Augustus a relative and adopted son of Julius Caesar. The red thread tying up a large number of people ethnically, religiously and culturally different that were the inhabitants of various lands and widely different environments was the power of Rome which lasted about five centuries. After the great *Pax Romana*, which had been kept under close control, broke down, each component went its way. The geographic extremes, Indo-European of the east and Indo-European of west, as defined above for the purpose of this study, are the present subject. They evolved in different directions and for many centuries there were only scattered contacts and trade between India at the eastern end and the European part of the Mediterranean in the west. It is however clear that the basic Indo-European substratum was never lost, there are greater or lesser remains of the common heritage in both India and the Graeco-Roman cultures. The powerful binding element among all the people classed as Indo-European, was the sharing of essentially similar languages, sharing word roots and above all sharing grammar and syntaxes. First Greek, then Latin were the languages used in the development of modern experimental science, because of the precision and accuracy of Latin.

The Iliad is based on the legends and myths that tell of the gods and heroes of the mythical past and on the poems and writings of rhapsodists, aedes and cytharists. The forefathers describe how the culture of Greece was born, grew and expanded to the point of receiving an exclusive and respected name: **Hellas** (= Greece). The words Hellenism and Hellenic (= Greek) civilization do not designate a nation, state or government. They indicate a culture, an evolved civilization, ideas and an ideal, they remind also the word **Veda** and **Vedism** where the root "to see" is substituted, in the words Hellas and hellenism, by the intention of the verb "to think." To see and to think, Vedism and Hellenism are the corner stones needed to build cultures and civilizations.

The Odyssey is focused on the geographic expansion of the Greek people and their culture. The Greek culture grew to maturity in the fertile fields of philosophy, arts and sciences. Greece was eventually occupied and politically ruled by Rome, but as the poet Horatius (= Horace, 65-8 BC) said: "*Graecia capta ferum victorem cepit et artes intulit augusti Latio. . .*" (= captured Greece captured the rough [wild] conquerors and introduced the arts into supreme Latium).

Since it is impossible to separate the two civilizations, the Greek and the Roman, the cultural symbiosis is known as the Graeco-Roman classical culture.

There are about ten to eleven centuries between the age when the facts described in the Iliad and the Odyssey took place, and the age when the Aeneis was written. The Aeneis is the Roman epic, also in hexameter poetry, that puts on record the evolution of the Graeco-Roman culture. It marks the end of the age of the Roman Republic and the beginning of the age of the Roman Empire and is well documented by historians, scientists, technicians, legislators, emperors and leaders in all fields.

Differently from the Homeric poems (Iliad and Odyssey), the Aeneis was written in a culturally refined and learned society, a powerful nation called Rome, just emerged from the period of civil wars that followed the assassination of Julius Caesar. The spirit of the Republic of Rome was curtailed to open the doors to an empire that dominated much of the civilised world known at that time in the west, the Roman Empire that lasted about five or six centuries. The fall of the western Roman Empire is dated 476 AD or about 568 AD, the time of the invasion of Italy by the Germanic Indo-European tribe of the Longobards.

The dominant philosophical tendencies of the Greek culture combined with the pragmatism of the Romans would not have developed into a great power if it had not been grafted into the strong Indo-European tradition, itself enriched by inputs from other cultures and civilizations of many different people. After the Aeneis there was no second Virgil able to produce masterpieces comparable to the two Homeric epics. The power and occasional lyrical beauty, respectively in Greek and in Latin of the three epic poems, has remained unrivalled to this day in the west. The most recent, authoritative and complete publications on these subjects are by Canfora, (2001) for the Greek literature, by Codino and Calzecchi-Onesti (1990) for the Iliad, by Heubeck (1991) for the Odyssey, by Paratore (2000) for the Latin literature, by La Penna and Scarcia (2002) for the Aeneis, Menghi (2003) for the geographic/historic perspective of the Greek civilization, among many other authors, ancient and modern.

The Indian civilization is a unique phenomenon. As already pointed out by ancient authors, Arrianus of Nicomedia being one of them, India did not wage wars against its neighbours and had no expansionist tendencies. India is indeed generated and evolved from inside out, hence the profound meaning and symbolism of the concept of *swayambhu liṅgam.* India has always walked its way free and indifferent and developed in splendid isolation, with the most individual and liberated attitude; nowhere alse can a *person* feel as free as he wants to be, as in India. Nowhere else are the concepts of *liber arbitrium* and *dharma* more alive and remembered, with its duties and privileges, responsibilities and rewards as it is in India, as *ṛṣi* Vaśiṣtha saw and lived by Varuṇa, the unfettered elder son of Āditi, the eternal ever-great unbound Mother of infinity, Varuṇa the great Asura Varuṇa is for many the Great God and Master of each one of us human beings, gifted with the power of reason and discrimination. However this is not the place to enter into philosophical reasoning.

The *Ṛgveda* is not a poem, it is also not a treatise in history or science, it tells of myths and legends as a substrate for a philosophy of life, together with the other Vedas, and other ancient texts and Vedānta, are a remarkable product of the human mind. These texts put on record the origin, evolution and development of the Indo-Arya civilization. There is no concern with absolute chronology, notions about comparative time and historical time sequences and genealogies are diffuse and have been laboriously reconstructed by scholars. There is no preconceived plan, no preconceived philosophy. The Vedas have no boundaries and are a presumably useful support to be considered by the individual mind at any time throughout life. The *ṚV* is the root of all the Vedas and though what has come down to us is probably only a fragment of the entire corpus of the Vedic lore. It is evident that the Vedas are a unique ageless composition that reflects the human eagerness to learn, to know, to understand and to think and work strenuously to conquer material and spiritual wealth. There are various singers of the different hymns, united into ten books. Most of the poet/singers are classed with the seven original *ṛṣis*. The Vedas are unique and cannot be classed in any literary category except for the fact that they are composed in metric poetry comparable to musical composition, similarly to what must have been the compositions of the aedi and rhapsodists of the very ancient pre-historic times of the Indo-European of east and west.

The *Rāmāyaṇa* and the *Mahābhārata* are closer to the western concept of epic poems, though accurate chronology and time sequence of the events narrated are often difficult to trace. The Indian epics grew with interpolations and additions over an unspecified number of centuries, based on the conviction that there is only One Absolute Truth, the Godhead itself. No single man can perceive the entire truth, hence the expressions, narrations and statements made at different times and conditions by enlightened wise men, women and children are recorded because they **may or may not express some partial truth** not previously **seen** by others. Inevitably contradictions may be found in the Śruti and *Smṛti,* they are the result of the acquisition of new knowledge and progress in science. Different viewpoints and conclusions are left open until when proven wrong and until knowledge is streamlined, if possible. There is throughout the unshakable belief that only the Absolute Truth exists and that man will never be able to reach full understanding of the world of which he is part and of the entire cosmos. Humility and a constructive critical attitude are the corner stone of wisdom. Mathematics of simple matters such as the Greek numbers *phi* or *pi,* or the series of prime numbers and other aspects of concept of "infinite" as evidenced by mathematics are perhaps the best approach to the study of the problems posed by Vedānta.

The *ṚV*, the epics, the Itihāsas, the Purāṇas and other ancient texts continue to grow from the heroic age as we know it and of which there are archaeologic datable remains that go as far back as when the Indo-Arya lived a pastoral life in the plains of R. Gurgan off the eastern part of the southern Caspian Sea. Culture was enriched and diversified later with the development of agriculture on those lands. With the development of agriculture the entire cultural spectrum was widened, migrations, contacts with other people, trade and new environments, enriched folklore and technical expertise resulted in better nutrition and health. Socio-economic organisation could become well established. The Indo-Europeans of the east were slow in adopting a script and relied mostly on individual and collective memory for the transmission of knowledge, they believed in example, a rigorous training and a simple way of life, they believed in teaching and learning from earliest childhood and throughout life, hence the importance of the brāhmaṇas, *ācāryas* and masters among the Indo-Aryans and the magi among the Indo-Iranians. The phantastic feats of memory of the elders were successful and today, even after the epics were written down, a rich folklore known to village story tellers, a variety of performers of dramas, legends and myths can maintain the sacred fire of tradition alive among the people at large. One of the nearest points of cultural contact between Indo-Europeans of east and west is the culture of the story-tellers, the recitations of the epics, the memorising of ancient text, the ability to improvise mythological and historical scenes and dialogues or entire genealogies, such are the pandits who memorize the Bhṛgu Saṁhitā or have similar cultural erudition and ability in the performing arts. Improvisers and story-tellers and brāhmaṇas, who memorize the four Vedas, or at least one Veda, are fast disappearing. Story tellers that go from festival to festival throughout the country to sing — a popular tradition in Italy as in India — are becoming more and more rare and we can only hope that "modernisation" will not destroy intellectual culture with the same fury as it is destroying natural and ancient or archaeologic remains.

Even after cities and fortified *pur* were developed, the Indo-Aryan man remained essentially bound to nature and considered himself part and parcel of it. From the heroic age to present days, India remained true to the belief that man cannot exist disjoined from Nature, because **Nature is real and** is perhaps the **only reality**.

Part IV

Summary and Conclusions

THE stated scope of this book is to produce a concise study of some aspects of the Indo-European family of languages and people, namely the evolution of the cultures of the Indo-Europeans (Indo-European) of the East, here called Indo-Aryans and Indo-Iranians, as well as of the Indo-European of the West, specifically the Graeco-Roman civilization. Customs and habits of the Indo-Iranians and of the Indo-Aryans of Central and South Asia and Asia Minor, and the customs and habits of the Indo-Europeans of the west who belonged to various stocks that lived in ancient times in the lands around the Mediterranean and Black Seas are discussed here. The present study stops at the last century BC after the short-lived reaction to the despotism of Gaius Julius Caesar (100-44 BC) promoted in the west renewed debates on philosophical matters such as Ethics, Fate and Destiny, Freedom, Individual and Political Liberty, and other topics taken up at open dialogues and discussions (= *disputatio* in Latin). The study of the evolution of Indo-European civilizations in Europe and Asia Minor in the Christian Era is beyond the scope of this book.

There were no dramatic breaks of continuity in the evolution of the Indo-Iranian and Indo-Arya civilizations from the ancient past and before AD times, apart from Zoroastrianism, Jainism and Buddhism and other minor sects who diverted from the mainstream of cultural development though they continued to profess the basic ideal of a naturalistic and simple way of life comparable to that of the Vedic people. Different use and interpretation of the word "god" led to distinct philosophical schools. Kochhar (2000) gives a short summary of the Indo-European family of languages [and people].

Sources for the knowledge of ancient times are found in the Avesta, in the Vedas and Vedānta, and in the Epics of east and west first transmitted orally from generation to generation. Records in writing among the Indo-Europeans of the east, started when man first used cuneiform script and Sanskrit-derived languages to record Peace Treaties, matrimonial alliances and letters or other documents of national and international importance. Written records go as far back as the first half of the second millennium BC. Recent publications give the results of new scientific methods and techniques applied to the study of the ancient past. I would mention only two of the most recent, Cavalli-Sforza and other scientists-applied genetics and DNA research methods to trace the origin of different human populations. McGovern and others use new chemical and other methods and techniques applicable to the analysis of very small amounts of materials from archaeological or other ancient remains. These sciences are fast evolving and readers should be on the look-out for the extremely interesting new knowledge being produced in quick succession.

The ancient-most records *in writing* of the Indo-European were produced in Asia Minor, West Asia and Mesopotamia and go as far back as the middle or first half of the second millennium BC. They were followed by texts written in an alphabetic script derived from the Phoenician alphabet that evolved into the Greek alphabet, a script used to this day. The language is classic Greek, an Indo-European language, even closer to Sanskrit than Latin. There were several variants of the Greek language and many different dialects in the Hellenic world which was a composite of various people who used the Greek spoken language and script regularly. The oldest texts refer to the history of Athens and her first kings called *archontes*. Later texts include philosophic, dramatic or epic material. Myths and legends, archaic beliefs and stories are the bulk of the oral tradition, which was sung by poet singers of east and west. Like the Greek, Latin script is phonetic, but originally Latin had only 14 different signs (= letters) while the Greek alphabet had 24, with low and high key for all the letters. Latin was originally written with capital letters only.

(A) People and Environments

For the purpose of this study, the Indo-European of the Graeco-Roman and Hellenistic civilizations of the Mediterranean Sea, Asia Minor and West Asia are here called the "Indo-Europeans of the west." The "Indo-Europeans of the east" are here understood to be the Indo-Aryans and Indo-Iranians who migrated from the Indo-European original homeland in the Eurasian steppes and moved southwards along the eastern and western margins of the Caspian Sea, then westwards over Asia Minor as far as Greece, and southwards to the Iranian plateau, or eastwards towards India. Other Indo-European clans also arrived in Greece coming from the Eurasian steppes and entered mainland Greece from the north, mainly Macedonians and Thracians and others coming from the lands around the Black Sea. Indo-Aryan clans coming from the Eurasian steppes who had settled east of the southern Caspian Sea in the plains of R. Gurgan, eventually moved further eastward until they settled in what are now northern Afghanistan, Pakistan, India and beyond, while other groups of Indo-Aryans moved westwards from the plains of R. Gurgan and eventually reached as far as the Aegean Sea and Greece. The Indo-Iranians migrated from the original Indo-European homeland in the Eurasian steppes and eventually moved southwards towards the Arabian Sea and occupied the countries known as Phars (= Fars), Elam and the Zagros (= ancient Indo-European root words) regions. The Indo-Iranians migrated also eastwards towards Central Asia, and occupied the regions called Chorasmia, Sogdiana, and perhaps further eastwards in lands of Central Asia (*fig.* 1, *apud* Girshman). We are not concerned here with the Indo-European Turks who migrated north-eastwards and are still now the major component of the people of the Altaï Mountains and produced over the centuries a most interesting literature.

The Indo-Aryans who crossed Central Asia and Asia Minor moving westwards, were among the first to have important cultural exchanges with non-Indo-European people pre-existent in the Mediterranean basin, they were indigenous people, Semitic and Egyptians. In the east, the Indo-Arya were followed by the Indo-Iranians who settled in the lands of present day Iran, from the Aral

Sea in the north, including the lands of Sogdiana and Chorasmia, west of R. Amu Darya and those between the Rs. Amu Darya and Syr. Darya. These natural migratory routes centuries later became the regular main trade routes between the "West and the far East," better called "Occident and Orient," and among others incorporated parts of the famous "Silk Route." Another route followed by the Indo-European in their movements towards Europe, went around the coastal plains of the Black Sea. After occupying the fertile plains of R. Danube they again moved southwards towards Macedonia, Thracia, Greece and Italy. Different clans of Indo-Europeans migrated into mainland Central and Northern Europe. We are not concerned with them here.

Western and Central Asia, especially Mesopotamia and Asia Minor witnessed the rise and development of some of the ancient-most great civilizations as well as the clashes of different cultures. Trade, metallurgy, development of arts and crafts, urbanisation, martial arts and matrimonial contracts contributed to a high level of acculturation of humankind. Enrichment and cultural evolution and refinement of all people, Indo-European, Semitic and others, followed the development of extensive agriculture and the use, distribution and control of water resources. Agriculture and animal husbandry became widespread without displacing pre-existing animal husbandry and pastoralism as sources of food, wool, hides, leather, horns and the manure needed for developing agriculture. Salt, cereals and vegetable fibres, metals, copper, zinc, iron, bronze, gold and silver could travel far and wide thanks to the development of trade routes by land and sea. Trade was the most important factor for the growth of permanent wealth and development of technicalities.

The spread of the ancient Egyptian civilization appears in the context of this study only as the Egyptian pharaohs moved their armies along the Mediterranean coast as far as present day Palestine. The until-then undisputed Egyptians, in the person of the young pharaoh Ramses II, were not adequately prepared to face the advanced warfare competence of the Indo-Aryans. After the battle of Kadesh, (1275 BC) Egypt was forced to agree and seal a peace treaty with the Indo-Aryan Hittites. It stopped forever the pharaonic advance into Asia and their attempt to remove the Hittite control over Syria.

The web of trade routes by land and sea favoured all people, but at places some populations were isolated due to difficult access to their settlements, such as the high mountains of the Hindukush, the Karakorum, the Himalayas, the Altaï mountains, and they became "cultural pockets," for instance in Afghanisthan. These "relict" populations are interesting because they preserve ancient cultural traits in their customs, habits and in the spoken language.

MIGRATIONS: INDO-ARYA AND INDO-IRANIANS

Twentieth century archaeological, ethnological and linguistic studies backed by scientific research and sophisticated techniques provided new insights into the origin and evolution of the cultures of south and central Asia. It is well established that the original homeland of the proto-Indo-European groups of people, particularly those who called themselves "Arya," were the steppes north of the Caspian and Black Seas, and eastwards as far as the Aral Sea and the lands between rivers Oxus (= Amu Darya) and Jaxartes (= Syr Darya) and as far westwards as the basins of Rs. Volga, Dnieper and Don, more specifically the lands between them. The Volga flows into the Caspian and the Dniepr and Don into the Black Sea. Over many generations, following the course of these rivers the Indo-Europeans living in the Eurasian steppes, migrated along the eastern coastal zone of the Caspian Sea southwards towards more fertile lands and better climates. Some groups moved in a western direction north of the Black Sea and around the western littoral of that sea, notable among them the Scythians and the Thracians. We are not concerned here with the Indo-Europeans who moved towards Central Europe and those who at a late date reached Macedonia, Greece and Rome. We here consider only the descendents of the original proto-Indo-Europeans who lived in the northern area of the Caspian Sea, where they split in two groups before moving southwards (*fig.* 1).

Various groups or tribes originated from the proto homeland of the Indo-European. For what concerns the present subject matter there were in the east two main groups, the Indo-Aryans and the Indo-Iranians (Ghirshman, 1977 p. 73, J. Markwart and A. Christensen, *apud* Ghirshman) whose geographic location was discussed by H.S. Nybeg (1938, *apud* Ghirshman, p. 73): "entweder ist Vouru-kasha das Kaspisches Meer und Raha die Volga, oder

Vouru-kasha ist die Aralsee, und Raha der alte Jaxartes, der heurige Syr Darya." The Avestic River *Raha* = *Ranha* is identified by some authors with the Vedic Rasa. As discussed above, based on the authors mentioned, and based on Avestic myths describing the hydrology of the area and on the study of ancient historians and geographers, I believe that there is no doubt that Vourukasha is the Aral Sea and River Raha is the Jaxartes more recently called Syr Darya. Summing up, according to the detailed texts of the Avesta describing the hydrological regime of their ancestral homeland, the very ancient Indo-Iranians lived in a place near the sea called Vourukasha and along the margins of a river called *Ranha,* identified by some authors with the R̥gvedic R. Rasa mentioned seven times in the *R̥V*. The river *Ranha* is most probably the present day R. Syr Darya (= Jaxartes). Again in the Avesta (Yasht 13, 143-144) the people of five countries are mentioned from this region whose names are Indo-European, they are: Aryans, Turanians, Sairimians, Sainians and Dahinians. It is well known that the people we now call Iranians originally called themselves Arya, from which came the name Iran. Recent archaeological studies tend to confirm this view of the distribution of Central Asian tribes in the fourth millennium BC and perhaps earlier.

The first group of proto-Indo-Europeans, known at present as the Indo-Aryan, migrated over the lands along the eastern littoral zone of the Caspian Sea and by the fourth millennium BC were well established in the lands off south-eastern Caspian Sea in the fertile plains bathed by the hydrological system of R. Gurgan and the eastern Elburz mountains. Already by the third millennium BC the local culture had developed into a flourishing rudimentary urban economy based on the domestication of the horse, the development of perfected wheels, carts and chariots, a simple type of war trumpet indicative of the rise of martial arts and of an organised society. Agriculture and trade based on manufactured goods were already developed as evidenced by material remains, a valuable source of information of the degree of development of the local culture. For unknown reasons, the Indo-Arya Indo-European were again divided into two groups and migrated from the Gurgan River plains in opposite directions. One group went eastwards into what are now

Afghanistan, Pakistan, India, where their descendants still live, along with people of different or related origins.

The group of Indo-Aryans who went westwards eventually reached Asia Minor, Anatolia and the Mediterranean. After migrating along the fertile southern rim of the Caspian Sea they crossed the northern parts of Mesopotamia. Archaeological remains indicate that they arrived in Mesopotamia about the nineteenth century BC. From there they extended into western Asia Minor. Dated artefacts and historical records show that the ancient Vedic or pre-Vedic culture of the Indo-Arya was **still alive and strong** among the Hittites and the ruling class of the Mitanni kingdom in the second millennium BC. The very ancient phase of the Indo-Arya who moved and settled in the north-eastern area of the Iranian plateau is dominated by datable potsherds of the so-called black-grey pottery ware and other artefacts already in the late fourth millennium and throughout the third millennium BC.

There are no reasonable explanations of the causes that impelled the Indo-Aryans to abandon the fertile soil of the plains of R. Gurgan, where they had completed the domestication of the horse and produced the "turkoman" breed, famous for its beauty, size, strength and endurance. Transport carts and wagons were developed and ornaments were produced in quantity based mainly on works in gold. The groups of Indo-Aryans who reached Afghanistan eventually entered into major India settled in the beautiful valleys of the lower Hindukush such as Swat, the lower Himalayas and the plains of Pakistan and India. Four-wheel wagons with solid wheels were drawn by specially trained oxen.

The other group of Indo-Arya who moved away from the plains of R. Gurgan migrated westwards along the plains of the southern Caspian Sea and occupied the Iranian plateau, Anatolia and Asia Minor. The noun *samudra* (= sea, ocean) to which the Vedas refer is not the Indian Ocean as often repeated in translation, but the Caspian Sea, the Aral Sea and most probably also the Black Sea. All of these have slightly saline waters as they are left-overs from the large rather shallow sea that covered the entire region in previous geologic eras. Knowledge of the Indian Ocean came late and was first known only from hear-say and through traded goods. The conch and other marine shells rich in mother-of-pearl used to manufacture jewellery was traded as far as Babylonia as attested from searches at Mehrgarh and in Mesopotamia.

Archaeological findings show that Indo-Iranian Medes and Persian tribes were well established in western Iran earlier than the twelfth-tenth centuries BC (Ghirshman 1977, p. 47) and produced a grey-black pottery which differs from the earlier painted pottery and had different shapes. These people also came from the north or from the north-east and had scarce use of iron. Herodotus (I, 215) says that the "Massagetes" who came into Iran from the north-east, did not know iron and silver, though iron ore was smelted into metal in what is now western Iran since the fourteenth century BC.

MIGRATIONS — THE INDO-IRANIANS

The Indo-Iranian group originated from the first split of the Indo-European into Indo-Aryans and Indo-Iranians, when they were still living and moving in the Indo-European homeland in the Eurasian steppes, as far east as the Aral Sea and the lands between the two main feeders of that sea, the Rs. Amu Darya and Syr Darya. The Indo-Iranian are first found in north-eastern Iran about two millennia **after** the Indo-Aryans had reached the same general area. The Indo-Iranians later moved along two main routes, one along the eastern and the other along the western margins of the Caspian Sea (*fig.* 1). The western group probably crossed the Caucasus Mountains going southwards, towards the second millennium BC. The eastern group of Indo-Iranians moved along the northern, then the eastern littoral of the Caspian Sea before reaching north-eastern Iran. These tribes eventually reached Afghanistan and came in contact with the Indo-Aryans who had preceded them in parts of what are now Afghanistan, Pakistan and India; they eventually became established in Sindh and India.

The Indo-Iranians who followed the western route migrated as far south as Phars in Iran, the kingdom of Elam and the Zagros Mountains where they settled in earlier sparsely populated areas. The Indo-Iranians who over many generations migrated along the eastern coasts of the Caspian Sea, went beyond River Oxus (= Amu Darya), and as far as River Jaxartes (= Syr Darya), where Alexander the Macedonian met them many centuries later. Rivers Amu Darya and Syr Darya are fed by opposite watersheds of the Pamir Mountains. Both these rivers flow northwards into the Aral Sea which has slightly saline waters and a relict ocean fauna, such as seals.

This general scheme of the early migration of the Indo-Europeans agrees with Firdusi (940?-1020? AD) who classed Iranians in eastern and western, respectively belonging to the Turan and Iran countries, as mentioned in the *Shah Namah*. The conclusions mentioned above are the most convincing considering all types of evidence and some authors go as far as believing that the homeland of the proto-Iranian Indo-European is Chorasmia, the northern part of the land between rivers Oxus and Jaxartes and west of the Aral Sea.

Climates changed over the past millennia. It is known that changes towards progressively greater aridity have plagued Central Asia since a few millennia ago. Also the Arabic peninsula was covered with vegetation until early historic times and the trough of the south-west monsoon continues to shift eastwards in South Asia, leaving increasing aridity behind it. Climate changes and incursions of hostile tribes coming from the north could also have been partially responsible for the centrifugal migrations of many tribes, rather than just wander-lust.

Due to migrations, displacements and wars, all the Indo-Europeans of the east found themselves living for varying lengths of time under different environmental and climatic conditions, they thus gained much practical experience and evolved quickly into advanced cultures that developed into several great civilizations. Needless to repeat here the imprint that the environment, including climate, has on the culture of emerging civilizations. Suffice it to recall the importance of the sciences: the study of nature, numbers, geometry, astronomy and hydrology for all practical aspects of agriculture and cultural life of mankind. In the west, science was recognised as an important branch of learning in its own right only late. The Greek Thales (624-623? — 548-543? BC) of the island of Milos in the Peloponnese, predicted accurately the solar eclipse that took place on 28th May of the year 585 BC. Since ancient times he has been considered in the west as one of the "seven sages" and founder of Greek science. The Greek Pythagoras (570-*c.* 490) from Samos on the coast of Asia Minor identified "the number" as the order in the universe and "the soul and nature" as life. Following the ancient oral tradition, neither Thales nor Pythagoras left anything in writing and whatever we know of their teachings is through the texts written by their disciples; one of them called Philolaos established the principles of the theory of numbers and explained the "Pythagoras theorem." Science was perhaps born earlier or at about the same time among the Indo-Europeans of the east, where also nothing was put in writing, knowledge was transmitted orally and by practical training and demonstrations. In east and west science was initially kept religiously secret, as a precious endowment of the learned. The geometrician Pythagoras, the astronomer Thales and the fifth century Parmenides "father of logical deduction" were members of secret societies as much as the ancient Egyptian priests and the Indian brāhmaṇas. Numbers and numerology preceded the invention of a script and of writing; the exact times cannot be defined in either east or west. The decimal system was invented independently by the Maya, in the Yucatan peninsula of the Gulf of Mexico and much earlier by Indians at an unknown early point in time. Āryabhaṭṭa in the sixth century AD used the decimal system for the mathematical calculus and the "sign" zero must have already been regularly used before him. In Āryabhaṭṭa's words: "from place to place each is ten times greater than the preceding."

STRUCTURED SOCIETIES AND ARCHITECTURAL STRUCTURES

With increasing knowledge, inevitably a class of learned men is born and societies become structured very early, though this does not necessarily imply the development of urban life. In India to this day society is clearly structured even, or specially so in villages, with duties and activities attributed to everyone according to local conditions and needs, though lifestyles continue to be of the rural type characteristic of farmers and shepherds. Refinement of culture and growing factual knowledge eventually develops into urban civilizations that flowered at different times all over the world. Evolution of culture also induces the creation of "temple cities," separate and away from the bustling central administrative capital where the king usually resides. Temple cities harboured the *philosophers* (= friends of knowledge), an ancient term which includes scientists and priests who are often one and the same; they are the learned men who know and must write and read.

Allen (2003), defines as "pentadic" the structure of the society described in the *Mahābhārata* and draws a parallel with the society described in the Iliad wondering whether the similarities are due to borrowing or common origin. Quoting from Allen: "Dumézil's main thesis is that the proto-Indo-European speakers tended to organize their conceptual world in terms of a hierarchical triadic classificatory scheme." Dumézil's opinion is closely followed also by Haudry (1981). Allen expands at both ends the triadic Dumézil scheme and draws a pentadic scheme. Allen correctly concludes that "common origin" does not exclude "borrowing" among cultures, which is an obvious and undoubtedly correct conclusion as also is its corollary that could be expressed as: different origins do not exclude borrowing. In my opinion, however, the common error of the three authors mentioned, is to compare the cultures described in the *Mahābhārata* with those in the Iliad as "proto-Indo-European." From this fundamental error they develop a complex theory on a false basis. In fact the culture described in the two epics is not that of proto- or pre-historic cultures. The societies described are already developed technically, literarily and religiously. Furthermore, the culture described in the Iliad is more primitive and less evolved than the culture described in the *Mahābhārata*. The Indian epics do not refer to brief periods of time; they include also the developments that occurred over centuries, as is obvious from the many interpolations made in the original text. On the other hand the Greek epics refer to short periods of time, though they also mention some changes that took place after the Mycenean age and during the Doric invasions and early Greek period. Evolution of primitive cultures inevitably leads to a "triadic" or "pentadic" structure, whatever we wish to call it. The word "evolution" involves the notion of increasing complexity; this is particularly true of the evolution and development of human societies. At whatever stage of development, all groups of humans out of necessity have a leader or ruler who ensures concerted efforts of all the members of the group and an organisation based on division of labour and attributes, the individual *timai* of men and gods. Therefore the "triadic" or "pentadic" schemes or theories give no explanations; at most they illustrate the structure of human society at similar or comparable levels of development. The comparison of the structure of the Greek and Indian societies of the Iliad and the *Mahābhārata* offered by Dumézil, Allen and Haudry does not hold.

There is no "society" if it is not structured, an "unstructured society" is a contradiction in terms and would be nothing more than a loose congregation of wandering human beings. There is always a ruler (= king, leader, chief etc.), there are learned men (ācāryas, purohits, teachers, masters, priests, artisans and engineers) and the *demos,* the people at large which form the mass of the population, each person doing his (or her) own allotted work and being conscribed and trained for war when the King decides to fight. The so-called "triadic or pentadic structure of the proto-Indo-Europeans" are not much more than a photographic representation of situations, there is no need to elaborate useless theories that neither explain or improve understanding. Obviously strong and young soldiers look forward to the promised booty, and the officers look forward to glory and pride in addition to wealth, the traditional carrot placed in front of the donkey. Obviously also the learned priestly class knows that there is power and wealth where there is knowledge and science. The society described in the *Mahābhārata* was far more organized for warfare than the Greek society of the Iliad, therefore even from this point of view a comparison between the two is useless.

The error of authors as those mentioned above, is to consider the epics as representatives of the structure of *proto-Indo-European cultures.* The common roots are to be found much deeper and earlier in time than the corresponding stages of the personalities of the epics of east and west or the duration of the phases of the war. The structures considered by the authors are the same among all cultures at comparable levels of development and come much later than "proto- or pre-historic" levels of cultural evolution. There is no need to push readings into theoretical straight-jackets such as castes, professions, arts and crafts that are the same in the development of all cultures. If generalised, Dumézil's and Allen's theories are interesting, but they cannot be restricted to the Iliad and *Mahābhārata* and are not much more than a picture, rather than an understanding or explanation of civilizations where society is already diversified into specialized professions.

Religions and philosophies are a different matter, not to be confused with this issue.

Culture is created and enriched in many practical or religious ways, for instance in arid zones of Iran architectural competence was enriched with the construction of massive "pigeon towers" built to enable man to collect the guano produced by the droppings of the birds, to fertilize the fields. The same habit prevailed in the south of France where "pigeon towers" only recently abandoned may be seen all over the Lot and Provence fields. Again, ziggurats were inspired by the grandiosity of mountains, a common element of worship especially among Indo-European people. They were built over the simple original platforms made for religious performance of the rites and worship of Fire and for astronomical observations already in 2200 BC in Sumer. Ziggurats are man-made stepped pyramids, an imitation of Sacred Mountains and were, according to the Sumerian tradition, made by "men coming from the east who worship mountains." The first recorded arrival of Sumerians in Mesopotamia was from the sea about the fourth millennium BC and they are known to have spoken a "non-Semitic language."

The oldest ziggurat in ancient Iran was in the kingdom of Elam at Dur Untashi near Susa, built at about 1200 BC and served both as tomb and temple (Pope, 1969). Ancient ziggurats were made, like the oldest Sumerian, Mesopotamian and Harappan structures, with sun-dried bricks. Next to nothing is known of the links if any, between the ancient Sumerians of Mesopotamia and the people of southern Iran and Elam east of the Zagros Mountains or with the Indus Valley civilization, also called Harappan civilization. Little is known about the relationships between the Indo-Arya and the Harappans and the entire Indus-valley civilization. We will not touch the problem here. Religious architecture however, tends to be conservative, such were also ziggurats that continued to be built during many centuries, as well as Fire temples whose platforms were shaped as stepped pyramids.

For more than practical and survival reasons, irrigation ditches assumed impressive proportions and canals were dug for navigational purposes linking different hydrographical systems, to facilitate fluvial navigation or access to the sea for trading purposes. The Rs. Tigris and Euphrates were linked by a man-made canal since ancient days. Climates determine architecture of common buildings, temples, city plans. Geography and topography determine road building. Trade was an important activity since pre-historic times, we find all over the Semitic and Indo-European worlds well planned webs of roads by land, river and sea for the transport of goods, as early as the beginning of the last millennium BC in Major India (Lahiri, 1992) and probably earlier. An exception to this was the closed kingdom of ancient Egyptian dynasties where transport of goods was by barges and sailing boats that plied R. Nile throughout the millennia. The Indo-European Hyksos introduced the horse in Egypt during their brief stay in the pharaonic kingdom. The Phoenicians, the Pelasgoi, the Feacians and other pre-Hellenic autochthonous people were the master navigators of the entire Mediterranean Sea. The last of the three channels that linked Egypt to the Red Sea was dug out during the reign of the Greek Ptolemy dynasty and was, like its predecessors, dried off by massive silting caused by desert sands brought by wind storms.

ECOLOGY

No nation can flourish in isolation from its environment, this is particularly true for what concerns the Indo-Aryans among the Indo-Europeans of the east who moved into sparsely populated areas where they had to adapt lifestyle, agricultural practices, social development and habits to the physical imperatives and requirements of the environment. Polyandry for instance, is a habit primarily acquired by trader-shepherds of high mountains because of the recurrent long absence of married men for up to two years at a time, due to the constraints inherent in transhumance over high mountain passes which are closed for many winter months at a time. In remote environments, such as the Himalayas, a woman is often implicitly understood to be married to all the brothers of the family, since the day of her marriage to the eldest. It is the only way to ensure the birth of a sufficient number of offsprings to keep the family and lineage going. Some of the brothers always stay home during the long periods when the father and other brothers are absent for trade or for grazing the family flocks at high pastures. Such is the seed of the story of Draupadī in the *Mahābhārata* who was married to the eldest Pāṇḍava, but spent one year with each brother in turn, though each also had his own wife.

Institutionalised polyandry, the practice of levirate or the cohabitation with the husband's brother during the husband's absence or after his death, are accepted even if not the rule of many societies down to the present. The wife does not become impure by sexual intercourse with the husband's brother or brothers, but all her children are considered to be children of the first rightful husband. This practice reflects the great socio-economic and religious importance of the brother, especially the elder brother who takes over the functions of the father and becomes the head of the family when the father passes away. Individuals did not have a long life expectancy under the trying living conditions of life at high altitude. All brothers of the same family are the *alter ego* of each other, but the eldest has the authority and commands respect because of his heavy duties which he usually shares with the father when alive and takes over entirely when the father passes away. Indo-European people of west and east were patriarchal societies and very similar situations existed until recently in Greece, Italy, Portugal, Spain and others, until when traditions became diluted by "modernity," whatever that may signify. In India, elder brother and elder sister, *dīdī* are in fact second father and second mother to the younger brothers and sisters throughout life.

Such normal customary family habits also tend to strengthen the bonds of friendship and mutual assistance among all the daughters-in-law of the extended families living in mountain ranges. The solidarity and power of womanhood is the focus of a beautiful and most important book by Anjali Capila (2002). The crucial role of the forest in distant regions calls to memory a beautiful hymn of the *R̥V* (X 146) in praise of the Lady of the Forest, *Araṇyāni.* Isolated populations and populations under stress tend to follow similar rules and procedures every where, including xenophobia, as a form of protection.

Finally, solidarity among the various families of the clan, the tribe or lineages is of basic importance for survival under the trying conditions and hazards of life. Some reasons and causes of polygamy spring from the same root, namely the prolonged absence and uncertain return of the husband who is away for trade or for the grazing of the flock at high altitudes where nutritious grass grows quickly and sheep and goats will produce best quality wool. Some of the best hunters, mariners, traders, warriors or mountain people often died early and the family or clan should ensure that genetically good offsprings (= "good race") were produced. Hence also early marriages, soon after the onset of puberty. My own grandmother and great-grandmother of ancient Florentine lineage in Italy were married at sixteen years of age and my father was married at age 19, **before** he left as a volunteer for the First World War. Among the Aztecs, the hero and magnificent volunteer warrior who would be sacrificed one year after victory, was given the choicest virgins for company and pleasure before his still pulsating heart was ripped from his living body and offered to the gods.

INDO-EUROPEANS OF THE WEST

The Indo-Europeans of the Mediterranean Sea and inland Europe were themselves a mixed assemblage of various tribes and lineages and their vocabularies were different enough to hinder communication, though the grammar and syntaxes of the language were the same as Greek or Latin and neo-Latin languages. Latin languages are remarkably close to Sanskrit and Sanskrit-derived languages as Filippo Sassetti (1540-1588), the Florentine writer, notary and trader who lived for some years at Cochin (Kochi) and then died in Goa, noticed already in the sixteenth century AD. There never was a single homogeneous Indo-European nation in Europe, the mixing of different Indo-European people from Asia Minor and continental Europe started very early and reached its peak, but not the end, during the time of Imperial Rome. Culturally the Hellenic world, and later its heir Rome held together an assemblage of the city-states of Greece and Magna Graecia and then a variety of many nations under Rome, until the fall of the Roman Empire in 476 AD. The environment was as varied as the people, except for the socio-economic and climatic regulator, the Mediterranean Sea. The number of different species of flora and fauna had been greatly reduced by the glaciations that wiped Europe clean of a very large variety of species; very soon Indo-Europeans brought with them and introduced useful species from Africa and Asia for food, fibres, vegetables, meat and so on.

In the Mediterranean world there were also autochthonous populations in Greece and Italy before the advent of the Indo-Europeans. There were ancient civilizations, the Egyptians, various groups of Semites and the Sumerians of unknown extraction. There were also other Indo-European people and autochthonous populations of different origins scattered over the entire Mediterranean world and adjacent areas. Important among them were the Sumerians who invented the first syllabic phonetic form of writing, the cuneiform script. There were Phoenicians and Pelasgians who were master navigators and pirates, the various powerful Mesopotamian kingdoms, all of them over-shadowed by the mighty Egyptian pharaohs. When the Indo-European of the east crossed Asia Minor from east to west and arrived at the edge of the Aegean Sea, they already had been in direct or indirect contact with most of these people through trade, exchange of goods, metallurgy and other technical knowledge, wars and slavery. Concubinate by abduction of women as booty or by royal decree was common as well as "political marriages" among members of the nobilities.

The Indo-Aryan kingdom of Mitanni reached its maximum extension around the fifteenth and fourteenth centuries BC. The kingdom extended in a general direction from north to south, from the Mediterranean coast in the north down to the Zagros Mountains and the Persian Gulf in the South. Their neighbours were the Indo-European Hittites in the north and the Babylonian Kassites to the south and east of R. Tigris. Apart from the Mitanni, the Hittites were the other powerful Indo-European nation in all of Asia Minor and West Asia. At one stage they occupied most of Asia Minor. The Mitanni and the Hittites were Indo-Aryan as proven by the religion, the names of the gods, of the kings, nobles and warriors of the ruling class; the bulk of the people was of different ethnicity. The Medes were western Indo-Iranians who are first met in western Iran towards the end of the second millennium BC. There were also other pockets of Indo-European and other people whose independence and identity never survived for long periods of time; they were absorbed in one or other powerful group, as for instance the Hurrites, non Indo-European people who were ruled by a dominant class of Indo-Aryan nobility.

AUTOCHTHONOUS PEOPLE

Among the people whom the Indo-European met during their migrations, were the *Pelasgoi*, some ancient Italic tribes, the very ancient people of Greece, North Africa and Central Asia, the coasts of Asia Minor, all of them non Indo-European. Each of the composite assemblage of people of different background and geographic origin contributed to the development of the multifaceted civilizations of the Mediterranean region. The Hellenic civilization itself was not a single self-contained nation. Without being a federation of States, it had a loose political structure centered on the greatness of Athens, the mother of all city-states. The Hellenic world was knit together by the notion and concept of the "*polis*" (= the City-state) and the supremacy of Athens which was the prototype and philosophical model and ideal to be followed. Of all the many *polies* and small city states, Athens was the first, the most learned and admirable, **THE Polis**. Greek culture, including the different aspects of Greek religion and philosophy, was transmitted down to the present thanks to the learning of the men of the many *polies* scattered over the Mediterranean, thanks to the Museum and to the Library of Alexandria in Egypt, thanks to Rome, and finally thanks to the patient work of medieval monks and friars who were those who copied all that could be copied, even if the sleepy scribes in poorly lit and cold libraries would occasionally, willingly or unwillingly, introduce errors or "improvements" in the texts of often poorly preserved ancient manuscripts. The language was always Greek or Latin, both of them Indo-European languages.

RELICT INDO-EUROPEAN POPULATIONS IN EAST AND WEST

Relict is the name given to species or populations of biological species that remained isolated over very long periods of time, centuries, millennia or geologic eras. Because of genetic drift, climatic adaptations and inbreeding, isolated populations are at phenotypic and genotypic variance with the original genetic pool. Such isolated or semi-isolated groups of individuals have survived in remote places, having little contact with individuals or populations of the same species living beyond their domain. Isolation of humans is never complete but habits and folklore tend to remain static except for the addition of details and new myths whose origin and evolution are influenced by the local environmental, ecological and socio-economic constraints. Only a few examples are cited here.

In the reports of his travels in Afghanistan, Robertson (1894, 1896) describes the habits of the people of some of the tribes with whom he stayed for shorter or longer periods. Details of daily and family habits match rather closely with those of the people of high altitude elsewhere in Asia, specially the Himalayas and the Hindukush, Gilgit, Hunza and Chitral. The building and plan of the houses with central hearth, the closeness of the cattle shed, the family structure and division of labour, the fierce wreaking of vengeance and violent punishment, the importance of certain festivals, specially the festival of the winter solstice and the preparation of grapes' wine, fermented grapes juice or "new wine" which is not much more than what in Italian is called *mosto* and which is exactly what Ulysses served to the Cyclop Polyphemus to make him dead drunk, and above all the ferocious aggressiveness and cleanliness of the various lineages were among the most marked characteristics of the people with whom Robertson lived for more than one year. Up to the time when the people were Islamised, the temples were structures open to the sky, as they were among ancient Indo-Europeans everywhere. Open air temples and sacred enclosures are still common in the high Himalayas. They were ornamented with zig-zag motifs and other repetitive geometric designs, similar but different from the western Indo-European "Greek" geometric designs easily weaved on hip-stretched looms. The designs are still repeated, for instance by the people of the high ranges of the Beas River in the Kullu-Manali valleys and high passes of the Himalayas and by local Kalash and other *pahārī women* (= mountain women). They are closely comparable or even identical to those of the ancient Indo-Iranian and Persian motifs, such as represented on temple walls and ziggurats. As a child in primary and secondary Italian schools I still learned how to produce such designs and "Greek borders" in drawings or embroidery work. Many

Christian churches were also opened to the sky until the middle ages, in fact, they were just sacred enclosures with the *sanctum sanctorum* well protected at the centre of the cross-shaped plan of the church.

SUMMARY

In the west, the fragmented geography of the Mediterranean world, the multitude of islands, the all-important presence of the "salted sea" (the salinity of the Mediterranean waters is several times higher than that of the inland "seas," Caspian and Aral) and the high development achieved by some of the civilizations that preceded the Indo-Europeans of the west, favoured a fragmentation of the Graeco-Roman world into many nations, each marked by particulars of the local environment and by the influence of Semitic, autochthonous and Egyptian civilizations. The Mediterranean Sea is invariably characterised in the epics of the last millennim BC as "great" or "salted sea," evidently to differentiate it from the less extensive and lower-salinity inland seas.

In the east, the massive continental mass of Asia, its peculiar and varied climate and geography favoured the formation of well characterised nations each covering large areas adjoining to each other and linked by a web of major and secondary trade and pilgrim routes. In Greece coastal and inter-island navigation developed relatively early, but long distance sailing and rowing developed late. Special sea-going crafts are typical of the Indian Ocean, such as the Tamil *"kattu-maram"* (= katamaran) and the ubiquitous sewed planks crafts, large and small. The city of Salala on the Oman coast on the Indian Ocean became famous for the high quality and sea-worthiness of the *dhows* and other craft built there. Sindbad was an Omani trader/adventurer, but that is another story.

The Mediterranean Sea remained and became strong and rich ever more because it was the common denominator of ancient and burgeoning cultures. The vast and generally continental, monotonous landscape over vast areas of Asia favoured the formation of extensive countries and nations, Indo-European or other with well structured and developed cultures dominant over large areas. With acculturation and inevitable division of labour all populations become subdivided into specialized classes or castes. The division of people into castes can be more or less strict, but is everywhere inevitable because it is necessary. Slavery was widespread and even Athens, famous for its democratic regime, maintained slaves who had none of the rights and privileges of the Athenian citizens. Rome was not a declared democracy but only Roman citizens had the right to vote and had other privileges. Slaves had no privileges though they had some rights and a special class of magistrates, the *edili* had the prescribed function of surveying for the welfare, availability of water and food of the *plebe*, the populace of free men and women who were neither slaves nor citizens, all workmen, artisans, free workers (= *liberti* = liberated slaves), and slaves, none of them with the rank of Roman citizen. To be an Athenian or a Roman citizen was a privilege by birth or special decree from the authority.

(B) Myths, Legends, History and Geography

THE BIRTH AND USE OF MYTHS

As opposed to legends, myths are phantastic imaginary stories alive in the collective memory of people. Legends are traditional stories that may have originally been based on actual facts, historical happenings or major natural events like earthquakes or floods, magnified by phantasy and hero-glorification at every re-telling. Myths and legends are the root of the folklore of all cultures and play an important role in their being and becoming. Popular knowledge and wisdom whether derived by actual observation and experimentation or pure imagination, may acquire powerful symbolic value at the individual, clan, nation or entire mankind levels. It may become crystallized as proverbs, aphorisms or anecdotes and "sayings." Myths and legends are born at any time of the history of man. Arbitrarily, history has been defined as the period beginning with written testimony of known facts. However even in the contemporary "age of reason" new beliefs may arise and older ones may be validated or abandoned. Man has **faith** in the stories he wants to believe in, irrespective of whether they are **real truth** or just **wishful thinking** or dictated by **fear.** Superstitions belong to the latter category, though there may have been a rational seed that created the superstition to begin with.

History should be and pretends to be an impartial, chronological narration of facts and events, their origin, succession and evolution. History should therefore be studied methodically and scientifically. It is of importance to groups of people and nations. Unfortunately however myths, legends and history have always been and are regularly used to serve political intentions. Paraphrasing Dandekar, I would say that myths and legends are like magics, they are not mistaken religion, but mistaken history and mistaken science.

Myths and legends serve the very important role of strengthening the self-respect of individuals and the collective power of groups of people and nations. Assurance and determination are fortified by self-respect but, as everything else, excess of it degenerates into arrogance. Arrogance is a behaviour and frame of mind used by dictators, tyrants, absolute monarchs or others at all times to manipulate people or armies for good or for evil. Alexander the Macedonian and Napoleon Bonaparte who took Alexander as his model, were masters of the art. A typical example is the encouragement given by Napoleon to his troops on the eve of the Battle of the Pyramids: "Soldiers, forty centuries watch you from the top of these pyramids!" Incidentally it should be noted that the words "dictator" (= one who dictates the rules) and "tyrant" (= one with authority to interpret and use the law according to his own discretion), originally did not have a pejorative meaning and many tyrants and dictators of ancient Greece and Rome, served their city or state with admirable wisdom. The prototype is Solon (638-559 BC) of Athens. It has been only the *abuse* of power that has led to the pejorative connotation of the words.

There are innumerable historic examples that show the persistence of tradition even when new laws, rules, habits or politics try by all means, including violent repression, to eradicate them. Often, however, changes are attractive and the ancient tradition is adopted under a new robe, a sort of disguise to make it acceptable to the new authorities or the people. Since myths and legends often have a somewhat cryptic meaning to begin with, instead of being abandoned, they become entangled in cultic practices and recorded in the stories that make up history. Ancestral memory remains rooted in the collective memory of the people, the more so the more restricted their ecumene (= living domain, from the Greek *oikoumene* = the inhabited world).

Myths, legends and history are alive, they have had a beginning and as every thing else, they also evolve. Moved from an original cause, they have had and continue to have effects and consequences as long as the original cause persists. With time myths and legends acquire philosophical and religious characteristics and an important cultural role, but when they become mixed with civic or religious cultic practices confusion is created and may grow into individual or collective folly. Of this there are innumerable historic examples of all types and magnitude, from the ancient past down to present days.

There are many historical "truths" which could have been myths, and many myths whose origin could have been some historical truth. The legend of the rape of the Sabine women by Romulus and Remus and their companions is obviously a myth created to glorify the leaders and "legalise" the heinous crime of abduction of the wives of the men who had given land to the twins to build the new city of Rome. Romulus and Remus, according to one of the legends, were twin sons of god Mars and founders of Rome. A crime should not blemish the fame of the burgeoning power, but the word "crime" has and always had only a meaning relative to the time and culture where the "crime" occurred. On the other hand the myth of the advent and teachings of goddess Demeter is most probably historical fact, blown up by phantasy and enthusiasm. Which history becomes myth or legend and which myths are history, depends on the evolutionary stage of the culture in which they are first created or born by spontaneous generation among the people, the "hearsay," the whispers that spread like bushfire.

THE LIFE AND WORLD OF MYTHS

Myths and legends must have existed since human speech developed, as proved by cave paintings and other primitive forms of expression, perhaps myths acquired a mental form even before speech was structured into a "language." If this is so, there must be myths common to all mankind. In fact, though details vary, we find creation myths and glorification of human reproduction in all cultures, focused on primary and secondary or enhanced secondary female sex organs and ithyphallic male figures. At the individual and collective level all people share common curiosity: who are we? Where do the world and we come from? What is death? What to are we subject? Where to find help or protection? Answers to these and other fundamental questions vary as a function of the level of culture at the time and place where the myths were born. The pertinent question here is whether Indo-Europeans of east and west as the term is used here, share some myths. The answer is yes.

Myths of the creation of man and origin of the cosmos occur among all people. Their origin is lost in the archaic past, their structure and story are entirely dependent on the environment in which they were first born, they involve rivers, seas, mountains, lakes, rains, forests, caves, springs, lightnings, all natural phenomena, and above all frightful episodic events, such as earthquakes, floods, volcanic eruptions, swamp and other natural fires. They involve living plants and animals, friends and foes, the invisible powers of good and evil, such as winds, thunders, lightnings and other sounds and above all, the mysterious powers of Life, Death and Reproduction.

Myths are typical products of the proto-history of people, they are derived from the urge to understand or "explain" the otherwise unexplainable. Imaginary superhuman beings are created, powerful animals or theriomorphic monsters part animal and part human, with man's power of reason and the physical capabilities that man does not have. They often symbolize unfulfilled aspirations, such as flight or invisibility and may become friendly servants or fearful enemies who can only be defeated with the help of gods. A late historical example is the man-headed winged huge bulls that guarded the monumental pavilion at the entrance of the temple of Persepolis (521-463 BC), capital city of the Indo-Iranian tradition, destroyed by Alexander the Macedonian to establish his supremacy.

While myths are often the intellectual fulfillment of impossible-to-realise desires, legends are usually embellishments of acts and facts of the past history of people and nations. Legends are more often than not self-glorifying stories, tools frequently used by rulers to persuade the people they rule to whatever they want them to do or believe, including the divine origin and divinity of the ruling king or dynasty. The legends concerning the semi-god Herakles or that of the Argonautes of the Indo-Europeans of the west, or the epics of east and west are part of the history of the geographic expansion of Indo-Europeans into new lands.

MYTHOLOGIES OF FIRE

Only man can make and use fire, this ability was the key to man's evolution and development. World-wide, the mythology of fire is among the richest and most deeply rooted. Fire is revered as a manifestation of God and also as a god in its own right, it is worshipped as the spirit or *essence* of fire and its power, eternity and divinity. In its popular acceptance, fire provides the indispensable energy for all basic needs, for cooking, for warmth, for making artefacts and for disposing of corpse liberating the spirit and providing the link and communion of man with God.

The fire god, Atar in the Avesta and Agni in the Vedas, remained the omnipresent god to this day among all the Indo-European of the east, Indo-Arya and Indo-Iranians, Parsis and Hindus. The worship of fire in all its different forms is at the origin of Zoroastrianism, Mazdeism and Vedism. Fire worship has remained in its original central place and form among the Parsis. While fire retains its central place in Hinduism, a large number of other divinities or manifestations of God were added to the Hindu pantheon, each god and deity with characteristics of its own. Among Indo-Europeans of the west, fire had originally a prominent place, but over the centuries fire was more and more respected for its utilitarian aspects, rather than as a deity. The Great Olympian gods overshadowed the fire god. Fire remained an indispensable means for Hephaistos (= Hephaestus, Vulcanus) to do his work and produce metal artifacts which became gradually more and more important as martial arts, communication and trade were developed.

Indo-Europeans of east and west are not the only people who regard fire with respect and awe even if often, for forgotten reasons and weakened religiosity, fire worship has been lost. Fire towers of impressive size were built for religious purposes in Central Asia since very ancient times and were still being built after the Islamic conquest. Fire is the centre of Zoroastrianism as a symbol of the religion and philosophy of the eternal battle of Good against Evil. The role of fire, the god and of common fire among the Indo-Aryans was summarized by Vannucci (1999). Fire as energy can rightly be considered the ancestral hub, the navel (= *nābhi*) of Indo-European myths.

Both Indo-Europeans of east and west recognized the importance of fire as a natural physical phenomenon and as a symbol and abstract concept of power, energy, heat, capable of purifying and sublimate matter into spirit (= transform from material to ethereal). Fire can be produced ritually by friction of the *aranis* (= sacred fire-sticks) and can be stored alive under ashes. It should be kept perpetually alive, man requires the presence of some form of fire continuously and forever, including as life energy. Fire is the First God (*ṚV* I; 67, 3) universal in time and space (*ṚV* III; 26, 7) and can be understood as the universal energy. God Agni as the Absolute Truth (*ṚV* I; 145) represents the human quest for knowledge and wisdom. There are many myths related to common fire, its origin and uses in every culture.

In the west the myth of Prometheus tells how fire was originally an exclusive commodity of the gods, therefore the Titan hero stole fire from them and gave it to Man. But the gods were very possessive, probably they did not want man to develop and grow in knowledge, strength and power, so Zeus punished Prometheus, had him chained to the Caucasus mountains and ordered a dirty vulture (or eagle) to feast on his continuously growing liver for all eternity. To date, nobody has found Prometheus chained to the rocks of the Caucasus and fire continues to be respected and used by man in a variety of different manners.[1]

The Caucasus Mountains cross the land between the Caspian and Black Sea from west to east, they appear very often in the myths and legends of the Indo-Europeans of the west. They are often represented as a monster, as a formidable difficulty or hazard that man must vanquish. This is a sure sign that the crossing of that chain of mountains during the migrations of the Indo-Europeans moving southwards from the Eurasian steppes towards what is now Eastern Turkey, was an arduous period in the history of the great displacements southwards of the same Indo-European tribes.

ARCHAIC MYTHS

Apart from fire, archaic myths of the Indo-Europeans of east and west refer to unfulfilled aspirations or to the sublimation of special wishes, such as extraordinary physical power, the ability to fly, great speed of displacement and ubiquity, invisibility, immortality, good health and food, water in arid lands, warmth in cold winters, eternally calm seas coupled with fair winds for sailors and above all, a great, healthy progeny. Myths are often ideological substitutes or wishful thinking needed to appease the eager human mind, as in (*R̥V* X, 86), where the logical ape Vrishakapi represents the flickering, never appeased mind of inconstant man. The entire saga of Gilgamesh and the ill-fated flight of Daedalus and Icarus are examples of impossible-to-fulfil wishes. Nobody, not even Zeus, father of gods and men can oppose Fate.

The desire of immortality is inherent in man, but all the myths teach that immortality of the body is impossible, thus the gods have provided substitutes for deserving humans: paradise, heaven, reincarnation, transforming the spirit of sages into heavenly *immortal* bodies such as constellations, stars, planets, satellites, sacred mountains, rivers, springs, caves, plants, animals, volcanoes and other environmentally meaningful structures or "eternal," though not immortal, human beings.

Most significant is the position of very high respect held by the horse among the Indo-European people. The personality of Hippolytus (= Gk. *hippos* = horse), son of the Athenian hero Theseus, himself son of Poseidon is the personification of the nobility of the horse who does not stoop down to treachery. Hippolytus is killed by Poseidon because of the curse made by Theseus who believes the calumny raised against the noble and pure Hippolytus who dies rather than disclose the name of the vile stepmother who had accused him of having made advances to her. Hippolytus is the title and subject of one of Euripides' tragedies.

As an example of the high esteem in which the horse was held, we may recall the Kalash people of north Pakistan. Funerary wooden statues of deceased respected men were a rule, however, specially distinguished individuals, usually valiant leaders were figured on horseback and wearing a tall conical pointed headgear similar to the mitra of the *magi.* A most interesting collection of those carvings is curated in the Anthropological Museum of Florence, Italy, including a near-life-size man on horse back.[2] In the original homeland the carvings have probably disappeared after the Islamisation of the "kafirs," however, stylized horse-heads were still implanted on the outer walls of open-air temples in honour of gods Mahāndeo, Sajigor and goddess Jestak of the temples at Rumbur in Chitral when Loude and Lièvre spent long periods living with the local people (Loude and Lièvre, 1984 and other publications by the same authors).[2] Primitive or very ancient art forms disregard portraying the likeness of humans or revered animals, like the horse; the representations are stereotypes because the intention is just to sacralise an idea or concept, the essence or spirit, the "*forma*" of the deceased is more important than the material aspect. The image has the intention and is used only as a reminder of a virtual reality that man cannot produce or reproduce. In fact, painting an exact likeness would almost be a profanation of the represented symbolic being whose physical body is only the useful vehicle of the all-important spirit, a concept alive and respectfully followed in Hinduism and Buddhism.

Accordingly the religious wooden carvings are not intended to portray the semblance of the deceased or of the horse. When the gods visit the people on the occasion of the main festivals, god *Imra* (= Indra) and his horse are seen only by the oracle who is imbued with super-human powers when in trance, but Imra and his horse are invisible to the assembled people. What is all important is the representation of a feeling, an idea, a concept, a belief, i.e, the creation of a materialised symbol as a reminder, a mark of respectful devotion. External resemblance is as unimporant as a discarded dress or piece of clothing.

The horse has played a fundamental role in the evolution of all the Indo-European people. The antiquity of these myths is attested by the association of the extremely useful and strong horse (= reliable, unable of treason or telling lies, truthful and faithful) with the sun, often represented as a stylised bird made of "pure" bread offerings at the most important festivals, such as the winter solstice among the Kalash people. The bird-shaped sacrificial bread offerings are reminiscent and have the same stylised design as the bird-shaped altar built for the greatest Vedic sacrifice, the Soma sacrifice. Among the most ancient gods of all people, Fire and the Sun in its own right or as the greatest fire, are common among all cultures. In Greek mythology Phoebus Apollon, the Sun-god, arrives at dawn on his glorious chariot drawn by beautiful white stallions harnessed in a front row as were the *quadrigae* first used in the horse races of the earliest Olympian games at Olympia, traditionally said to have been organised by Heracles in honour of the Great Zeus, father of all men and all gods.

ARCHAIC MYTHS AMONG RELICT SOCIETIES

I would finally mention the rare persistence of traditionally violent acts, such as murder for revenge and ritual bloody sacrifices which occur in the remote mountain areas of the island of Sardinia in Italy, called Barbagia. Two psychiatrist medical doctors, Sanna and Lorettu (Sanna and Lorettu 2000), carried out a detailed and very thorough study of the perverse and cruel aspects of what is locally considered to be remains of a "cult of Dionysos." I mentioned above that the original, primitive form of the personification of violent manifestations of nature had received different names at various places and times, or just remained un-named. One such archaic name of the entity that would eventually be called Dionysos was *"Bromios"* (= foul smelling, rough, stormy, violent, unrestrained, loud-voiced, cause of clamor and confusion). The word in Greek literally means "stench." The archaic names of the negative, destructive aspects of nature were later incorporated in the personality of Dionysos who, being the manifestation of all nature, includes also wild, cruel, destructive, bloody aspects as well as positive traits. Undoubtedly some of the exalted ferocious aspects are traceable to the tragic consequences of violent natural forces, but the immediate causes of the "cult of revenge" in Barbagia was interpreted by the authors as due to extreme isolation and "mountains against plains" rivalry and jealousy of the people. The interesting aspect of the isolated traditional practice is that it is commonly said and "known" to be a survival of very ancient rites in honour of god Dionysos. In my opinion, it is an example of how mistaken (= perverse) cultic practices can engender collective folly. The area called Barbagia (= barbarous land) is remote and isolated, typically a relict place and people whose culture evolved in the wrong direction.

There should not be unwarranted mixing of myths with cultic practices. The region where the authors studied the socio-psychological-political-isolation and other causes of homicide, cruelty and defacement of the dead body for revenge purposes, is characteristic of a relict society. It is a good example of the degradation and ethical regression of religious practices induced by hardships, poverty, persecutions, ignorance and most probably, also degenerative genetic inbreeding and mental instability.

The extremes of orgiastic festivities in the name of the Dionysan religion during the decadence of Imperial Rome are another example of degenerative isolation. The Roman nobility was isolated and entangled in the vicious circle of unbridled licentiousness, a social rather than geographic isolation.

ARCHAIC MYTHS OF EAST AND WEST

There are some parallels between archaic myths of Indo-Europeans of east and west that reflect basic human tendencies. One category is what has been called "creation myths." Each in its own way describes the creation of the world or of the entire universe based on the forgotten memory and nostalgia of the ancestral homeland and as a function of the present living place. More often than not people, specially leaders, rulers, kings and emperors like to trace their ancestry back to one of the main, if not the highest, divinity responsible for the act of creation of the universe.

The archaic and very ancient myths of the Indo-Europeans of the east, both Indo-Arya and Indo-Iranians are well known. The parallels between the Avesta and the *Ṛgveda* are the best proof of the common origin of the two cultures. Among them, of particular interest here is, in the Avesta: Yasht V dedicated Ardvi Sura Anahita, the wet, strong, immaculate one (= River Volga according to some authors, R. Oxus or Amu Darya (= R. Jaxartes or Syr Darya according to others). Rivers are feminine in the Vedas and equally immaculate and purifying as is the prototype, the Gaṅgā. Yasht X is dedicated to Mithra, the perfect, impartial, very ancient, correct and loyal god Mithra (= loyalty, friendship, honesty, faithfulness) who is often associated to Varuṇa, the unfettered Āditya of the Vedas. At a later stage Mithra represents respect for the Law. The Niyayesh, is a very ancient hymn in which Atar (= Agni, fire) is all Goodness and is the first and central god in the two mythologies, Avesta and Veda. Also Yasht XIV commemorates god Verethragna (= the slayer of the demon, corresponds to the Vr̥tra-slayer = Indra). The inversion of roles between gods and demons in the Avesta and in the Vedas is well known and will not be discussed here. Finally, Ahura (= Asura-Mazda) the Great Wise Wizard has his counterpart in Varuṇa, "the Great Asura" in the *R̥V*. The Indian *kavi* are poets, the singers who retell the myths to man, while the *Kavi* (= proto-historic kings) covered by divine glory (Curtis, 1994) are the very ancient pre-historical kings of archaic times whose dynasty came after the Paradata series of mythical kings of Iran (as in the Shah-Namah). We should also note that the ancient Indo-European root *mithra* is the same for "uterus" (= matrix) and "measure" (= metre).

Most of the archaic myths of the Indo-Europeans of the west are lost. The *aedes* and the rhapsodists left nothing in writing; the entire tradition was exclusively oral. From Homer and Hesiod we know that there was a considerable, perhaps voluminous body of myths which were used and codified by them not earlier than eighth century BC, when Homer and Hesiod produced their own creation myths. We also know from these poets themselves, that they created an entire new pantheon and grafted what was best suitable of the ancient tradition into the theogony and theocracy which they produced. The Creation myths produced by Homer and Hesiod are clearly more influenced by Semitic myths from West Asia than by the naturalistic philosophy of their Indo-European ancestors. Not surprisingly the latter survived to this day, while the Great Olympians are mainly remembered through the figurative arts and the theatre where the characters include Olympian gods.

THE EVOLUTION OF MYTHS

In the evolution of cultures myths and legends can be transformed in three different manners: (1) the basic concepts and the story are unchanged, only minor details of the story vary according to changed habits and customs due to environmental, geographic and historical changes at various places; (2) the name and concept remain unaltered but the story varies; (3) the name and heroes are changed, but the concept and celebrations are basically the same as in the original culture.

1. As first example of myths that remain basically unchanged over time and place, I recall the Hindu ceremony of the first feeding of cooked food found or grown in nature, which is given to the baby after weaning. It is called *Annaprāśana,* a very ancient ceremony whose origin is lost in time. It represents the entry of the new human being into the Hindu world**, because he is now eating food made by the gods** namely *boiled rice,* and he is no longer entirely dependent on mother's milk. ***Anna Perenna*** was the name of a Roman festival that took place on the full moon day and night nearest to the Ides of Mars. The popular festival is described by the Roman poet Ovid (43 BC-18 AD) in his book called *Fasti* (= Feasts) in which he describes the feasts of Republican Rome, their meaning and their origin. *Anna* is an ancient Indo-European root for "food." *Perenna* means "throughout the year," hence the English word: *perennial* (= lasting forever, or for one year, a full solar cycle).

   There are many different myths about Anna Perenna, a sure proof of the archaic very ancient origin of the ritual. One of them, reported amongst others by Ovid (*Fasti* 3, 657) tells that the nymph *Anna,* daugther of the Titan Atlas, would have given the first food to child Jupiter (= Zeus). The traditional feast was celebrated in a grove one mile away from Rome, near a bridge over R.Tiber called *"Milvius,"* historically famous for its participation in the rebellions of the plebe against the patrician rulers, a sort of *Place de Grève* of ancient Rome. *Anna Perenna* in all the myths in which she plays a role, is always associated with food and feeding of the very young or very hungry. As a curiosity I would mention that in Tamil language, the word "Anna" is an affectionate epithet for "elder brother," an important element in the family circle because he is the one who next to the father provides for the needs of his younger siblings. "Anna" is specially important to his sisters. Incidentally, the Latin *Anna* is not related to the Hebrew *Hannah.*

2. The second type of cultural evolution is that in which name and concept remain unchanged but the story or the geography varies. The Vedic R. Rasa has been identified by earlier authors with the Avestan R. Ranha, said to flow into the Great Vourukasha Sea (= Aral Sea, most probably) that encircles the Earth. The Vedic Rasa is taken to be a tributary (= affluent) of the largest river known by the Indo-Aryans, the Indus where they arrived many centuries after leaving the area bathed by the Ranha. As mentioned above the Ranha corresponds to the Jaxartes (= Syr Darya) most probably not to the Volga as hypothesized by some older authors. The rivers kept their personality but were transferred elsewhere, they were ideologically kept "near by," "at hand" for whenever needed. Another example of added attributes and names changed after migrations took the people to new areas, are the Avestan Tishtrya and the Vedic *Tr̥ta*. The Vedic God *Tr̥ta* is a personification that emerged later than the Avestan Tishtrya and only after acquiring more attributes, duties and activities with the passage of time.

3. The third type of cultural evolution is that at different times and places names change but concepts and celebrations have the same meaning as in the original culture. One example is the joyous ritualistic game called "The Thrust," or "throwing [of the stone]" among the Indo-Europeans of the west. As far as we know the game originated with goddess Demetra (Homeric Hymn II, 260-69) who instituted the practice when Queen Metaneira accused Demeter of trying to kill child Demophont, her son. Truly what goddess Demeter was doing was conferring immortality to the child by exposing him to the fire god daily every night. The child was unscathed by fire, but when his mother shouted an alarm after what she saw, goddess Demeter cursed her for lack of faith. She then determined that in her own honour

two groups of adolescents would throw stones at each other on a prescribed date, but they would not be hurt. A similar ceremonial game takes place annually in the Kumaon area of the Himalayas under the supervision of an organizer Pande brāhmaṇa. Nobody gets hurt, similar to what happened with child Demophont who never was hurt by Demeter's failed attempt at giving him immortality through fire. The medieval "proof by fire" to which suspects of lying, of perjury or blasphemy were submitted to prove their honesty, may have the same root as well as the practice of firewalking which is common in south India and other places. Firewalkers say that faith and belief are needed not to be burned. True belief never fails a clean character. The same myth was narrated in Egypt, where goddess Demeter was impersonated by the Egyptian goddess Isis.

THE DAWN OF HISTORY

Scholars usually define history and historical times as the stage when knowledge of the past and present of civilizations was entrusted to written texts. In other words, history only "begins" after writing was invented and facts were documented in writing. It is possible to accept this definition provided it is agreed beforehand that it is nothing more than a convention and not a true definition. In fact it is impossible to assign a birthdate to history. The ancient undated pictographs of caves showing hunting scenes, menhirs and carved stones, remains of artefacts of pre-historic man and hominid species that lived prior to our own species, are historical records though not in writing, therefore the invention of a script cannot be considered *the* "beginning of history." The recording and transmission of history starts with the individual education of the infant, his initiation into the community and participation in the collective memory of the people. Contemporary historical analyses show that though less phantastic, modern "historical" texts can be no less ambiguous, false and biased as the oral or written history of the past. In fact cave paintings and other similar "pre-historic" records are authentic, correct and unwritten informative pieces of history.

In the historical period the deep gap between philosophies and religions of Indo-Europeans of east and west became evident, as east and west went each on a divergent path, always more pragmatic in the west where man is deemed to be the centre and scope of creation, and more ecologically sound in the east where man is considered to be one of the very many elements of nature. Man is a member of nature endowed with the powers of reason and discrimination, therefore capable of holding the reins of his own destiny within the limits imposed by physical forces of nature. In the east the oral tradition was considered to be the only correct manner for transfer of Śruti, the sacred revealed truth of the Vedic religion. The sacred texts, Śruti and Smṛti and the epics were written down relatively late and the alphabet used, *Devnāgarī* or *nāgarī*, borrowed largely from the Greek and earlier scripts which in turn had borrowed from Phoenician and other pre-existent *alphabets* (= *alpha-beta*, the first two letters of the Greek alphabet).

Early history can be gleaned from archaeological and other sources including the writings of the Egyptian, Sumerian, Semite, Greek and Latin authors, scribes, painters, carvers, pre-historic cave-painters who held no taboo against using written texts and other evidence. It is interesting to compare reports of the same historical events written by different scribes in different languages. The official report of the battle of Kadesh (year 1275 BC) is a case in point. The reports written in Egyptian hieroglyphs as well as those in cursive Egyptian script refer repeatedly to the "unethical" behaviour of the Hittite army which did not follow the rules of battle usually imposed by the Great Pharaoh and fully respected until then. The reports by the Hittites in cuneiform script give details of the superior war tactics and battle strategy of the Hittite generals. Neither version is used in the final official text of the treaty (Table 1) drawn between the kingdoms of Hatti and Egypt. The text is bilingual and bi-script. Evidently the historical truth is a vicarious element. In this case, as in many others, there are three "truths," the Hittite, the Egyptian and the international treaty, the latter is fortunately cold and objective, and it was sealed in 1259 BC.

There was no ill-will or deliberate fraud on either side, it was just the result of different points of view. The Egyptian battles were

Table: 1
Synchronism between Egypt and Hatti

EGYPT	HATTI
Pre-dinastic Period (5000–3000 BC)	Ancient Kingdom of 16th century
Protodinastic Period (2650–2150 BC)	1531 — Conquest of Babylonia (3000–2650 BC)
Old Kingdom (2650–2150 BC)	Middle Kingdom (15th to Middle 14th century BC)
First Intermediate Kingdom (2150–2100 BC)	
Middle Kingdom (2100–1750 BC)	Empire (Middle 14th century to 12th century BC)
Second Intermediate Period (1750–1540 BC)	
New Kingdom (1540–1070 BC)	1275 — Battly of Kadesh
19th *dinasty* and(1295–1190 BC)	1259 — Peace Treaty between Hatti Egypt
Sethi I–II Ramesse I–II Merenptah	1246 — Wedding of Ramesse II with an Hittite princess
Third Intermediate Period (1070–715 BC)	
Late Period (715–332 BC)	
Graeco-Roman Period (332 BC–313 AD)	
Alexander the Great (332–323 AD)	
Roman Period (30 BC–313 AD)	
Coptic Age (313–640 AD)	
Arab Conquest (640 AD)	

Table: 2

Synchronism from XIV to XII centuries BC
(in the 14th to 12th centuries BC)

EGITTO	AMURRU	UGARIT	KARKAMISH	HATTI
		14th centuries BC		
Amenophis III		Ammishtamru I		Tuthaliya II
	Abdi-Ashirt			Arnuwanda I
	Niqmepa			Tathaliya III
	Baaluya			
Akhenaton	Aziru	Niqmadu II		Suppiluliuma I
Tutankhamun			Sharri-Kushuh/	
Ay			Piyassili	Arnuwanda II
Horembeb				Mursili II
		13th century BC		
		Ar-Halba		
	Du-Teshub	Niqmepa	Sahurunuwa	
	Duppi-Teshub			
Ramesse I				
Sethi I	Benteshina			Muwatalli II
Ramesse II				
	Shabili			Urhi-Teshub/
	Benteshina			Mursili III
				Hattusili III +
				Puduhepa
		Ammishtamru II	Ini-Teshub	
	Shaushgamuwa	Ibranu		Tuthaliya IV +
				Puduhepa
Merneptah		Niqmadu III		
Amenmesse		Ammurapi		Arnuwanda III
		12th century BC		
Seth II			Talmi-Teshub	SuppiluliumaII
Siptah				
Beya				
Tausert			Kunzi-Teshub	
Setnakh				
Ramesse III				

Source: Guidotti, M.V. and F. Pecchioli Daddi, *La battaglia di Qadesh*, 2002. Inside of back cover, ed. Superintendenza dei beni archeologici della Toscana, Firenze. Courtesy of the Archaeological Museum of Florence.

ceremonial and revolved around the "divine" figure of the King of Kings and his showmanship; naturally the Egyptians were shocked at the Indo-Aryan eagerness to win the battle. The Indo-Aryans had behind them a long story of aggressiveness, wars and battles waged to win at all costs within their own Code of Conduct, well detailed in the Indian epics but unknown to the Egyptians. There was no absolute truth and no breach of honesty in the different wordings of the early and the final treaties drawn between two widely different cultures. There was, however, a proof of chivalry, honesty and generosity of two great warriors who acknowledged each other's valour, the young pharaoh Ramses II and the Hittite king Muwatalli II. The final treaty bears the seals of both parties, in the interest of all the people. Peace reigned in the area for about 200 years and was fortified by mutual cultural enrichment and ceremonial weddings at the highest levels.

Modern historians, however, tend to recognise documents as historically most important and valid only *when there are* quantitative data. As an example of a very important, historically reliable ancient document mention could be made of the document promulgated by the Indo-Iranian Persian king Darius when he organised his Empire by fixing the tributes to be paid to the Emperor by each satrapy. Thus the sixteenth District, which included the people of Sogdiana (= *sogdoi* in Greek), had to contribute annually 300 talents (Herodotus III, 93), although there were veteran Sogdians who had already fought in the army of king Xerxes (Herodotus VII, 66).

EVOLUTION OF KNOWLEDGE AND WISDOM, PRIDE AND ARROGANCE

While there are limits to the desires of enhanced individual physical competence, many persons are apparently convinced that there are no limits to the growth of intellectual capability. With its growth, arrogance and pride also became widespread, man started very early to move in a direction that will spell self-destruction. Though many anchorites, prophets, saints and scientists have seen and warned that man advances fast towards disaster, the principle of inertia is operative and humanity continues to move with accelerated velocity towards self-annihilation. Man as a biological species has probably already crossed the line of no return.

Summing up, the forces of nature which are Varuṇa's *pāśa* (= fetters, limitations), were seen in ancient times as the reality which man must accept in order to survive. The man-made laws for living together in a community, usually called the social behaviour of man, are the acculturation passage from the level of a diffuse cultural condition to the state of an organized civilization. Adaptation to material and immaterial reality creates myths about the tangible and the intangible. In the East, **all** the manifestations of "reality" were considered to be part of the **Absolute**, unimaginable, indescribable, the Truth in Space and Time, everywhere and nowhere at the same time. Polytheism is one way of trying to visualise the infinite facets of the Absolute. In Greece there was a break-away from the original basic nature religion when Homer and Hesiod created the new Olympian religion strongly influenced by a Hurrite legend rendered in cuneiform script and Hurrite language in a Hittite text of the thirteenth century BC. Homer and Hesiod built the Olympian pantheon on the older autochthonous nature religion of ancient Greece. As knowledge evolved, concepts became more precise and myths were revived, they were stripped of the phantastic and were re-interpreted with the interpolations of new myths. Finally "scientific" explanations become the only ones believed in, though science itself evolves and yesterday's truth could become tomorrow's mistakes. For instance, some of Varuṇa's *pāśa* are now called the *"Law of Universal Gravitation"* expressed by a convincing mathematical formula for which we are indebted to an obliging ripe apple that providentially selected the right time to hit the ground in front of a daydreaming genius called Isaac Newton (1642-1727). However, even before the mathematical formula was written, empirical ballistics was good enough to win duels and wars.

By relating myths to the time when they were first produced it is possible to draw pictures of early and changing aspirations of individuals and nations. For instance, to the desire of immortality of the body, follows expansionism of the nation and the growth of the ego of kings, warriors, leaders of nations and so on, each in his own field with evergrowing lust for glory and wealth. To the desire to fly followed flying machines, eventually successful. Monsters like Scylla and Caribdis of the Straits of Messina are now correctly explained by the occurrence at odd timing of the tides in the seas at either end of the Straits, predictions can be accurate. Most of the findings of science have been useful but too many have been used for evil purposes.

In the course of the evolution of thinking man, man learns, or should learn, how to use the power of Reason and Discrimination with which he is endowed to acquire knowledge and develop wisdom. Knowledge without wisdom can be extremely dangerous. Regrettably only too often in the history of mankind knowledge and wisdom were changed into Pride and Arrogance.

(C) Destiny and Fate

The uncontrolled desire of knowing the immediate and distant future is innate in man. Innumerable ways of foretelling the future were invented by men, they are collectively called the "Art of Divination." Logical and "scientific" methods and techniques were devised since the ancient past. Some were honest, serious attempts to read into the laws of nature and thereby learn how to predict the future, such as astronomy, physics, chemistry and natual sciences in general, others were and still are nothing more than conscious or subconscious guesswork or downright frauds. Evidently the desire of foreboding the future is related to the unavowed wish for immortality, long life and glory.

MEANING OF FATE AND DESTINY

In the east and down to the early last millennium BC, in the areas under Indo-Iranian and Indo-Arya influence, the basic philosophy of life had not changed much since pre-historic times. However, one of the fundamental differences between ancient Indo-European of west and Indo-European of east is the attitude towards destiny.

Destiny can be defined as the "predetermined cause of individual or collective course of events that *usually* cannot be changed by men." Though they are not the same, Destiny is sometimes mistakingly taken as synonym of "Fate" (= *fatum,* "what has been spoken" or "an utterance," from Lt. *fari* = to speak). Future events can be revealed by the utterance of a prophet, a seer such as for instance the famous Sibylla of Cumae near present day Naples in southern Italy. The response of the prophetess could be a prediction of the future or an advice about what destiny had in store. Fate, however, was understood to be the indescribable Power underlining the sayings of the prophet. Fate is the predetermined Power on Earth or beyond that cannot be controlled by persons or gods. Fatalism is not passive or lazy resignation but an unconditional faith in God. **Fate is an unchangeable Cause; Destiny is the means to enact the consequences of the Cause.**

Marcus Tullius Cicero (*De Fato*, 44, 45) talks of antecedent or "preceding" causes, they are inevitable and are called Fate. Cicero distinguishes very clearly between "eternal causes" (= *fatum*) and "near and immediate" causes that are in the hand of man to change. The "immediate causes" are not named by Cicero in the *De Fato*, but he obviously refers and describes what in one word is called Destiny (= *destinum*). Only later commentators caused the confusion between *fatum* and d*estinum.*

Fatalism is the doctrine according to which all events are predetermined by a Power conventionally called Fate. It cannot be changed by human beings. Final Destiny is inevitable, but details of the ways that lead to the end, can be influenced by man, gods or chance. Fate is manifest as the "life" (= movement) of astronomic bodies, planets, satellites and above all, Sun and Moon and all the fixed laws of Nature which are beyond the control of man. The Arab word *qismah* (= portion) and *qasama* (= allotted, fate, fortune) refer to what is allotted to each person and that too cannot be changed, it is usually used in a negative sense. The word has entered the English language vocabulary as *kismet*. The words destiny, fate and fatalism have been used in a variety of ways with the result that misunderstandings are common.

The word *Fatum* in Latin is the past participle of the verb f*ari* (= to say, to express a prophecy or an utterance, to speak). The meaning is that *fatum* is the vaticination (= prophecy) that can be revealed by the *vates* (= seers, prophets). Fatum as a noun is used in Latin with the meaning of: *what has been said and cannot be altered*. Or: *what is said is said, and what is, is*. The word Destiny comes from the Latin: *destinare* (= to determine, to give a destination), used in the same sense as the original meaning of predetermination and an *inevitable* course of events that can, however, be influenced by the will-power of man or men, or by accidental causes.

The difference between the subtle meanings of Fate and Destiny is that, the word **Fate** refers to events past, present and future that no power can alter, not even the most powerful gods. Fate could occasionally be revealed to seers, prophets, men and women gifted with the special power of vaticination. In contrast **Destiny** is the cause of individual or collective predetermined events that may be influenced or altered under very special conditions or the will of gods.

Fate is something that **IS,** like *ṛta*, that "**is what is**," such as the laws that govern the cosmos. Fate is the result of a decision taken; it is impersonal, untouchable and unchangeable. Fate is not necessarily the physical reality, but is just what "has been determined," which means that before or after the decision was taken matters could be different. It is presumed that decisions are taken by entities with the authority to do so: such as gods who have the competence and authority to see, influence and determine details of the future. Following a petition, the gods can change details of the destiny of men, without altering their ultimate Fate.

The Vedas define very clearly the concept of *ṛta*, there is no question of where, when, how *ṛta* came into being, or how long it will last, who "made" things as they are or how they were made and how they operate. The concept of *ṛta* is independent of any Myth of Creation. It is a statement based on the knowledge and understanding obtained from the observation and study of the world around us and all Nature, physical, chemical and biological. The idea or concept of Life (= life energy as different from dead spoils of plants and animals) is different from *ṛta*. *Ṛta* is not a god, it is an inescapable fact, a situation, it is the dynamics of Nature and of all the Cosmos. Science in the modern acceptance of the word is the knowledge of *ṛta*.

In the Latin language, the neutral noun Fate, a past participle, is a statement as the neutral noun *ṛta* also is, like *ṛta* it implies that it is perceived by men only as the result of the study and vision of a prophet, a *ṛṣi*, a sage, a scientist, a seer gifted with the power of "unveiling Truth," though he cannot change the **Truth that IS**. Fate, like *ṛta*, is final and irrevocable. Zeus himself, the Great Olympian god, father and ruler of gods and men was unable to alter Fate, but he could influence individual destiny.

Though the different meaning between destiny and fate are deep-rooted and clear, the common usage of the words is blurred. We find the following synomy in dictionaries and vocabularies. *Fate = destiny, kismet, lot, portion, predestination, that which is inevitably destined to occur. Destiny = fate, fortune, the power or agency held to predetermine events.* (Webster's Dictionary). About fortune as a synonym of Destiny, Webster's says: *inevitable or necessary lot to which a particular person or thing is destined*. Though the difference between the meanings of words fortune, fate and destiny is profound, very soon they became mixed up in the west. They usually are not used correctly or clearly, as may be seen from the transcription from Webster's where explanations and definitions go round in a not-so-merry go-round.

Finally, the word *aisa* in Greek is akin to the inflection *est* (= it is) of the Latin auxiliary verb *esse* = to be. The same word *hai,* in colloquial Hindi is often used as an interjection meaning: so, it is, very good, it is decided. It can be used as a question or as a sign of approval. Also in Italian, the inflection *è* = it is, is used in the same way, with nearly the same pronunciation as in Hindi. The use of the word *aisa,* in ancient Greece had the value of a decree.

FREE-WILL AND WILL-POWER

Cicero (106-43 BC) analysed the concepts of free-will, will-power and other religious and philosophic aspects of the Graeco-Roman religion in the last century BC in a trilogy called: *De divinatione* (= On divination), *De natura deorum* (= On the nature of the Gods) and *De Fato* (= On Fate). Cicero declares himself an anti-fatalist and an eclectic philosopher. He discusses the concept of Fate under three aspects: first, as a problem in Logics since Fate is one of the "non-contradiction principles"; second, from the ethical point of view, since the problem is entirely one of personal human responsibility; and third, from the point of view of the laws of Physics (= Nature) since Fate is an inescapable causality. In the original Latin language, Cicero uses the word **Fate.** The word Destiny (= from Lt. *destinum*) was improperly used by later authors indifferently as a synonym of Fate, causing the present day conceptual confusion between the meanings of Fate and Destiny. The antecedent or "preceding causes" (Cicero, *De Fato* 44, 45) are inevitable and are called **Fate,** they are eternal. Cicero distinguishes "eternal causes" (= Fate) from "near" or "immediate" causes that are in the hand of man to change. The immediate causes are not specifically named by Cicero, but they obviously refer to individual fortune, "good or bad luck" and destiny = *destinum.*

Cicero, as an antifatalist makes the distinction between the immutable Fate determined by Nature (= Physics) and the voluntary acts of man. Since man is different from animals because he is endowed with powers of reason and discrimination, he can use his will to change the evil tendencies and wrong acts into good and correct behaviour. Man is endowed with will-power, and therefore has the freedom to select his own course of actions, he has the *Liber arbitrium* (= free choice), but only within the constraints of Fate. Fate is expressed in Vedism as Varuṇa's *pāśa.* While Fate has the force of an independent and inescapable necessity above Chance, free-will is in the hands, mind and will-power of each and everyone independent of Reason.

In conclusion, certain **causes** induce events which man cannot change. Other **causes** are such as man can alter the results and consequences of the original cause. Here enter the concepts of free-will and will-power of man. This is the belief of Vedic man, there are acts that are in man's power to change independently of Fate, but each one of us bears the responsibility and consequences of his acts.

FATE AND DESTINY AMONG THE INDO-EUROPEANS OF THE WEST

The idea/concept of Fate falls within the philosophical approach to the problems of freedom and responsibility of the adult man or woman. Liberty or freedom to make choices and take independent decisions implies both ethical behaviour and logical use of the relations between causes and effects. Cicero in the *De natura deorum* and in the *De Fato* reports discussions between imaginary members of different philosophical schools, the Academicians, the Sophists, the Epicureans, the Stoics and others. Though he adopts a correct impartial attitude, he offers some arguments in favour of the Epicureans, mainly the naturalistic attitude of Lucretius (Titus Lucretius Carus, 96?-55 BC) and alternately those of other masters. The best known expounder of the Epicurean school was Democritus (460?-357? BC).

The important point regarding the subject of this book is that in Greece the concept of the *polis* and later in Rome that of the *State*, represented by the acronym S.P.Q.R. (= *Senatus Populus Que Romanus* = the State and the People of Rome) created an attitude of undiscussed obedience to the authority. The dominant role of the Polis or of the State was such that throughout the Graeco-Roman world authority and dictatorships were the rule. This served well the pragmatism of Rome, but differently from Rome, the independence of the many city-states of the Hellenic world had prompted the development of philosophical schools, including experimental science, that questioned human bondage. The early myth of Prometheus and the story of Medea are representatives of the struggle of the ancient Greeks towards freedom of the mind and will of man according to the dictates of Reason.

It was only natural that in Rome, after the despotism that cost his life to Caesar, the newly acquired freedom would renew philosophical discussions on subjects related to Gods, Nature, Predestination, Fate, Destiny and the like. For Rome, this liberty was short-lived, the Republic (= *res publica* = community matters, public thing, commonwealth) was soon replaced by the powerful Empire. How much freedom did individual rulers or states have, or should have, was one of the most fundamental questions discussed. There was no final answer; there could not have been one, either by Cicero or by any other learned philosopher or statesman on the eve of Imperial rule under Caesar Octavianus Augustus (63 BC-14 AD). At the level of philosophical debates, it appears plausible that Cicero believed that there is a Power above all, even higher than the gods themselves, which holds the reins of acts and facts of past, present and future. This Power is called Fate. It is "higher" even than astronomical or other high-level physical powers which are regulated by and for eternity. These events are pre-ordained and may be predicted, such as the phases of the moon, equinoxes and solstices, solar or lunar eclipses, the reproduction of animals, the germination of the seed, growth of plants, flowering and production of new seeds, and so on. These are the laws of the cosmos which man or Jupiter himself is unable to interfere with. This is Fate which is believed to govern everything on Earth. From the belief in Fate springs divination, the art of foretelling future events or revealing occult knowledge by means of augury or supernatural agencies, but divination cannot change the working of Fate, it can only study nature and give a probabilistic vision of the future through the prophet's responses. In fact the answers of the oracle, for instance the famous oracle at Delphos, was usually just the offer of a choice between two advices or it sounded the alert of probable dangers. It was implicit that divination cannot change Fate; divination could at most reveal Destiny under specific instances.

Destiny, the course of events at the individual or national level is influenced also by other people's individual or collective fortunes and by unpredictable events such as storms, winds, floods, droughts, landslides or earthquakes, enemies, natural calamities or wars that cannot be influenced by persons or nations. Finally Cicero clears the point with the conclusion that there is a fundamental difference between what happens because of "Fate," and what is preordained but independent of Fate, and can therefore be changed, which is called Destiny. Destiny can to a certain extent be manipulated by the will of individuals or nations and can lead to folly and disasters if the manipulations are senseless. Human actions are caused by the will of individuals or nations, hence fatalism, in the present popular sense of the word, has no reason to exist. Finally Cicero admits that there is a certain amount of *liber arbitrium* granted to man by the gods, but freedom and liberty are not without duties. Most important are the duties and responsibilities towards the *Polis* and the State. Since man has will-power, he has freedom, he has the liberty of choice and freedom to take decisions, for the consequences of which he will be rewarded or punished but he cannot escape from Varuṇa's *pāśa*.

For the Greek, Fate was always a final inescapable dictate from which men or nations would never be able to extricate themselves. Solon (630?-559 BC) the Greek legislator-founder of the greatness of the city of Athens, called *aisa* the inner voice that guided him, which he believed to be goddess Athena herself, so *aisa* (= decision) was always final. In a celebrated poem Solon warned the citizens of Athens that "our city will never fall because of a decision of goddess Athena, but it is the citizens themselves who, in their folly, may cause disaster." Disobedience to destiny or the course of events prescribed by the gods, spells disaster. Five centuries later Cicero reiterates that Fate is the inescapable future but, he says, Destiny is a warning. In conclusion, the Graeco-Roman civilization was based on the reasoning that there is a clear difference beween **Fate** which is beyond human and divine power to change and **Destiny** which is "written in golden letters by Fate" but can be annulled by the "ability of man to perceive or see his own Destiny" (Cicero). Will-power can influence only immediate personal acts and the short-term course of events.

Destiny is often called *moira,* a word with many meanings in Homer, such as death, decision, destiny, duty. These many meanings give an idea of the complexity of the philosophical concept of destiny among the Indo-Europeans of the west, both Greek and Romans.

FATE AND DESTINY AMONG THE INDO-EUROPEANS OF THE EAST

In the east the power of Fate is recognized but is not linked to any particular god. Fate is akin to *ṛta,* the Law and Order of the Universe. The destiny of the individual person is related to the person's past actions in the present or in earlier lives. It is analogous but not the same as *karma.* In the concept of *karma* the ideas of reincarnation and palingenesis are intrinsic. In other words, though there is a Power called Fate, man as a conscious being with the power of reason, has limited possibilities to take final decisions, but he should be aware that he will bear the consequences if he does not follow the overall dictates of Fate, the impersonal Power that knows best. The very ancient god Varuṇa, the unfettered son of Āditi, mother of Infinity, holds the *pāśa,* the fetters that restrain and govern cosmic and individual acts, behaviour and moods. Man's will and actions are eternally restrained by the Great Asura Varuṇa's fetters.

For the Indo-European of the east, everything is sacred; it is part of the Absolute Self, the Self-Existent. The individual Self is an infinitesimally small part of the Absolute Self, it is not free from making mistakes, even committing sins, for the simple reason that man is endowed with reason and will power, both of them boons or curse liable to become misleading. It is in the interest of the individual self to listen to the "voice within," the "ideas" which usually come to each one of us, if one cares to listen even to the unexpected. For this reason, it is wrong to say or think: "I have an idea," rather than saying that "an idea has come into my thoughts . . . though I know not wherefrom, how, when, why and so on."

SUMMARY AND CONCLUSIONS

Finally, in Homer and Hesiod the gods themselves in their own or other forms, whisper advices in the ears of those heroes who are their friends and to deserving princes and commoners. The gods may be invisible, but the message is received by the human brain that reacts accordingly. If the given advice agrees with what has been predetermined by Fate, the undefined Power or Agent stronger than the gods and higher than Zeus himself, man will be fortunate to follow the advice. However if matters had been predetermined otherwise by the fixed laws of Fate, man and even the gods will be unable to change the course of events.

Among the Indo-Europeans of the east the belief is that man often acts guided by some inner inexplainable impulse, usually not heard as a spoken word. The spontaneous inner drive, the "inner self" is part of the Absolute, the Self Existent which, everything considered, always works for the best and least-harmful decision. The Absolute Power beyond and above human will and beyond all the manifestations of God is the Law and Order that governs the Cosmos, the Vedic Ṛta. In Vedism and Vedānta everything is sacred, there is no higher or lower. The **Absolute Self** is one and unique, with no beginning or end. The word fatalism as commonly used at present, is an improper derivation from the concept of Fate; it is often wrongly interpreted as an attitude of dejection, weakness, laziness and carelessness. The admission that Fate exists should stimulate each one of us to recognise and pursue the correct actions, rather than drop into a passive pessimistic attitude.

The concepts of Fate and Destiny are clearly represented in Homer's epics. The Greek Odysseus (= Ulysses) spends ten years after the arson of the city of Troy on his return journey home to Ithaca. All his men die and his ships are destroyed in a variety of ways during the long journey home, everything happens as a punishment for his sins. His major sin had been to act on his own accord rather than according to the dictates of the gods and to cause the burning and destruction of Troy in a treacherous, rather than valiant manner. He is cleansed of his sins and pays for them with his perils, or as Solon would say, his folly. Ulysses' destiny is to pay for his sins but due to his merits, he is granted pardon and he returns home to Ithaca in time to save his deserving wife Penelope and good son Telemacus from the tyranny of the Procians.

Again in the Odyssey, Zeus is aware that "it has been said" that Hector, the finest of the Trojan Princes will die in battle at the hands of Achilles, the great Achaean (= Greek) warrior. Zeus cannot change Fate and knows that Hector will have to be killed by Achilles. Nevertheless he persuades Hector, his protege, to go into battle. This was not a malevolent act; on the contrary, Zeus will not and cannot go against Fate, he will not save Hector's body, but he orders the "Gods to free Hector from the cycle [of life and death] and to liberate from evil suffering the souls of men" (pers. note from an Orphic hymn). Thus the great Trojan Hector is given the opportunity to show his mighty valour for the last time, his honour will be enhanced, his faith in the gods will be rewarded and he will pass down into history as a great warrior, a great prince and God-fearing hero.

The episode of Vāli's death at the hands of prince Rāma is another example showing that Fate cannot be altered. Due to Vāli's earlier noble behaviour and previously acquired merit and exemplary life, and due to the merits of his brother Sugriva, the act of justice could only be carried out by the righteous unerring arrow of Lord Rāma, but the noble Prince cannot be seen to bend the bow under cover of a tree. Fate cannot be altered. Sugriva's brother has to be killed but there is no sin or blemish on the head of the executioner whose hand is held by Justice that will bring back on the path of righteousness the course of Fate.

The concept of god and religion is strongly influenced by the environment in which people live and where their culture evolved. Temples are permanent structures because they are the abode where man captures and retains his gods. But temples are not an entirely suitable substitute for natural structures not made by man, such as the world of nature, the grandiosity and marvels of mountains, rivers, trees, the earth that nourishes plants and animals with whom we share the bounties of nature that will always be greater than anything that man can make. Nature and all natural processes must be taken care of because man is dependent on them for his own survival and life.

Since everything is interrelated and interdependent, and because nothing would go awry, everything functions according to the eternal laws, everything has its duties, responsibilities and rights. Everything living and non living must be taken good care of, it is irreplaceable. Everything that **IS,** that exists, has a life and power of its own, everything is **sacred**; it is sacred because it **exists.** Man is no exception and man has his place in the world, with duties and rights if, and only **if,** he abides by the laws of *ṛta*. The order of the universe is the sacred law that governs everything, including the individual doings, those of the family and of the community.

Sins are whatever actions at variance with *ṛta* the universal law that shapes destiny, a virtual ethical space in which man moves freely because of his *liber arbitrium,* his freedom to decide about his own actions. The freedom to decide is a heavy responsibility; only a being endowed with reason can and must have the freedom to make choices. *Ṛta* cannot be disregarded, hence the importance of education and teaching, and even the sages, as all other human beings, had to spend long years of study and training. Training and education are lifelong imperatives and reminders of the need to abide by the laws of nature, a principle that should be strengthened in the education of all human beings. Bypasses spell disasters, it is *folly.*

When men began living in enclosures, walled or not, in cities, city states and states bigger and bigger with emphasis on man-made laws and rules rather than on the eternal laws and rules of nature, the concept of validity and reaches of Destiny and Fate were discussed at length. Some philosophies rejected the principle of the *liber arbitrium.*

The Athenian concept of the "polis," the city-state governed by responsible rulers was developed during the second millennium BC and was extended to the concept of "state." The idea of the "polis" or of the "state" is not an idea or a natural phenomenon or an "affair" of the natural world into which *Homo sapiens sapiens* evolved. The state, like religious dogmas, is a man-made institution, hence the concept of destiny when extended from the individual level to the community level, the State is governed by man-made laws which can and should be discussed, differently from what happens with *r̥ta*, which is far beyond and above human dialectics.

Different schools of philosophy and different religions diverge on these matters, but are all concerned with the theoretical and practical implications of fate, destiny and the freedom to make choices. Man should be prepared and instructed on the responsibilities attached to this freedom, and all freedoms. Education based on a "philosophy of life," on wisdom based on knowledge, provides the tools for taking informed decisions.

In the east, the concepts of *karma* and *dharma* define clearly individual duties and responsibilities, merits and demerits for transgressing the law, all of them reflected **by** and **in** the individual *karma*.

(D) Philosophies and Religions

I have argued earlier that "philosophy comes before religion" (Vannucci 1994, 1999) in the sense that religion, as the belief in Powers and Forces which are governors of the universe, can arise in the mind of Man only **after** people have observed and reasoned about the world around them, its origin, dynamics and evolution. I have also argued that rather than *cogito ergo sum* (= I think, therefore I exist), it is more Cartesian, if I may say so, to believe that *sum ergo cogito* (= I exist, therefore I think) for the simple reason that there cannot be thinking before existing. Since there can be existence before thinking, humanism is implicit in the famous aphorism of the French mathematician Descartes (1596-1650). In the east humanism entered into naturalistic reasoning only after man understood that he is one of the infinite elements of the complex natural system called and governed by the laws of the cosmos, called *r̥ta*. Man however admitted that he may, perhaps, be the only element endowed with the power of reason and discrimination. In other words, there can be existence without thinking, but there cannot be thinking without existing.

Man originally saw himself as part of the universe around and inside him, he naturally must have wondered about what are the relationships with others like him and with the whole of nature. It must have taken scores of generations before some understanding of the functioning of nature dawned on primitive human minds. The way from "instinct," whatever that means, to reasoned behaviour was an adventurous and hazardous one. This early cultural period is the time when philosophies are born and may eventually develop into experimental science and structured religions. The latter are often the fruit of "revelations." This development was first taken by mythical or not-so-mythical beings, like Museus, Fanes, Protogonos, Erikepaios, Orphaeus, Viṣṇu, Śiva, Kr̥ṣṇa, Zarathushtra, the sages of ancient traditions often referred to as "the seven sages" and so many others from all cultures.

When there is a strong will to know and an inner urge for explanations, religion and what became known as "science" may become a reasoned and conscientious substitute to accept ready-made understanding. But *blind belief* is a form of escapism and an easy way for just survival and not beyond. With *reasoned belief,* often assisted by "revelations" or "visions," methodic, structured religions are born as the fruit of observation, experimentation, experience, practical and traditional knowledge and above all, critical reasoning, *kr̥ttikā.* Hence complete respect and obedience to the master who has already walked the long path. Whatever the origin, religion becomes the bond between man and gods, powers often not known in themselves, except from the effects of their existence. Religions are the promise, the hope, the help, the psychological support and answer to otherwise unanswered questions. But before the concepts of Life, Death, Reproduction, Health, Disease, Sleep, Dreams and the multitude of aspects of life beyond just being alive and reproducing, other thoughts crept into the mind of early men, women and children of our species. They were the practicalities related to better lifestyles and technical developments that in turn allowed for more time for thinking, planning, and understanding.

The idea of a Supreme Power or Powers would have taken shape initially. Man the hunter knew well that everybody needs a head, but there can be only one head for each body. With increased knowledge, the next step would have been to *believe in* and *bow to* the Great Power for protection and help to satisfy the daily needs. The need to communicate with the Great Power must have created spontaneous prayers, gestures, performances gradually codified into rituals and rites, ceremonies, cultic practices and liturgy (*Lt. liturgia* = public rites, ceremonies or services, as opposed to secret ceremonies or rites, mysteries). Mystery in Greek means a secret, or a closed and reserved practice, rites or habits usually considered to be sacred.

PHILOSOPHY AND RELIGION

The unique characteristic of the evolved human mind is the passionate urge to know and understand what is perceived by the sense organs, including the mind. *Philosophy* as the conscious pursuit of knowledge and wisdom is the study of the laws, causes and effects of natural phenomena and their representation *in* and *by* the human mind. Philosophy deals with observation, experimentation, reason and logical deduction. Ethics is the aspect of philosophy that deals with correct behaviour. But "correct behaviour" is an ambiguous term whose meaning varies from one culture or civilization to another, one gender to another; it varies with age and varies with individual convictions as well. Willing or not, ethics has nothing to do with logics. However, logical deduction and ethics may be vitiated by preconceived assumptions, insufficient knowledge or individual personal convictions. These and other forms of biased reasoning may transform philosophy into religion, or they may become a religion based on preconceived thinking. The transition from objective to subjective reasoning is a dangerous and slippery path; the weary mind can easily fall into a bottomless pit.

There are basically two types of religion, revealed and *natural*. Revealed religions develop from the teachings of prophets who received knowledge and orders directly from their God. Natural religions develop from the observation of natural phenomena and from the study of the relations between causes and effects. Natural and revealed religions may become fused into a single body by the establishment of dogmatic creeds. The word *dogma* in Greek comes from the verb *dokéo* (= it seems to me) and its meaning evolved historically into "supposition," then "opinion" and finally acquired the meaning of a *decision, an irrefutable decision.* Dogmas are man-made by highest level authorities.

Empirical studies usually evolve into mathematics and experimental science. The word *reason* is used here to describe the mental processes that search into the powers and forces that act on material and immaterial events and their functioning. Revealed religions are built on the indisputable concept of *Faith.* Revealed religions require the devotee to have faith even before he acquires knowledge. Nature religions are based on *Reason,* though they also require belief conditioned by observation of the phenomena and forces which are usually best known through their effects. Rather than blind faith, nature religions teach that the perception and discrimination of causes and effects of the forces of nature may be due to the "vision" or "internal" reasoning that dictate the teachings of sages and prophets. Natural religions require that the devotee acquires knowledge and as much understanding as possible along the path that leads to faith and devotion, a reasoned rather than blind faith.

Rajagopalachari in a short introduction to the Bhaja Govindam of Ādi Śaṅkara discusses briefly the concepts of knowledge and faith, or jnana and bhakti, and shows how intelligence matures into wisdom when knowledge is fully developed in the hearts of man, wisdom becomes devotion. Rajagopalachari closes his talk on Ādi Śaṅkara with the perfect aphorism: "*jñāna* and *bhakti* are one and the same" (= knowledge and devotion are one and the same). In other words, there is no knowledge without devotion and no devotion without knowledge. Or, according to C.V. Ramachandra Aiyar who declares in a translation of Ādi Śaṅkara's Gītā Bhāṣya: "Devotion is part and parcel of both Action and Knowledge."

INDO-EUROPEANS OF THE WEST

Homer lived about the ninth century BC, Hesiod in the eighth century and the mathematician Thales (640?-546 BC) in the seventh/sixth centuries BC. They were Greeks, though not all of them born in mainland Greece. They belonged to the Greek world, a politically loose group of small states united by a common language and culturally assembled around Athens, the great city of mainland Greece. Homer, Hesiod and Thales were philosophers in the original sense of the word "philosophy" (= friends or lovers of knowledge, wisdom). Philosophy includes religion as well as all branches of knowledge at present understood as "science." Homer and Hesiod developed a religious system based partly on ancient autochthonous *and* partly on imported beliefs, myths and legends. They expressed their erudition and wisdom in poetry. Thales and Pythagoras (570-490 BC) left nothing in writing, they expressed their findings numerically and in prose, what we know of their teachings is only through their disciples. Thales is considered to be the initiator of Greek culture though Anaximander (611-547 BC) preceded him with his treatise on nature, called *Physika.*

Between the four of them, Homer, Hesiod, Thales and Pythagoras all aspects of human culture are included, from revelation and theoretical discussions, to practicalities such as geometry and topography, from revealed beliefs to mathematics, astronomy and astrology and natural sciences.

The culture and civilization of the Indo-Europeans of west is fragmented in space (geographically), in time (historically) and ideals. Southern Europe is the only place where, in past millennia and for a relatively short time, two initial species of the genus *Homo* probably co-existed. There may have been exchange of genetic material between the two "species," or "sub-species" of very early man, commonly known as the Neanderthal and the Cro-Magnon or *Homo sapiens.* The Cro-Magnon people arrived in Europe, as far as known at present, about 43,000 BC (Cavalli-Sforza 1996), somewhat earlier than the disappearance of the Neanderthal. The numerical presence and the population density of these early groups of people was very low and scattered over a vast area.

Archaeological findings and traditional lore show beyond doubt the *non-Hellenic* or *pre-Hellenic* origin of sanctuaries and the performance of funerary rites at places which were later built over by Greek people and inhabited by Greek gods. Specially significant for the present study is the sanctuary of the two Olympians, Phoebus Apollon and his twin sister Artemis (= Diana) at Delos (island in the archipelago of the Cyclades in the southern Aegean Sea) where according to legend they were born. On Mount Cimmeros, the highest mountain in Delos, there are pre-historic remains dated probably from the late third millennium BC, but it is not known exactly to what culture they belonged. It is known that in historical times young girls still danced and sang songs in honour of a goddess whose name was forgotten in a language that nobody could understand, during the spring festival at Delos. In historic times, Apollon moved from Delos to Delphi in Phocea, where the famous Delphic prophetess, the Pythia, gave her often nebulous but frequenly correct responses to kings, princes, generals and all powerful men who interrogated her about the future.

Of the many mysteries of ancient times, the Orphic are the only ones who left written records. There is no doubt that the Orphics followed the teachings of the great poet-singer Orphaeus who celebrated Dionysos as the latest of the Powers who fashioned Nature, **after** the Demiurge (*demos= people+ergon= work*) had created the world and the people therein. Dionysos is the recent-most, or last of the many mythical beings who, taken together represent all aspects of nature.

The mysteries performed at Eleusis are probably the most important of all the ancient mysteries of the Graeco-Roman world. Based on responsible agriculture as the practical and wise use of mother earth, the myth proceeds into problems of the spiritual beliefs of man, the senseless fear of death of the body and the desire of immortality of the soul. The value of the teachings of both the Low and the Great Mysteries was so meaningful that they could only be overcome by the material destruction of Eleusis at the hands of the Goths in the year 396 AD, who obeyed the order given by Christian monks. Knowledge and wisdom from the Mysteries of Eleusis were divulged only orally, and as far as we know nothing was ever put in writing.

THE GRAECO-ROMAN RELIGION

Among the Indo-Europeans of the west, the original nature religions were discarded but could not be entirely ignored by the man-made new Greek religion created by Homer and Hesiod. The new religion availed itself of the rich mythology of the heroic pre-historic age of Greece, much older than the last millennium BC. The new religion created a theocracy to strengthen what would become the ruling class of Greece and Rome.

The pre-Homeric culture of the pre-heroic age of Greece was essentially of non-Indo-European extraction and was mainly based on telluric myths and legends, as far as can be deduced from scarce very ancient archaeological remains in mainland Greece and in the Aegean islands, dated earlier than the arrival of the Greek people. The genius of Homer, followed by Hesiod, was to incorporate in their poetry, which deals mainly with gods, wars and feats of the Indo-European heroes and warriors, also myths and legends, as well as the knowledge and experience of the various local people. The newly created Greek religion, known at present as the Classical greek religion of Ancient Greece, was built on the pre-Homeric tradition based on the concepts of Time, Space, Evolution and Development. It taught that there is nothing fixed and immutable forever.

The Great Olympian gods were the sovereigns who ruled the world where autochthonous populations had lived before them in tune with the life on land and in the sea for an untold number of generations. The ancient tradition was undoubtedly a liberal philosophy of nature, but legendary figures older than Homer, such as Museus and Orphaeus are not mentioned in the Iliad, the Odyssey or the Homeric hymns, though the tradition of the ancient poet-singers, the *aedes* and *rhapsodists* existed since at least almost a thousand years prior to Homer.

The most genuine (Lt. *genuinus* = natural, unspoiled) representatives of the ancient tradition are the legends and cults of Fanes (= the Manifest) one or several mythical beings called by many names, such as Protogonos, Erikepaios, Metis, Eros Primigenius, Eros Proterogonos and others. All of these ancient *personalized* concepts were gradually incorporated in the multifaceted and evolving personality of the god later labelled Dionysos, which is the **good** first principle of nature, as repeatedly mentioned in Orphic hymns. The Orphic texts also include praises of the fully evolved personification of human ingenuity, competence and generosity, the paragon of which is Demeter (= Cerere for the Romans).

The Orphic texts, or what remains of them, are the earliest and most reliable description of the acts and teachings of Dionysos, including the cultivation of grapes, of Demeter or the domestication of nature through agriculture, and to a certain degree also through forestry, first developed by Ariadne, the spouse of Dionysos. The classical Greek culture ascribed the authorship of the *Ieroi* (= sacred texts) to Orphaeus and of an early, pre-Hesiod *Theogonia* (= origin of the Gods) to Museus. Tradition held that both Orphaeus and Museus were living long before Homer and Hesiod and were the fathers of the oral tradition.

SUNSET OVER THE OLYMPIAN THEOCRACY

By the third century BC the existence, the form and the acts of the man-made Homeric gods were openly questioned by the new schools of philosophers, later better known as *scientists*, and by the *praxis* of Rome. The classical Greek religion was respected until when it continued to be useful for political purposes of the intellectual Hellenistic civilization and Roman expansionism, it then faded away. Cicero's religious trilogy, the *De divinatione*, the *De Natura Deorum* and the *De Fato*, bear testimony to the spiritual and religious crisis that gripped the thinking elite of the Senate and People of Rome (S.P.Q.R. = *Senatus Populus Que Romanus*) in the last centuries BC. They had been preceded by the great dramatists of Greece, Aeschylos, Sophocles, Euripides, Aristophanes and others. Cicero was a highest level magistrate and had also spent some years as *Pontifex Maximus* (= Highest Priest). He describes debates that would have taken place in the seventies of the last century BC among representatives of different philosophical schools and he openly discusses his own beliefs, disbeliefs and opinions about the State religion. Had he lived at the time of the Roman Catholic Church Inquisition of the middle Ages and early Renaissance periods, he would have been burned at the stakes.

The classical Greek religion of the last millennium BC was very soon exposed to the findings of the philosophers and scientists. Skepticism developed early, even before the religion could establish many dogmas or a pre-fixed complex liturgy, except for ritual sacrifices and ritual libations. Several independent schools of thought, many of them linked to mystic practices, such as the famous Orphic mysteries or the Eleusinian mysteries and others, replaced to a certain extent the State religion and the reverence to the ideal *polis*. The mysteries went each its own way.

RELIGION AND CIVIL LIFE IN THE WEST

The members of the discussions (= *disputatio*) of Cicero's books are based on historically known scholars and some of them were also high priests of the State religion and were advocates of the need to safeguard the teachings of *the tradition of the ancestors*. Some of the most erudite were *Pontifex Maximus* Gaius Aurelius Cotta, academician, *Pontifex Maximus* Lucilius Balbus, Stoic and Velleius, Epicurean. All of them, whether state clerics or not, were authentic representatives of the cool headed, conservative Roman oligarchy. They were interested in safekeeping their status and semblance as much as the apparel, cultic practices and ceremonies for political and social reasons and interests of the State and of themselves. In the last century BC skepticism in Rome had already contaminated the sacred-most values of the proud Roman tradition, as clearly shown by the debates and letters exchanged between the learned men. Thus new values from forgotten wisdom were sought in the ancient myths of the Heroic Age and in the beliefs of other cultures. Already Chrysippus (third century BC) director and systematiser of the Stoic School of thought, had recognized the value of the most ancient pre-Homeric poems of Orphaeus and of the teachings of the legendary Museus, celebrated in the Orphic hymns. Chrysippus linked ancient myths with the "new" science of Nature. It should better be called *the renewed* science of nature. Chrysippus was followed by Diogenes of Babylonia and others who applied the use of reason, rather than blind belief to verify the validity of the Olympian religion. To quote from Aurelius Cotta (middle last century BC): *I, as Pontifex Maximus consider that the current religious ceremonies and liturgy must be scrupulously observed. . . however I would like to be convinced not only by faith but also by rational proofs that the gods of Rome exist.*

Though Cicero objectively discusses the different points of view of the various philosophical schools and though he declares his faith and belief in the gods of Rome, indirectly he contributes to destroy the official religion of the Roman state by rationalising the issues of the religion itself.

What is interesting in the present context is to register the effort spent by the philosophers of the last decadess of the Roman Republic to "prove" the existence, acts and facts of the decrepit Olympian gods, while in the daily routine the gods were already superseded by ancient, earlier or older beliefs, both autochthonous and foreign. Many ancient concepts deprived of their religious significance and value and stripped of the phantastic myths in which they were clothed, are alive to this day as wholesome habits and customs. Many others are still remembered as "superstitions," a few are forgotten, and they may have been reborn under a new physiognomy.

RELIGIOUS VACUUM AND NATURAL PHILOSOPHY

Innumerable examples could be drawn, but that cannot be done here for lack of space, suffice it to say that Hellenistic science and Roman practical mind and experience delivered a final blow on the Olympian gods. When faith in the Olympians failed, it was replaced by faith in *immortal Rome,* the "invincible empire" and its traditional values. Thus the seeds of degradation created by the irrational desire of political immortality were introduced in the system. Rome as other great empires finally collapsed because they ignored the lesson that nothing is static, immortal or unchangeable forever. Roman Caesars died off as well as the last dynasty of pharaohs of Egypt, the Greek Ptolomees. Apart from religion, the Graeco-Roman and the Egyptian civilizations in the West left a legacy in science and philosophy to which is due much of the development of the west in terms of applied science, philosophy and knowledge, but unfortunately, not much in terms of wisdom, except for some magnificent figures. Failure cannot be avoided where and when there is no opportunity or space for evolution of the mind and adaptation of the cultic practices to changes.

Natural philosophy, with its queries and doubts becomes religion when blind faith and dogmas replace scientific observation and experimentation. Blind faith causes stagnation while nature religions evolve with the development of knowledge. Ceremonies and rituals are, according to the epicurist Velleius, *always growing and perfected* or as Dandekar says, "also the gods evolve" or, as I would say, the *understanding* of the gods evolves. Or, as argued by Vedānta, knowledge leads to devotion. All these are different manners of saying the same thing, increase of knowledge leads to better understanding, hence reasoned devotion rather than blind faith.

Natural religious practices are attuned to the reality of the environment which was beyond man's power to change. Ancient basic religious manifestations were gradually perfected into "participatory rites" (Dandekar) and "sacrifices" were a form of instinctive natural worship where worshipper and worshipped become one and the same. The man-made classical theocratic Graeco-Roman religion was short-lived, indirectly it caused a reaction that paved the way to a return to philosophy entrenched in logics and sciences. This rational movement of open-minded constructive criticism of the man-made Olympian religion is particularly pointed in Aristophanes' comedies and the famous Greek tragedies. From Magna Graecia to the expanding Roman Republic and Empire the traditional knowledge and experience of the many people, barbarians or civilized with whom the Indo-Europeans of west came in contact, were absorbed in the Graeco-Roman culture. An example of this is the "romanisation" of the very ancient Vedic and Avestan god Mithra, the supervisor of honesty and justice, observer and guarantor of the fulfilment of promises and treaties. From this point of view, Mithra became very powerful during the Roman Empire and had an indirect role to play in the incorporation and development of the science and philosophies of Hellenism into the humanism of later centuries in Italy. In the Christian age, Mitra survived spiritually in the personality of John, the very pure young disciple of Christ and guardian of fidelity of all deals.

The Graeco-Roman religion is a good example that man-made, dogmatic religions can live only as long as the political will and the fanaticism that created them are still alive.

SURVIVAL OF TRADITIONAL KNOWLEDGE AND WISDOM

Traditional Greek myths are about human dreams and aspirations, some of them were incorporated by Hesiod in the system which he created. There is not much in common between the classic Greek myths of the Indo-Europeans of the west and the myths of the Indo-Europeans of the east because the hedonistic Greek civilization and Hellenism were more influenced by Egyptian and Semitic myths and technical development than by the local nature religion that preceded them. What is common between Indo-Europeans of east and west are gestures of greeting, thanks and invocation, of supplication, of well wishing, details of rites and secret meanings of rituals, family life and the education of children, the fundamental role allotted to women in the family and community, though nominally they were a patriarchal society. This and more are typical of Indo-Europeans of both east and of west. There are root words in common and the use of case endings, specially the use of the dative case, of some verbal inflections specially the use of the gerundium, the past and present participle, still widely used in modern Indian languages, the frequent use of the subjunctive mood, the use of the infinitive, specially the personal infinitive that survives to this day also in the Portuguese language, and others. Even more significant than the affinity of word roots is the similarity of the syntaxes of Greek and Latin with Sanskrit and Sanskrit-derived languages.

All religions aim at acquiring intimacy with the god or gods of man's beliefs; this is what the word religion means. How this intimacy is developed varies in the various cultic practices. Modern comparable religious studies are more often focused on this aspect of religions.

The archaic myths of Vedism were assembled over a period of many centuries, about two millennia or more. They are based on the observation and study of nature, aimed at acquiring wisdom and giving a functional body and structure to human society. The archaic myths of the Avesta, or what we know at present of the Avesta, are also based on the study of nature and on the development of appropriate lifestyles according to the features of the environment. Among the Indo-Iranians there was an early development of technologies, especially for water resources use and management, and of agricultural practices. Fire as universal energy was the central point of cultic practices.

In Greece archaic myths, though of primary importance were overshadowed in the first quarter of the first millennium BC by the snobbish state religion which nevertheless absorbed freely non-Indo-European beliefs from local land and sea people, also from the Egyptians and Semitic cultures. What the Semitic, Egyptian and Greek systems have in common is the concept of Revelation that makes of man the centre around which revolves the universe. All three systems are focused on man who is the centre of the world and who received the dictates of God or gods directly or through the word of prophets. This biased idea was successful to establish a direct or second hand contact with the gods and proved to be a factor that favoured the development of humanistic and applied arts and science. As opposed to this, among the Indo-Europeans of the east, the basic idea is that **Man as a biological species is not** the centre of the universe, he is rather a part of it, even if an important part from man's point of view, but man is only one of an infinitely large number of elements of the universe for both good and bad. Definitely, however, man is a unique member of the world because he is endowed with the powers of Reason and Discrimination.

Conceptually Vedism and Vedānta did not change from ancient past to present, however the accelerated "technical developments" of the past few centuries AD, has induced unavoidable changes in lifestyles and "simplifications" of the daily cultic practices. Historical facts such as the destruction of the sacred books of the *magi* of the Zoroastrian religion by order of Alexander the Great equally caused a serious change in daily religious habits and in the culture of the ancient Indo-Iranians, though the phenomenal expansion of military power and increasing wealth under the Achaemenid dynasty had already initiated the progressive change of the originally simple lifestyles of ancient Persians into a life of luxury of the kings and of the nobility, even before the destructive wrath of Alexander the Great almost achieved total destruction. Comparable upheavels tend to alter also the practices of Hinduism as heir of the Vedic religion.

The highly structured society of the Indo-Europeans of east, both Indo-Arya and Indo-Iranians during the last centuries of the last millennium BC is one of the basic factors responsible for the stability and development of the nations historically derived from the Avestic and Vedic cultures. Among the Indo-Europeans of west, Hellenism became well-established because of the high reputation of its philosophers, including what we would today call scientists, its dramatists, and the respect for the concepts of the *polis* and politics and of the city of Athens. The Roman supremacy was forcibly established because of its pragmatism, its military power, the power of rhetorics and its political stronghold. The fascination that Rome had over most of the world known at the time was due more to the iron grip that Rome held on the people than to the wisdom of its learned men, though senators were often also high rank officials of the priesthood, the Curia of Rome, who watched over the observance of tradition and of the Law. Finally Roman roads, water resources management and *circenses* (= martial arts and what are called at present "sports" held in the circuses) were the knots that held the Roman web together under the *aegis* of the undiscussed strict Roman law.

What is interesting in the present context is the effort spent by the philosophers of the last decades of the Roman Republic to "prove" the existence of the Olympians, while in practice they were mostly if not only remembered in state ceremonial occasions. In practice it was the human heroes and warriors or the nature gods or some specific concept, like the festival in honour of *Anna Perenna,* who were worshipped. This attitude can be easily sensed reading the Orphic texts, some of which are briefly mentioned here: (1) "Initially, before Eros [Primigenius] mixed all the elements [i.e, before the creation of the world], the immortal Olympians did not exist." (2) "Museus and Orphaeus showed us how to purify ourselves through" sacrifices, [sporting] games and initiation ceremonies, *long before Homer and Hesiod.* (3) Wisdom of those "who have reached the state of "bliss," after a good life and good *passage to another stage. . ."* (4) "The real God is the beginning, the end and the middle of all that exists . . . *according to the laws of nature."* (5) "God is the Demiurge (Gk. = *demiourgos,* (Lt. = *demiurgus,* a name created by Plato to designate a hypothetical creator of the original material world)." Sings Orphaeus: "The Great Chronos (= Time) made the shining egg in the divine Ether." In other words, in Orphism **creation** means to "produce from nothing," which is beyond human competence and undersanding. The meaning of "fabrication" is different from "creation" in that it implies the mixture of at least two elements: **matter** and **form**. Fabrication is within the ability and competence of man, creation is not. These and many other verses indicate the formulation and later survival of ancient nature cults during the reign of the Olympian gods throughout the centuries of the immensely powerful Roman Empire.

A parallel study of the concept of Time in east and west is extremely interesting, but beyond the scope of the present exercise. The Orphic mysteries were centered on the "forms" and teachings of all the personalities that came to be known under the name of "Dionysos," in the various evolutionary stages and aspects of the god. The Orphic and Eleusinian mysteries survived all the political, religious and historical vicissitudes of Rome.

NATURE GODS AND GODDESSES

Among the gods of the Indo-Europeans of west, only the great nature gods, Dionysos and Demeter survived to this day. It is not relevant to speculate whether Dionysos is a name that covers a single god under many manifestations, or whether there were many nature gods in the ancient Indo-European world of the west who were eventually integrated in the single personality of Dionysos. The earliest archaic god that we know of, was frightful and powerful, a personification of the unleashed wild forces of nature. Probably one of his first names was *Bromios* (= stench), he represents man the hunter, eater of raw flesh, performing bloody sacrifices. Dionysos/ Bromios was followed by a host of gods and godlings, some are mentioned above, each hallowed at different places and times and with a variety of attributes.

The Hellenic world was small when compared to the vastness of Asia Minor, Central Asia and Major India, but each part of it has peculiarities of its own, hence the various names and characteristics of Dionysos and of the deities and superhuman beings which form his retinue. At present Dionysos is best known as the mighty god in whose honour the Athenians created initially a rich literary world of tragedies, human dramas and comedies. The latest Dionysos was very close to the nature gods and godlings of the Indo-Europeans of east before becoming the great god under tyrant Pisistratus of Athens (560-527 BC). There is a close similariy of the earlier Dionysos and smaller deities of the archaic myths of the Indo-Europeans of west, the nymphs, fairies, maenads, demons, with the theriomorphic forms and metamorphoses of the Indo-Europeans of east. Some other significant similarities are: representation of seasonal cycles, cycles of birth, death and rebirth and cycling and re-cycling of everything in nature, including man. The Greek seasons follow Dionysos the leader and are called *Horae* (= hours). When he is shown accompanied by the *Horae,* Dionysos is usually represented as a bearded and composed mature leader. Also in the east there were only three seasons to begin with, they were then multiplied to six to better accommodate the monsoonal periodicity.

Plato accepted from Egypt the doctrine of metempsychosis via the Orphic mysteries which have many points in common with Vedism. Also the concepts of the individual *liber arbitrium* (= free will) and personal responsibility in relation to fate and destiny, duty and rights is inbuilt in Vedism, Vedānta and were later crystallized to the level of religious injunctions. Orphism is very ancient and much older than Homer.

The basic difference between Indo-Europeans of west and east is that in India there never was a single all-encompassing god of nature (Dionysos) and a goddess of agriculture and god-given food (Demeter). There was instead, and there still is the presence of innumerable gods, godlings, spirits, deities, nymphs and fairies in each cave, tree, spring as in the archaic religion sung by the *aedes* and almost forgotten in Homer and Hesiod's religion. It is significant, however, that the commonly and frequently used words privilege or privileged (Lt. *privilegius* = *privi,* ancient, prior, earlier, original + *legis* = law) goes back to very ancient or archaic facts, rites or rules. The word also recalls one of the names of mother earth, *Pṛthvī* the original nourisher and food provider. The word for "death" of the body in the Eleusinian mysteries was: *"the privilege of death,"* death of the body is the birth of the spirit in a new form of life, until when a new incarnation will transfer the spirit of one cycle to the cycle of another body.

The help of etymologists is here and elsewhere requested and required to search for archaic roots that could be meaningful and of yet unrecognised similar derivations between Vedic Sanskrit and Latin or Greek.

Another important archaic similarity between Indo-Europeans of east and west is that in the east cyclic aspects of nature are under the tutelage of Viṣṇu, the Preserver, while in a similar manner they are under the tutelage of Dionysos in the west. Needless to say that rites, rituals and all other details of the religious practices devoted to the two gods are entirely different. The idea or the "pure reason" in a Kantian sense is one, while the "forms" or "modalities" vary. It is also significant that Viṣṇu a minor god in the ancient-most Vedic hymns grows in importance with time, while cultic practices become more complex in parallel with the growth of human knowledge.

Similarly the cult of Dionysos grew in complexity with time, and included processions, games, feasts that were open to the public as were also the Lesser Mysteries of the cult of Demeter. The participation in the Great Mysteries required secrecy and was reserved to the initiated few. The religious split between east and west was sudden and dramatic when Dionysos became institutionalised in Athens with the development of the theatre.

Points of contact of ancestral hereditary and traditional basic archaic beliefs between east and west are numerous, but there are no similarities or parallels between east and west after the "urbanisation" of Dionysos. This point of rupture in the "career" of the god explains the frequently noticed but not explained contrasts, or as Delcourt (1981) puts it, "contradictions" among the poets and dramatists of ancient Greece which she could not explain. In my view it would be astonishing if there were no contradictions in the descriptions of the moods, behaviour and acts of Greek gods focused by Graeco-Roman poets and dramatists from the sixth century BC onwards. The Greek gods are man-made and they are moved by very human passions. Their acts are introduced, shown and explained in different manners by the dramatists and writers in general, both Greek and Roman because the authors are as human as the gods and heroes who are actors on the scene. In other words, gods and heroes are described by human beings according to each writer's own point of view, influenced in turn by his own passions. The Greek gods, being as human as they are, can be interpreted from as many different angles as the human authors who give them a role in the Olympus, in real life or in the amphitheatre. This could not be otherwise and is not astonishing since the Olympian gods were tailor-made by Homer, Hesiod and the philosophers and authors who expressed their own convictions, ideas and opinions through the theatrical *dramatis personae.* Incidentally, the word *"persona"* means: "the voice, or sound, that comes through." The actors of the Greek and Roman theatres wore masks, tragic, hilarious or otherwise that marked the character *personified* by the actor.

PHILOSOPHY AND RELIGION AMONG INDO-EUROPEANS OF THE EAST

Zoroastrianism as a philosophy and religion has survived down to the present day, in spite of persecutions and changes in the many environments where the members of the community lived. There have been no radical philosophical changes in the fundamental belief that there is an eternal fight between Good and Evil. Each human being has to make a choice and decide on what side he or she stands. Of course the ways and means to achieve the goal must have evolved with time in tune with the changes of the environment and the development of science and technologies. I do not think, but am no authority on the matter, that there were any major changes in beliefs and cultic practices of Zoroastrianism. Basically the principles and aspirations of Vedism remained equally unchanged. Vedism and Zoroastrianism are good examples that, as a rule, what survives of all cultures through the ages is the ancestral substratum, fundamentally based on the realities of nature, including man.

The Indo-Europeans of the east who arrived in Europe from Asia Minor, reached the shores of the Mediterranean at a time when local nature religions were overshadowed by the official religions of the State. Furthermore, the religions of the Indo-Arya and Indo-Iranians had already suffered the influence of the religions of the many people with whom they had been in contact during the period of probably two-thousand or more years they spent on the grand movement westwards (fig. 1).

INDO-ARYA AND INDO-IRANIANS

What is specifically interesting here is to compare the myths of the Indo-Aryans and Indo-Iranians, well defined groups having the same ancestry and archaic culture that split in two major groups already in the second millennium BC or earlier, according to dated archaeological findings.

Among the Indo-Iranians, fire worship remained centered on ethical matters, specially the eternal fight between Good and Evil. Among the Indo-Aryans, religion became diversified into beliefs and worship of all the multiple manifestations of the Supreme Power, the Absolute Being, the Self-Existent. Indo-Iranian mythology begins with the dynasty of the Paradata (in the Avesta) where the first man, *Gayomartan* (later *Kiyumars*) is the great hero who becomes king because of his courage. He is the excellent king, he and his successors establish dominance over land, plants, animals and man. After many generations and with considerable magical power and technical advance, he achieves victory of Good over Evil (Shah-Namah of Firdusi, "completed" in 1010 AD).

The acts and facts related by the Indo-Iranian myths cover the entire repertoire available to all mythologies of the world, including theriomorphic creatures and monsters which often are personifications of Ahriman. Div and Ahriman are the names of a group of enemy kings and people who perhaps lived in the land bordering the southern Caspian Sea in the sixteenth century BC, according to some authors (Curtis 1993). Ahriman is chief of all demons and enemies, the *daeva*. Would this be a sign of the split between Indo-Iranians and Indo-Aryans? Alternately or concomitantly would this be a sign of competition among rival Indo-European clans and the cause of the split of the Indo-Aryans themselves, some of which went eastwards and are later found in India and some went westwards and are later found in the Indo-European kingdoms, kings, rulers, warriors of Anatolia and other parts of Asia Minor and as far as Hellas (= Greece)?

Indo-Iranian myths continued to evolve and flourish as late as the sixth century BC and include the historical personality of Zoroaster who organized the religion now known as Zoroastrianism and is contained in the Zend-Avesta.

The Indo-Aryan mythology has not ceased to grow since the archaic period. Characteristically nothing is ever lost by the Indo-Aryan cultures, the complexity and richness of mythologies and folklore is ever-growing irrespective of internal contradictory statements, always respected and sometimes accepted, even if with reserve, on the ground that different opinions "could be" correct, or perhaps, "even if not correct," should be considered. The critical attitude of accepting with reserve all teachings is what has favoured the development of mathematics, astronomy and all sciences in Major India. It is also what has developed into the proverbial religious tolerance of Hinduism. The word "critics" (Lt.*criticus* and Gr. noun *kritikos* and verb *krinein* = to discern, to separate) is cognate to the word *kṛtya* and *kṛttikā* in Sanskrit (Vannucci 1999). The Avesta is based on similar concepts. In conclusion, philosophy is the fruit of rational thinking which gives to man his assigned place in the world. Belief in the knowledge acquired can become the basis of religion. Finally, all religions create their own philosophy whether Vedānta, Thomism, Islam or others.

There is one point in common to all religions, the inevitable belief in revelation. The so-called "revealed religions" teach that God himself talked to prophets. Nature religions believe that revelation derives from observation, study, meditation and concentration which enable specially gifted persons, the "seers," to unveil (= discover) truth, directly, without an intermediate prophet. This type of revelation, of unveiling the truth is the fruit of reason and experimentation, not the fruit of blind belief. Such are, among the Indo-European of the east, the Vedas and Vedānta which are Śruti, or "revealed Truth." The Avesta occupies a similar position among the Indo-Iranians, where the **Great Sage Ahura Mazda** had the power to reveal his visions (= understanding and wisdom) to man.

IN CONCLUSION

Greek Olympian gods were symbols of the ruling theocracy which demanded undivided loyalty.

There are two basic trends that mark the Graeco-Roman religion. First, beliefs are mainly produced for the use of the cultured elite; the

Gods demand or impose loyalty to both the civil and religious authority which is usually two in one and are the POLIS in Hellenism and the STATE in the Roman tradition. Second, religion provides the *demos* with a template of habits, customs and festivals to give it a feeling of belonging and participation in the life of the nation. In Rome these habits were re-inforced, the Olympic religion was declared a state religion, but the basic faith of the *demos* continued to be naturalistic. For this reason, the strongest unbreakable oath was: **"by bread and salt."** Blasphemy or swearing were addressed to the Gods: *by Jupiter, by Bacchus,* but never *by Iacchos* (esoteric name of Bacchus = Dionysos).

The role of religion in the civil life of the Polis is clearly discussed in "The frogs" of Aristophanes that figures Dionysos, there called by his mystic name "Iacchos," travelling to Hades, the nether world, to select which one of the great philosophers could return to Earth to save Athens from a dangerous period of civil degradation. We can say that the Great Olympian gods and minor Greek deities are characters who played a role in the development of the Greek civilization through the State theocracy; however it was the discussions on the nature of man in relation to the Olympian gods that confirmed the down-to-earth strength and power of Rome.

The Vedic gods **exist** independently of mankind, they are manifestations of the realities of the ecosystem man lives in as a member and participant of the great cosmic drama.

Whatever we say or do, at all times and situations, it should be clear in the mind of each one of us that the word **religion** = organized, systematized religion, is not a synonym of **religious spirit.** Mysticism is independent of religions.

(E) Gods and Heroes

Nature gods are similar in east and west, they are a function of local environmental constraints, they exist as such since the dawn of Time, they were not *made* by man but they are *perceived* or understood and explained by man to men and therefore they are real as could not be otherwise. The importance of *ācārya*s, masters, guides, learned men, sages and all teachers for the development of cultures and civilizations cannot be overemphasized. Olympian and other man-made gods have a different origin and are different in east and west, they are adapted to local needs and social imperatives of the people and governments, and they reflect the tendencies and wishes of the leaders and of the people, Indo-European or others. Parallelism and similarities can therefore be found between nature deities of east and west, but not or only very rarely, between man-made gods of east and west whatever the religion. Mysticism and mystics are of the same kind all over the world and similarities among mystics of any religion can usually be readily seen. Nature gods appear spontaneously during the early stages of cultural evolution of all people. Nature gods or man-made deities or gods often become the centre of "official" religions.

Heroes of the epics of all mankind are initially super-men or idealised super-men capable of incredible heroic feats; they can be "deified" thanks to their heroism. The acts may be accomplished either for their own benefit or for specific groups or in favour of all mankind; they build up traditions and are taken as exemplars for the education of the masses and future generations. Heroes belong to ancient pre-historic times or to evolved historical stages of cultural evolution, they belong to different civilizations, their personality and the stories of their exploits may have as much influence on the people and on their daily life as the gods themselves. Heroes may have been imaginary or real, kings, warriors, artists, prophets, saints, or any other exceptionally gifted person. Every and all civilizations have their heroes.

Epilogue

BEFORE closing I would like to apologize for repetitions found in the text. Repetitions are intentional and inevitable because each culture must be studied as a whole as well as from different viewpoints and perspectives, and in relation to other cultures, hence the repetitions. Cultures evolve and change with the passage of time, with changes in the environment, changes in the surroundings and climates, changes in the ecological, human, cultural, historic and political neighbourhood. The only exception is that of cultures that develop in isolation. The Indian culture and civilization is unique from numerous points of view, much is due to the fact that it evolved from within and to a high degree it developed in splendid isolation. Cultures grow and develop with the acquisition of scientific knowledge, and with the growth of expertise in technical matters due to trade, wars and competition with other cultures. In the present text many questions are raised and a few answers are tentatively offered, many hypotheses are left open to future studies, much understanding could be reached by looking at matters from new perspectives, some of which I have tried to point out. Many more are only briefly mentioned.

Sarianidi (1996,) wrote a "Conclusion" for his chapter on *Food-producing and other Neolithic communities* which is here transcribed in full because it gives the key to understanding the very early movements of the people that are the subject matter of this book. Sarianidi expresses clearly and convincingly what could very well serve as a preamble to this book that is essentially concerned with post-Neolithic ages.

The culture of Neolithic agriculturists and of cattle-breeders of Iran, Afghanistan and Soviet Central Asia shows that a transition to the forms of economy, usually termed the Neolithic revolution, took place here almost simultaneously with similar developments in western Asia. A new way of life is clearly represented here by comfortable houses with accurate trimming of interiors, bright ceramics and wide use of ornaments. This qualitative leap in social development prepared the necessary base for the creation of ancient civilizations. At the same time inequalities in the course of historical development become clear: the ancient tribes of Iran and southern Turkmenistan passed to the new forms of economy, while in other areas of Soviet Central Asia and northern Afghanistan the transition was delayed. Tribes of hunters, fishers and food-gatherers, maintaining many archaic features in their culture, were contemporary with sedentary communities in oases. The lines of cultural links that emerged during the Palaeolithic epoch not only keep their importance but also become stronger — a fact which played an important role in the diffusion of cultivating cereals and of cattle-breeding.

The subject-matter of this book begins with the emergence of the poorly known groups of people conventionally known as "Indo-Europeans" who evolved from the upper Palaeolithic into the Neolithic Age through the development of what is usually called "food-producing communities" and "food-producing cultures." Their remote ancestors were pastoral-agricultural communities, as revealed by archaeological research in eastern Europe, Central Asia and adjoining areas.The general sketch produced by Ghirshman, 1977, (*fig.* 1), was enriched with much knowledge and insight by research carried out during the last quarter of the nineteenth century. Volumes one and two of the multi-author *History and Civilizations of Central Asia*, a UNESCO publication, synthesize in a detailed and authoritative manner the results of long-lasting field work and other studies concerning the emergence of Neolithic cultures and early civilizations in Asia. Specially noteworthy for the specific interest of this book, are the results of the research by Askarov, A. (1996); Dani, A.H. (1996); Ghirshman, R. (1938, 1977); Gimbutas, M. (1963, 1970, 1974); Harmatta, J. (1996 a, b, c); Masson, V.M. (1996); Masson, V.M. & Sarianidi, V.I. (1996); Lal, M. (1996); Sarianidi, V. (1996); Thapar, B. K. (1984). These and others have made important contributions to field and laboratory work, as discussed in volumes one and two of the UNESCO series mentioned above.

After comparing dates, historical evidence and cultural levels of Proto-Indo-Europeans, Indo-Europeans of east (Indo-Aryans and Indo-Iranians) and of Indo-Europeans of west (here considered only the Roman-Greek civilizations), I follow with a few selected conclusions considered to be particularly significant in the context of this book — many more questions and hypotheses could be made. Further research in the following and other areas of research will undoubtedly prove to be interesting and could offer answers to the many questions raised above;

- Indo-Europeans of east, both Indo-Aryans and Indo-Iranians arrived at the eastern Mediterranean region, first in the island of Crete and in the Aegean Sea and its main islands, in more than one wave, at different times and at different levels of cultural evolution. When they reached the Mediterranean Sea region they already had acquired much cultural interaction with other people, not only Indo-European but also Semitic, Egyptian and autochthonous people. The influence of Indo-European of east was prominent in Greece already in the Mycenean Age, and perhaps earlier than 2000 BC. It was followed by what has been called the "Doric" invasion of Greece that in turn preceded the religious reform moved by Homer and Hesiod. Also other Indo-European people at more primitive cultural levels arrived in Greece coming from the north. Primitive autochthonous non Indo-European cultures were settled in the Greek peninsula already as early or earlier than about 6000 BC, when primitive agriculture was first introduced in Greece. Hellenism was a well defined and evolved culture that nevertheless remained open to foreign influences compatible with its peculiar type of humanism. The "isolationism" of India and allied cultures and civilizations such as those of Nepal, south-east Asia, Thailand, Myanmar, Bali and others promoted developments of each culture in its own way and along its own path that may be "evaluated and timed" against the development of the civilizations of the west that followed a winding path and much mixing with other cultures and civilizations. The Vedic Indian civilization grew in relative isolation and remained relatively impervious to foreign influences until recently.

- The Homeric reformation was the indirect cause that prepared the fertile soil on which flourished the revolutionary artistic/ scientific/philosophical cultural "explosion" of the Greek humanistic movement against the Olympians. The revolt that followed few centuries after the Homeric reformation was a revolt against the man-made gods who often behaved in a not-very-godly manner. It was an ethical revolt of thinking men, personalised by Prometheus, the rebellious and powerful "titanic" personality, and other characters of the Greek tragedy. The revolt is clearly and openly stated by the dramatists, by Aristophanes and others, who openly ridicule the Greek gods. This revolt was integrated in the Roman culture and civilization and influenced the history and development of "western" culture for ever after. Constructive *criticism* and a positive *critical* attitude were undoubtedly one of the most important factors that promoted the development of Indo-Europeans of east and west since early historic and even prehistoric times. It is given an important role in the *ṚV* as *Kṛtya* or *Kṛttikā* (*ṚV* X, 85, 29), a word root shared with Greek *Kritiké,* from the adjective *kritikos* and the verb: *krino*= I judge, therefore = I discriminate; I separate (see. Vannucci, 1999).

- The two main branches of the Indo-Europeans considered here are the Indo-Aryans and the Indo-Iranians, though originally they all called themselves Arya. They eventually settled in "Major India," including north-eastern Iran, formerly known as Chorasmia and Sogdiana and south as far as the Arabian Sea and the Zagros mountains. The Harappan civilization, also called the Indus River culture and civilization, may have originally been formed by distinct groups of Indo-Europeans who migrated from Central Asia into the large hydrological system of the rivers fed by the melting snows of the southern Pamir and the Hindukush ranges, known as *Sapta Sindhava* (= the lands of the seven rivers) that extends into the hydrographical system of R.Indus and its affluents, known as the land of the Five Rivers, the Punjab. Unfortunately language and script of the Harappans are still undeciphered. Most probably the Harappans gradually moved southwards along the course of rivers and downstream of the Indus, as far as the

Arabian Sea. The hypothesis is put forward that the Sumerians were a group of Harappans who sailed or rowed hugging the Makran coast from the delta of R. Indus as far as the then separate mouths of R. Tigris and R. Euphrates. Ghirshman, Kochhar and others have already advanced the well founded hypothesis that the Harappan culture may have been introduced into Sapta Sindhava, coming from Central Asia, Sogdiana or Chorasmia. The help of scientists and scholars is urgently needed to study these problems.

- The area of the delta of R. Indus has "since ever" been worked and re-worked by tides, earthquakes, floods, alluvial deposits, erosion and silting, man-made embankments and canals. Some occasional particularly violent episodic events of this sort in the delta area of R. Indus could have caused migrations of local people westwards along the Arabian Sea coast, hopping from "hor" to "hor" (khwar = lagoon). Travel by sea would be easier and safer than travel overland. Alexander's admiral Nearchus proved this point, he arrived at the mouth of R. Tigris for the appointment with Alexander the Great before Alexander who arrived exhausted after a perilous journey by land and finally died, perhaps of malaria, in 323 BC.
- Ancient and not-so-ancient people migrations favour transfer of all aspects of culture. Very ancient nature gods and religions are comparable in east and west up to when urbanization and acculturation introduced new gods, new cultic practices and new philosophies in the west. At that stage the Greek culture diverged from the Indian which continued on its way of nature philosophies that evolved into Vedānta, Jainism, Buddhism and other philosophical systems with no loss of their innate characteristics of ancient nature religions and philosophies.
- Heroes and wars are comparable in east and west, including logistics and war tactics and armaments. What changes, are the ethics of heroes that follow the prevailing religion, philosophy and social imperatives of the local community.
- Habits and customs of the heroic age of Indo-Europeans of east and west are comparable, many details survive even in developed cultural stages and modern Latin and Sanskrit-

derived languages. "Gods" and "Heroes" are not as useful to identify affinities or differences between people as are the study of the origin, maintenance and survival of habits and customs.

- Studies of the Malayalam language of Kerala and search of possible relationships with Sumerian, Sanskrit or affinities with languages of Mesopotamia and Baluchistan, should be undertaken.
- Anthropological and linguistic studies of the language, habits and customs of Kampa or Champa, Dard and Kalash people and other minorities, are recommended.
- More ethnological research into traditional habits and customs, such as *balletys* of the Greek and *bagao* of India, is needed.
- More research on *soma, homa* and wine should be done.
- . . . and many more . . .

Finally, on re-reading the classic Greek tragedies and comedies as well as the writings of the Roman philosophers, what is most striking is that in spite of superficial differences, the *essential* cultural habits remain unchanged, such are the key role of the mother, of the education of the child, of the unconditional respect and obedience to the father and to "Truth, and the abhorrence of lies."

Many other topics for research offer ample possibilities of interesting cultural work. It has taken much will power to decide to close this work. There is much more available evidence that can be used to support the hypotheses and ideas that surfaced during the studies and readings for this book, which I believe would be interesting to follow. The deeper we delve into the subject, the greater is the number of important points that should be noted and discussed. Due to my advanced age and because I am not an expert in archaeology or anthropology and above all due to my ignorance of several of the recently developed scientific research methods and techniques that could be used to prove or disprove earlier statements, or my own interpretations, I decided to write down this "epilogue" which is more like an apology for leaving without closing the door behind me. In fact, research could never close doors, it can only open doors. This is one of the fundamental axioms of the Vedas and Vedānta.

I depart with many unanswered questions. I tried not to lengthen the text unduly and hope that brevity would not become obscurity. I would like to suggest as insistently and politely as possible, that etymologists, ethnologists, archaeologists, anthropologists and the many other *ists* who are better qualified than myself, carry out research into this most interesting and fertile area of studies, which is the behaviour of past generations of men, women and childrens. I take leave wishing the best of lucks, hard work and sincere intellectual enjoyment to readers and all those who will carry on the work.

Notes

Introduction

1. There are significant differences in the past history of the various people who spoke, or still speak a variety of closely related languages. The word *Indo-European* is used to designate the people who speak Indo-European languages regardless of ethnic connotations or ethnic affinities. In this study I designate Indo-Europeans of the east the people who called themselves Aryans, namely the Indo-Aryans and the Indo-Iranians. The Indo-Iranians may in turn be distinguished as Indo-Iranians of east, the Turanians of the Avesta and of the *Shah Namah* of Firdusi, and the Indo-Iranian of west, the Persians. The original Indo-European groups or clans who called themselves Arya, moved away from the original Indo-European homeland, at present believed to be the Eurasian steppes north of the Caspian and Black Seas and as far as the Aral Sea. Archaeological findings indicate that migratory movements southwards along the eastern shores of the Caspian Sea, eastwards towards the plains south of the Aral Sea and towards present-day Iran, began in the fourth millennium BC or earlier. The Indo-Aryans and the Indo-Iranians were closely related clans from the same original stock of Indo-Europeans, as attested by their language and culture, including a social structure based on patriarchy associated with much power allotted to the mother who ruled the family. The Indo-Aryans who migrated along the eastern shores of the Caspian Sea and settled for centuries along the banks of river Gurgan (= Gorgan) that flows into the south-eastern end of the Caspian Sea, eventually migrated south-easterly towards Afghanistan and

India. Later, in the first half of the second millennium BC they moved westward as far as Asia Minor, the islands of the Aegean Sea and mainland Greece and eventually lost their identity as members of a separate culture. Differently from the Indo-Aryans, the Indo-Iranians migrated away from the northern steppes of the original Indo-European homeland and split into two major groups, one settled in the lands around the Aral Sea while the other gradually occupied the then sparsely populated regions of the Iranian Plateau as far as the Zagros (an Indo-European root-word) mountains and the Persian Gulf. Both Indo-Aryans and Indo-Iranians are here collectively called Indo-Europeans of the east. They mixed with other people Indo-European or not, and fought wars with other Indo-Europeans during the period that preceded the last century BC. The general result of these movements, peaceful occupation of lands, many wars and isolation, is that the Indo-Europeans of the east, retained many of the fundamental characteristics of their clans, presumably also of the culture of their original Indo-European homeland, over many more centuries than the Indo-Europeans of west. Many of these characteristics survived the long evolution of the Sanskritic and the Avestan cultures and are still alive nowadays in India and among the Parsis as Zoroastrianism. The Greek culture and civilization is the focus of the Indo-European of the west, who suffered also the influence of Indo-Europeans coming from the lands around the Black Sea and from the plains of the Danube. They were greatly influenced also by ancient autochthonous people of West Asia, of the Mediterranean islands by the great Egyptian civilization and by various Semitic and other cultures. The eastern Mediterranean lands and islands were the great cultural melting pot of the most ancient "Old World" cultures.

Comparisons between mature and advanced cultures of the "Indo-Europeans" of east and west are futile, it would be like comparing oranges against apples, both are fruits but beyond that, not much more could be said. Schrader (1890) was probably the first scholar who suggested an eastern origin of the people who produced a certain type of pottery typical of early Indo-Europeans. More recently Gimbutas published several papers and books to support the view that early Indo-European people lived in Ukraina, South-East Russia. According to Gimbutas (1974) there is a continuity from the Srednij Stog II Culture, about 4400 BC (= Kurgan I) to the Kurgan II Culture (about 3400 BC), followed by the Kurgan III Culture, about 3500-2900 BC and the Jamna Culture on R. Volga, third millennium BC. All of these are characterized by circular tombs. The basic traits of these cultures are the same as those of the archaic cultures of the people of the steppes north of the Black and Caspian Seas, usually believed at present to be the homeland of the Indo-European, though *kurgan* type tombs are not yet known from the Indo-Iranian and Indo-Aryan cultures.

Palaeontologically speaking, the horse evolved as a species from perissodactyl ancestors (= mammals with an odd number of toes in each foot) of the Asian steppes. The remote ancestors of the horse were not bigger than a large size dog and were first domesticated for meat as food, sinews, leather and hoofs. Later, horses were trained in Central Asia for traction and riding and were selected for tall stature. The horse arrived in Europe as a fully evolved species as known at present. All the sites excavated by Gimbutas include normal size horses and remains of horse sacrifices. The archaeological research of Gimbutas strengthen, rather than contradict, the findings summarized above, that place the homeland of the Indo-European ancestors of the Indo-Aryans and Indo-Iranian tribes or clans, in the Eurasian steppes north of the Black and Caspian Seas. The fourth millennium BC and perhaps earlier was undoubtedly a time of migrations of groups of people. Most probably migrations were not uni-directional and occurred as successive "waves" of people displacements. The migrating tribes or clans of Indo-Europeans most probably were formed by a restricted number of families and did not include many individuals. For this reason we find Indo-Europeans as the ruling class over populations of different origin. Such is the case among others and much later, of the Indo-Aryan Hittites, the Mitanni, or the Greek Ptolemies of the last centuries BC, who were the last pharaonic dynasty of ancient Egypt. Displacements must have occurred at various times and different directions for a variety of reasons and due to a variety of causes. Such may have been epidemic diseases of people and domestic animals, floods and other catastrophic natural events, opportunistic occupation of newly found and sparsely inhabited lands, wars and feuds between related and foreign families and clans, invasions by entire populations of enemy people and so on. Migrations became possible due to the ancient Indo-European feat of domestication of animals and plants. Distant voyages took place after the breeding and training of strong horses and bullocks for traction, after the invention of the wheel, of carts, of boats, of textiles, of pottery, of the metallurgy of copper, bronze and later, of iron. The development of animal husbandry and the symbiosis of man with domestic animals, rearing of cattle, goats and sheep for wool, hides, and horns were the indispensable arts that gave to the human species some freedom above slavery to the environment. The development of temporary or permanent settlements grew with the practice of agriculture. The decisive factor for evolution of the Indo-European ancient cultures was the development of articulate languages with a grammar and syntax accurate enough to convey exact teachings and clear thoughts. Archaeology provides data about what happened before and after the fourth millennium BC and where it happened.

2. After the fall of the Champa (= Kampa, Campa) kingdom in Vietnam in relatively recent historical times, people of Indian origin who were ethnically different from the local population, were left landless and with no source of income. At present their descendants may be found in small groups roaming about the land, carrying their children and meagre belongings on their shoulders, poor among the poorest. Quoting from Spallanzani, 1997, Pl. 2, a chart made by the Venitian cartographer Ramusio in 1550 shows the kingdom of *Campa* (italian pronunciation = Kampa) still flourishing in the sixteenth century, in the present day area of Vietnam, where well preserved temples with carvings in *nagari* script are common (pers. observations). Comparable nomads are found all over Europe where they are called gypsies and call themselves *Roman* or *Rom.* In India and in Europe they used to

travel in their brass-work decorated wagons offering their skill as *loharis* and fortune tellers to people living in farms and local peasants of hamlets and villages. Nowadays in the west they continue to be nomads without regular work because they do not care to settle down, they move around in latest model trailers and sleep under tent or pre-fabricated houses when they settle temporarily.

3. Both temporary and permanent migrants usually carry with them the memory and names of their original habitat. The collective memory of the people, blown up by new experience and new knowledge, contributes to build up tradition and culture. The feats of ancestors, good or bad, are remembered as myths, idealized as songs, announced as epic poems to produce the folklore that mothers, grandmothers, poets, singers, oracles, learned people and priests cultivate and teach to the younger generations. Finally, a very special type of displacements, individually or in groups of even-minded devotees, are *pilgrimages* to places known for their purity and holiness, frequently considered to be the site where miracles are known to occur or have occurred in the past. Respect and awe at sites where the presence of above-human powers is felt by many, such as volcanoes, mountain tops, springs, caves, shrines, tombs, temples or even single trees, springs or fires, are visited by inspired persons and all those in need of emotional and psychological support. Under diverse names, pilgrims, saints, anchorites and visionaries are special specimens of mankind.

4. The "Pax romana," or "Universal Roman Peace" was achieved thanks to the tolerance of Imperial Rome that respected other people's customs, habits, rules and religion *provided* the supremacy of the law of the Empire was recognized, respected and obeyed, and dues were paid.

Part I - The Scenario

1. Maps based on the maps and descriptions made by classic Greek and Roman authors give an idea of the geographic distribution of the Indo-European tribes and clans and their neighbours. Ancient text in cuneiform, in Egyptian hieroglyphs

and cursive script, in Greek and Latin scripts put on record episodes of the last millennia BC and early AD centuries which are of great relevance for understanding historic developments which took place in the Mediterranean Sea regions, where Indo-European and non-Indo-European people extended their irresistible urge to know more about the world and of the Ocean Sea beyond the Pillars of Hercules. One Pytheas, son of Crinas, a Greek from Massalia (= *Massilia*, present day Marseilles), "because of sheer curiosity and eagerness to see new environments" armed and manned a *pentecontere* (large cargo ship with fifty oarsmen) and sailed beyond the Pillars of Hercules hugging the coast in a clockwise direction, up to the "ultimate Thule," the British Isles, Iceland (?) or most probably northern Norway. He evidently sailed beyond the Arctic Circle since he described the "year divided in six months of night darkness that alternate with six months of daylight" (transl. into Italian by G.M. Rossi, 1995). According to Pytheas the travel took place during the reign of Alexander the Great (336-323 BC).

2. Pytheas also mentions one Tasus, a Phoenician of Tyre as one of his precursors, and a Punic man from Chartage, called Imilcone brother of Annone, who sailed along the northwestern coasts of Europe as far as the British Isles. Another distant sailor was Scylax from Caria who sailed beyond the Pillars of Hercules hugging the African coast southwards. An ancient tradition says that the Phoenicians had achieved the circumnavigation of Africa, sailing from east to west and there are stories about other sailors who sailed very far. A few returned home, others did not, but what is sure is that whatever the origin, the urge to "go beyond" is typical of Man the Discoverer, Man the Adventurer, whatever his origins.

3. Whatever their origin, the Indo-European coming from Asia Minor or West Asia who migrated to south Europe and the land bordering the Aegean Sea met with autochthonous populations some of which had already reached a high cultural development. The Egyptians and Phoenicians played a highly meaningful role in the development of the Greek culture and

civilization, as attested by some of the most ancient myths that had firm roots in Greek mythology long before Homer's singing of the major Greek epics, and before Hesiod's writing of the *Theogonia*. In fact Io, daughter of Inacus, a fluvial god of the city of Argus in the Peloponnesus in mainland Greece, was loved by Zeus (= Jupiter) disguised as a cloud, she was transformed into a young cow because of Hera's jealousy. Io was continuously molested by a horse-fly (genus *Tabanus*) that relentlessly pushed her out of Europe. After some adventures she was finally restored to human form on the banks of the R. Nile by a gentle stroke from Zeus and she gave birth to Danao's remote ancestors. In the Iliad Greeks are alternately called Acheans, Argives, Danaes (from Danao), as different from the Trojans, themselves Indo-Europeans coming from a different lineage. Another early myth tells how Zeus who, disguised as a bull kidnapped Europa, daughter of a Phoenician named Agenore, took her to Crete where she gave birth to Minos who later became king of the island. The many women loved by Zeus gave origin to lineages spread over the then known western world. This parentage of ancient Greeks was a bond that united members of the Hellenic world and created the great cultural movement called Hellenism. It could also be used as an argument to favour bonds among the *polies* of the Hellenic civilization, and between them and the Great Athens. Temples and shrines to Olympic gods and goddesses and to their extended human families were scattered over Africa, Europe, Asia Minor and West Asia.

4. The place where Mycaene was built, not far from the city of Argos in the Peloponnesus, had been occupied by local people even earlier than the Bronze Age and was settled by Greeks since the middle of the second millennium BC. Most of the pre-Homeric myths referred to in the Iliad and the Odyssey are about family stories and genealogies, political, military and trade relationships among the many people, who lived in the Mediterranean Sea islands and the lands around it. Iliad II, 484-779 gives details of all the people who sided with the Achaean League, as well as the number of ships and men that they sent to the Trojan War. It equally gives details of the Trojan

forces (Iliad II, 780-877). Non Indo-European participants are mentioned from both sides, Achaeans and Trojans.

5. Since ancient times man admired and worshipped mountains. Ziggurats, terraced pyramids several stories high were built in ancient Sumer already around 2000 BC (Pope 1969) by men "who came from eastern lands" and could not bring with them their mountains, so they made their own "Holy Hill" or "Mountain of All Lands," the mythical Mount Merus of ancient Indians and Greeks. The dates coincide with the time of the migrations of the Indo-Iranians southwards. Later the *shikara* and the *gopuram* of Indian architecture reflect the same eagerness to reach as high as possible with nothing more than human ingenuity, means and power.

6. Migrating Indo-Europeans probably were not very numerous in numbers of individuals. The Indo-Aryan Hittites were the ruling class of a population of a different origin, the Hurrians, most probably not Indo-European. The last dynasty of ruling pharaos of Egypt, the Ptolemies, were Greek. The dynasty was founded by Ptolomeus Soter I, son of Lagos who was related to the Royal family of Macedonia. The Sumerians who "entered Mesopotamia from the sea and spoke a different [non-Semitic] language arrived there in small numbers" and to this date their original homeland is not known for sure.

7. The nobility of the horse was immortalized by Euripides in the mythical character called Hippolytus (*hippos* = horse), son of the Athenian hero Theseus, falsely accused by his stepmother Phaedra of having raped her while Theseus was away on a pilgrimage. Hippolytus denies the accusation but rather than revealing the foul play of his step-mother Phaedra, he leaves Athens after being cursed by his father. As requested by Theseus, Neptune causes the death of Hippolytus and the great hero Theseus is punished for his thoughtless decision by discovering the truth only too late. The noble character of *Hippolytus* is thus vindicated.

8. Often-repeated physical acts and manners at the individual or collective levels, tend to become a "habit" of the person or society. Habits, such as removing footwear when entering a

temple or home, usually become engraved in the individual or society's memory and behaviour, they are repeated "automatically" without giving a special thought to the act. Usually, but not always, only favourable habits become "customs" of the whole community and thereby are engraved in the collective memory as a tradition carried over time and evolution of the society itself. Using a Latin term, *consuetudo* (= characteristics, usual = custom in English), customs become "consuetudinal" (= constant use, habitual, inveterate) meaning that they may be repeated "instinctively" and without any conscious thinking or will. Habits, in English but not in the Latin-derived languages, are gestures, attitudes, interjections, sleep or food preferences unique at personal, family or group level repeated as a matter of fact. They often become idiosyncrasies.

9. Cavalli-Sforza mentions that very little is known about the arrival of *Homo sapiens sapiens* in Asia, except for the arrival of modern man in China, dated 67,000 years ago.

10. The *paredros* was in Greek mythology the masculine figure that "sits next to" (= attends on) a goddess, particularly the Mother Goddess or Great Mother or Earth Mother to whom the *paredros* voluntarily submits his personality and acts. Dionysos was the *paredros* of Demeter.

11. Agriculture was developed in the Fertile Crescent of Central Asia surely since about 6000 BC, perhaps earlier. It was practised by Etruscans who taught the art to the Romans. Developed agricultural practices were introduced in Italy by Greeks and other Indo-Europeans of the west coming from Asia Minor, prior to the foundation of Rome. The credible legend of the arrival of Demeter in Attika, peninsular Greece, "who came from the east" about the middle of the second millennium BC, is linked to the cultivation of bread wheat (= AABBCC or hexaploid wheat) and to the practice of rational agriculture, including legal aspects of land demarcation and ownership. Agricultural practices were already well known to Homer who describes, among other features, an invasion of grasshoppers who were fought away with fire (Il. XXI, 12-14).

12. Rivers of the Indo-Europeans of east are usually personified as goddesses. One of the few notable exceptions is R. Brahmaputra, a masculine deity. Contrarily, the rivers of the Indo-Europeans of west are personified gods. R. Ilyssos is one of the two sacred rivers of Attika and is masculine; it watered the Rharian plains north of Athens where Demeter's wheat was first planted. The rituals of the mysteries of Eleusis initiated by Demeter, goddess of methodical agriculture, included special propitiatory rites to god Ilyssos. I have no knowledge of large or medium scale irrigation works in Attika or in the whole of Greece in prehistoric times, but large to very large irrigation works were well developed in Central Asia, most ancient being those of Mesopotamia, including the canal that linked the Tigris to the Euphrates, made by an ancient Semitic Queen and her people. Important hydrological works were made already in ancient Iran and India and continue to be carried out.

13. The full text of the Iliad and the Odyssey, the two epic poems traditionally believed to have been sung by a blind poet/singer called Homer in the eighth century BC, were written and left unchanged to this day, with no additions or deletions. The same may be said of the *Theogonia* produced by Hesiod in the eighth-seventh century BC. The Indian and Iranian epics once formulated, memorised and written down, were never changed. No modifications, no additions or deletions were made, the text and the lay-out remained as originally planned by the authors. The same could be said of the Aeneis of Virgil. What we have of the major Graeco-Roman poems is usually the final, perfect, entire outcome of the author's work. On the other hand, traditionally in India no knowledge and nobody's opinion is ever lost, if worthy. Knowledge or just opinions and arguments are stored in the collective immense Indian memory in some way or the other. Interpolations and additions in the *Rāmāyaṇa* and in the *Mahābhārata*, as well as in many other major literary Indian works from the Purāṇas to the Ītihāsas, are frequent and extremely valuable not only in themselves, but also for the wealth of information they provide since they are true cultural archives, though often beautified by phantasy. The wealth of literary production in many different languages of India is so

great that the main difficulty is to determine the dates of the original writing and those of the modifications made later by different scribes or authors. The *Shah-Namah* of Firdusi written more than two thousand years after the facts described took place, is more than an epic poem, it is a historical text with interpolations of popular stories, legends and personal details on the character and life of kings and heroes, and details of ancient habits and customs of the Indo-Iranians, including those of AD times. The Vedas and the Avesta are extremely valuable receptacles of the knowledge and wisdom of the very ancients, regardless of time, place, accuracy or paternity of acts, facts or precision and credibility.

14. Everything changes with time, trade of slaves in British India was a common practice (Yule *et al.*). Following are a few notes copied from Col. Henry Yule. 1637- ". . . the most effectual and speedy method for supplying our settlements upon the West coast with slaves . . . from Madagascar . . . delivered by the captains of those ships to our agents at Fort Marlborough at the rate of . . . 15 shillings a head . . . (Court letter of Dec. 8 by Rev. James Long). 1676 ". . . of three Thieves two were executed and one made a slave" (The Court of St. George, March 7). —1764, 20 shillings was "the price for every slave shipped at Madagascar to be divided 13s 4d a head to the Commander is to be further allowed . . . 6s 8d and the Chief Mate 3s 4d. The surgeon is to be allowed 10s for each slave landed at Fort Marlborough (Court letter of Feb. 22 in Long, 368). — 1778, ". . . charge sheet of the Calcutta magistrate . . . showing slaves and slave-girls of Europeans, Portuguese and Armenians . . . to be punished with the *rattan* for running away and such offences (Echoes of Old Calcutta, p. 117 seq.; other newspaper extracts). —1782- ". . . to be sold at auction . . . two slave girls about 6 year old (India Gazette, July 27). —1794- ". . . 50 Rupees Reward for Discover . . . a Malay Slave . . . run off . . . stole a Silk Purse with 45 Venetians, and some Silver Buttons . . ." (Bombay Courier Feb. 22) and others. In ancient Greece, **citizens** of the *polies* who were the illustrious men who honoured their city in war and peace, the administrators, politicians, warriors, philosophers or scientists were free and had time enough to

cultivate and develop their talents, became famous and rich only because they could rely on the slavery of other men. These men, women and children were the *ilotas* who worked the lands around Sparta and the men and women of the "democratic" governments of Athens and the other *polies* who were not "citizens" by birth-right and therefore had no right to vote or any other right. In Athens and other polies there were also free men who were not slaves but did not have the right to vote, such were artisans, small traders and small landowners, free professionals and *liberti* (= liberated slaves).

15. The word *samudra* appears in a late hymn by sage Savya, *ṚV* I; 56, 2. It is a hymn in praise of Indra who, strengthened by Śakti, the Goddess of Power, and after defeating Vṛtra and binding Shushma, is glorified and supported by libations offered by the sacrificer. Indra is praised as *samudra,* the great body of water (or flood, or abundant rains). He is credited for having set the waters free, defeating drought. The songs that the community sings in his praise flow as abundantly as in large bodies of water. *Samudra* is a noun used regularly in Ṛgvedic and post-*ṚV* literature to designate things infinitely large, such as the Great Ocean. The word describes adequately the large "seas" with which the Indo-Aryans were familiar, the Caspian and Black Seas, most probably the word includes also the Aral Sea. These three seas cover such a large area that the sun may be seen to rise or set directly from the water, depending on the viewpoint of the observer, on the western or eastern shore.

16. Aristotle was only partially successful in educating Alexander, the son of Philip II, king of Macedonia, who would be known to posterity as Alexander the Great (366-323 BC) because of his extraordinary military genius and bravery in battle. Alexander was prone to uncontrollable fits of anger and bursts of pride. One of his greatest cultural sins was to order, as tradition would have it, the arson of the leather sheets on which parts of the Avesta were engraved in golden letters and this was only one of the episodes when he forgot his master's teachings. One of his greatest merits however, was to take with him in his long

military campaigns his learned friends who left to posterity valuable reports of their observations on people, environment, plants and animals of the places and lands conquered by Alexander. The example was followed with excellent results by Napoleon Bonaparte in his campaign of Egypt.

17. A common trait of all the Indo-European was the habit of undertaking distant migrations and travels. In ancient times there was a general pattern of migration of large groups which included men, women, children, carts, wagons and all the paraphernalia of people on the move, such as domestic animals, stores of food and of seed for planting in the lands to be colonised. Such major displacements were rare and slow moving; they were preceded by movements of smaller groups of scouts, hunters and warriors, usually guided and advised by experienced leaders. Mass migrations did not take place blindly or in a vacuum, they were carefully planned over generations, traders had come and gone over routes already known and they had reported on goods for commerce and trade and most important, they also reported about climates and seasons. The "wars of conquest" of Alexander the Great, had been planned long in advance and had been preceded by the campaigns of his father king Philip II of Macedonia. The young king Alexander was well informed by spies and ambassadors that he and his father before him had sent to kingdoms abroad. Similar situations are well known also from the Indian epics and history. Crowding at home may be one reason for the travels of the Greeks but wanderlust and search for essential goods, like metals or salt were sufficient attraction to sail or travel afar. The Greeks expanded the Hellenistic world by founding colonies always further west and east on the coastal areas of the Mediterranean and the Black Sea. Some of these colonies evolved and developed as major cities, such as Massilia (= Marseille). The warriors of the many people of the Achaean League that besieged the city of Troy were also the oarsmen who manned the ships of their kings on the way to and back from Troy. At that time there were only very few large ships that required to be manned by up to 50 oarsmen, the majority carried only a handful of men. A catalogue of princes,

warriors and ships is given in the Iliad (book II), it gives detailed information on the size and spread of the Greeks in the Mediterranean area at the height of the Mycenean civilization period. Migrants take with them patronymics (names of the ancestor's lineage), geographic, trade and caste names. To mention a typical example; the word *satrapes* in Latin and Greek is the title of the ruler of a territory given in a feudal system of government to a faithful warrior, general or other dignitary by ancient Persian kings. The territory was then called *satrapy* and the same word was used by Alexander who gave several *satrapies* as a reward to his most faithful and reliable generals. After Alexander's death many satrapies became independent Hellenistic kingdoms. The word *satrapes* in Latin and in Greek (with a slightly different pronunciation), is derived from ancient Persian *khsathrapa,* where *khsathra* = kingdom (= ruler, warrior, caste) and *pa* = father (= lord, patriarch) are ancient Indo-European root words, as *kṣatriya* in Indic languages.[19] The last pharaonic dynasty of Egypt, the Ptolomies were Greek, had Greek names and spoke Greek, but the mass of the people were Egyptians. A city near present day Delhi, in India is called Gurgaon, a name perhaps carried over from the ancient city Gurgan and the river (= *Gorgan*) that drains the fertile plains off the south-eastern Caspian Sea where the very ancient Indo-Arya people had lived for many centuries before splitting in two groups, one moving eastwards and the other westwards towards Asia Minor.

18. When the Indo-European arrived in Asia Minor and Greece they met some highly developed Mediterranean civilizations at different levels of cultural development. The Egyptian civilization was very advanced in the science of astronomy and recorded exceptional phenomena, such as the passage of planets and comets, the revolution of the planets and the position of fixed stars that are benchmarks useful to draw correct chronologies. The Egyptians had been present in the eastern Mediterranean since centuries but had not ventured far at sea. It was typically a river-basin culture totally dependent on the hydrology of R. Nile that has no important affluents. The eastern-most Mediterranean was dominated by Semitic

cultures that extended inland as far as the Mesopotamian river-dependent cultures with which they traded actively. The Phoenicians had a highly developed maritime tradition. The Pelasgians were considered by *Herodotus (I,* 56), probably erroneously, to be the autochthonous population of Greece, developed on the border of the sea. The biological and ecological environments were new to the tribes of Indo-European who settled in Greece. The Indo-Europeans adapted quickly to the new environment, including to the vast salty Ocean, different from the large bodies of water which they called *samudra,* the Caspian and Aral Seas, with low salinity water. However the Indo-Europeans learned quickly to man and build ships and navigate to and from the isles and westwards towards the setting sun. The ancient god Dionysos in one of his early incarnations was an expert navigator, perhaps a Pelasgian (from *pelagus=* high seas).

19. We will not deal here with root words. Any etymological dictionary gives hundreds of root-words common to Indo-European languages. Specially frequent is the correspondence between Indo-Arya and Indo-Iranian words and between these and Greek and Latin. We are concerned here mainly with concepts, ideas, habits and customs.

20. The Pelasgoi were considered by Greek authors to be one of the autochthonous people of Hellas, they were most probably centrally located in the island of Crete. According to Herodotus (I, 56) the "Helle nic race or lineage descends from immigrants, mainly Doric people. The Pelasgoi are autochthonous." In I, 27 Herodotus also says that Phrygia, Lydia, Armenia, Cappadocia and all of Asia Minor is inhabited by Greeks. The affinity of the most ancient myths of the Indo-Aryans, Indo-Iranians and Greeks and the time and routes taken by migrations suggest that ancient Indo-European myths arrived in Greece over two routes, one from Asia Minor via the Indo-Europeans of east, the other by the over-land route from Europe, brought over by different groups of Indo-European. The similarities of the "original" myths are striking and cannot be due to chance and transfer of cultures alone. Homer and Hesiod superimposed

the new Olympic pantheon over the archaic traditional gods, myths and legends of the heroic age and arranged all of them into an imaginary whole. The result was the epics and the *Theogonia*. Hesiod does not describe only the genealogy of gods and men, he gives a succint cosmogony (= origin of the cosmos) as well. He lists the lineages derived from the gods who had sons and daughters from local women and men who in turn contributed to the "ethnic" expansion of Hellas and to the formation of Hellenism. Zeus himself produced gods, goddesses and heroes and a numerous progeny following the advice of his parents, Gaya and Uranus (*Theogonia,* 895). The Theogonia was not only a religious work; it also functioned as leverage for the development of the ancient western scientific, political and artistic scene and history. The many lineages initiated by the rich and varied love-making of Zeus was used to justify the Greek ambition and expansion over the Mediterranean, the coastal Black Sea, Asia Minor and western and Central Asia where "lived the descendants" of the very prolific Zeus, Father of gods and men.

21. There are innumerable examples of wooden structures destroyed by fire since ancient times the world over. One of the early records from the ancient Greek world is that of the temple of Athena Assieses near Miles on the east coast of peninsular Greece (Herodotus I 19). As late as the early Middle Ages in Italy the first church of the largest abbey of the rich Benedictine Order (St. Benedict, 480?-543) was made of wood and eventually was destroyed by fire. Early Greek statuary was also made of wood, and equally made of wood were most of the oldest medieval churches in Italy. The traditional Indo-European ancient and some of the old sacred enclosures were open to the sky as were also some of the very large non-wooden medieval Christian churches that were drawn out of a large place in the centre of the town. Sacred areas open to the sky and natural grottoes were common as places for worship and study among the original Indo-European and Indo-European-derived Asian and Mediterranean religions. The altar was built inside a protected or fenced-off enclosure, the *sanctum sanctorum* and the entire architectural structure was planned and could be

used to harbour old persons, women and children if the city was under siege or in times of wars and pestilences. The cathedral of Florence was constructed as sturdy as a fortress and the high dome over the transept was built only *after* the infamous pest that decimated the European population in 1348-1351 AD. At that time the population of Florence was 70,000 people, 58% of which died of the pest.

Part II - Gods

1. About the fourth millennium BC, the people who were eventually called Sumerians arrived in southern Mesopotamia, and settled in a country that later was called Sumer after them. Local ancient tradition and cuneiform texts confirm that the Sumerians arrived from the sea. Tradition also reports that Seven Sages initiated the local "rough, uncivilized" people to "matters pertaining to civilized life." Among the new arrivals, the Seven Sages were different from the local people and spoke a different language. The Seven Sages would have actively contributed to the acculturation of the local Semitic people of Akkad, a land north of what was to become the land of Sumer. The Sumerian society was based on matriarchy; they were few in numbers and became the only heirs of the mixed culture of Sumer. Triads of gods are common in most cultures and many religions. Numbers three and five are common also in nature as units of symmetry, such as number of sepals, carpels and petals of flowers and fruits. Five is the number of digits of hands and feet, of fore and rear members of vertebrate animals and is prominent in man's anatomy, it is easy to count up to five. Seven is the next prime number; it is different and not easily related to common natural features. Concern with numbers and the need to count is probably among the first expressions of language. Primitive numerology could be the first seed of science, the first reasoning developed by thinking man. The links between arithmetic and mathematical realities and the evolution of human culture are undeniable, though there is no explanation on how these links work. One most interesting numerological relationship is the frequent occurrence of the Fibonacci number, expressed by the Greek letter **Phi**,

surreptitiously present in everyday life, in nature and in human culture and artefacts.

2. Gaya "with the ample chest" (*Gaya eurysternos* in *Theogonia, 117 et al.*), the Universal Mother in Greek mythology, reminds Aditi of the original Indian (= Indo-Arya of the east) mythology. Gaya (= *Gaya pelore*), the extraordinary genetrix, is the prodigious, portentous, fertility goddess, the mother who produces the very powerful Typhaeus, her son from her second spouse Tartarus (= the Nether world) after her first mate Uranos had become unable to generate more progeny following the treacherous castration inflicted upon him by his son Chronos. *Gaya pelore* is Mother Earth, the Great Mother with an infinite capacity to produce and reproduce, Gaya (= Ge, Gea) is also a symbol of fertility. In Indian mythology Āditi is the Mother of Infinity with an immense capacity to generate great sons, immortal principles and powers, but Pṛthvī like Gaya, is everybody's mother, she is earth, who was born from Puruṣa's feet (*ṚV* X, 90). In Greek mythology Zeus (= Jupiter) castrates his bad tempered father Chronos (= Time) son of Uranos, but in the Indian mythology and lineage of gods and goddesses, there is no castration of Time. Differently from Zeus, Naṭarāja, Lord of Dance (= king and regulator of movements, an expression of the life-principle) dances over and subjugates the demon Kāla (= Time, passage of time). Castration of men defeated in battle or guilty of criminal actions is mentioned as a punishment in AV VI, 138, 2 (= "let Indra with the two pressing stones crush both his testicles"; the same technique is used to castrate bullocks and horses to this day). Time appears to be very small under Naṭarāja's feet, evidently Life as a principle cannot be subjugated by Time and in one or many forms Life will go on, independently of Time. There is no life without movement, no time-limit to the Life-principle, though life cannot be represented or perceived except by the feeling of being alive. It was the furious tandava dance that set Life in motion with the mysterious vibrations of the sound of the sacred syllable AUṀ. Life is a non-explainable natural force and all that man can do is to sing and dance to celebrate the eternal life principle. This the ancient Indo-European of east and west

knew very well, there were no celebrations, sacred or profane without songs, dances, games and libations. In fact there was nothing profane in the life of man and all nature. I believe that these must have been basic ideas or beliefs of all the Proto Indo-Europeans. The famous statue of the Great Mother Cybele later identified with Artemis (= Diana), goddess of fertility at Ephesus in Indo-European Phrygia (western Anatolia, on the mouth of R. Meander, at the end of the "royal route" that linked Mesopotamia to the Mediterranean Sea) is shown covered with a large number of egg-shaped breasts and is a late representation, second century AD, of an ancient fertility cult in that region. The Great Mother of Fertility corresponds to Gaya which existed already in the archaic ages of Greece. Pausanias (I, IV, 5) confirms reports from Herodotus about a temple, the *Metroon* (from the root for *matrix*), built on an ancient sacred place, dedicated to *Agdisti* (the root *Ag* = to drive, to push, to guide forwards; *agdisti*= ? to go far) the very ancient mother of all gods, the Great Mother. The prefix *ag* could be a reminder of ancient times when life was based on pastoralism and the most important occupation of man was to *push forward* the herds of sheep from pasture to pasture. The name *Agdisti* of this "very ancient universal mother," reminds the name *Āditi*, the Great Mother holder of the *pāśa* that drive forward all the *beings* and their actions. The most ancient gods mentioned in the *R̥V* were generated by Aditi, but only Varuṇa was not bound by fetters. Other Āditiyas were Mitra, Aryaman, Bhāga, Dakṣa, Br̥haspati, and more were added with time.

3. Alalu and Aṇu were the original ancient-most gods of the Akkadian and local Mesopotamians; they were the founders of the dynasty of god/kings. *Aṇu* is comparable to the ancient Uranos of the Greek pantheon and the Uranus/Gaya pair. Aṇu is dethroned and Kumarbi fights with him, then swallows his genitals to prevent production of more offsprings from his lineage. For the Vedic man, gods **exist** and need not be generated or castrated. In India ritual castration of youngsters and adult men with total excision of the genitals occurs ritualistically among some aberrant sects such as the Hijra (eunuchs).

4. Hermes, son of Zeus and Maya (= magical power), was his father's swift messenger with winged feet. Hermes was knower of medicine, secret doctrines, arts and creeds, he was the handman of Zeus (= Jupiter) in all matters. Large and tall squared off stones or megaliths later called *menhir* in Europe could be as tall as man or more. They were placed upright at the gate, or in the *agora* (market place) where they marked limits or other boundaries that should not be violated. In the Hellenic world these megaliths initially represented Hermes in human form, ithyphallic and facing out from the territory protected by his menacing presence. Like the mimetic colours and forms exhibited as warning by animals from insects to vertebrates. Like the monkeys with an erect genital organ sitting motionless with their back turned away from the troupe they guard, the ithyphallic Hermes was a warning not to trespass. The property was well guarded. Later, in Roman times, the boundary between adjoining fields of different owners was guarded by a squared tall stone on top of which the bust or just the head of a two faced austere god, *Janus bifrons* (= two faced, or two-fronts Janus) reminded the neighbours not to violate each other's property limits, *sub poena* of becoming liable to prosecution. Under an evolved culture and strict regulations and rules, a bearded stern faced adult would no longer need to be exhibited in an ithyphallic pose to command obedience and respect for the law.

5. The reason and purpose for transcribing the early Hittite text (thirteenth century BC) from the Hurrian original, are not known. The text probably reflects the original religious thought of the non Indo-European Hurrian people and its influence on the invading Indo-Aryans. The fusion (?) of the two traditions, one local and the other immigrant, produced a text in a script that belonged to neither, it shows that at least one of them had its most ancient roots in archaic attempts to "explain" and understand cosmogony and theogony. This is not the only text that travelled from Asia to Greece in writing or through the oral tradition. Neither the Hittites nor the Hurrians had a script in the second half of the second millennium BC. It is significant that the castration episodes of the early god-kings created by

Hesiod are absent in the Vedic or Avestan traditions while castration of men as punishment or other reasons, was an allowed practice duly regulated by the AV. Therefore, the inclusion in the western mythology of such episodes is due to direct transfer from the older mythologies, whether Semitic or other local non-Indo-European traditions. Alternately it could also mean that the absence of castration of Time (= *Kāla*) in the archaic Indo-Arya tradition is due to the realistic, though symbolic myths of the Vedic tradition that reflect more closely what would have been the early Indo-European religion. Naṭarāja is Life, expressed by movement, songs and games, he dances over Time, a non-destructible demon that can be subjugated and therefore mentally, and therefore only symbolically castrated and rendered harmless only by Life, with no need of a bloody intervention such as physical castration. Going back to the time of first appearance of the myths, we know that archaeological findings confirm an early separation of the Indo-Arya clans that moved eastwards towards the "land of the seven rivers," Sapta-sindhava and the Punjab, the hydrological system of R. Indus, from those who moved westwards towards Asia Minor and Anatolia. It was Indra, a very ancient god who released the flow of the Seven Rivers after he controlled Vr̥tra.

6. Initially the westward migrating Indo-Aryans were groups of warriors, priests and artisans. Archaeological remains suggest that these groups were followed by a portion of the bulk of the population that had been left behind to colonise the lands where the advanced group had earlier settled. They relied for food, raw materials and labour on the people of the west on whom they now ruled. They quickly adopted the invention of a phonetic script; the cuneiform script invented by the Sumerians, and would have had to learn the local languages. The names of gods and most important elements of the Indo-Aryan culture that could now be written down would have lived on with the original tradition. The entrance of Indo-European into the island-dotted Aegean Sea was linguistically easy. The most ancient Indo-European civilization of the Mediterranean was that of Crete, born around 2300 BC, it reached its maximum

power around 1700 BC. Cretans spoke and wrote an Indo-European language considered to be a form of archaic Greek, as attested by the Linear B script deciphered by Ventris.

7. Both Vṛtra, defeated by Indra and Typhaeus, defeated by Zeus, are superhuman beings often described in non-human form, they are very strong and choleric, they can cause great damage to Mother Earth. Undoubtedly Indra Vṛtrahan and Zeus who defeated the Thracian god or demon Typhaeus, were archaic gods or powers of the Indo-European religion from the time when the images of man and god were not seen as very different from each other. Indra and Zeus share many features. The human form, Indra or Zeus, has long fights and finally defeats the non-human monstruous form, Vṛtra or defeates Typhaeus respectively. Other ancestral godly figures of the Indo-European are Gaya (= *terra mater,* Mother Earth), usually called *Gaya pelore.* Vṛtra, Typhaeus or Kāla cannot be definitely destroyed because they have an eternal role to play in the symphony and reality of nature and in the preservation of Life, an undefinable principle, hence subjugation under the dancing feet of Naṭarāja.

8. The archaic Dionysos under his early name of *Phanes* was one of the first principles. He is so ancient that there are temples, shrines, sanctuaries or just natural sites sacred to Dionysos under any of his many names, everywhere in the ancient Hellenic world, even before the arrival of the Greek people. Nothing survives eternally; nothing is fixed in time though time is a measurable, virtual non-entity that **exists**. Time changes everything along its way. What is perceived by living beings are the physical consequences and aspects of the passage of time, such as rhythm and harmony which become movement, music, dance and games, or ageing of the body. Life is the result of the interplay of all movements, at a higher more complex level time is manifest as joy, harmony and melody that are the result of the integration of movements at all levels. There is an infinitely large number of factors at play in the cosmic drama; they are manifest in the different aspects and metamorphoses of all forms of life. Astral bodies move, they are alive, even if alive under a form different from our personal life. The *tandava* dance does not symbolise only the victory of

Life over Time, it symbolizes also the constant transformation of everything in nature. Many centuries later the French chemist Lavoisier (1743-1794), based on his experiments formulated the "Law of Conservation of Matter: "Nothing is created, nothing is destroyed, but everything is transformed."

9. The description of the primordial boisterous and howling Dionysos, or that of the god of Tempests is similar to the description of the Vedic god Rudra, the personification of the violent aspects of nature in the imagination of primitive man. The myths relating to Rudra refer to the oldest gods, they put on record the impression and ideas that man had about nature and his place in it.

10. Among the advanced Indo-European civilizations of the Eastern Mediterranean, the oldest was that of the island of Crete, (2300-2000 BC) facing the western end of Asia Minor and linked to it by the islands of Rhodes and Carpathos and the many islands of the archipelago of the Sporades. Homer (Odyssey XIX, 172-79) says that "there are many people in Crete: the magnanimous Eteocretans, the Achaeans, the Cidonians, the Doric and the Pelasgians. Achaeans, Doric and Cidonians are Indo-European; some authors include also the Pelasgians among the Indo-European, which is very doubtful. Homer further adds that there are ninety cities, including Knossus the Great "where reigned Minos great friend of Zeus." This was the knowledge at the time of Homer, **after** the Doric invasion of Greece. The basic language and culture of Crete were Indo-European; the Great Mother Goddess was most probably the cultic centre of the religion, as she was in Phrygia. She was shown in a statuette dated 1600/1500 BC recovered from the excavations made at Knossus, bare breasted and clothed in a full length skirt, holding a wrigling snake in each lifted hand and with a cat sitting on her head. Other well defined language groups in the Homeric epics are the Achaeans, Mycenean and post-Mycenaean Indo-European and the ancient Indo-European Troyans of Asia Minor. In the Graeco-Roman tradition Zagreus was known as an ancient Thracian god incorporated late in the personality of Dionysos: Dionysos Zagreus. The qualifying adjective "zagreus" suggests that the

god was born, or came from the Zagros Mountain region. The details of the ancient myths are interesting because they tell us where and how myths were first born in the mind of man, thus at the time of the great upheaval of the revolt of the Titans against Zeus, the ancient Zagreus was torn to pieces by the infuriated maenads, followers of Dionysos but the pieces were then put together by Athene and he was reborn as Dionysos Zagreus, the Thracian god. These myths obviously represent the clashes of the various people for occupation of the lands of the Mediterranean region. Wine in ancient Crete was called *oinos* (= akin to *haoma* and soma) hence the Greek word "*eno*" (from which "enology," the science of wine) and the more recent Latin name *vinum.* The habit of drinking wine was believed, in ancient Greece, to have been introduced from a more ancient civilization, that of Crete. The rebirth of Zagreus as a Thracian God, his name and the habit of drinking wine also point at an active exchange of arts and customs between the still primitive Thracian culture and probably western Indo-Iranians, very early during the age of the Mycenean and early Cretan civilizations of the second millennium BC.

11. The State religion of the Graeco-Roman civilizations had been codified by Hesiod and Homer. The myths and legends on which the State religion was founded were respected and kept alive even after Rome gradually annexed the various components of the Hellenic world and absorbed the culture known as Hellenism. Myths and legends were the strong scaffolding on which were built the collective memory and religious practices of the many *demos* of the Graeco-Roman world of the eastern and central Mediterranean world. New episodes and interpretations were added to the archaic tradition as well as old legends and myths by the Greek historians and dramatists. Much of the ancient tradition was kept alive by the "Mysteries" and the interrogation of the oracles. Delphi and Epidaurus were among the most revered centres of pilgrimage. The origin of the religious practices at Delphi is lost in time and there is archaeological evidence of rites and sacrifices offered to *Earth* older than the advent of Apollo (= Phoebus Apollon). Homeric Hymn III with 546 verses and

Hymn XXI are bench marks for understanding the personality of Apollo. An updated critical review of what we know at present of the Oracle at Delphi can be found in Delcourt (1981). The wealth of songs and visions of the Orphic mysteries recall the golden ancient past lived represented by Dionysos, god of nature described in a manner comparable to the Golden Era of the Vedic religion. The most salient philosophical traits of the Delphic Orphism are its pessimism and its concern with immortality and metempsychosis. Orphaeus is a philosopher who sees the full potential of man, **if** and only **if** integrated with Dionysos, Nature personified. To understand nature by intuition and by mental concentration is the duty of man. One of the songs says: ". . . far from birth peregrination . . . next to Orphaeus the initiated to the cult of Dionysos and Kore, they pray to escape from the circle and be liberated from evil." Another song says: ". . . according to Orphaeus it is impossible to be liberated from the circle of Fate and birth, unless by the will of the gods to whom Zeus ordered to comfort from sufferance the souls of men bound to the circle (= cycle)." Dionysos is the cause of purification and therefore he is the redeemer. The most famous sanctuary dedicated to Asclepias was in the Argolid part of the Peloponnesus; it was built in the sixth century BC and was taken care of by the lineage of the Asclepiades during the many centuries of activities of the sanctuary. As god of Nature, Dionysos was reputed to be versed also in the use of medicinal plants. The theatre of Epidaurus, famous stage for the performance of the great tragedies (Aeschylus, Sophocles, Euripides, sixth and fifth centuries BC) based on the contrasting responsibilities that arise from the fact of "being human," was built in the fourth century BC. The theatre is preserved practically intact to this day and has also been studied in detail for its perfect acoustics; it could seat fourteen thousand persons. In 1683 Anthon Van Dale wrote a *De oraculis veterum ethnicorum* (= About the oracles of the ancient people) in which he showed that the activities and authority of the oracles, including those at Delphi, survived for centuries even after the advent of Christianity.

12. Nonnos tried to find common grounds between the ancient religions and Christianity in the very human endeavour to establish good relations between Man and the Divine.

13. During the Greek hegemony and throughout Hellenism, there was a tendency to call "Indians" all the people of Asia Minor, West and Central Asia and those living all the way eastwards towards R.Indus. Most probably this was due to the fact that the rulers and dominant classes of this vast region were since the early second millennium BC originally Indic speaking people. Several clans or tribes of Indo-European people arrived in Asia Minor coming from over the Caucasus, following the earlier arrival of the Indo-Aryans and Indo-Iranians.

14. There is a basic similarity between **Rudra** (Vedic), **Phanes Proterogonos** (archaic Greek) and **The God of Tempests** (Hittite text of a Hurrite ancient myth).

15. McGovern (2003) reviewed the present knowledge, including the results of his own research and that of his colleagues on the history of grapes culture (= viticulture) and of the art of making grapes' wine (= viniculture). The author was successful in writing an extremely interesting, informative, scientifically documented and lively text rendering the results of extensive and intensive scientific research described in a book that reads easily as a most fascinating detective novel. From the point of view of the present study I now wish to focus only on the brief remark about the identity of Vedic *soma* with Avestic *haoma* (pp. 208-209). McGovern writes that Russian archaeologists studied fortified settlements in the Karakum desert east of Bactria and Sogdiana, dated second millennium BC. In addition to wine, traces of *Ephedra, Cannabis* and *Papaver* were found in drinking cups, however the remains of these plants were *not* associated to, or in the same container as remains of grapes' wine. In my opinion this is easily explained because wine, a fermented drink keeps for long periods of many years if well prepared and conditioned. Wine had to be imported in the regions mentioned where wine was not produced at that time. Libations with wine and pouring of some wine in the fire were part of the rites for propitiation of the gods. The three plants

mentioned were most probably also used in association with, but not mixed with wine. The plants mentioned grow wild or may be cultivated *in loco* where grapes do not thrive. Watery extracts or the juices of the plants do not undergo a process of fermentation before libation at the same sacrifices when and where wine was offered to the gods, therefore fresh plant extracts would be offered from different cups than those used for wine libations, but could be consumed at the same time and same sacrifices. When libations with *soma* or *haoma* were made with pure wine the offering was restricted to sprinkling some drops or pouring small quantities of wine into the sacrificial fire. Most authors at present identify the *soma* plant with *Ephedra*. The findings of McGovern reflect different cultic practices at different places rather than identification of strict ubiquitous rules. Vannucci (1999, Appendix) gave a short discussion in favour of identifying soma with grapes wine. It is also known that the "soma" used during sacrificial libations over the centuries was not always prepared from the same plant, but from a reduced variety of species because of local and temporary absence or availability of appropriate substitutes of the *"real soma plant."* The practice of using surrogates of grapes' wine for ritualistic practices continues at present (verbal information from authoritative sources). Probably the correct explanation is a compound of different partial interpretations of a complex problem that was stretched over millennia and over an extensive geographic area. McGovern's findings are important.

16. Zeus was the Father of gods and men. After castrating his father Chronos, Zeus actively produced as many divine or semi-divine offsprings as possible. Evidently the supremacy of Greece had to be justified far and wide. Zeus created gods to incorporate a functional assembly dwelling on the highest mountain of Greece, the Olympus, thereby he generated lineages of semi-gods, heroes and other notable persons belonging to many parts of the then-known western world. Some of those more often remembered are: 1. Demeter, an ancient immigrant into Hellas (= Greece) coming from the east, she had to be Hellenized by her intimacy with Zeus. The offspring

of that union was Kore, the young girl abducted by Aidoneus. 2. Io, daughter of the fluvial god Inachus in the Argolid region. She was a priestess of Hera, fell in love with Zeus and was transformed into a young cow to protect her against Hera's (= Juno) wrath. She travelled widely and went as far as "India" through Arabia and was later restored to human form by a touch of Zeus. She was identified with the Moon and the Egyptian goddess Isis. She was the mother of Epaphus, ancestor of Danaus. 3. Europa, daughter of the Phoenician Agenor, and mother of Minos, king of Crete. 4. Danae (= judge, feminine gender), daughter of Acrisius king of Argo and mother of Perseus. She was visited by Zeus disguised as a shower of gold. 5. Latona or Leto, daughter of a Titan from Lycia (?), mother of Apollo and his twin sister Artemis (= Diana) born on the floating island of Delos that was anchored to the bottom of the sea to facilitate Latona's labour and delivery. 6. Māyā (Lt. = Skt., māyā, magics, illusion), mother of Hermes who, according to some late authors, stole Apollo's cows and hid them in a cave (similar to the Indra/Vala episode of the stolen cows). 7. Alcmena, mother of Herakles, the strongest of all, champion of gods and men. 8. Semele, daughter of Kadmus native of Thebes in Egypt and founder of the citadel of Thebes in Greece, mother of Dionysos. 9. Leda, wife of Tyndareus king of Sparta, later deified as Nemesis, goddess of Justice, loved by Zeus who changed Leda and himself into a couple of swans. She laid an egg from which emerged the twins Castor and Polydeuces (= Pollux) and also Helen of Troy (?). These and many other Greek myths are evidently based on a fusion of local archaic knowledge with folklore enriched at different times and occasions with Egyptian, Semitic and the Indo-European oral tradition.

17. Prayers are usually considered to be one, if not the first manifestation of religiosity. On closer analysis, invocations which evolve into songs, bowing, stooping or kneeling into competitions and games (= sports) and dances "by prescribed steps" are equally significant archaic manifestations of religiosity. Songs, dances and games gradually lost their exclusive religious aspect and became manifestations of the

culture of the civilizations that developed in west and east. These aspects of cultic practices are typical of all so-called "primitive religions." In India and Greece the tradition of ritual songs, dances and games was preserved and continued to be developed as cultural manifestations as well as the expression of gratefulness for the participation of man in the cult of the divine. The best example of a game created as a ritual on which there is historical evidence (Homeric Hymn II, To Demeter), is *Balletys* or the "Thrust." As late as the sixteenth century Galileo Galilei studied the laws of the free fall of objects under the pull of gravity using his own heart-beat as a measure of time, for lack of a more precise field instrument for the purpose. The first theatres (= amphitheatres = half of a sphere) built in Greece were attached to temples, sanctuaries, or sacred areas that included shrines, store-houses, hostels for pilgrims and other structures related to cultic practices in addition to the temples themselves. Apart from the *agora*, the Greek theatre was the centre of the community's cultural life, including ritualistic feasts and ceremonies organised by the state who selected poets, musicians, actors, and dancers. In older times the audience interacted with the "chorus," ideas and problems of the *polis* were freely discussed in the theatre, during the performances, as in the *agora* among all the citizens. The representation of the famous tragedies and comedies of the classic Greek dramatists were the opportunity for the people to think about problems relating to administration, law and justice. The large temple cities of south India were independently inspired on the same principles and continue to play an authoritative role in the life of Indian people, though architecture, orgnization and scope are based on different principles and ideals and are determined by different laws and rules. The passage of time, however, continues to be measured by music, songs and rhythm.

18. Demeter was undoubtedly one of the oldest divine personalities of the ancient ages of Greece. Scholars who tried to establish her chronological age agreed that she existed already in the archaic, proto-historic period of Greece. She was a guest of the archont/king Keleus (= Celeus) and everything considered,

her appearance in Greece can safely be put to the middle or early second half of the second millennium BC.

19. Prof. Menghi (2003) sees in Pythagoras; theories (570-490 BC born in the island of Samo on the western coast of Asia Minor) the "influence of Indian doctrines on the nature and destiny of our psychic component; equally strong is the influence [that the Indian doctrines] will have on Plato's thoughts (427?-347 BC) and on Christianity". . ."the *Number* [for Pythagoras and his school] is the Principle of Order in the Universe. . . . as are also astral movements that can be expressed by numerical constants . . . all worldy phenomena . . . have a rational physical and numerical structure." Philolaos, a disciple of Pythagoras produced the final theoretical form of the idea of "number," under the name of "Pythagoras theorem."

20. The word *maryanni* refers to the *marya.* Chakravarty (1997) quoting Wikander, considers the word *maria* = Skt = *marya,* "a band of young men moving in groups (*cf.* sardhas, gana, vrata)." The words *marya* and *mariyanni* sound Indo-European, Sāyaṇa (apud Chakravarty *l.c.*) interprets *maryah* as *maraka manuṣyarūpa va,* different from the Latin and Greek name Maria, feminine, and the masculine form Mario that are known to have been taken directly from the Hebrew *Miryam.* Whether a coincidence or not, what is interesting here is that the "Maruts are often described as *maryah;* they are "*rudrasya maryah*" *cf.* Chakrabarty (I.64.2; VII. 56.1). The Maruts are an important part of the retinue of Indra, they are "storm gods, soldiers, strong and vigorous" (Chakravarty, *l.c.*). Their image recalls some of the characters of many of Dionysos' retinue, specially as described in Nonnos.

21. From the linguistic point of view the Homeric hymns, the epics and the *Theogonia* have many archaisms that help to place them chronologically. Some of the Homeric hymns are marked as having been produced several centuries *after* Homer. Finally the Orphic mysteries can be mentioned as a source of understanding of the close relationship between them and the Dionysian mysteries. The written tradition also points at the correct notion that the Orphic and Dionysian mysteries had much in common also with Vedic lore. As an example, the

teaching of nature's cycles, including the life-death-life cycle (Cassola, Orphic Hymn 53, 7), or the seasons "who run in circles," are a recurring theme also in the figurative arts. Merkelbach correctly points at the close relationship between Virgil's Georgicae and the mysteries. Merkelbach quotes from the Georgicae I, 168: *divini gloria ruris* (= the glory of the field of the divine, or, the divine glory of the fields, *transl. mine*). Both Merkelbach and Cassola traced the myths of Dionysos back to geographical sites, to the ritual *trieterides*, bi-annual festivals in honour of Dionysos linked to the many myths related to the Titans and to domestic and foreign deities, tracing back logically the origin and changes of the legends over time. Building on the basic characteristics and original personality of Dionysos, Cassola, Merkelbach and a few others cleared much of the superstructure of newly invented stories accumulated over the centuries, they could thus produce a clear image of the nature of the god, its origin, complexity, meanings and final return to the original violent personification that is still alive in remote corners that have been under Indo-European influence. On the other hand many modern authors have lumped together all the bits of information available in whatever text or popular legends, with the result that little reliable, reasonable or logical information may be found in the personality described by them. To quote only two, I would mention Graves who, in the Index of his encyclopedic "The Greek Myths" writes of Dionysos "the lame God"! Otto (1933) impressed by the furious traits of the primitive Dionysos and his possible identity with the Thracian Zagreus repeatedly describes Dionysos as "demented, mad, crazy, frantic, insane." Though this may be correct about occasional aspects of the multi-faceted god, the adjective cannot be generalised to the complex figure as a whole. Cassola (1975) produced learned and detailed commentaries of Homeric Hymns I, VII and XXVI and studied original sources to validate the character of Dionysos from what is known in grammar, language, chronology, geography and all legitimate sources other than Homer and Hesiod, such as Aeschylus, Sophocles and Euripides, the fathers of the Greek tragedy. Merkelbach (1988) gives clear and documented analyses of myths and legends as well as historical information. He is successful in putting into chronological order the cultural evolution of the Greek understanding of the myths. It is obviously impossible to draw a parallel between Dionysos and any of the Vedic gods because the fundamental concepts and ideas are different. Several modern authors attempted to draw such parallelisms; they are, amongst others, the unconvincing efforts made by Danielou who saw an identity between Śiva and Dionysos, and other far fetched simplifications, always more or less ridiculous.

Part III — Heroes

1. The word "hero" has an approximate but stronger synonym which is *vir*. The noun *vir* needs to be understood. *Virus* in Latin means *poison*. *Virus* comes from the ancient Lt. *visos* from an Indo-European root-word *wisos* (or *wisos*, spelling has a different *letter i*) that means poison also in ancient Indic languages. About the IV century BC *wisos* changed into *virus* with the same meaning (= poison). In Lt. the present participle of the verb *virere* = to become green, greenish, to be green is *virens-virentis*, with a variety of meanings, including *virulence* and derivates. The word *virtus-virtutis*, Lt. for *virtue* is an abstract noun that designates a *virile* (= virtuous) man having all qualities and *wiro* was the ancient name given to a *virile man*. How *wiro* = poison changed into *Vir*, a superior specimen of man, I could not find out. The word for man= *homo* in Italian, is known to be derived from Lt. *humus*= earth, soil, fertile soil, therefore the name *homo* in colloquial Italian characterizes man as an *earthern creature*, a being of and from the earth. The word *Mann* in Germanic languages is believed to be derived directly from the Indic *manuṣya* = thinking being, a mortal being *not* a god. In Greek and Armenian-derived languages, man as a mortal being is known as *brotos*. The root-word *wisos* is already found in Tosco-Umbrian, a very ancient language of central Italy (Tuscany and Umbria). It is also found in Baltic languages and early Indic roots. In Rome, the honourific *Vir* was given as a qualifying adjective to men valiant in any field of learning or action. The sense of the noun *Vir* is better understood from the

use made of this noun when, during the Roman Republic, the Senate nominated a group made of three illustrious, wise and law-abiding men to govern the State during particularly difficult or dangerous periods, these were the Triumvirates (= group of three notable men, the authority of three *vir*). Biographies of great leaders in war and peace, literates, learned men, philosophers, wise rulers and other notable people were often titled *De viris illustribus* (= About illustrious Men), following the example of Cornelius Nepos, contemporary of Caesar, and of the historian Svetonius of the second century AD, whose major works were also titled *De viris illustribus*. Svetonius became famous because he was often quoted and copied in the following centuries. Even St. Jerome (340?-420 AD) followed Svetonius and titled his major work: *De viris illustribus*. Much earlier the name *Mahāvīra* was used in India for the *Great Man* of Jainism. The feminine for Vir is *Virago*, meaning a woman having the strong character, physical power and courage of a man and a *Vir*. Rani Jhansi is an appropriate Indian example. In medical sciences the meaning of the words *virus, viral* and other related words are derived from the original *wisos* (= poison). Many interesting speculations could be made on the evolution of the meaning of the original root word, but this is not the place. Chakravarty, U. (1997) correctly mentions Mahāvīra, along with Buddha, Jesus and Chaitanya as great personalities of the past who were "mythologised." Bhargava (2001, 1st ed. 1956) writes "long before Siddhartha and Mahāvīra there were teachers who denied the sanctity of the Veda." In *R̥V* VIII; 61, 10, a Valakhilya hymn, the *mahāvīra* is mentioned as a cauldron, a synonym of the *gharma* cauldron the contents of which are poured into the fire at the *pravargya* rite, introductory to the Soma sacrifice. Bhargava also mentions the *mahāvīra* as the vessel used during the *pravargya* which is regarded as *makhasya sirah* (Bhargava chapt.VII, note 52). Again quoting from Bhargava (*l.c.*, v. I, p. 26), Makha was a particularly famous demon who stood by the gods, though opposed to them. ". . . The myth says that the splendour (= *yasas*) reaches him first and that he runs away with it and remains standing leaning against his bow. The bow string snaps and severes

Makha's head which becomes the *Pravargya* (*ap.* TM Brahmana VII 5.6). I will refrain from trying to interpret these and various other extremely meaningful myths.

2. The Homeric heroes of the Mycenean Age were the kings of many small "kingdoms" of peninsular Greece, the Aegean islands and the western coast of Asia Minor, they were relatives and companions of the king of Mycene, the capital city of the Mycenean civilization whose king was Agamennon, leader of the Achaean princes who moved to the war that ended with the capture and destruction of the city of Ilio (= Troy). Horses, chariots and bronze armaments were specially made for, used and personally paid for by each warrior. The "soldiers" and common people were poorly armed and played only a minor role in battle. They were however indispensable as oarsmen, smiths, carpenters, servants, providers of food and water, shepherds and agriculturists. Along with pleasure women they were mostly ranked as slaves (= Lt. *servus* = servant), many were recruited locally after landing ashore and were captured during preliminary scouting inland.

3. The Homeric hero is the lord of a city, island or land that may include smaller cities, villages and ploughed or otherwise cultivated fields. The warrior-king and his family are powerful as long as the head of the family is victorious and is capable of asserting his superiority over other kings by any manner, including diplomacy or plunder. The great Homeric hero is not troubled by ethical scruples as long as he is under the protection of an Olympic god or other deity. At a certain stage of development all cultures select the image and model of some "ancient sage" (= patriarch, patron, master, teacher), known to be a wise and learned man. The word sage is from the Latin *sap* (= *sapere*, to know; from popular latin *sapjus* = knower, clever). The English word *sage* is from ancient French: *sage*, (= correct, honest, well behaved). Ancient *sages* were eternally remembered in many countries the world over, mostly they are said to be seven in number and they have different names. As mentioned above, numerology and basic arithmetics, may have been the first step in the development of the human brain, thought and

expression, perhaps also language. Āryabhata in the sixth century AD defines the decimal system that involves the use of the sign "zero" (= *śūnya*, void) and an Indian table dated 595 AD indicates that the decimal system was already in current use in India at that time. The *golden ratio* (= golden mean), the symbol of which in modern mathematics is the Greek letter *phi* (= the Fibonacci number) primarily studied and calculted by the mathematician Fibonacci (born in Pisa, Italy about 1170, died 1240), is found everywhere in nature and may have been used, knowingly or "instinctively" since very ancient times, for instance in building the pyramids, in forming the polyhedrons of Plato or just in the choice between order and disorder and the best choice in music and in the harmonic arrangements of parts, structures and designs, as well as in accountancy, as proven by the notary/accountant and painter Piero della Francesca (about 1412-1492, born in the Tuscan village of San Sepolcro) and divulged by Luca Pacioli (born in 1445 in the same village), also a notary and known as the "father of accountancy."

4. The so-called *Habur ware* pottery is known from archaeological findings to have been in current use since about 1800 BC in a vast area that goes from the Mediterranean shores as far as the Zagros Mountains, Kurdistan and Azerbaidjan areas. The *Habur ware* is characterized by black circles and cross-hatched triangles. It indicates the area of Hurrite expansion. The Hurrite belonged to the same ethnic group as the people who established the kingdom of Urartu around the area of Lake Van, but spoke a related but more archaic language. Their early displacements from the mountains had been towards the end of the third millennium BC. The Hurrite formed the mass of the people of the Mitanni kingdom the rulers and upper class of which were of Indo-European origin. The Indo-Arya entered in the Mitanni area about the seventeenth or sixteenth centuries BC. In contrast with the *Habur ware* the most common pottery of the Mitanni is differently shaped, has white opaque designs on a black background. The designs vary in the different regions, east of R. Tigris there are birds similar to those of the painted pottery of pre-historic Iran. In the western region (Atchana),

there seem to be dominance of Cretan designs (from Ghirshman, 1977).

5. Aristotle (384-322 BC) saw and tried to analyse the reasons of the conceited attitude of the Greeks who considered themselves the topmost people of the world known to them. Menghi (2003, p. 10) quotes from Aristotle's *Politica,* VII, 7. (pers. transl.): "The people who live in cold regions and those of Europe [including the Scyths] are very courageous, but they are somewhat short of intelligence and hability in the arts, therefore they live free, but they do not have political institutions and cannot dominate their neighbours; the Asian people [Persians] instead are naturally intelligent and are clever in the arts, but have no courage and for this reason they are always in servitude. On the other hand the stems (= lineages) of the Hellenes which occupy the central region, can participate in the character of both, in fact they [the Hellenes, the hellenic lineages] have courage and intelligence, they therefore live always in freedom, [Hellas] have the best political institutions and the possibility to dominate all others, if constitutional unity will be achieved." This quote, among other reasonings, shows why the Greeks and later the Romans called barbarians all the people who did not speak Greek or Latin or had no "constitutional unity" and lived like hordes "moving from place to place." Nobody could be initiated in the mystic rites, such as the Eleusinian or Orphic mysteries, if they did not speak Greek or Latin. The quote from Aristotle also indicates how early the Greek philosophers liberated themselves from the Olympian man-made gods, by introducing Reason above blind faith or credulity.

6. The city of Troy (= Ilio) became regionally important after the seventeenth century BC, though archaeological excavations show that a city grew on the same place since about 3000 BC and was destroyed and rebuilt several times. The remains of the city called *Ilio* in the Iliad are those at archaeological levels VI and VII. The findings also show that a widespread fire destroyed the last city (level VII), hence the conclusion that the Iliad and Odyssey are based on pre-historic facts, namely the existence, siege, pillage and arson of a city caled **Ilio** (= Troy).

The name Troy comes from the name of the region where the city had been built, the Troade and became rich with trade. Archaeologically determined dates and information from the epics show that the ruling class and the warriors were Indo-European but there is not much information about the *demos* (the populace, the people at large). The rural area, agriculture or pastoralism are not discussed in the Iliad. Pelasgoi and perhaps also other non Indo-European groups are mentioned in the "catalogue of the ships" in book II as taking sides with Achaeans or Trojans. The culture of Troy was Indo-European and the dates suggest that Troy was a front settlement of the Indo-Arya advance westwards. The conquerors who built the great city of Troy had become very rich over the years because of the strategic position of the city, thanks to which they could control navigation and trade between the Aegean and the Black Sea coastal areas which was gradually colonised by the Greek. Hence the fundamental importance, for the Greeks to keep the access to the Black Sea open and free from having to pay duties to the Trojans.

7. The Iliad begins on the 51st day of the siege of Troy when Achilles, son of the sea goddess Thetys and of Pelaeus, a semi-god grand-son of Zeus, rages for days because Hector stole his pretty slave Briseis, though her father had already paid the ransom. Temperamental Achilles withdraws from the war and causes great damage to the Achaeans, until he is coaxed back to battle by goddesses Hera and Athena. The Iliad closes after ten years of siege, with the killing of Hector, a Trojan prince, by Achilles, in revenge for the slaying of his friend Patroklos. The Iliad ends after the exequies of Hector are completed and the corpse is buried. At that time, corpses were either cremated or entombed. The Iliad is historically important because it is a bench-mark in the evolution and spread of Greek culture and lifestyle, eventually called Hellenism. From the point of view of this study, the Homeric poem shows clearly that the evolution of the fundamental Indo-European culture of the west spread, and perhaps was even strengthened by the wars waged between different clans of Indo-Europeans. The same may be said about the great Bhārata War. The Homeric poems are also

a primary source of information on the Mycenean culture and the cultural developments achieved by the Greeks up to the eighth-seventh century BC, when the poem was put in its final form. Menghi (2003), and others before him, sees a direct influence of Indian doctrines on early Greek philosophers, such as Parmenides (fifth century BC) and mathematicians and philosophers such as Pythagoras (570-about 490 BC) who belonged to the aristocratic class and were both born in *Magna Graecia,* and not in peninsular Greece.

8. From the beginning of the last millennium BC the Greeks greatly expanded their zone of influence. By the sixth century they extended westwards as far as Sicily, south and western Italy, southern France, Spain and eastwards all around the Black Sea. There were only three *polies* on the northern African coast, all in eastern Lybia (Barce, Cyrene and Apollonia). The Greeks had at that time actually colonised the entire Greek peninsula, Crete and the eastern coastal lands of Asia Minor facing the sea. They were surrounded by Iberians in the Iberic peninsula, by Celts in what is now France, Italics and Etruscans in Italy, Illirians north of Macedonia. North African shores and the south-eastern Mediterranean along Palestine and Phoenicia were already under the sphere of influence of the Phoenicians. Most *polies* were not much more than trading emporia placed where there was a suitable harbour. Athens was topographically protected on the land side and its harbour, the Pyraeus was of easy access from the sea, therefore the city was never short of supplies and could prosper in peace. The original Indo-European world was land-locked, except for the mildly saline waters of the Caspian and Aral Seas, thus when the Indo-Europeans arrived at the Aegean Sea, they found themselves suddenly facing a large salt-water dominated environment punctuated by small islands. They had to learn from the local people how to navigate and use the sea. After the destruction of Troy the Greek expanded mainly in a westward direction.

9. One of the most important differences between the evolution of the Indo-European civilizations of east and west is that the art

of writing was learnt, adopted and used early in Greece but only several centuries later in India. There is therefore written testimony of the state of knowledge in early Greece, while there is mostly the oral tradition to testify on the corresponding developments in India. Philosophical knowledge in Greece, defined as "the research of the principles and of the causes" (Livio 2003), was open and included all sciences, while the main corpus of the philosophical knowledge in India was written down late and with a phonetic script developed from foreign models. In the west the teachings of the masters could be recorded in writing and the books could be stored in Museums and Libraries, the most important being those at Alexandria of Egypt. The use of the art of writing and the role it played for the technical and scientific evolution of cultures cannot be over emphasized. A single example taken from mathematics, the basis of all applied and theoretical sciences, is mentioned here. Euclides (third century BC), was a Greek who worked in the museum/library and lived in Alexandria. He followed the line of great mathematician/philosophers: Thales (640?-546 BC), Pythagoras (died 497 BC) and Plato (427?-347 BC) who were among the most influential. Among the most fundamental discoveries of ancient Greece, I would recall only one which is the formulation of a ratio called "the **golden ratio**" which is found everywhere in nature and man-made structures and in everything where there is harmony pleasing to the sense organs of man, it is determined mathematically. Euclides repeatedly discussed what he called "the extreme and medium proportion" (= golden ratio, golden mean, etc.) in the treatise called "Elements" that has been reproduced in all languages and is the most translated and read of all books ever. In the Euclidean "Elements" the properties of the golden ratio are stated, illustrated and the geometric method to obtain an approximate representative number is defined in writing. The golden ratio could not be calculated in ancient times, because the "sign zero" had not yet been invented. In modern mathematics the "interminable" number known as the Fibonacci number, is now written as the Greek letter **phi** from Fibonacci who first calculated the number and described the properties of the golden ratio, in his famous book the *Liber abaci* (= The abacus book) published in 1202. The treatise opens with the following sentence: "With the nine Indian cyphers 9 8 7 6 5 4 3 2 1 and the sign 0 . . . it is possible to write any number, as shown below." The number calculated from what Euclides had called "the proportion between the extreme and medium," the present day Fibonacci number, whose symbol is the greek letter *phi* = 1,6180339887. . . is an "interminable" or "unlimited" number, because there will never be a repetition of figures for as long as we go on dividing. In other words, it is neither an "entire" or round number nor a round fraction. Fibonacci also showed the mathematical properties of this universally occurring ratio, as discussed by the astrophysicist Livio in his fascinating book "The Golden Ratio, The story of a number and mystery that survives over three thousand years." This was the mathematical ratio described geometrically in the Euclidean "Elements" and mathematically calculated by Fibonacci, published in the *Liber abaci* in 1202 AD.

10. The mixing of people and cultures was favoured by trade by land and sea routes. This is evident from the transfer of myths and legends from one culture to another, with due adaptation of names, environmental features, customs and habits of the people and their rulers. One example of transfer of culture and of the changes that occur in the process of adaptation of old myths to new environments is well illustrated by the transfer of the myth of child Demophont (Homeric hymn to Demeter, mentioned above) to the Egyptian mythical *corpus.* The Egyptian version of the story of Demophont was divulged in Egypt during the Ptolemaic age, and is only one of the several cultural traits imported from Greece, at the late stage of the ancient Egyptian BC culture. The myth says that Isis brought up the baby prince, son of king Malcandrus whose queen was variedly known as Saosis, Nemanus or Astarte (Semitic goddess of fertility) suckling him from her finger tips, instead of her breasts. One night Isis "burned away the mortal parts of the baby" and when the real mother shrieked in panic, Isis flew away as a swallow and the baby missed the chance of becoming immortal but became instead the wooden pillar that sustains

the roof. The story of burning the "mortal parts" of the child to secure his immortality is told step by step with the name changed from Demeter to Isis and corresponding changes to reflect the new relationships (Brunner-Traut, 1963) among people and places. Another interesting transfer of legends is the story of Sindbad (the name could come from the Persian Sindbad, "the man from Sind"), the famous Omani adventurer and trader who sailed from the Arabian Sea to as far east as Tien-tsin Province in northern China in the eighth century AD. Quoting from Khawam (1985) who translated the full story of Sindbad from the Arabic original manuscripts into French, we learn that only as late as the eighteenth AD century the "adventures of Sindbad" were introduced in the famous "Thousand and One Nights." The full version of the story of Sindbad was incorporated in the "Strasburg manuscript" of the "Nights" as late as 1831. The complete translation of Khawam's text is very informative and gives many details of the seven voyages from Baghdad to China, sailing from the port of al-Basra. Sindbad was a merchant who spiced his business travels with phantastic accounts of the adventures into which he was dragged by his insatiable curiosity. Many western authors compared Sindbad to Ulysses. The differences however are radical. First: Sindbad's travels were taken at the time of Khalif Harun-al-Raschid of the Abassid dynasty of Baghdad (786-809 AD or 170-193 by the Islamic calendar), about 1500 years *after* the approximate dates of the travels of Ulysses, when the art of navigation and naval architecture had been greatly improved; Second, Ulysses (= Odysseus) was a prince and warrior, while Sindbad was a merchant and adventurer; finally Sindbad's travels took him to many really distant lands and real, though then unknown people who spoke entirely different languages, while Ulysses was restricted to the Mediterranean Sea where Greek was widely spoken. What both have in common, are the descriptions of places and habits and accurate recording of names. Sindbad's ships were sea worthy enough to sail long distances and they have reputedly been used as models of the ships for which the city, of Salala in the Sultanate of Oman, is rightly famous. Both Odysseus and

Sindbad are great story tellers and give a good idea of the world of their times. Sindbad is an excellent personification of Arab traders, merchants and mariners who plied the Arabian Sea, the Indian Ocean and the West Pacific as far as Kyushu in Japan and Tien-Tsin Province in northern China, and all the coastal places and islands on the way. Sindbad is the epitome of the spread of Islam eastwards over oceans and seas in a manner comparable to what had been the spread of Hellenism in the Mediterranean Sea, the Atlantic Ocean and the Black Sea, a little over a millennium earlier. These two major movements had profound consequences on the development of cultures and civilizations worldwide.

11. Among the many recurrent and significant Indo-European root-word one frequently found is the prefix *pri* = what comes first (Lt. *pri* = first as in *primus*), *primo* Lt. *pri*mitive, *primus, pri*me, *pri*mary, *prim* (as precise, proper), *pri*mavera (= first flowering, spring, the spring equinox coincides with the beginning of a new year), *pri*meval, *pri*mordial, *pri*vilege and others. What "**comes** first" is not necessarily *original,* that means = *what* **was different** *at the beginning.* Significantly calendars, seasons, weeks, days, astronomical laws, astrology and others are terms whose meaning is common to all Indo-European people. Greek and Roman calendars can be easily calculated from ancient times to present day western Gregorian calendar (since 1582), which was an improved version of the Julian calendar, introduced by Julius Caesar in 46 BC and used throughout the Roman territories. Significantly *Pṛśni* is the mother of the Maruts and, according to Sāyaṇa, she is the many coloured Earth, or earth (= soil) in its multiple aspects (*ṚV* VI, 6, 4). *Pṛthvī* (*ṚV* X, 90, 14) is the original earth, origin of everything and all, and *Prithi,* is the first anointed king. The prefix *pri* is onomatopoeic and the word implies that it will be followed by a series of "things" similar to itself and that will evolve from it. Curiously enough, number one in Icelandic, a language that was isolated during many centuries, is *ek* as in Hindi.

12. Homer tells us that Dardanus, the ancestor of the Trojans, was the son of Zeus and Electra, a mortal woman. Dardanus was

the legendary founder of Dardania "a city older than Troy." This coincides with the conclusions of modern archaeology which found five levels, or layers of cities older than Troy at the same place and under the city called Ilio that was conquered by the Greeks shortly before the end of the mycenaean civilization, and before the Doric "invasion" of Greece. The Straits of Dardanelles bears the name of the very ancient hero called Dardanus who aimed at having control over the waterway that connects the Aegean sea to the Black Sea and coastal plains. Dardanus was successful and his distant successors amassed a great fortune that was lost in smoke by the arson caused by the Achaeans. Virgil in a late account makes Dardanus the ancestor of the Italic people. Dardanus was father of Erictonion, at one time the richest man on earth.

Part IV — Summary and Conclusions

1. Homer and Hesiod created a religion usually known at present as the classical Graeco-Roman religion. It was a superstructure built on a pre-Hellenic rich foundation of legends and myths, the corpus of the cultures of the eastern Mediterranean autochthonous populations, already influenced by the ancient myths and history of Semitic populations of West Asia and to a lesser degree, also by the culture of the Egyptian civilization. Following the "urbanization" of the cult of Dionysos, the great tragedies of Aeschylus, Sophocles and Euripides and the satyric comedies of Aristophanes among others, discussed already in the sixth-fifth centuries BC, the inevitable conflicts arising from the religion and acculturation of the Athenian citizens on one side and the moral and legal organization of the *"polis"* (= State) on the other. They realized that there was a price to be paid for the passage from a generalized culture to an organized class system, namely the State with its rigid rules, laws, regulations and justice. Hesiod described the first step of the conflict between man and man-made gods and described the revolt of the Titans against Zeus; the second step was the result of the "urbanization" of Dionysos by will of Pisistratus, "tyrant" of Athens. Dionysos became the patron of the classical Greek theatre, authors could draw freely from the mythology

that preceded them. Ancient nature religions correctly describe the "fetters" (= bondage, limitations) imposed on man as a biological and social species by its very nature, those of a biological being. The urbanisation of Dionysos engendered new and earlier unforeseen limitations on the personal lives of men and women who were now forced to admit and bow to the laws of the *polis*. Desires and aspirations of the new class of persons, the citizens, were curtailed by the desires and aspirations of other citizens like themselves living in structured communities regulated by The Law. Citizenship had been secured at the very high cost of new socio-biological individual constraints added upon the natural fetters common to all living beings. In the Introduction to the *Theogonia* Hesiod declares that he is concerned only with Truth devoid of all the phantasies created by earlier generations of poets. The beginning of the *Theogonia* (= origin of the gods) is nevertheless not new, it is a very close repetition with changed names, of a Hittite text of the thirteenth century BC written in cuneiform script and Hurrite language that described under different names the original dynasty of the gods exactly in the same sequence and details as repeated in Hesiod's *Theogonia* of the eighth century BC Greece. The newly born Olympian dynasties of gods and humans, and Athens as a State, acquire each a status of its own that are seen as the means to fulfil the Destiny of the community ruled by the *polis*. However, some men or women were torn to pieces by an unremitting urge to declare their freedom and independence to satisfy their natural passions, good or bad regardless of the punishment that Zeus or other gods would inflict on them for the great sin called rebellion. What greater sin could there be than trying to escape from the iron grip of the father of all gods and all men, though he himself indulged in all desires and pleasures, right or wrong? Yet, some men and women did challenge Zeus and faced his wrath. There are few stories as powerful and poignant as the conscientious rebellion of the Titan Prometheus, a super-man who finally succeeds in his self-imposed task of stealing fire from the gods and giving it to men. It is the openly bold declaration that man can conquer man-made gods, if they are sincere and determined. Only two examples need be mentioned here: **A.** - The story of ancient characters in Euripides' tragedy called "Medea." Ancient tradition from the Heroic Age tells how Medea, gifted with magical powers and daughter of Eeta, king of Kolchides, betrays her family and country for the sake of her love for Jason, leader of the expedition of the Argonautes. She instructs him on the way that leads to, and how to obtain the "golden fleece." She abandons her country and family to give her support to Jason. But on their return to Corynth in Greece, after ten years of happy married life Jason abandons Medea and their two children, to marry the young daughter of the local king. Medea is banned from Corynth because she plans revenge. Rather than being repentful for her earlier betrayal against her *State and family in Kolchides,* Medea's anger now grows to the paroxysm of killing her own children to punish Jason for abandoning her. The pre-Homeric legend goes on saying that Medea ran away from Corynth and found refuge among the *Arya of Phrygia in Asia Minor* and "those people" as a mark of gratitude for her teachings called themselves *Medes.* In Pausanias' words (II, 3,8): "After killing her children Medea went to Athens and married Aegeus . . . then conspired against the Athenian hero Theseus and had to run away from Athens. She then arrived in the land then called *Arya* and gave her name to the people who are now called Medes from "Medea". . . She had a son from Aegeus . . . whose name was *Medo.*" The arrival of the Medes is known approximately, it is therefore possible to date the settlement of the Indo-Arya in Asia Minor to the pre-Homeric Age, prior to historically known dates. The arrival of the Medes is therefore not later than the early second millennium BC or alternately, the myths and legends about Medea were grafted later into traditional or historical records. The Medes play a very important role in the evolution of the Indo-Iranian history; they can be identified with the present day Kurdish population. **B.** - Another important myth is that of Prometheus, discussed by Aeschylus in the trilogy: "Chained Prometheus," "Liberated Prometheus;" "Prometheus Carrier of Fire." Of the three tragedies only the first has come down to us complete, only paıts of the second and just one verse of the third. Initially Prometheus is chained to the Caucasus Mountains as a punishment for bringing fire to mankind. Prometheus is a rebellious Titan who symbolizes the conflicts between man and law, nature and pre-ordained destiny, natural and state religions, individual freedom and tyranny of the state that all prompt Prometheus to exclaim desperately: "O Art, how much weaker thou art than Destiny!." Prometheus is cruelly punished by Zeus but he is finally pardoned because, *and only because* Prometheus finally accepts the unavoidable limits imposed on his freedom to ensure ethical lifestyles and community understanding among men, while Zeus recognizes and endorses the dignity of the human personality and accepts the rules that extend the limits of the ambitions and desires of man. Zeus has to accept and endorse the *physis* (= physical nature) and the *nomos* (= laws and regulations) of man's status and pardons Prometheus. Thus, paraphrasing Prometheus: "Art may become as strong as Destiny." Like Medea, Prometheus had challenged Zeus boldly well-knowing that he would have to suffer terrible punishments, but his urge to safeguard human dignity is stronger than all other sentiments and cannot be controlled. In the tragedy, Aeschylus equates the rebellious Titan Prometheus and his urge to know and do, with the nobility of Heroic Man. Even the dubious character of Medea retains, in Euripides' tragedy, a certain dignity in her determination, her urge to act, to fulfill her destiny, even if knowingly evil. In Greek humanism destiny is devoid of ethical worries of good or bad, only consequences matter. Prometheus is an admirable hero, a great man, a Titan who finally accepts the unavoidable limits imposed on his freedom for the sake of the community, while Zeus has to bow low and agree to grant some freedom to Man for the sake of fulfilling the destiny allotted to man. Zeus' reasoning seems to be that man would not be able to fulfill his destiny without the free use of fire. And fire has here the double meaning of a tool as means to an end, and of a symbol of freedom and determination to achieve the proposed end. Aeschylus, Sophocles, Euripides, returned to its honourable place the nobility of the condition of *Man* that had been lost in the vitiated Olympic world of Homer and

Hesiod. Greek humanism is at the opposite end from the Indian humanism that accepts human frailties as natural and unavoidable, but at the same time tries to educate and strengthen by all means all members of society at all ages, pushing them away from what is obviously bad or evil. Human nature, individually and collectively, must be reconciled with the *physis* and *nomos* of the naked biped, using Diogenes' words, who has the power of reason and discrimination independently of the Olympian gods. Mātariśvan is mentioned 24 times in the *R̥V* alone. He is a deity often identified with or representing Agni (= Fire), at times the two gods appear to be interchangeable. Mātariśvan is rich in treasure, wealth, he is a light winner who finds a pathway for his offspring, the fire produced by friction of the *aranis* (= firesticks) to receive the libation of soma. He was sent as a messenger by Vivasvān (= brilliant as the morning sun) to take Fire who was hiding in heaven, to Bhr̥gu (*R̥V* I; 31, 3- *R̥V* VI, 8, 4)). Mātariśvan is skilful, has power and mind (*R̥V* X, 105). In the religion and philosophies of the Indo-Europeans of east, fire and Mātariśvan are simply what they really are, good and generous, teachers of the value, role and importance of man-made fire, itself a god. All mankind owes much to fire and to the messenger Mātariśvan to whom mankind is grateful for having acquired the skill. Mātariśvan is worthy of the songs of praise (*R̥V* III; 26, 2) addressed to him, whatever his nature.

2. There is a good collection of wooden statues of Kalash men, their ancestors and their horses, as well as tools, utensils and other artefacts in the Anthropological Museum of the Department of Natural History of the University of Florence. Not a single carving has the least intention of portraying faithfully the deceased or the horses. All the carvings are just symbolic reminders. One of the most interesting is registered under No. 32841, and is part of the collection made by prof. Paolo Grazioli during the Italian Expedition to the Karakorum and K2 peak, 1955-1960. It is an equestrian statue made of deodar wood (*Cedrus deodara* = Skt. *Devadaru* = wood of the gods, made specially according to tradition for Prof. Grazioli,

and purchased at Chitral. The horse and his mount are almost life size and typically there are no saddle or stirrups, the human figure bears a conical headdress similar to the *tiara* worn by the earlier Persian kings, and later also by the *magi* of the east and other noblemen.

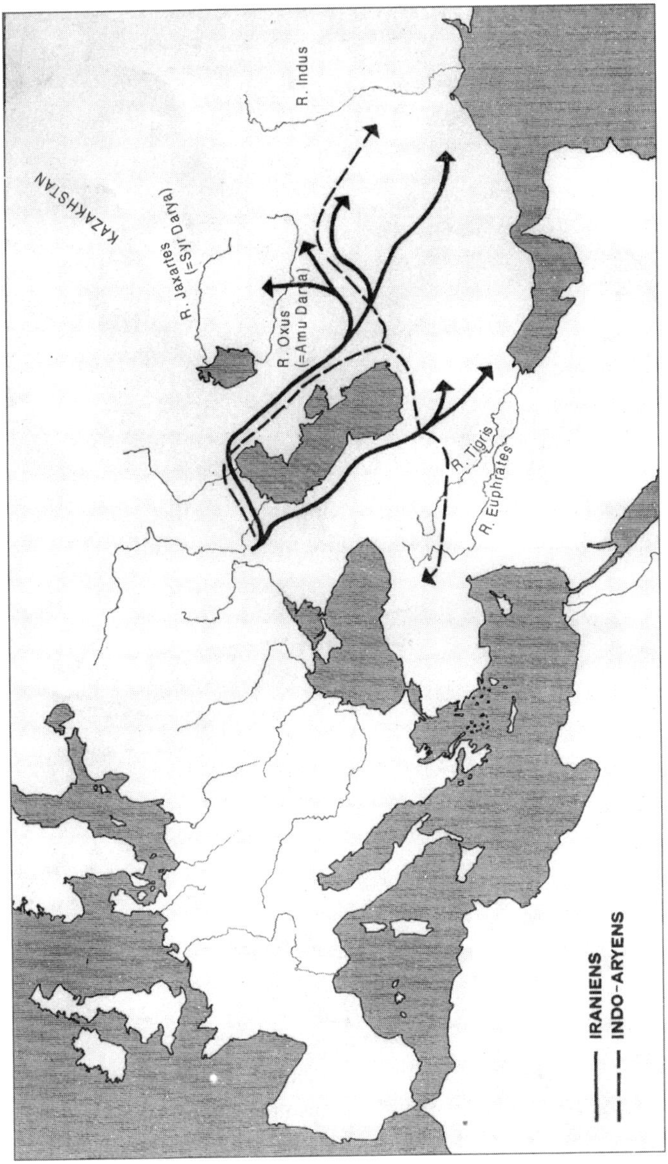

fig. 1. Chart of the migration of the Indo-Aryans and of the Indo-Iranians, *(apud* Ghirshman, 1977, *fig* 5).

fig. 2. ***Egyptian Chariot,*** New Kingdom, XVIII dynasty. Courtesy of the Archaeological Museum, Florence, cat.n° 2678.

fig. 3. Carvings showing Pharaoh Thutmosis IV on his war chariot with eight-spoke wheels and the charioteer next to the king, holding the reins. Smaller, single-man chariots are also shown, they have four-spoke wheels and are also drawn by two horses, in: Guidotti, M.V. and F. Pecchioli Daddi, *La battaglia di Qadesh,* 2002, pp. 44-45. Ed. by Superintendenza dei beni archeologici della Toscana, Firenze. Courtesy of the Archaeological Museum of Florence.

fig. 4. Inner cover, *La Battaglia di Qadesh,* M.V. Guidotti and F. Pecchioli Daddi, 2002, Asis Minor and West Asia, inside of front cover. Courtesy of the Archaeological Museum of Florence.

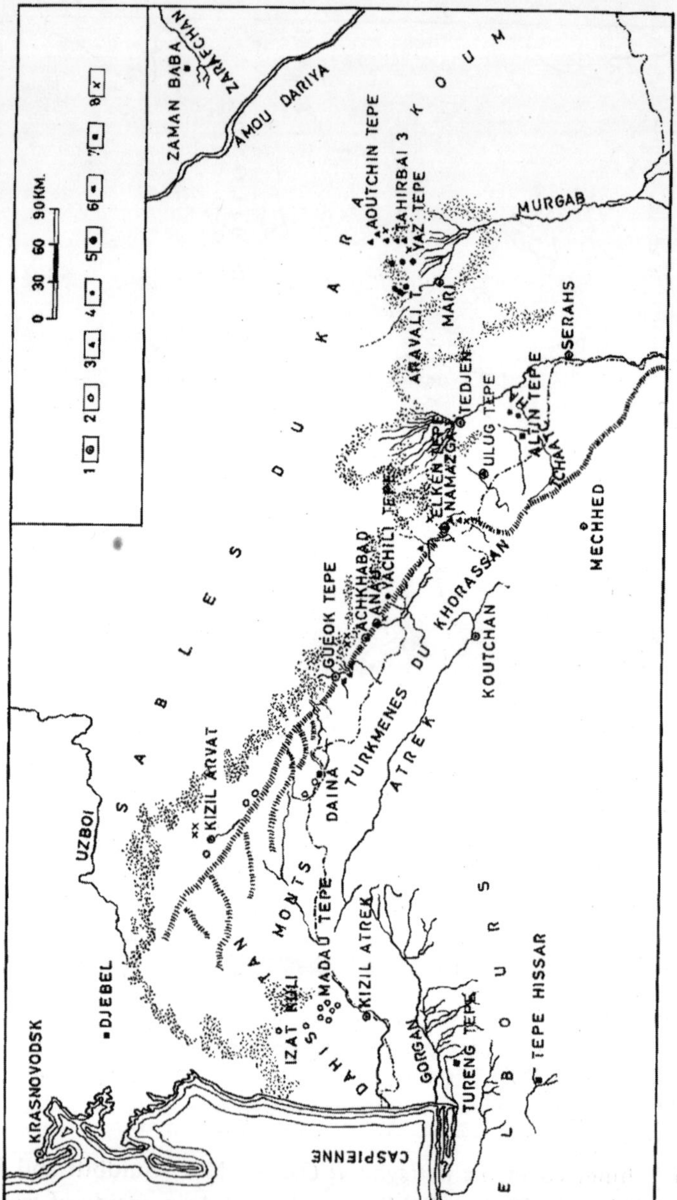

fig. 5. Southern Turkmenistan, late Bronze Age and early Iron Age from Ghirshman, 1977, *apud V.M.Masson*, 1959, *fig. 31.*

Bibliography

Allen, N.J., 2003, "Mahabharata and Iliad: a Common Origin?" *Annals of the Bhandarkar Oriental Research Institute*, LXXXIII

André, J. & J. Filliozat (transl.), 1980, *Pline l'ancien, Histoire Naturelle, Livre 1*, publ. Paris: Les Belles Lettres.

Anonymous, 1893, *South India*, Delhi: Rupa & Co.

Aristophanes, *Le Rane* (*Frogs*).

Arrianus, *Indikè; Anabasis*, Complete Greek and Italian texts.

Arrighetti, G., 2000, *Hesiod, Theogonia* (first ed. 1984). Complete Greek and Italian texts, Milano: Rizzoli.

Arrighetti, G., 1989, *Frammenti Orfici*, ed. Milano: Associati.

Aeschylus, *Tragedies*, specifically: *Chained Prometheus*.

Askarov, A., 1996 (first ed. 1992), The beginning of the Iron Age in Transoxiana, in: *History of Civilizations of Central Asia*, I, Paris: UNESCO.

Askarov, A., V. Volkov and N. Ser-Odjav, 1996, Pastoral and Nomadic Tribes at the beginning of the first millennium BC, in: *History of Civilizations in Central Asia*, I, Paris: UNESCO.

Bajpai, S.C., 1987, *Lahaul-Spiti*, New Delhi: Indus Publishing Company.

Bhargava,P.L., 2001, *India in the Vedic Age* (3rd ed), New Delhi: D.K.Printworld.

Bottero, J., 1994, *Babylone et la Bible*, Plurielle: Hachette.

Bottero, J., 1998, *La plus vieille religion*, Paris: Gallimard.

Bowra, C.M., 1961, *Heroic Poetry* (first ed. 1952) London.

Brunner-Traut, E., 1963, *Altaegyptische Maerchen*. It. transl. *Favole e Miti dell'antico Egitto*. 1999, ed. Milano: Mondolibri.

Burkert, W., 1992 (first ed. 1979), *Structure and History in Greek Mythology and Ritual*, publ. Univ. California. Ital. transl. *Mito e Rituale in Grecia*, ed. A. Milano: Mondadori.

Calzecchi-Onesti, R., 1990, *Iliade*. Complete Greek and Italian texts. Einaudi, Torino (see: Onesti).

Canfora, L., 2001, *Storia della letteratura greca*. Milano: Mondadori.

Capila,A. 2002, *Images of Women in the Folk Songs of Garhwal Himalayas*. New Delhi: Concept Publ. Co.

Cāssola, F. 1997, (first ed. 1984), Introduzione a: *Herodotus Istoriai*, books I-IX

Cāssola, F. 2000, (5th ed.) *Inni Omerici*, Introduction and Notes. Complete Greek and Italian texts. Milano: Mondadori.

Casson, L. 2001, *Libraries in the Ancient World*. New Haven: Yale Univ. Press.

Cavalli-Sforza, L. 1996, *Gr̥nes, Peuples et Langues*, Paris: Odile Jacob.

Cavalli-Sforza F. & L. Cavalli-Sforza 1995, *The Great Human Diasporas*, Reading (MA) Wesley: Addison.

Cavalli-Sforza, L. & M. Feldman 1981, *Cultural Transmission and Evolution. A Quantitative Approach*. Princeton Univ. Press.

Cavalli-Sforza, L Wang W.S.Y. 1986, The Impact of Farming on the Expansion of Human Populations, in: *The Origin and Domestication of Cultivated Plants*, (C.Barigozzi ed.) Amsterdam: Elsevier.

Chakrabarti, D. K. 2001, Archaeological Geography of the Ganga Plains, in: *India, an Archaeological History*, Kolkata: Permanent Black.

Chakravarty, U. 1997, *Indra and other Vedic Deities. A euhemeristic study*. New Delhi: D.K.Printworld.

Christensen, A. 1943, *Le premier chapitre du Vendidad et l'histoire primitive des tribues iraniennes*. Kopenhagen 1943 (in: Ghirshman 1977).

Chuvin, P. 1992, *La mythologie Grecque*, Paris: Flammarion.

Cicero, Marcus Tullius, *De natura deorum* (complete Latin and Italian texts) 1967, Introduction and Notes by V. Pizzani, Milano: Mondadori.

Cicero, Marcus Tullius, *De Fato* (complete Latin and Italian texts) 1994, Introduction and Notes by F. Antonini, ed. Milano: Rizzoli.

Codino, F., 1990, *Preface to Homer's Iliad* (complete Greek and Italian texts), ed: Torino: Einaudi.

Curtis, V.S . (first publ. 1993 by Trustees of the British Museum) *Persian Myths*, British Museum Publ.

Dandekar, R.N. 1997, *Indological Miscellanea,* Pune, India.

Dandekar, R.N. 1979a, *Vedic Mythological Tracts, Select Writings I,* Delhi: Ajanta Publ., Pune: Bhandarkar Inst. Press.

Dandekar, R.N . 1979b *Insights into Hinduism, Select Writings II.*

Dandekar, R.N. 1979c *New light on the Vedic God Savitr,* in: R.N.Dandekar, *Select Writings I,* Poona: BORI.

Dandekar, R.N. 1981, *Exercises in Indology, Select Writings III,* Delhi: Ajanta Publ., Pune: Bhandarkar Inst. Press

Dani, A.H. 1996 (first ed. 1992), Pastoral-agricultural tribes of Pakistan in the post-Indus period, in: *History and Civilizations in Central Asia,* I. Paris: UNESCO Publ.

Dani, A.H. & P. Bernard, 1996 (first ed. 1994), Alexander and his successors in Central Asia, in: *History and Civilizations in Central Asia,* II. Paris: UNESCO Publ.

Dani, A.H. & V.M.Masson, (ed.) 1996 (first ed. 1992), *History of Civilizations of Central Asia,*I. The dawn of civilization: earliest times to 700 B.C. I, 525. Paris: UNESCO Publ.

Dani, A.H. & B.K.Thapar, (1996, first ed. 1992), The Indus Civilization, in: *History of Civilizations in Central Asia, I, The dawn of civilization: earliest times to 700* BC.

Darmesteter, J. 1977 (first publ. 1865), *The Zend-Avesta,* ed: Benaras: Motilal Banarsi Dass.

Delcourt, M. 1981, *L'oracle de Delphes,* Paris: Payot.

Dutt, R.C. 1910, *The Ramayana and the Mahabharata in English Verse, Selected Parts*

Euripides, Tragedies, here specifically *Medea* and *Hippolytus.*

Firdusi, 1967, *The Epic of the Kings, Shah-Nama,* ed. Royal Inst. Teheran and UNESCO

Fisher, J.F. 1987 (first publ. 1986, Univ. California), *Trans-Himalayan Traders,* ed. Varanasi: Motilal Banarsidass.

Ghirshman, R. 1938, *Fouilles de Sialk, prr̥s de Kashan 1933, 1934, 1937,* Paris: Librairie Orientaliste Paul Geuthner, 2 vols.

Ghirshman, R. 1963, *Proto-iraniens. Mr̥des. Achéménides* in: Paris: Ghirshman 1977.

Ghirshman, R. 1977, *L'Iran et la migration des Indo-Aryens et des Iraniens*, Leiden: E. J. Brill.

Ghosh, R.N. 1977, Protogeological Studies on the Ancient Water Regimes of Rajasthan Rivers, in: P.Agrawal and B.M.Pande (eds.), *Ecology and Archaeology of Western India*, Delhi: Concept Publishing Co.

Ghurye, G.S. 1979, *Vedic India*, Popular Prakashan.

Gibon, McGuire, 1986, *Journal of Eastern Studies*, 35, 1.

Gimbutas, M. 1956, *The Prehistory of Eastern Europe*, Journ. Indo-European Studies.

Gimbutas, M. 1970, Proto Indo-European Culture. The Kurgan Culture during the fifth, fourth and third Millennia BC, in: *Indo-European and Indo-Europeans*. Philadelphia: Univ. of Pennsylvnia Press.

Gimbutas, M. 1974, *Journ. Indo-European Studies*; 2

Graves, R. 1960 (first ed. 1955), *The Greek Myths*, ed. Penguin Books.

Guidotti, M.V. and Daddi,F.P. (ed.) 2002, *La battaglia di Qadesh, Ramesse II contro gli Ittiti per la conquista della Siria*. Ed. Superintendenza dei beni archeologici della Toscana, ed. Sillabe Firenze: publ. Museo Archeologico Nazionale.

Hancar, F. 1956, *Das Pferd in praehistorischer und frueher historischer Zeit*. Munchen.

Hancar, F. 1934, *Kaukasus-Luristan,Eurasia Septentrionalis Antiqua*. Helsinki.

Harmatta, J. 1996a (first ed. 1994), The emergence of the Indo-Iranians: the Indo-Iranian languages, in: *History of civilizations of Central Asia*, 1, UNESCO publ.

Harmatta, J. 1996b (first ed. 1994), Languages and scripts in Graeco-Bactria and the Saka kingdoms, in: *History of civilizations of Central Asia*, 2, UNESCO publ.

Harmatta, J. 1996c (first ed. 1994), Languages and literature of the Kushan Empire, in: *History of civilizations of Central Asia*, 2, UNESCO publ.

Harmatta, J. (ed.) 1996 (first ed. 1994), *History of civilizations of Central Asia*, UNESCO publ.

Haudry, J. 1985 (first ed. 1981), *Les Indo-Européens*, Paris: Presses Univ. France.

Herodotus, *Historias*, Books I - XII.

Heubeck, A. 1991 (first ed. 1981, see Privitera), Interpretation of the Odyssey, translation from German into Italian by E. Livrea in: *Odyssey* (1991), complete Greek and Italian texts, Mondadori

Homer, 1900, *Iliados,* complete Greek and Italian texts. Preface by F.Codino, transl. by R. Calzecchi-Onesti. ed. Einaudi

Homer, 2004 *Odysseia,* full Greek and Italian texts by Privitera, G.A. ed. Mondadori.

Homeric Hymns, 2000 (first ed. 1997), transl. and notes by Filippo Cāssola. Milano: Mondadori.

Jones, S. 1967, *The political organization of the Kam Kafirs,* a preliminary analysis. Kopenhagen.

Keshwani, D.G. 1980, Echanges commerciaux de l'Inde avec l'Asie du Sud-Est, in : *Relations historiques ā travers l'Océan Indien.* publ. Paris: UNESCO.

Khawam, R.R. 1985, *Les aventures de Sindbad le Marin.* Transl. of complete original text, Paris: Phébus.

Khorshid, F.H. 1986, *La lingua Kurda e la distribuzione geografica dei suoi dialetti.* Trad. Shorsh A. Surme, Venezia.

Kirk, G.S, 1962, *The Songs of Homer,* Cambridge.

Kochhar, R. 2000, *The Vedic People.* Hyderabad, Orient Longman.

Kramer, S.N. 1983, *In Search of Sumer.* Journ. Amer. Oriental Society, 103.

Kramer, S.N. 1994 (first ed. 1959), *L'histoire commence ā Sumer,* Paris: Flammarion.

Kramer, S.N. and J.N.Bottero 1889, *Lorsque les dieux faisaient l'homme.* Mythologie mésopotamienne, Paris: Gallimard.

Lahiri, N. 1992, *The Archaeology of Indian Trade Routes up to c.200BC.,* New Delhi: Oxford Univ. Press.

·Lahiri, N. 2005, *Finding Forgotten Cities,* Delhi: Permanent Black.

Lal, M. 1985, Settlement Patterns of Painted Grey Ware Culture in the Ganga Valley, in: V.N.Misra and P. Bellwood (eds.), *Recent Advances in Indo-Pacific Pre-history,* Leiden: E.J.Brill.

Lal, M. 1996, The Painted Grey Ware Culture of the Iron Age, in: *History of Civilizations of Central Asia,* 1, publ. Paris: UNESCO.

LaPenna, A. 2002, *Introduzione,* Eneide di P. Virgilio Marone., ed. Milano: Rizzoli.

Lirvre, V. and J.Y.Loude, 1990, *Le shamanisme des Kalash du Pakistan,* ed. Paris: C.N.R.S.

Livio, M. 2002, *The Golden Ratio,* publ. Broadway Publishing Group, Random House Inc.

Loude, J.Y. 1987, Frtes d'été chez les Kalash du Nord Pakistan, in : *L'éthnographie,* 100-01.

Loude, J.Y. and V.Lirvre 1980, *Kalash, les derniers infidrles de l'Hindukush,* Berger-Levrault, Paris: Espace des Hommes.

Loude, J.Y. and V.Lirvre, 1984, *Solstice paien,* Paris: Presses de la Renaissance.

Longo, *(see Merkelbach 1988).*

Lord, A.B. 1960, *The Singer of Tales,* Cambridge, Mass.

Macleod, R. 2001 (ed.first ed. 2000), ed. *The Library of Alexandria*

Markwart, J. 1938, *Wehrot und Arang. Untersuchungen zur mytischen und geschichtlichen Landeskunde von Ostrian.* Leiden 1938 (apud Ghirshman 1977).

Masson,V.M. 1996 (first ed. 1992), The environment, in: *History of Civilizations of Central Asia,* 1, publ. Paris: UNESCO.

Masson, V.M. and V.Serianidi, 1996 (first ed. 1992), Food-producing and other Neolithic communities in Khorasan and Transoxiana: eastern Iran, Soviet Central Asia, in: *History of civilizations of Central Asia.* 1, publ. Paris: UNESCO.

Mazumdar, R.C. 1988 ed. *The Vedic Age,* Bharatiya Vidya Bhavan.

McGovern, P.E. 2003, *Ancient Wine, The Search of the Origin of Viniculture,* Princeton University Press.

Menghi, M. 2003, *Atlante dell'antica Grecia,* DeAgostini, Novara.

Merkelbach, R. 1991 (first ed. 1988, *Die Hirten des Dionysos), I misteri di Dioniso.* Ed. Genova: Blengino.

Munduruku, D. 2001, *As serpentes que roubaram a noite,* ed. Peiropolis, S.Paulo.

Munduruku, D, 2001, *Meu vo Apolinario,* ed. S.Paulo: Studio Nobel.

Munduruku, D. 2003, ed. S.Paulo: Fundarao Peiropolis.

Mylonas, G.E. 1961, *Eleusis and the Eleusinian Mysteries,* Princeton Univ, Press.

Nonnos of Panopolis, middle 5th century AD, *Dionysiaka,* transl. M. Maletto, notes by F. Tissoni, Introduction by D. DeCarmo, books 1-24, publ. Adelphi, Milano. Books 25-39, 2004, transl. G. Agosti, ed. Rizzoli.

Nyberg, H.S. 1938, Die Religion des Alten Iran. Leipzig.

Otto, W.F. 1993 (first ed. 1929), *Les dieux de la France,* ed. Payot et Rivages

Otto, W.F. 1997, (first ed. 1933), *Dionysos.* Il nuovo Melangolo, ed. Genova

Parpola, A. 1999, Formation of the Aryan Branch of the Indo-Europeans, in: *Archaeology and Language* III: *Artefacts, Languages and Texts,* London: Routledge.

Parry, A. 1971, The Making of Homeric Verse. The Collected Papers of Milman Parry, Oxford 1971 (*apud* Alfreed Heubeck) in: *Omero, Odissea (1991),* publ. Arnoldo Mondadori.

Parry, A. 1928, *Les formules et la métrique d'Homṛre,* in : Heubeck,A. 1981, (*apud* Privitera, 1981).

Pettinato, G. 1992, La saga di Gilgamesh.

Pizzani, U. 2004 (first publ.1967), *Cicerone, sulla natura degli dei (De natura deorum).* Introduction and full Latin and Italian texts, A. Mondadori ed.

Pope, A.U. 1969, *Persian Architecture* .Asia Publ. Inst. Kobe, Japan, Oxford Univ. Press.

Potts, D.T. 1990, The Arabian Gulf in Antiquity, in: *Prehistory to the fall of the Achaemenid Empire,* 1, London: Clarendon Press Oxford.

Privitera, G.A. 1991, *Odysseia* (first ed. 1981) complete Greek and Italian texts, Oscar Mondadori ed.

Virgilius, *Aeneis,* complete Latin and Italian texts.

Puri, B.N. 1996, The Sakas and Indo-Parthians in: *History of civilizations in Central Asia,* II, UNESCO publ.

Puri, B.N. 1996, The Kushans in: *History of civilizations in Central Asia,* II, UNESCO publ.

Pytheas, son of Crinas, Greek navigator from Massala, *Finis Terrisö,* transl. by G.M.Rossi, ed. Sellerio, Palermo.

Radhakrishnan, S. 1974 (first publ.1953), *The Principal Upanishads.* George Allen and Unwin, New York: Humanities Press.

Rau, W. 1974, *Vedic Texts on the Manufacture of Pottery,* 23, Baroda: Oriental Inst. Baroda.

Rau, W. 1976, *The meaning of Pur in Vedic Literature.* Muenchen: Wilhelm Fink Verlag.

Renfrew, C.A. 1994 (first ed.1988) , *Archaeology and Language, the Puzzle of the Indo-European Origin,* Cambridge Univ. Press

Robertson, G.S. 1884, *Kafiristan.* The Geographical Journal, 4. London

Robertson, G.S. 1894, *The Kafirs of the Hindukush,* 1969 ed. by Sang-e-Meel publ., Lahore.

Sanna, M.N. and L. Lorettu, 2000, *L'omicidio per vendetta in Barbagia,* ed. Carlo Delfino, Sassari.

Sarianidi, V. 1996, Food-producing and other Neolithic communities in Khorasan and Transoxiana: eastern Iran, Soviet Central Asia and Afghanistan, in: *History and civilizations of Central Asia,* I, Unesco publ.

Sax, W.S. 1991, *Mountain Goddess,* New York: Oxford Univ. Press.

Scarcia, R. 2002, *Notes on the Aeaeis, P.Virgilius Maronis.* Complete Latin and Italian texts. Milano: Rizzoli.

Schaffer, J.G. and B.K.Thapar, 1996 (first ed.1992), Pre-Indus and early Indus Cultures of Pakistan and India, in: *History and civilizations of Central Asia,* I, UNESCO publ.

Sharif, M. and B.K.Thapar, Food-producing communities in Pakistan and northern India, in: *History and civilizations of Central Asia,* I, UNESCO publ.

Sharma, J.C. *Cham Temples of Vietnam,* Conference delivered at I.G.N.C.A. New Delhi, Oct.27, 1994.

Schrader, O. 1890, *Prehistoric Antiquities of the Aryan People,* London.

Schuré, E. 1899 (first ed.) *Les grands Initiés.*

Soane, E.B. 1918, *Report on the Sulaiman District of Kurdistan.* Calcutta.

Spallanzani, M. 1997, *Mercanti fiorentini nell'Asia portoghese (1500-1525),* ed. S.P.E.S. Firenze.

Swaminathan, T.B. 1999, The Carpenter and Pithagoras Theorem, in: Vannucci, *Human Ecology in the Vedas,* Delhi: D.K.Printworld.

Thapar, B.K. 1984, Six Decades of Indus Studies, in: B.B.Lal and S.P.Gupta (eds.). *Frontiers of the Indus Civilization.* Sir Mortimer Wheeler Commemoration Volume, Delhi: Books and Books, for the Indian Archaeological Society.

Vannucci, M. 1994, *Ecological Readings in the Vedas*, New Delhi: D.K.Printworld.

Vannucci, M. 1994a, *Conscious and Unconscious Time*, publ. New Delhi: I.G.N.C.A.

Vannucci, M. 1995, *Common Roots or Transfer of Culture?* In: Prakriti, ed. K. Vatsyayana, New Delhi: I.G.N.C.A.

Vannucci, M. 1998, The Origin of the Cult of Demeter: the Story of Hexaploid Wheat, in: *Annals Bandarkar Oriental Research Inst. LXXIX*, Pune, India, BORI. 1999.

Vannucci, M. 1999, *Material and Immaterial Reality*, in:Vannucci 1999, New Delhi: D.K. Printworld.

Virgilius, Publius Virgilius Maronis, The *Aeneis*, Complete Latin and Italian texts.

Vian, F. 1960, Le mythe de Typhé et le problṛme de ses origines orientales, in: *Eléments orientaux dans la relation grecque ancienne*, Paris: 1960 and later eds.

Wasson, R.G., A.Hofmann and C.A.A.Ruck, 1996 (it. transl. first ed. 1978), *Alla scopeta dei misteri Eleusini*, ed. URRA. First ed. Helen and Kurt Wolff Book, Harcourt Brace Yovanovich, New York.

Young, T.C. 1965, *A Comparative Ceramic Chronology of Western Iran 1500-500BC*, in: IRAN, III.

Young, T.C. 1967, *The Iranian Migration into Zagros*, in: IRAN, V.

Yule, H. and A.C.Burnell, 1985 (first publ.1886), *Hobson-Jobson. A Glossary of Anglo-Indian words and phrases.* Publ.Routledge & Kegan Paul, Kitab and Chennai.

Index